City of Saints

THE MIDDLE AGES SERIES

Ruth Mazo Karras, Series Editor
Edward Peters, Founding Editor

A complete list of books in the series is available from the publisher.

City of Saints

Rebuilding Rome in the Early Middle Ages

Maya Maskarinec

PENN

University of Pennsylvania Press
Philadelphia

ART HISTORY
PUBLICATION INITIATIVE

This book is made possible by a collaborative grant from the Andrew W. Mellon Foundation.

Published by
University of Pennsylvania Press
Philadelphia, Pennsylvania 19104-4112
www.upenn.edu/pennpress

Printed in the United States of America on acid-free paper
10 9 8 7 6 5 4 3 2 1

Library of Congress Cataloging-in-Publication Data
Names: Maskarinec, Maya, author.
Title: City of saints : rebuilding Rome in the early Middle Ages / Maya Maskarinec.
Other titles: Middle Ages series.
Description: 1st edition. | Philadelphia : University of Pennsylvania Press, [2018] | Series: The Middle Ages series | Includes bibliographical references and index.
Identifiers: LCCN 2017046025 | ISBN 978-0-8122-5008-4 (hardcover : alk. paper)
Subjects: LCSH: Christian saints—Cult—Italy—Rome—History—To 1500. | Christianity—Social aspects—Italy—Rome—History—To 1500. | Christianity—Social aspects—Europe—History—To 1500. | Rome (Italy)—Church history. | Rome (Italy)—History—476–1420.
Classification: LCC BX2333 .M38 2018 | DDC 235/.2094563209021—dc23
LC record available at https://lccn.loc.gov/2017046025

Contents

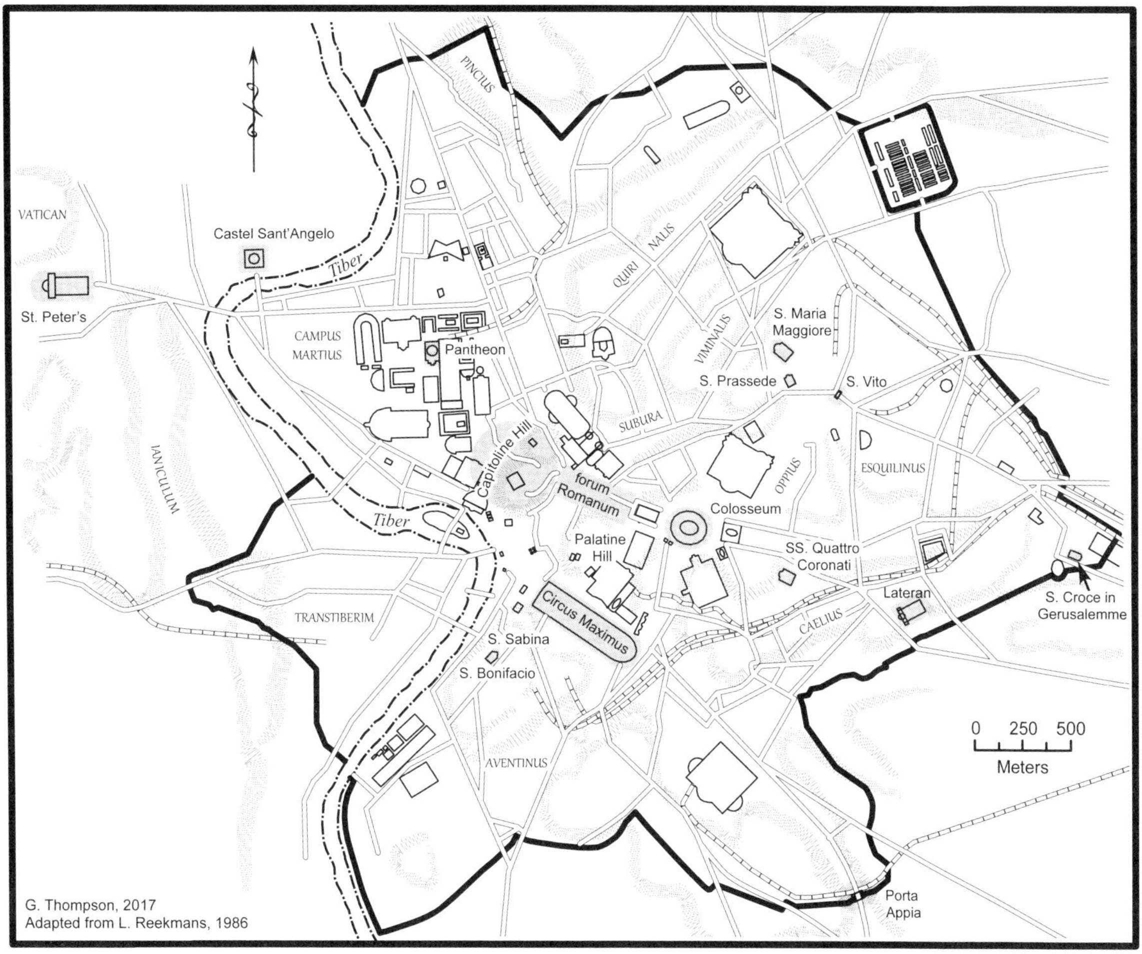

Map 1. Map of early medieval Rome. Map adapted by Gordie Thompson after Reekmans, "L'implantation monumentale chrétienne."

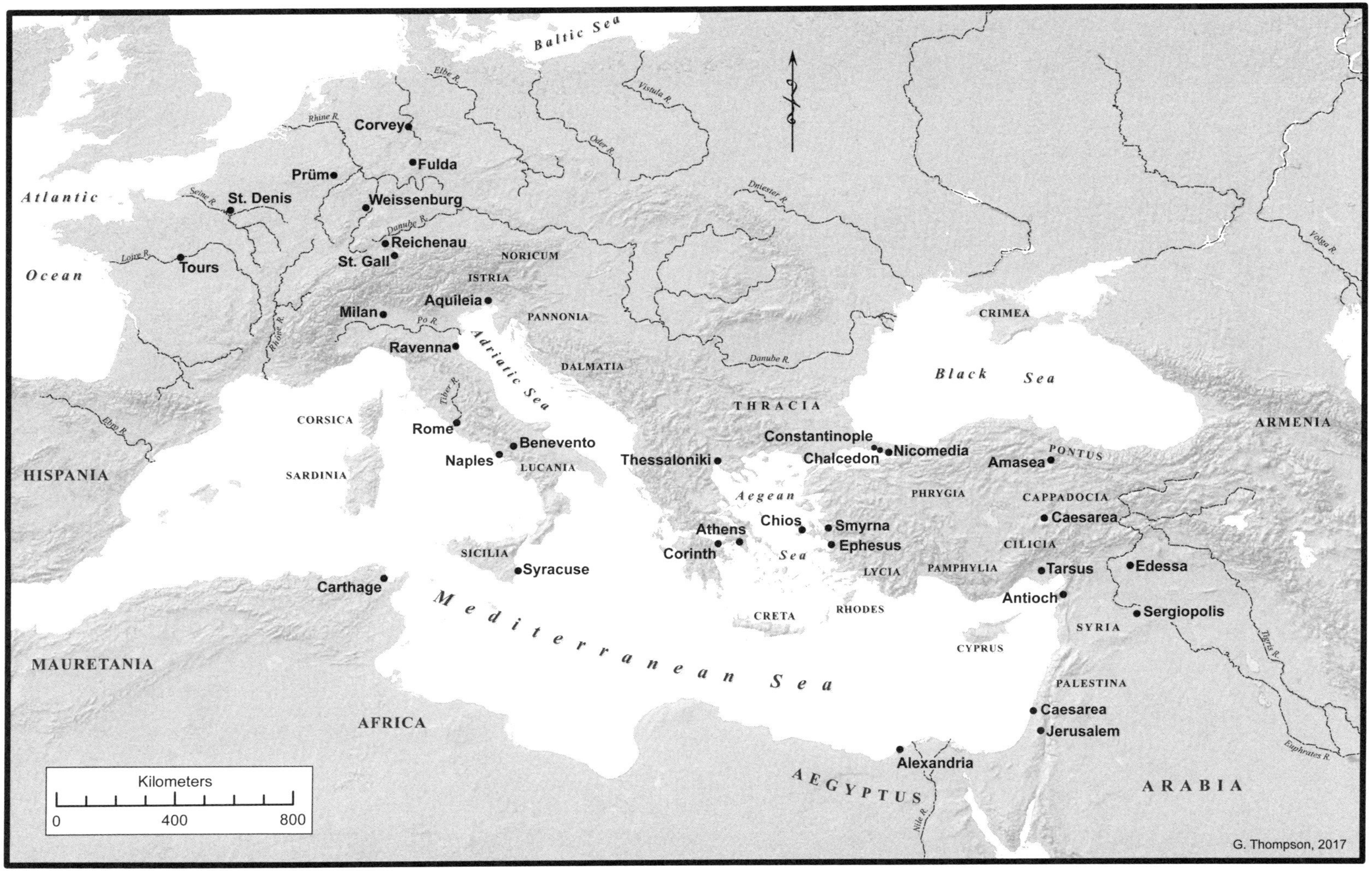

Map 2. Map of the early medieval Mediterranean. Map created by Gordie Thompson.

Introduction

In the mid-eighth century, Fulrad, abbot of the monastery of St. Denis, north of Paris, was "burning with great enthusiasm" to serve God by rendering due honor to the most blessed Christian martyrs.[1] The theological basis for Fulrad's enthusiasm, as our source (probably a ninth-century monk in the monastery of Corvey in Saxony) explains, is that God placed "Abel, Seth, Enoch, Noah, Abraham and the other patriarchs, prophets, apostles, martyrs, confessors, virgins, widows and praiseworthy monks" like "stars" to guide humankind through darkness.[2] Accordingly, Fulrad, together with an equally devout lay relative, begged the Frankish king Pippin (the first king of the Carolingian dynasty), that they—like other contemporaries—might go to Rome to obtain relics, that is, the bodily remains of saints.[3] Saints, individuals whose life or death had earned them a place in heaven, were theoretically no longer constrained by earthly boundaries. In practice, however, they tended to be most present, especially when performing miracles, in their relics. King Pippin assented, and the abbot and his relative set off on a long journey to Rome.[4] They returned having succeeded in their mission: Fulrad, with the bodies of the saints Alexander and Hippolytus, martyred in Rome; his relative, with that of St. Vitus, martyred, according to legend, in southern Italy, in Lucania, under the Roman emperor Diocletian.

It is easy to take for granted Fulrad's enthusiasm for Rome. The Carolingian fascination with Rome, ancient and Christian, is well documented.[5] Today, Rome, "the eternal city," continues to enchant us, drawing countless visitors from afar. This was the city that had given birth to the Roman Empire, whose wealth flowed back into the city, transforming it from brick into marble. This was the city where the apostles Peter and Paul had been martyred and that boasted grand basilicas dedicated by the first Christian emperor, Constantine. Not without reason, then, has the city often seemed—to scholars, inhabitants, and visitors alike—predestined for greatness.[6] But it was not: Rome's ability to reinvent itself in countless guises over the centuries was neither predictable nor inevitable.

Quite to the contrary, eighth-century Rome was a paradoxical place.[7] Once the head of the extensive Roman Empire, the city had shrunk physically, economically, and politically into a shadow of its former imperial self. Constantinople, not Rome, was now the capital of the much smaller Roman Empire, conventionally termed the "Byzantine" Empire,[8] and a new, Carolingian empire was soon to take shape in Europe under Charlemagne, the son of king Pippin. The bishop of Rome, the pope, styled himself the head of a "universal" church, but many Christians throughout the Mediterranean world had reservations about that characterization. No longer did peoples, products, and ideas from across the Mediterranean world stream into the city with the same great frequency. As archaeological work has shown, long-distance trade to Rome from Sicily, North Africa, and farther afield continued, although not with the same intensity, throughout the seventh century, but thereafter declined significantly.[9] Rome's population was a small fraction of what it had been in previous centuries, with pockets of habitation interspersed within its grand nineteen-kilometer wall. Precise numbers are notoriously difficult to obtain, but we may imagine a population on the order of a million in the early empire, declining to something around 50,000–60,000 residents in the later sixth to seventh centuries, and decreasing still further to 20,000–30,000 by the later eighth century.[10]

Yet, eighth-century Rome remained a monumental city with traces of its former imperial glory on view.[11] It had assertive spiritual and political overseers, the blessed apostles Peter and Paul, and Peter's living representative, the pope.[12] But Rome also had something more—another ingredient that acted as a catalyst to its remarkable transformation from a crumbling city with an imperial and Christian past to the spiritual capital of western Christendom. This feature inspired Fulrad's journey to Rome.

Rome in the early eighth century, as part of the Byzantine Empire, was shaped by its interactions with the wider Mediterranean world; it was also a city turning to face north of the Alps.[13] As a Mediterranean city, Rome housed saints, like Vitus, who were venerated, but *not* martyred, in Rome. These were saints whose cults had spread throughout the Mediterranean world but were not necessarily well known in the Frankish kingdoms or other communities north of the Alps. Eastern merchants, travelers, and refugees brought stories and relics of such saints to Rome, and in Rome, Roman administrators, ecclesiastics, and aristocrats actively participated in their cults. Adapted to Rome's multilayered imperial and Christian past, these new saints and their communities contributed to the city's dynamic sacred topography, magnifying Rome's allure to audiences north of the Alps. These saints and their communities are the missing ingredient that explains why Rome became the prime Carolingian destination for serving God with enthusiasm.

* * *

This book investigates this understudied category of evidence: saints who were venerated, but *not* martyred, in Rome.[14] It argues that these saints were critical to Rome's remarkable metamorphosis, against all odds, from an exhausted city with a limited Christian presence to a city filled with a seemingly inexhaustible reservoir of sanctity.

The period under study here, roughly the sixth to the ninth centuries, is commonly referred to as the early Middle Ages. It has also been called the Dark Ages, a description that does accurately reflect the paucity of surviving evidence. As their names suggest, the early Middle Ages and its counterpart, Late Antiquity (roughly the third to the sixth centuries), are periods that fall between the cracks of the traditional historical periodizations of Antiquity and the Middle Ages. Yet, scholarly work in the past fifty years, above all that of Peter Brown, has dispelled the notion of Late Antiquity as a "break" in history.[15] Instead we have come to see Late Antiquity as a vibrant period in its own right characterized by the reworking of Roman forms in new guises. Emblematic, for Rome, is the widespread use of spolia: reused architectural materials from the older imperial city creatively reconfigured into new, usually Christian, constellations.[16] This prompts the question of what happened next: how did Rome develop in new ways out of its late antique heritage?

* * *

Studying saints from abroad in Rome provides us insight into this transformation. There was nothing intrinsically different about how or why saints from abroad were venerated in the city in comparison with the veneration of saints martyred in Rome. Both types of saints provided patronage and protection to their communities. And yet, it is instructive to focus on the category of saints from abroad for two principal reasons.

First, patchy and often unsatisfactory as the evidence is, such an approach complicates our static picture of the early medieval city. It wrenches us away from the myth of the inevitable rise of a Rome destined for Christian primacy, shepherded through the "Dark Ages" by powerful popes.[17] By attending to the less studied evidence of saints' cults from abroad, we begin to hear a vibrant plurality of voices—of Byzantine administrators, refugees, monks, pilgrims, and others—as well as ecclesiastics, enmeshed in a wider world stretching across the Mediterranean and western Europe. Unexpected and unintended as their actions were, these individuals were as vital as any early medieval pope in shaping the saintly topography of Rome.

Second, although these saints were not necessarily "foreign" in the sense of being exotic or even obscure to Roman audiences (though some certainly were), the locations in which these saints were martyred (or, in the case of confessors, where they died) did matter. In the matrix of late antique and early medieval Christendom, a saint's identity was constituted by three basic coordinates: his or her name; "birthday," that is, the date of death and entrance into heaven; and place of death. Indeed, many of Rome's own martyrs, including Peter and Paul, had come to Rome only late in life, but belonged to the city by virtue of their deaths. In their posthumous travels, saints retained these coordinates, ensuring their identification in new surroundings. The ninth-century text that records how St. Vitus's relics were translated from Rome to St. Denis (and subsequently, as the text proceeds to narrate, to a monastery in Saxony) recalls that Vitus was martyred in Lucania on June 15.[18] Wherever a saint went, he or she bore this geographical marker, evoking a world beyond the confines of the saint's new community.

In Rome, the presence of these saints gave particular inflexion to the city, rendering it more than just another localized community. (Appendix 1 provides an overview of saints from abroad venerated in Rome from about 500–800.) Rome's Mediterranean sanctity contributed to and complicated its already rich late antique Christian and imperial heritage. From a Mediterranean perspective the presence of these saints in Rome was not remarkable: many cities throughout the Mediterranean world boasted a similar range of saints. From a Carolingian perspective, however, this diversity was more unexpected. Part of what made Rome so distinctive to northern audiences was that the city was home to this wider world of saints associated with distant locations. Given forceful organizers, which it had in a number of assertive early medieval popes, and given an actively engaged audience—above all the Carolingian elite—Rome could stand in as a microcosm of the macrocosm of "universal" Christianity.[19]

* * *

Saints were an integral part of late antique and early medieval Christendom.[20] The essence of an individual's sanctity was his or her *virtus*, "virtue," which rendered a saint closer to God than other mortals. Holy men and women were recognizable by their exemplary ways of life or feats of endurance; martyrs had secured their place in heaven by dying for the faith. Saints were intercessors between heaven and earth, offering assistance and protection, physical and spiritual, to the men and women who invoked them in their prayers. Saints had the ability to perform signs and miracles. Relics, the living remains of deceased saints, perpetuated their presence on earth.

Not that everyone agreed about the role of saints. How to recognize a saint and what powers saints and their relics possessed were difficult questions to answer. Pope Gregory the Great (r. 590–604), in his influential *Dialogues*, showcased holy men and women in Italy, the merit of whose lives, he explained, was to be measured by their good works, not their display of miracles.[21] Gregory emphasized the moral achievements—in particular humility—of the living, in contradistinction, so scholars have argued, to the dramatic deaths and posthumous miracles detailed in the hagiographical legends of many martyrs.[22] At the same time, however, Gregory was concerned to defend the cult of saints against more radical naysayers, such as those who denied that saints were still active after death.[23] Meanwhile, on a more practical level, the reliability of hagiographical texts and the authenticity of relics were perennial sources of concern.

For the present study, it is important to recognize the instability of a saint's cult. Every time a saint "moved," his or her sanctity needed to be reconstituted by the saint's new community. New buildings, artwork, reliquaries, and texts gave meaning to a saint in his or her new surroundings and, when they survive, provide indications of this process. The second point to be emphasized is that for all the agonizing about sanctity, past and present, more often than not, saints *were* taken for granted in early medieval Rome. For as we will see, saints were undeniably present in Rome: in the form of relics, but also in glittering mosaics, in the stories that circulated, and, above all, in the minds of the men and women who lavished so much time and care on their cults.

* * *

Roman sanctity did not emerge out of nowhere. Rome in the sixth to ninth centuries was part of a larger Mediterranean world in flux, and saints and their forms of veneration followed the same pathways as contemporary peoples, products, and ideas.[24] After its reexpansion under the Emperor Justinian (r. 527–565), the Byzantine Empire shrank, its unquestioned capital became Constantinople, regions throughout the Mediterranean turned in on themselves (as was especially apparent in the irresolvable doctrinal disputes), and the Carolingians appeared on the Mediterranean stage.[25] These changes affected individuals and communities in Rome and beyond.

This triangulation—the Byzantine East, Rome, and Francia—was manifested in the circulation of specific saints' cults. Alongside Roman and Italian saints, most commonly venerated in Rome were saints associated with the Byzantine Mediterranean: Constantinople, Asia Minor, the Levant, and Egypt. A shared Christian heritage explained why such saints could travel so easily and why they appealed to new audiences. As I emphasized earlier, it would be misleading to categorize such saints as "foreign" from a Roman perspective. A merchant from Rome who sailed the Mediterranean would have been more familiar with St. Menas—whose cult was based in Alexandria, but who was popular among sailors throughout the late antique Mediterranean (and to whom a church was dedicated in Rome)—than one of the more obscure of Rome's many "native" martyrs in the catacombs. Saints who belonged to the cultural *koine* of the late antique Mediterranean world readily settled in Rome.

Nevertheless Roman communities did adapt saints' cults to their new surroundings, to Rome's multilayered past. By A.D. 600 the city of Rome could look back on a thousand years of urban development. As the imperial capital, Rome had drawn in the resources of its far-flung empire, and the late antique city retained the imprint of this imperial—and pagan—legacy.[26] Although Krautheimer's assessment of church building in the early Middle Ages and his emphasis on the symbolic significance of salient architectural features have come under critique, his cultural history of Rome through its monuments, *Rome, Profile of a City, 312–1308*, remains the most eloquent and persuasive exploration of the continued impact of Rome's monumental past on successive generations.[27] Rome's urban legacy also shaped where and how saints' cults took hold in Rome—as emphasized by Louis Duchesne (d. 1922) and Albert Dufourcq (d. 1952) in their pioneering work on saints' cults in late antique and medieval Rome.[28] Preexisting buildings were repurposed as ecclesiastical dedications, legends of saints interacted with the monuments and stories that were already in place, and regions throughout Rome had resilient reputations to which new communities and their saints adjusted. Saints from abroad were changed in Rome even as they changed the city.

From a Carolingian perspective, then, these were saints that were at once "foreign," unfamiliar saints associated with distant locations, and "Roman"—saints validated and desirable because they were to be found in Rome. Saints from abroad contributed to Rome's unique profile of sanctity that so captivated visitors, like Fulrad, from north of the Alps. In turn, Rome became a transportable resource that could be disconnected from the city and carried—especially in the form of relics—to new locations.[29]

* * *

My study is guided by two images of Rome: Rome as an "ecosystem of sanctity" and Rome as a "storehouse of saints." The introductory walk through mid-eighth-century Rome (Chapter 1) and the following four chapters consider Rome's ecosystem of sanctity. Rome was a living, breathing, ever-changing city, and saints both contributed to and complicated the relationship between its communities and the city's densely built environment.[30] My primary aim in these chapters is to make tangible some of the dynamic interactions that built up Rome's firm foundation of sanctity. The focus is on the neighborhoods in Rome where saints from abroad had the strongest impact on the transformation of the city: the Forum Romanum and the Palatine, where Byzantine administrators took an active role in reshaping Rome's imperial past; the Tiber bend, a hub for traders and other travelers from the Mediterranean; and the Aventine Hill, with its cosmopolitan elite. Chapters 2 through 4 proceed roughly chronologically to trace how the influx of saints into Rome was affected by the Byzantine conquest of Italy in the sixth century, the shifting contours of the seventh-century Mediterranean, and expanding papal prerogatives in the eighth century; Chapter 5 takes a longer-term perspective appropriate to the Aventine's distinctive traditions of sanctity.

Saints from abroad helped mold Rome's unique ecosystem of sanctity—a city of saints embedded in an imperial and early Christian past. Consequently, they also helped mold the mental landscape that arose out of this living and changing city: the idea of Rome as an inexhaustible storehouse of sanctity. Chapters 6, 7, and 8 tackle the processes that were most influential in unifying and propagating Rome's sacred topography: the papal interest in collectivities of sanctity and the Carolingian interest in appropriating, codifying, and magnifying Rome and its sanctity. An epilogue returns briefly to the city of Rome. My hope is that readers will come to share the excitement that Fulrad and others like him felt when they encountered or imagined Rome.

CHAPTER 1

A City of Saints

Sanctity added another dimension to the ecosystem that was Rome. Saints did so by their physical presence in the city and by their stories that reached backward and forward in time. These legends knotted saints to the city and its past, opening up worlds beyond Rome: pagan emperors of bygone centuries, distant cities across the Mediterranean, and the heavens above. This chapter introduces this city of saints with a walk through Rome in the mid-eighth century.[1]

This walk is largely based on the storehouses of material about Rome that Carolingians collected. In particular I draw on two types of evidence: first, a remarkable ninth-century manuscript produced in the Frankish monastery of Fulda in Hessen (Germany): the Einsiedeln compilation (Codex Einsidlensis 326, ff. 67–97). This manuscript is a compilation of diverse materials, much of it related to the city of Rome. It includes transcriptions of inscriptions from Rome, "itineraries" through the city, statistics about Rome's wall, a brief liturgical description of mass at the Lateran, and a poetry collection. In Chapter 7 we will return to the Einsiedeln compilation to consider how this manuscript both collapsed the city into a static set of words on the page and magnified the meaning of Rome. In making use of the Einsiedeln compilation to reconstruct early medieval Rome, I am following a long historiographical tradition.[2] Second, and less conventionally, my walk makes use of hagiographical texts related to saints found in Rome. These are texts that most often survive today in the versions copied and circulated throughout the Frankish world, particularly at prominent monasteries such as Fulda.

Assisted by archaeological evidence from early medieval Rome, I layer these stories of saints back onto the Roman landscape. My aim is to convey a sense of the city's rich and multilayered texture of sanctity, showing how Rome's saints, almost all martyrs of imperial persecutions of bygone centuries, offered a firm foundation of sanctity that was embedded in the fabric of the city's imperial past. I also point out certain neighborhoods inside the city where the influence of saints from abroad was especially strong. We will revisit these neighborhoods in the chapters that follow.

* * *

In layering saints' stories onto the Roman landscape I draw freely on a wide range of early medieval legends from different sources. Some readers may object to this approach. Accordingly, I should emphasize that my aim is not to reconstruct the viewpoint of one particular observer nor present a comprehensive overview of all potential viewpoints; rather it is to present the sorts of associations that monuments in Rome would have evoked for contemporaries. Such an approach is justified by the fluid relationship between saints, places, and their stories.

The legends surrounding a saint were always in flux. Whether transmitted orally or in writing, stories changed, and in the best of circumstances we can never be sure exactly which versions of a saint's legend were percolating through the city. What any given individual knew about a saint was, of course, all the more unpredictable. Little is known about the precise practices of saintly commemoration in early medieval Rome. Saints' legends (martyrs' *passiones* or confessors' *vitae*) were certainly read aloud on the anniversaries of their feast days, even as a much more diffuse, muddled mix of anecdotes hovered around a saint.[3]

Take St. Anthony in Rome today. Anthony was a late third- to early fourth-century hermit in the Egyptian desert. His well-known *vita*, as refracted through twentieth-century literature and film, tends to follow certain recognizable outlines: a renunciation of city life, a struggle with demons, a stark asceticism. It is none of these traits, however, that draws crowds to his statue in the church of S. Eusebio in Rome on the Saturday after his feast day on January 17 (Figure 1). With their dogs, cats, birds, goldfish, and other animals, these pet owners come to have their animals blessed: Anthony's reputation for protecting animals is clearly evidenced by the pet pig who keeps his statue company. In reconstructing the sanctity of early medieval Rome, we must likewise remain open to such a plurality of stories and associations as refracted in contemporary sources.

As they fluctuated, saints' stories transformed their surroundings. Because saints had a more immediate impact on the places in which they were situated and the people with whom they interacted on a daily basis, the subsequent chapters focus on changes within specific communities. Yet a saint's sanctity could also pulse through the city and affect other saints, places, and people. The *passio* of Tatiana, a Roman martyr, slightly modified, became the *passio* of the Roman martyr Martina to whom a church was dedicated in the heart of Rome, on the Forum Romanum.[4] Adapted yet again, the narrative served to explain the fate of Prisca,

Figure 1. Statue of St. Anthony at S. Eusebio. Photograph by author, January 2014.

another Roman martyr, located high up on the Aventine Hill. Or, in the form of portable trinkets and other paraphernalia, saints themselves moved throughout the city. This chapter provides a glimpse of this larger world of Roman sanctity as background for the more microscopic studies that follow.

* * *

Let us begin our walk through Rome. Imagine a sunny day in early April 752.[5] You are entering the city from the northwest along the ancient via Triumphalis. Just before descending into Rome this road rises onto a slight hill (Monte Mario), where visitors for centuries have admired Rome from above. The undulating Tiber River weaves its way through the landscape. Sharp contours define the city: the nineteen-kilometer wall forms a clear boundary, although by no means a firm limit, to the sprawling metropolis inside.[6] The wall itself is a structure that can stand in, as shorthand, for the grandeur that is Rome. A meticulous count might verify that "there are 383 towers, 7,020 crenels, 5 small gates, 116 latrines and 2,066 large windows" in the wall.[7]

Out of the walls, like tentacles, stretch the cities' arteries, the sturdy roads—built up from the bedrock—that once connected Rome to its vast Mediterranean empire. In bewildering profusion, centuries of the dead cluster around these roads, clamoring for attention. Smaller steles compete with towering mausolea, each justifying itself with extensive inscriptions. Long names and titles, truncated to single letters, are the norm:

> C · DILLIO · A · F · SER · VOCVLAE / TRIB · MILIT · LEG · I · IIII · VIRO · VIARVM · CVRANDAR / Q · PROVINC · PONTI · ET · BITHYNIAE · TRIB · PL · PR / LEG · IN GERMANIA · LEG · XXII · PRIMIGENIAE / HELVIA · T · F · PROCVLA · VXOR · FECIT

With skill we can decode this inscription to learn the genealogy and career of a certain Gaius Dillius Vocula.[8] Among the many tombs are other messages too: a stele announces a customs boundary established by decree of Emperor Caesar Marcus Aurelius Antoninus Augustus, assuring merchants that they are obligated to pay their customs duties only once.[9]

There are merchants on the road, but they don't give a moment's pause to these inscriptions. More attentive to the verbal cues are pilgrims. On the road we might meet Fulrad and his lay relative, accompanied by a few servants and a Roman tour guide.[10] They are making their way through this pagan monumentality, searching out its Christian treasure: the bones of Roman martyrs. Fulrad (so we may imagine) has brought with him an itinerary that lists the extramural cemeteries around Rome and their saints and is trying to correlate the guide's information with this document.[11]

Spacious basilicas with glimmering mosaics are these pilgrims' most obvious destinations.[12] From Monte Mario we are headed to the most spectacular of them all, the Vatican complex, home to Rome's foremost saint, Peter.[13] We must certainly stop to pray near Peter's relics, but the basilica also has many other attractions to visit.[14] Its grand apse mosaic proclaims, “The seat of justice, the house of faith, the hall of chastity: this is what you perceive, what all piety inhabits.”[15]

The Vatican area around St. Peter’s is a small town unto itself. Here are houses, shops, and fountains. We can purchase trinkets or precious silks imported from the eastern Mediterranean.[16] There are monasteries whose monks serve the basilica. Two of these are dedicated to St. Stephen of Jerusalem: as protomartyr, he is always a dependable saint for a Roman monastery.[17] There are also *scholae*, associations of foreigners, united for mutual support and protection and providing assistance to their respective pilgrims or other travelers.[18] The Saxons are well established: not long ago Ina, king of Wessex (d. after 726), like his predecessor Cæwalla (d. 689), abdicated his throne and left the rainy British isle to settle in Rome. The Saxon *schola* is anchored by a church for the Virgin Mary, by far the most popular patron for churches in Rome.[19]

* * *

On the other roads leading into Rome are different, smaller, communities of the living providing for the dead. The monastic communities at these sites vary: some are male, some female, and there are also a few Greek-speaking communities.[20] Especially noteworthy are S. Paolo fuori le Mura, home to Peter’s counterpart St. Paul, on the via Ostiensis, and S. Lorenzo fuori le Mura, home to the Roman deacon St. Lawrence, on the via Tiburtina.

Each of these extramural basilicas is shaped by devotion to its patron saint. Entering the compact basilica of S. Agnese on the via Nomentana we are immersed in marble splendor.[21] From the main apse, St. Agnes, decked out in rich imperial garb, stares down at us (Plate 1). Two soberly dressed priests stand at either side of her. Shimmering stars hover in the dark blue sky above. On her tomb, below the altar, elegantly carved letters remind us of Agnes’s devoted preservation of her virginity, how she “of her own accord scorned the threats and rage of the savage tyrant,” a resolve that catapulted her to eternal majestic splendor.[22] A priest might read out Agnes’s *passio* for us, grimly detailing how the son of a Roman prefect had fallen madly in love with Agnes on her way home from school one day. He promised her all the wealth in the world if only she would not refuse him. Unimpressed, the little virgin refused and, even when dragged naked through the streets to a brothel, did not lose her trust in Christ.[23]

On the other side of Rome, along the via Ostiensis, past S. Paolo fuori le Mura, at the monastery Ad Aquas Salvias, we may visit a Greek-speaking community that boasts the head of St. Anastasius. Anastasius—Magundat before his Christian conversion—was a Persian by birth, a soldier in the army of the Persian king who deserted the army, traveled to Jerusalem, converted to Christianity, and then was martyred in Persia. In the first half of the seventh century refugees from the Jerusalem area, fleeing the Arab invasions of their homeland, brought the precious relic of Anastasius's head and also a copy of his Greek *passio* to Rome.[24] The community has since actively promoted the cult of Anastasius and translated the Greek *passio* into Latin. As the monks are proud to report, Anastasius has performed miracles in Rome, such as exorcising a demon from the daughter of Theopemptos, a Syrian immigrant to Rome.[25]

* * *

Yet for the most committed of pilgrims, these extramural monasteries will not suffice. Our quest thus takes us down into the depths of the labyrinthine catacombs. There altars, frescoes, and elegantly inscribed marble tablets (often, as at S. Agnese, flourishing the trusted name of Pope Damasus, r. 366–384) assure us that we are in the right place.[26] The pilgrims around us address their prayers to the saints or furtively glance around for an opportunity to snatch a few bones that would provide firm foundations for the dedication of a new church back home.[27] Some visitors scratch their names onto the walls. "I, Rapulus, a humble and unworthy monk," scrawls a visitor to the cemetery of SS. Marcellino e Pietro.[28]

Navigating these many shrines is a laborious and often perplexing task. The numbers and names of saints multiply rapidly. On the via Aurelia, "you go to St. Pancratius . . . and in that church you will go far under the earth and find the martyr Arthemius, and in another place, the martyr St. Paulinus, and in another niche the martyr St. Sophia and her two daughters, the martyrs, Agape and Pistis."[29] It is difficult to keep all these saints' stories straight. Gorgonius? Was he the saint buried on the via Labicana at the cemetery near the church dedicated to the empress St. Helena? Or was he the one who was martyred in Nicomedia on the orders of Emperor Diocletian and whose body was only later brought to Rome and buried on the via Latina "between two laurel trees"?[30]

Legends float through these realms and multiply. Damasus's inscription honoring Agnes begins, "Fama refert," crediting to tradition his account of Agnes's martyrdom. Alternate versions circulate. Damasus's verses suggest that Agnes suffered martyrdom by fire; his contemporary Ambrose of Milan recounts that she was decapitated.[31] Stories mingle and mix. Certainly if we are planning to bring home a few of these precious relics it would be best to have a *passio* transcribed.[32] In the end it will be the saint who proves his or her own sanctity, but some indications of authenticity would be desirable given all the bones and stories that circulate.

Altogether, these saints with their interwoven, at times contradictory, legends form the substructure of Rome's Christian past. Paul was the first of the apostles to reach Rome (we are told), but it is Peter to whom the stories ascribe much of the hard labor of conversion, not least in his dramatic face-off with the magician Simon.[33] Both Peter and Paul came from the "East," but were martyred in Rome, at opposite ends of the city. Thus, in the words of Damasus's epigram, "Rome has merited to claim them as citizens."[34] Later, some Greeks tried to snatch their bodies away from Rome. Unsurprisingly they failed.[35]

Peter and Paul were only the first of Rome's crown of martyrs. As Pope Leo (r. 440–461) explained, "Thousands of blessed martyrs, rivaling the Apostles' triumphs, have circled the city far and wide in purple-clad and ruddy-gleaming throngs, and crowned it, as it were, with a single diadem of countless gems linked by honor."[36] Processus and Martinianus were assigned to guard Peter and Paul, but after being baptized by Peter they were martyred on the orders of Emperor Nero.[37] Early bishops of Rome, many of them martyrs, had built up the Christian Church: Pope Marcellinus, who had his head chopped off on the orders of Emperor Diocletian, or Pope Sylvester who, according to one version of the story, cured the Emperor Constantine of leprosy and converted him to Christianity.[38] There are other imperial conversions too: St. Cyriacus exorcised a demon from Artemia, the daughter of Emperor Diocletian, and then baptized her. Cyriacus also baptized Iobe, the daughter of Sapor, a king of Persia, before he was martyred in Rome.

And there are the many less prominent men, women, and children, ecclesiastics and lay, Romans and foreigners, rich and poor, whose stories tell of their horrendous deaths under persecuting emperors. Whole families were martyred: the seven brothers, sons of St. Felicitas, each put to death in a different manner; or Marius and Martha, with their sons Audifax and Abbacuc, nobles of Persia who came to Rome to pray and were martyred under Emperor Claudius. There are the martyrdoms that set off chain reactions: the constancy of Saturninus and Sisinnius inspired Papias and Maurus to follow them to martyrdom. Then there are the saints who specialized in burying martyrs: the matron Lucina and the presbyter John, both of whom appear in numerous legends honorably burying other martyrs.[39] Most saints buried in the catacombs were martyred in Rome, but there are exceptions: on the via Appia we can visit the tomb of Bishop Quirinus of Sescia (today, Sisak in Croatia) who was martyred far from Rome, but whose relics were brought to the catacombs for safekeeping.

Again and again what stands out in these martyrs' stories is the violence of their deaths. The martyr Lawrence slowly burns to death on a grill, with enough time to joke to his executors that he needs to be turned over to assure even cooking.[40] Gladiators kill Almachius after he protests that pagan sacrifices should not take place to celebrate the first day of the new year. Angry pagans stone Agnes's sister Emerentiania to death while she prays at her sister's tomb. The schoolteacher

Cassian is killed by his own pupils, who strike him to death with their writing tablets and pens.

Still, there is more. These extramural basilicas, these catacombs with their blood-soaked stories, do not exhaust the sanctity of Rome. Inside the walls we find many more saints. Their stories, often transpiring across the Mediterranean world, render Rome a veritable Christian cosmopolis. Let us then draw our attention away from this "subterranean arsenal" of saints and proceed into the city.[41]

* * *

From the Vatican we enter Rome by crossing the Tiber where the river begins to bend back on itself. The dominant landmark here is an imposing fortress (Castel Sant'Angelo). It is covered with inscriptions that remind viewers of its original construction as an imperial tomb.[42] Hovering above this imperial titulature is an oratory for the archangel Michael, the commander of the celestial army who, with his invincible sword, conquered the dragon, Satan.[43]

We cross over the murky waters of the Tiber. After heavy rains the river always threatens to rise over its banks and sweep the city away. If we catch sight of a dragon or serpent floating by, it surely portends some coming disaster.[44]

* * *

Inside Rome, as outside the city, saints compete for our attention. Yet the clamor of daily life is much stronger, and with the vegetable sellers and grumbling fishermen it takes effort to remember that this is a sacred city. Only if we are attentive does this world of sanctity emerge.

The low-lying plain of the Campus Martius where we have entered the city is an especially dense thicket.[45] Without any hills from which to regain perspective, we can quickly get lost in the maze of little streets, losing any orientation. A lone cypress tree can serve as the most reliable signpost.[46] Aristocratic dwellings front the more prominent roads, but if we duck into the neighborhoods we find smaller ramshackle houses and heaps of trash among the large tufa blocks of ancient monuments.[47]

In this tangle of buildings we encounter presences familiar from outside the walls. Emerging into an open piazza (today the Piazza Navona), we spot a church dedicated to the young martyr Agnes. Avid connoisseurs of Roman saints' legends will identify this as a circus arena, the execution site of many Roman martyrs, surely including Agnes herself.[48] Nearby is a church for St. Lawrence, whose name, Sancti Laurentii in Damaso, alerts us that we can again find here the trustworthy hand of Pope Damasus at work in commemorating Rome's martyrs.[49]

At every step, if we stop to notice, there are strong saintly personalities. Around the corner from the piazza is a *diaconia* dedicated to St. Eustachius. The building is nestled up against the ruins of a spacious bath complex with high vaulted ceilings.[50] Such massive bath complexes are regular presences in the city: testaments to the pagan love for superfluous luxury, so a Roman tour guide might admonish you.[51] A crowd indicates there is an attraction here. Come closer, and it becomes clear that this in fact is a queue. Poor Romans and visitors are waiting as portions of grain are being handed out.

Diaconiae, such as that of S. Eustachio, are charitable institutions that provide provisions to the poor and travelers.[52] Some are built directly into or adjacent to preexisting imperial structures, allowing them more easily to store the grain that they distribute.[53] Some of Rome's *diaconiae* additionally provide facilities for ritual bathing. Although Rome's imperial bath complexes lie unused and in ruins, Rome remains a city of water. Its ancient aqueducts continue to pour water into the city, feeding watermills and filling public fountains.[54]

An island of welfare in the harsh city, each *diaconia* is headed by a prominent member of the Roman elite and maintained by a dedicated (male) community, often including Greek-speaking members of the Roman elite, some of whom are immigrants. Each *diaconia* is also dedicated to a patron saint or, in many cases, the Virgin Mary. These patrons are often saints from abroad who appeal to the *diaconia*'s diverse constituency.

At the *diaconia* that we now approach, our patron is St. Eustachius, whose noble status, devotion to God, and dedication to the poor correspond well to the aspirations of the *diaconia*'s members. Eustachius's *passio* is in Greek, but the community assures us that there is also a Latin translation available.[55] Let us stop to read his *passio* since its dominant themes—the definition of nobility in Christian terms, the fraught relationship between the Roman Empire and Christianity, and the travails imposed by travel and displacement—all recur in subsequent chapters.

Placidas, as he was called before his Christian conversion, was a nobleman and highly successful general living in Rome during the reign of Emperor Trajan. Although a pagan, Placidas and his wife and family exhibited all the characteristics of pious Christians: in particular, he (like members of his *diaconia*) ministered to the poor and suffering. God thus deemed him worthy for conversion. One day while Placidas was hunting outside of Rome, a cross with the image of Christ appeared between the horns of the stag he was following, and Placidas was converted to Christianity, changing his name to Eustachius. This was the start to an eventful life of travels and hardships, and thereupon he and his family began to undergo terrible misfortunes in the manner of Job. They were displaced to Egypt and separated from each other, but nonetheless Eustachius remained steadfast in his faith.

An invasion of barbarians threatened the Roman Empire, and Emperor Trajan sent messengers everywhere searching for his foremost general. The messengers eventually found him, and so Eustachius led the imperial troops to victory and, while on campaign, was reunited with his family. After traversing the Mediterranean, Eustachius returned to Rome with his family to celebrate his triumph, but not as he had expected. During his absence the emperor Trajan had died and been replaced by Hadrian, who, angered by the family's refusal to sacrifice to the pagan gods, had them all martyred. The many trials Eustachius endured, in Egypt and on the road, were crowned by his triumphal martyrdom back in Rome.

Eustachius's legend offers a triumphalist Christian reinterpretation of Rome's imperial past: the Roman Empire's military successes occurred not in spite of, but precisely on account of, Christianity. Paganism had been long defeated in the city and had become a straw man easy to vilify. Nonetheless this genre of hagiography, set during the reign of one of Rome's prominent emperors and addressing the compatibility of Christianity and empire, enjoys widespread popularity among audiences in mid-eighth-century Rome. After all the Roman Empire is still a relevant topic everywhere on view in the city.

That empire stretches back to the days of Augustus, but its current status is uncertain. Is the administration based in Constantinople, with its demands for taxes, really the successor of Augustus's Rome? More tangibly, on the ground, the imperial past persists in full force. Christian legends provided a way for audiences in Rome to engage with and make sense of their surroundings. Saints competed, clashed with, and inevitably, triumphed over the strong imperial past in which they were enveloped. As paragons of Christian fortitude in the face of hardship, individuals like Eustachius presented a model for contemporaries. Romans were encouraged to scorn their worldly surroundings, to abandon the decaying remains of pagan temples—or reclaim them for a Christian purpose. Moreover, as warfare or other disasters displaced people across the Mediterranean—the Lombards' ravaging of northern Italy or the Arab invasions, to name just two—these legends provided the reassuring message that Christians had seen worse and could triumph over any adversity.

Saints are presences everywhere in the city. They can serve many purposes. They are powerful patrons who perform astonishing miracles. Their stories provide entertainment and encouragement. Saints can also deliver more targeted political messages. Right around the corner from S. Eustachio, on the other side of the bath complex, we find an example of such a saint.

Here is a church for St. Apollinaris.[56] Apollinaris's *passio* transpires across the Mediterranean and returns us to the days of the pagan Roman Empire. More readily, the name "Apollinaris" calls to mind the northern Italian city of Ravenna, where Apollinaris had served as its first bishop.[57] According to his *passio* Apollinaris had been raised in Antioch and trained in Greek and Latin letters.[58] He then became a disciple of St. Peter, who sent him to Ravenna. In that city Apollinaris accomplished miracles, and destroyed idols and pagan temples, converting many people to Christianity. Arrested and imprisoned he was led as a prisoner throughout the eastern Mediterranean. He returned to Ravenna to be martyred.

The church for Apollinaris in the Campus Martius in Rome celebrates the link between Rome and Ravenna. More than a century ago, Pope Honorius (r. 625–638), who was eager to confirm Rome's relationship with its neighboring sees, had dedicated a basilica for Apollinaris in the portico of St. Peter's.[59] In the mid-eighth century, dedications to Apollinaris took on special significance. Since the mid-sixth century when Byzantine troops swept through Italy, Ravenna had been the Byzantine Empire's key administrative stronghold in Italy: it was thus much more firmly tied to Constantinople than to Rome. In 751, however, Ravenna was captured by the Lombard king Aistulf, and Byzantine troops had not yet mobilized to recapture the city. Was the church for Apollinaris in Rome an expression of Roman support for the beleaguered Ravennese bishop? Or was it a reminder of his subordination to Rome?

* * *

Let us continue our walk. Before we leave the Campus Martius we should make a stop at one of Rome's most famous churches: the Pantheon, or, as it was also called, the Rotunda. The church is entered (as it still is today) through the columned portico, whose entablature proclaims that Agrippa ordered its construction.[60] Inside, marble veneer coats the floor and walls. The oculus in the dome lets in sunlight and rain. Early medieval Rome boasted other round churches, and there remained other massive imperial domed structures on view in the city. Nor was this the only ancient Roman building that had been repurposed for Christian use. Such considerations notwithstanding, the Pantheon presented a spectacular experience to anyone who entered it. Befitting its magnificence, the church was dedicated to the Virgin Mary and all the saints: a tempera painting of Mary carrying her son proclaims her presence.[61] In the early seventh century the Byzantine emperor Phocas had allowed Pope Boniface IV to convert the building into a church.[62] Later that century when the Byzantine emperor Constans II visited Rome, he was so impressed by the building that he had its bronze tiles stripped off and shipped to Constantinople.[63] In the late ninth century, its fame was such that the Frankish bishop Ado reasoned that this building must have inspired the establishment of an annual feast day to commemorate all the saints.[64]

Let us continue onward. We have various options at this point. Most of these routes will take us to less densely populated areas of the city. We can follow one of Rome's straightest streets (via Lata) to the north, all the way to the Porta Flaminia and out of the city. Along the way are obelisks; columns with spiraling friezes that tell stories of bygone military triumphs; three- and four-story apartment blocks (*insulae*), crumbling but often still inhabited; and aqueducts, some in use, some broken. We will encounter the popular St. Lawrence again and a church dedicated to Pope Sylvester, whose reputation for defeating dragons contributes to his suitability as a saint to populate the urban wilderness.[65] Dangerous basilisks may well still be lurking in these many rotting buildings.[66]

Or we can head up the Quirinal or Viminal Hills. Here too the buildings thin out. Gardens, vineyards, and open patches of unused space abound. Oxen plow the fields; pigs root around in the soil. The large aristocratic Roman houses (*domus*) arranged around courtyards are often only partially inhabited. Still, there are some saints to seek out in these neighborhoods. High up on the Quirinal, near the massive baths of Diocletian, is a church for St. Susanna: a beautiful Roman girl, martyred under the emperor Diocletian in her own home that then became her church, the *titulus* S. Susanna.[67]

The *tituli* are among Rome's oldest churches and can be found in almost every neighborhood in Rome.[68] They are parish churches, each dedicated to its own saint and catering to its local community, but tightly integrated into the papal administration. In the forty days of Lent preceding Easter, the bishop of Rome will have celebrated mass in almost all the *tituli*, following an elaborate liturgical schedule that takes him throughout the city.[69] Processing through the different neighborhoods, the pope maps out with his feet the aspiration of a unified city.

If you ask an eighth-century ecclesiastical official, he will likely tell you that the *tituli* date back to the time before Constantine and were a pastoral system designed by early popes.[70] (Modern scholars generally agree that the *tituli* date, for the most part, to the fourth and fifth centuries and were the result of donations to the Roman Church.[71]) Many of the *tituli*'s legends tell of their patron saints as Romans, usually aristocrats, male or female, but also as presbyters, popes, or other individuals who were martyred during the reign of one of the pagan emperors, the Arian Constantius II, or Julian the Apostate.[72] At times these legends, as in the case of St. Susanna, also associate their saints in some way with the buildings that became churches for them.

* * *

There are still more neighborhoods to explore up on these hills. Somewhat more frequented than the Quirinal and Viminal Hills is the Esquiline Hill (best accessed

Figure 2. S. Vito. Photograph by Marion Riggs.

via a steep road, the ancient Roman clivus Suburbanus that leads up from the Forum Romanum): this is a verdant district with aristocratic mansions and crumbling apartment buildings, but few monumental temples from antiquity. Here we find the most prestigious of Rome's many Marian dedications: S. Maria Maggiore. Although it does not rival St. Peter's or the Lateran, S. Maria Maggiore is an old and hallowed church.[73] Pilgrims may venerate the crib in which Christ was born, and appropriately, here the Roman bishop celebrates Christmas vigil and midnight mass, as well as other important feast days, not least the Assumption of Mary.[74]

Nearby are two titular churches dedicated to distinguished Roman saints: St. Praxedis and St. Pudentiana, aristocratic women with whom the apostle Paul stayed during his sojourn in Rome.[75] Not far away, attached to an arch celebrating Emperor Gallienus and his wife, Salonina, is a *diaconia* dedicated to the child martyr Vitus—whose relics Fulrad's lay relative will acquire while in Rome (Figure 2). This imperial juxtaposition befits a saint who had briefly visited Rome to exorcise a demon from Emperor Diocletian's son before being martyred in Lucania in southern Italy.[76] Nor is the imperial past a mere backdrop. Many of the key terms celebrating the imperial family on the arch—clemency, virtue, piety, and sanctity—likewise occur in the *passio* of Vitus to describe him or his Christian God.[77] The Christian appropriation of Roman values is on display in the theater of Rome's monuments.

* * *

To find the heart of early medieval Rome, however, we must descend from these hills. The center, since time immemorial, has been the Forum Romanum, the low-lying plain where paths running throughout the city intersect.[78] Whether travelling from the Vatican to the Lateran, coming up from the Tiber's ports, or walking down from the agricultural fields in the hills, this is a convenient spot to stop and trade.

A steep ascent from the Forum brings us up the craggy Capitoline Hill. "The Capitolium is so called because it was the highest *caput* of the Roman city and religion," so Hrabanus Maurus, abbot of Fulda, a leading Carolingian theologian in the early ninth century, would write about the hill in his encyclopedic work *On the Nature of Things*.[79] Its name evokes grandeur, but there is not much reason to climb this hill today. It is certainly worth a visit for those interested in transcribing old Roman inscriptions but does not have much to offer anyone else.[80]

In the Forum Romanum we find few private houses and no *tituli*. Old Roman porticos shelter shops from the sun and rain.[81] Numerous ecclesiastical dedications are built into and around the imperial monuments. Many of these are associated with the Byzantine administration that retains at least nominal control over much of this area, and visitors from the imperial capital of Constantinople will recognize visual and saintly parallels between the Forum Romanum and the Augustaion, the forum in the heart of Constantinople. These are the result of a dialogue over centuries between the two cities that we will explore further in Chapter 2.

Moving on, we now have many choices. We may climb the Palatine Hill (Chapter 3) to visit the crumbling ruins of the imperial palaces and an imperial chapel for St. Caesarius, whose legend takes us to the seaside town of Terracina, south of Rome. This is again, at least nominally, imperial property, although not since Constans II in the mid-seventh century has any emperor stayed in these palaces.

If we head toward the Tiber (Chapter 4), we will enter a lively commercial district where Greek-speaking merchants and immigrants arriving from overseas congregate. Here construction is underway on a new *diaconia* (S. Angelo in Pescheria). It is being built into a preexisting imperial structure (the porticus of Octavia), whose monumental imperial façade proclaims its restoration by the emperor Septimius Severus.[82] Responsible for its construction is Theodotus, a member of the Roman elite, who has had a distinguished career in both the civil—that is, Byzantine—and ecclesiastical, that is, papal, administrations. Theodotus has served both as dux, the foremost Byzantine administrator in Rome, and as *primicerius notariorum*, the closest advisor to the pope.

A few years ago, Theodotus, together with his wife and children, dedicated a chapel (in S. Maria Antiqua) to the saints Julitta and Quiricus: a mother and her young son martyred in Tarsus in Cilicia during the reign of the emperor

Diocletian.[83] In that chapel, the whole family is depicted, richly dressed, juxtaposed with scenes from the *passio* of Julitta and Quiricus (Plate 2). His daughter wears a sumptuous necklace and earrings in the fashion of the Constantinopolitan elite; his wife, a dress decorated with large medallions and elaborately decorated shoes.[84] These are women with influence, though we rarely hear their voices in public.

Theodotus's new charitable foundation will be dedicated in his own name without any reference to his family. For the dedication Theodotus has assembled an extensive collection of relics from across the Mediterranean world. The *diaconia* will be dedicated to St. Paul, but in the inscription tallying the relics with which the *diaconia* is dedicated, pride of place (after Christ and the Virgin) is given to the archangels Michael and Gabriel (Figure 3). Thereupon follow more than fifty saints, most of whom are associated with locations in Italy or throughout the eastern Mediterranean. Some of these saints are familiar presences in Rome, such as Theodore, a soldier-saint who enjoyed great popularity among Byzantine soldiers; Cosmas and Damian, popular physician-saints; and Euphemia, whose basilica in Chalcedon, in Asia Minor, had hosted the Council of Chalcedon debating the relation between the human and the divine in Christ. Others, like Christopher, are less known in Rome. This is an inscription that demonstrates Theodotus's conversant participation in a shared eastern Mediterranean, Byzantine culture of Christian sanctity: a world of saints largely unfamiliar north of the Alps.

* * *

Crossing onto and over the Tiber island brings us to a bustling neighborhood on the other side (Trastevere). As we head away from the river the settlements thin out, but there are *tituli* to visit. We find a *titulus* dedicated to Mary and one to St. Cecilia, who like Susanna was a Roman martyred in her own home. There is also a *titulus* dedicated to St. Chrysogonus, a Christian tutor in Aquilea in northern Italy, whose exchange of letters with the Roman noblewoman Anastasia inspired her to persevere in her faith. Their intertwined *passiones* tell of how Anastasia followed her tutor to Aquilea, where he was later martyred; she herself was martyred on the island of Palmaria, off the coast of northern Italy.[85]

Unless we want to climb the steep Janiculum and leave the city, we must now head back across the Tiber and venture into the valley dominated by the Circus Maximus, past the *titulus* dedicated to St. Anastasia.

At this point we could climb the Caelian Hill. As in many of the neighborhoods we have already visited, many of the houses in this area have been abandoned or repurposed.[86] Such changes notwithstanding, this remains a neighborhood favored by wealthy Romans. Some of the older aristocratic properties have become

Figure 3. S. Angelo in Pescheria, Theodotus's dedicatory inscription. Photograph by author.

monasteries; most famously Gregory the Great transformed his family home into a monastery dedicated to the apostle Andrew (S. Gregorio al Celio).[87] Farther up the hill, past a distinctive round church for the protomartyr Stephen, is a Greek-speaking monastic community dedicated to Erasmus.[88] Erasmus was a hermit outside of Antioch until an angel sent him forth on a life of travel that ended with his martyrdom in Formia in Campania.[89] Immigrants arriving in Rome from across the Mediterranean, whether fleeing from Arab conquests or Constantinopolitan politics, could empathize with his hard life of displacement.[90]

Or, from the Circus Maximus, we could make our way out of Rome, departing through the Porta Appia. This was the route taken by St. Peter when, before his martyrdom, he sought to leave the city, only to meet Christ, who urged him to turn back.[91] This path takes us past the imposing structure that once comprised the Baths of Caracalla, now in part agricultural fields and storage space. Nearby is a *titulus* dedicated to Nereus and Achilleus, eunuchs who served in the bedchamber of the emperor Domitian and convinced the emperor's granddaughter Domitilla to preserve her virginity. They were exiled to the island of Ponza and then martyred in Terracina south of Rome.[92]

Or we could climb the Aventine Hill (Chapter 5). In the tranquil setting of this green hill overlooking the Tiber we can find some of Rome's most unusual communities and saints. Affluent communities with ties across the Mediterranean world have found a home here, promoting saints appropriate to their own distinctive backgrounds and their Roman surroundings. This route is not commonly taken.[93]

* * *

Today is Friday, April 7, 752: Good Friday. Our destination then should be the Lateran basilica. To get there from the Forum Romanum, we head along the via Sacra, once the path of triumphal emperors in Rome and still a major artery. We pass by the Arch of Titus with its depictions of the spoils from the Temple of Jerusalem carried in triumph through Rome. There is the massive Roman amphitheater (Colosseum). Some of its bays serve as residences, others as storage spaces. Workers are lugging away blocks from another section of the structure for use in new construction. Others burn pieces of marble in small kilns to produce lime, an increasingly prominent industry throughout the city.[94] There are also tombs to be found, mostly shallow graves covered with tiles.[95] Tombs are less visible inside Rome than outside the walls, but burials do take place throughout the city.

Heading up through vineyards and fields we pass a dedication to the unusual Quattro Coronati (Chapter 6): Roman soldier-saints commemorated, by papal decree, under the names of stone masons martyred in Pannonia. We continue walking, and just before we reach the city walls, the rural landscape again becomes more urban. We are at the Lateran.

Here is an ecclesiastical dedication to Christ: the "ecclesia Salvatoris" also known as the "basilica Constantiniana," serviced by the Roman bishop himself.[96] The papal residence (*Patriarchium*) is also here. Its current inhabitant is Pope Stephen II, only recently elected after the decade-long pontificate of Pope Zacharias and, like many of his predecessors, "of Greek descent (*natione Grecus*)."[97] On Zacharias's death in late March 751, a Roman priest, Stephen, was elected, but died only a few days later so that another candidate had to be found. Pope Stephen II, a Roman who inherited Zacharias's strained relations with the Byzantine emperor Constantine V, was then elected; a few years later he would travel north of the Alps to the Frankish king Pippin in Paris to request military assistance against the Lombards and to consecrate the Frankish king. But this is still to come.

Good Friday is an occasion that brings out the sounds, smells, and even the tangible presence of the holy in the city.[98] On Friday, at around the eighth hour, the bishop of Rome (the pope), barefoot, is surrounded by other priests, all likewise barefoot; they gather at the altar in the large church. Two white torches are lit. Then a procession begins, led by the clerics carrying the torches. The bishop, with his right hand holding a censer and with his left clutching the hand of the archdeacon, processes out of the church. Following him a deacon carries the True Cross in its bejeweled reliquary case (Figure 4).[99] The psalm, "Blessed are the undefiled in the way, who walk in the law of the Lord," accompanies them. Incense pervades the air.

Figure 4. True Cross reliquary. Lavorazione no. 1311, courtesy of the Biblioteca Apostolica Vaticana, with all rights reserved.

The slow, rhythmic procession transports us from Rome to Jerusalem, that is, to S. Croce in Gerusalemme.[100] This was a church established in the private palace of the empress Helena, the mother of Emperor Constantine, who had spectacularly discovered the True Cross during excavations in Palestine.[101] Furnished with relics of the True Cross, the Roman church could now stand in for the most holy of all holy cities: Jerusalem.

The procession enters the church, and the deacon places the reliquary on the altar. The pope opens the reliquary and kisses the True Cross, which smells sweetly of balm. All the bishops, presbyters, deacons, and subdeacons proceed to the altar, in succession, to kiss the cross. Then the cross is brought to the laity, men and women separately, so that they too may kiss it. Meanwhile mass has continued: a subdeacon climbs the pulpit of the church and pronounces a reading from the prophet Isaiah; the cantor sings. Neither the bishop of Rome nor his deacons take communion. At the conclusion of the mass the procession returns to the Lateran, again accompanied by the psalm, "Blessed are the undefiled in the way . . ." Tomorrow, the liturgical celebrations will continue at the Lateran.

* * *

Rome, not only in the eyes of our visitor but also from the perspective of its inhabitants, was one city. It was a city defined by its name, its walls, its bishop, its people, its past. And yet because of its large size and diverse population, it was also a city of distinctive neighborhoods, each with a life of its own. The four chapters that follow focus in on specific areas of the city, examining how and why saints from abroad were chosen as patrons for new ecclesiastical foundations and how, in turn, these saints and their stories continued to shape these neighborhoods.

CHAPTER 2

Imperial Saints Triumphant in the Forum Romanum

In this and the next chapter, we investigate saints who responded to the legacy of imperial Rome. In the early Middle Ages the Forum Romanum and the Palatine Hill were spaces steeped in visible reminders of Rome's imperial past. After the conquest of Italy in 554 under Emperor Justinian, they were also spaces supervised by the Byzantine administration. Greek- and Latin-speaking officials who answered to the emperor in Constantinople maintained their infrastructure and updated them to the exigencies of the new empire. Popes too vied to add their imprint.

The saints who came to inhabit these spaces had a double duty to perform: to respond to the dense Roman past in which they were engulfed and to "modernize" Rome into a Christian capital—a standard set by the new Rome, Constantinople. No wonder, then, that saints with imperial credentials, saints who bespoke the ideals of a vast and unified Roman Empire, were chosen for the task.

In this chapter, we begin our tour through Rome's multifarious sanctity at the heart of the ancient and medieval city: the Forum Romanum. We will observe how saints from the eastern reaches of the Empire—healing saints, soldier-saints, and administrative saints—arrived in the Forum when Byzantine military power was at its apogee: from shortly before the Justinianic conquest to the early seventh century. We will pay special attention to those saints who were brought by their new locations and legends into direct dialogue with Rome's monumental past. In Chapter 3, we will proceed to the Palatine Hill.

The Forum Romanum

The Forum Romanum is a low-lying plain roughly in the center of Rome that is easily accessible from most directions (Map 3).[1] It is nestled between the Capitoline

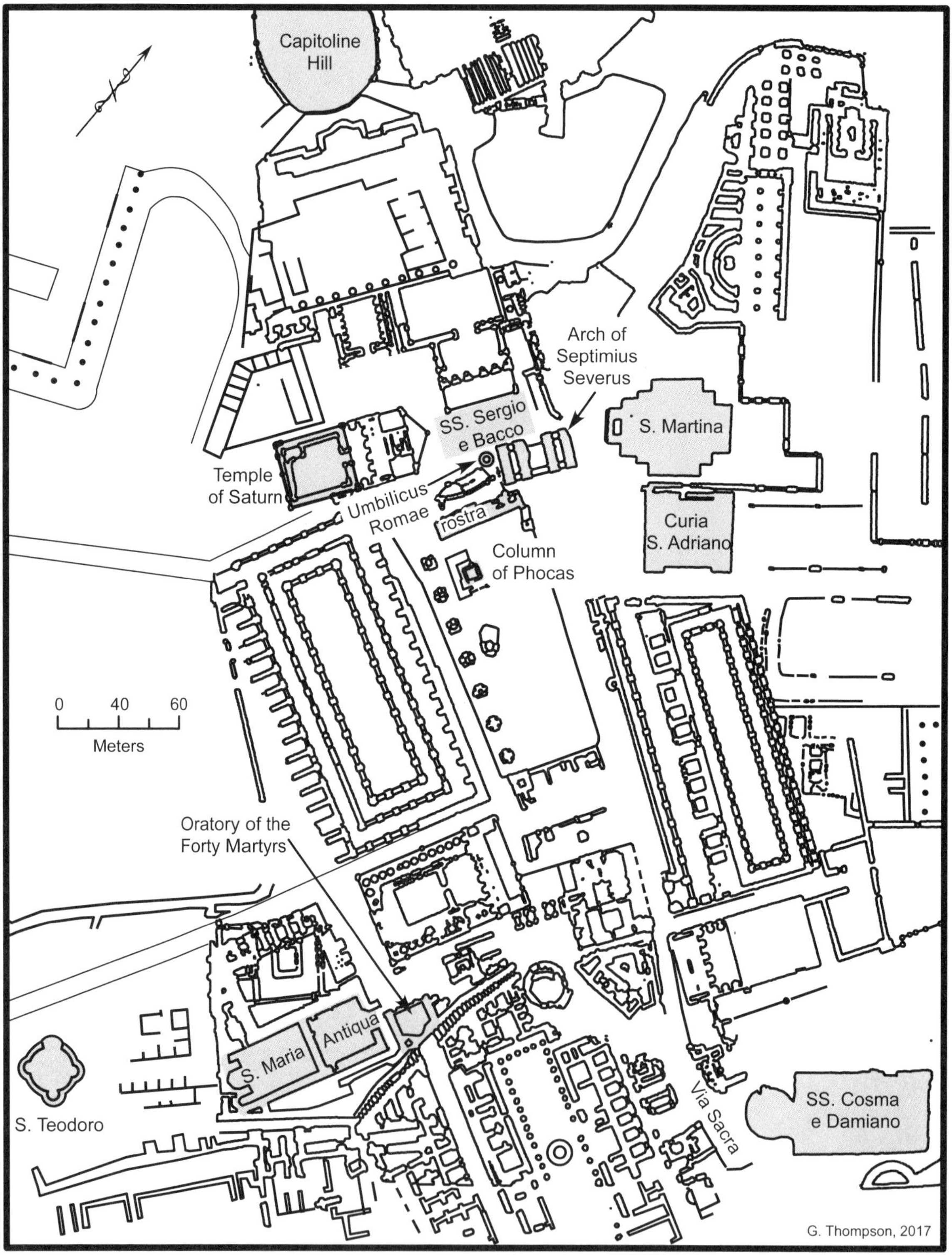

Map 3. Map of the early medieval Forum Romanum. Map created by Gordie Thompson.

Hill, with its grand temple of Jupiter Optimus Maximus, and the imperial residences on the Palatine Hill. Through the Forum runs the via Sacra, beginning outside the Forum near the Colosseum and continuing to the foot of the Capitoline Hill. This was the path taken by victorious emperors as they celebrated their military triumphs in Rome, a tradition continued by Christian emperors in Late Antiquity.[2] Such triumphs were, in turn, commemorated by travertine arches along the via Sacra, forcing on pedestrians these memories of imperial victory.[3] Throughout the Forum densely placed grand public buildings were interspersed with open spaces: public and private gatherings took place amidst colonnaded porticos, temples, and the clutter of centuries of commemoration.

Different eras of Rome's history collided in this space. Here were monuments that hearkened back to pre-Roman times—such as the Temple of Saturn evoking the golden age that had preceded the birth of Rome. Imprinted onto these earlier layers were the marks of emperors from Augustus onward. At the end of the via Sacra the arch of the Emperor Septimius Severus (r. 193–211) with its detailed depictions of Severus's military campaigns against the Parthians overshadowed the adjacent Senate house, the Curia. On the nearby speaker's podium, the Rostra, five enormous red granite columns, topped with statues, reminded viewers of the ubiquitous imperial presence. The Forum was also a particularly verbose area of Rome: high and low, from the façades of building to the bases of statues, inscriptions shouted out manifold messages of munificence, of concord, and of restoration, complicating the pictorial imagery.

At the same time the late antique and early medieval Forum Romanum was a space frequented by inhabitants of Rome and visitors alike, as they made their way from one part of the city to another or stopped to chat; buy, sell, or barter goods; or appeal to the administrators stationed in the area. Imagine the daily hum of sellers advertising their wares, of acquaintances exchanging the latest imperial gossip from Constantinople, of visitors asking for directions to the Vatican.

Beginning in the early sixth century Christian sanctity entered into this jumble of monumental past and daily life. Little evidence survives from this phase of the early medieval Forum: early excavations, in the nineteenth and early twentieth centuries, sought to retrieve the classical Roman Forum where Caesar was murdered and Cicero spoke, generally recording only the most monumental aspects (if that) of its medieval afterlife.[4] As a result, the history of the Forum's saints relies on scraps of evidence and plausible inferences. These nevertheless reveal the outlines of a dialogue between two cities, Rome and Constantinople, and the efforts by administrators and popes to refurbish Rome's Forum as befitted a Christian capital.[5]

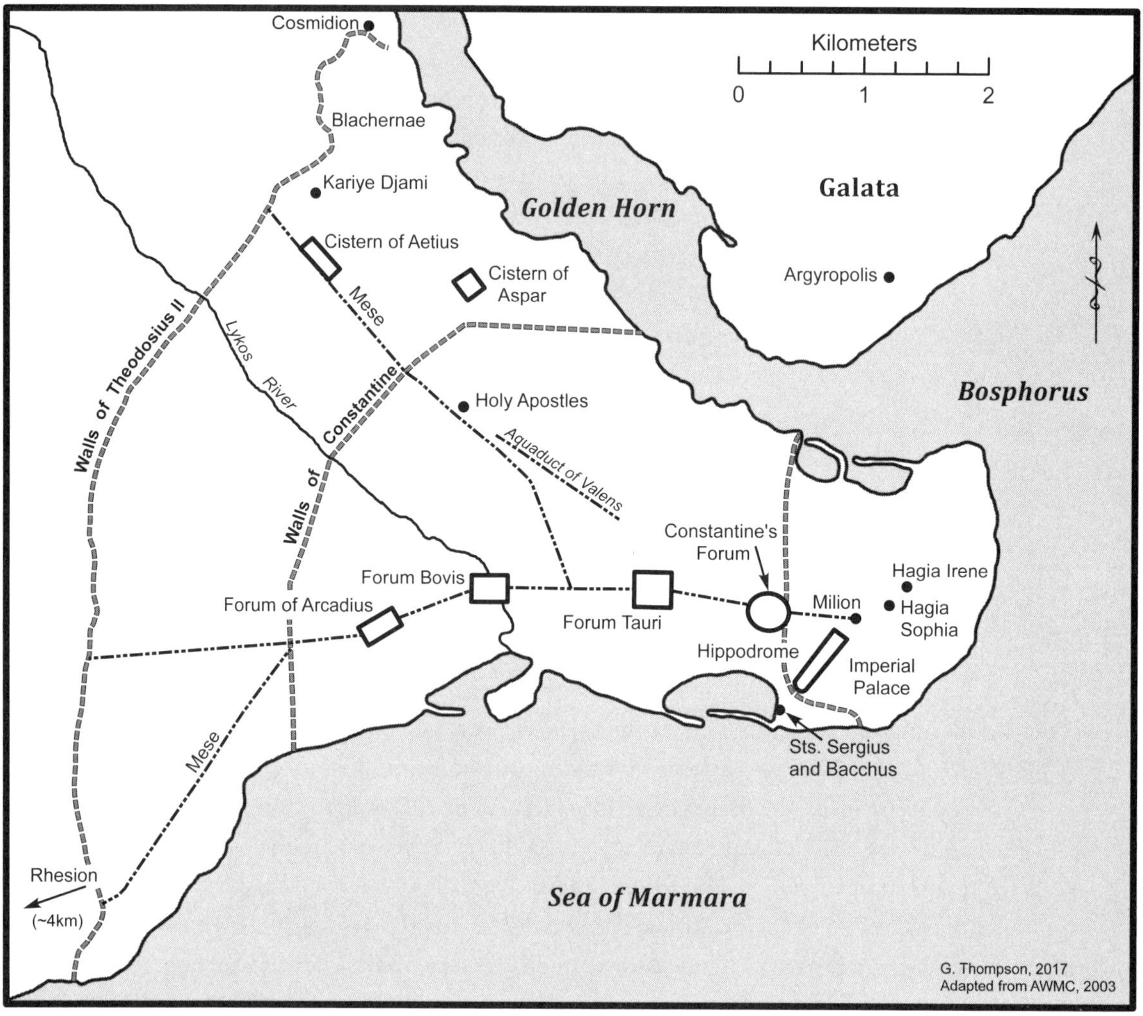

Map 4. Map of early medieval Constantinople. Map adapted by Gordie Thompson after "Byzantine Constantinople," by Carolyn Connor and Tom Elliott, © 2003 Ancient World Mapping Center, awmc.unc.edu.

Old and New Rome

Emperor Constantine founded his eponymous city of Constantinople on the Bosporus in 324 as a "New Rome," a city that was to mirror old Rome, the quintessential imperial capital.[6] Seven hills were marked out in Constantinople so as to parallel the topography of old Rome. Constantine and his successors provided the new capital with infrastructure that mimicked the old: an imperial palace, a senate, a circus/hippodrome, baths, and fora (Map 4).[7] Many of these monuments specifically reproduced older specimens in Rome. At the edge of the Augustaion,

Constantinople's equivalent of the Forum Romanum, stood a Milion, a monument marking distances to the major cities of the empire; it replicated a similar monument that stood in the west end of the Forum Romanum.[8] Columns with spiral reliefs, closely resembling those of Trajan and Marcus Aurelius in Rome, were commissioned by Emperors Theodosius (r. 379–395) and Arcadius (r. 395–408).

Whatever his intentions in founding Constantinople, Constantine could not have imagined the long-term consequences of his decision. In subsequent centuries old Rome slipped into the shadow of Constantinople, which grew in size and magnificence, benefiting from its strategic location and the generosity of eastern emperors. Its walls were strengthened; an ambitiously long aqueduct and large cisterns provided for the city's water supply. Still, as a city without a history of imperial persecutions, the new capital's Christian sanctity was in short supply. Nor did Constantinople have saints of the stature of Peter and Paul. Yet this proved to be no deterrent. The Churches of Holy Wisdom (*Hagia Sophia*) and of Holy Peace (*Hagia Eirene*), as well as relics brought from throughout the Mediterranean, began to orchestrate a majestic Christian topography.[9] The Church of the Holy Apostles boasted relics of three apostles: Andrew, Timothy, and Luke. Slowly but surely Constantinople detached itself from its reference point of Rome.

Meanwhile, fifth-century Italy was experiencing a period of chaotic political succession that saw a proliferation of alternative "Romes," each striving to acquire Christian sanctity to match its aspirations.[10] Milan, especially in the last quarter of the fourth century, could rightfully claim to be an imperial capital. In the fifth century Ravenna took center stage, first as the seat of Roman emperors; then as the capital for Odoacer (d. 493), a Roman military commander who ruled as king of Italy after deposing the young puppet emperor Romulus Augustulus in 476; and after that, as capital of the Ostrogothic kingdom of Theoderic (d. 526) who, with approval from the eastern Emperor Zeno in Constantinople, deposed Odoacer in 493.

Nevertheless, old Rome was not forgotten. Roman bishops, in particular Pope Leo (r. 440–461), emphasized their position as successors of St. Peter and the unique authority that this entailed for the Roman Church.[11] Emperors in the fifth century continued to regard Rome as the primary seat of government in the West, and its ecclesiastical primacy was routinely acknowledged.[12] On the Forum Romanum the local nobility continued to erect imperial portraits, whether or not these emperors resided in the city.[13] Throughout the city wealthy notables continued to lavish attention on private residences and Christian churches, despite the destruction caused by the Gothic Sack in 410 and the Vandal Sack in 455.[14] Spacious new Christian basilicas, such as S. Maria Maggiore on the Esquiline Hill, graced the aging city.

In 500, the Ostrogothic Arian king of Italy, Theoderic, visited Rome.[15] Eager to present himself in traditional Roman terms to the Romans, Theoderic orchestrated his ceremonial entry so that it climaxed at the west end of the Forum.

In front of the Senate house he gave a speech to the people that emphasized his respect for the venerable city and its notables. Theoderic was also attentive to his civic responsibilities. He focused his efforts on Ravenna, which he built up as a worthy Christian capital that would memorialize his achievements, but Rome also benefited from his patronage. Repairs done throughout the city included work on its walls, sewer system, the Palatine palaces, as well as buildings in the Forum Romanum.[16] Brick stamps attest to his restoration of a basilica complex fronting the Forum Romanum that, shortly thereafter, would become the first church on the Forum Romanum: SS. Cosma e Damiano.[17]

SS. Cosma e Damiano

Rome at the turn of the sixth century had no shortage of ecclesiastical dedications. In addition to the Constantinian foundations of the Lateran, St. Peter's, and S. Paolo fuori le Mura, there were more than twenty *tituli* throughout the city, as well as a handful of newer papal dedications, such as S. Stefano Rotondo on the Caelian Hill.[18] These churches were predominantly located in residential neighborhoods where they served their local congregations. Perhaps there was some reluctance to establish ecclesiastical dedications in public areas like the Forum Romanum that retained their own etiquette of commemoration and were deeply saturated with the pagan past. It is noteworthy that no surviving inscriptions or imagery from the late antique Forum explicitly reference Christianity.[19]

Only gradually, as Christianity pervaded all facets of urban life, would its absence in the Forum Romanum seem incongruous. By the sixth century legends told how the apostle Peter (and often also Paul) had defeated Simon the Magician on the Forum.[20] Simon had used his magical powers to fly through the sky to the amazement of the crowds that had gathered to watch. Then Peter, through his prayers, caused Simon to crash onto the paving stones of the Forum. Some versions of the story told how certain paving stones on the Forum marked Simon's crash or the exact spot where Peter and Paul had knelt to pray to God.[21] Why then were there no man-made markers of Christianity's triumph in the Forum?

In the early sixth century, Pope Felix IV (r. 526–530) took the lead and dedicated a church along the via Sacra.[22] For the dedicatee he did not choose Peter or another local Roman saint, but rather the eastern healing saints Cosmas and Damian. This choice reflected the political complexities of the period. The conversion of the space surely required the permission of the Ostrogothic administration in Ravenna, but it was above all a dedication that took its cue from Justinian in Constantinople.

In 526, the same year Felix IV became pope, King Theoderic died, and the young Athalaric, under his mother Amalasuntha's regency, succeeded him as king of Italy. The following year, a new emperor, Justinian (r. 527–565), was proclaimed in Constantinople. Amalasuntha was in a weak position and looked to him for protection; at the same time Justinian had ambitious plans for the empire and was eager to foster closer relations with the Ostrogothic kingdom (which nominally still remained part of the Byzantine Empire). In 527, Justinian, while promulgating a law against heretics, made a special exemption for the Arian Goths: "We have decided to relieve them somewhat of the severity [of the edict], and permit them to be among the *foederati* and enjoy their honors insofar as we please."[23] For the sake of empire, Justinian was willing to overlook differences in how the Goths construed the relationship between Christ and his Father.

Justinian and his consort Theodora had no shortage of ideas for how to forge an empire, including by fighting wars, promulgating laws, and sponsoring buildings. Another tactic was to promote theologically inclusive saints who were to mend the theological and political factions fragmenting the empire. Cosmas and Damian, well-known saints with a reputation for healing that crossed confessional borders, were a sensible choice.[24]

The pair of saints, martyrs of the imperial persecutions who had steadfastly clung to the Christian faith despite threats and tortures, were already familiar throughout the Mediterranean world by the time Justinian came to power. There were dedications to them in Cyrrhus in Syria and Aegeae in Cilicia (on the southeast coast of Asia Minor), the sites most closely associated with their martyrdom, and also farther afield, including in both Constantinople and Rome.[25] After Cosmas and Damian appeared to Justinian in a vision and cured him from a grave illness, as the contemporary Byzantine historian Procopius reports, Justinian developed a special interest in their cult. In Constantinople, he undertook to restore the Cosmidion, a healing shrine dedicated to Cosmas and Damian, located in the northwestern suburb of Blachernae.[26]

Meanwhile throughout the empire, Justinian and Theodora sponsored or encouraged dedications to the saints.[27] In Antioch, a city strategically situated on the empire's eastern frontier but with a strong faction opposed to the Chalcedonian orthodoxy, Justinian and Theodora's extensive building program included a church for Cosmas and Damian.[28] The city of Cyrrhus in Syria was refurbished, in honor of its church to Cosmas and Damian. New churches were dedicated in the region of Pamphylia and in Gerasa in Palestine.[29] The saints appear in the mosaic program of a grand newly built church in Poreč in Istria, and in Ravenna the Chalcedonian bishop Peter II (r. 494–520) included the saints in the mosaic program in the *capella arcivescovile*, the chapel inside the episcopal palace.[30] After

Ravenna was conquered by Byzantine troops, private individuals dedicated a small church, S. Michele in Africisco, in 545, and included the saints in its mosaic program. To these varied locations Cosmas and Damian brought their therapeutic abilities, forging a unified path to salvation across the empire.

Salvific Healing on the Forum

Pope Felix's dedication to Cosmas and Damian anchored Rome into this wider web of Justinian's vision of a unified Christian Roman Empire.[31] Moreover, Cosmas and Damian were saints who could tackle the perilous past that enveloped the new church. On the ground, the physicians provided for salvific healing amidst the rotting temples that surrounded them.

Visitors entered the new church from the via Sacra by way of a vestibule, a small round building, the so-called Temple of Romulus.[32] (Today the Temple of Romulus has been "restored" to its pre-Christian appearance, and the main hall of the church, which has been altered considerably over the centuries, is entered from the via dei Fori Imperiali.) They were greeted by a traditional Roman façade: a bronze door flanked by two porphyry columns topped by an entablature (Figure 5).[33] As far as we know there were no visible indications that this was a Christian church—although an inscription referencing Constantine could have conjured up Christian, and Constantinopolitan, associations.[34]

Entering the vestibule, which was located at an angle to the main hall of the church, visitors would have begun to glimpse the mosaic that dominated the small hall (Figure 6). Except for the mosaic, Felix seems to have left the building largely unchanged; marble revetment on the floors and walls remained in situ. Yet the impact of the mosaic cannot be overemphasized. Since the length of the hall was not much greater than its width (18 m × 23 m), the enormous mosaic must have presented a dramatic spectacle to its viewers, as it still does.[35] The mosaic has undergone significant restorations over the centuries (especially in the seventeenth century and especially the figure of Pope Felix), but its overall composition remains intact.

Against a deep blue background with reddish clouds stands an enormous golden Christ. To either side of Christ stand Peter and Paul, who are introducing Cosmas and Damian, holding their martyrs' crowns, into Christ's presence. On Christ's far right is Pope Felix IV (labeled), holding a model of the church that he has dedicated; on the far left (also labeled) stands St. Theodore. The shimmering display of the mosaic presents a dramatic expression of the power of God, encapsulated by its inscription's proclamation, in gold letters, of the "sure hope of health/salvation (*spes certa salutis*)" that the saints will provide.[36] Enclosed but visible within the altar were relics that made tangible the saints' presence.[37]

Figure 5. Temple of Romulus: vestibule of SS. Cosma e Damiano. Photograph by author.

The saints' ability to provide salvation of body and soul is spelled out by their *passio*.[38] This popular text, which circulated in various versions in Late Antiquity, in Latin as well as Greek, vividly celebrates the power of God to triumph over all adversities. During the reign of Emperors Diocletian and Maximian a report came to the pagan officials of Aegeae (in Cilicia) that "certain Christians [Cosmas and Damian] industrious in the art of healing are travelling through towns and villages curing the ill and those plagued by impure spirits, in the name of him whom

Figure 6. SS. Cosma e Damiano, apse mosaic (significantly restored). Scala / Ministero per i Beni e le Attività culturali / Art Resource, NY.

they call Christ, and making many signs they do not permit men to worship the gods with sacrifices at the temples."[39] Cosmas and Damian are then brought before the judge and questioned, and Cosmas explains that he and his brother are Arabian citizens without earthly wealth. After refusing to perform pagan sacrifices, the saints undergo not one but a series of executions: they are cast into the sea in chains, burned in a fire, stoned, and shot with arrows, but each attempt fails to kill them. Throughout their tortures they sing hymns praising the power of God. When sent into a burning fire, the martyrs praise God, asking him to "free us from our enemies, lest those who do not know you should say, 'Where is your God?'" In response, a sudden earthquake causes the flames to leap forth and destroy a multitude of pagans, while the martyrs themselves are left unharmed.[40] Repeatedly Cosmas and Damian are accused of sorcery; repeatedly they insist that they are Christians. Finally they are decapitated, although not before uttering a final prayer praising God. Thus the legend contrasts the invincible power of God, who by his miracles repeatedly intervenes on behalf of his saints, with the futility of pagan superstition. These are saints who can mobilize God's protection in the face of pagan threats (real or imagined) to life and limb.

This message of Christian triumphalism is reaffirmed by the presence of St. Theodore, who is portrayed on Christ's far left. Theodore was a soldier who refused to conduct sacrifices in Amaseia in Pontus.[41] When given time to reconsider his decision, he instead took the opportunity to burn down the temple of the mother of the gods during the night. He was then sentenced to starvation, but the Holy Spirit came to nourish him during the night. Cosmas and Damian's miracles included the destruction of pagans; Theodore destroyed a pagan temple. Together the saints pugnaciously opposed the pagan gods as they cleansed the Forum and introduced the true hope of salvation.

Rome as a Battlefield: The Gothic Wars (535–554)

Cosmas and Damian have retained their church on the Forum to the present day, but the fiction of imperial unity that they presented did not last long. The soldier-saint Theodore prefigured what was soon to come. Only a decade after the dedication of the new church, in 535, Amalasuntha was murdered, and Justinian appointed Belisarius commander of a military invasion that was to put the Italian peninsula firmly under Constantinopolitan imperial control. This bloody military campaign lasted nearly twenty years. Rome became a battleground, facing long sieges and changing hands five times.

The scenes of devastation are difficult to imagine.[42] Procopius reports that during the first siege of Rome in 537–538, Romans fighting off a Gothic attack from atop the mausoleum of Hadrian (the modern-day Castel Sant'Angelo) resorted to breaking statues and throwing them onto the heads of the invaders.[43] One night, in desperation, some Romans pried open the doors of the small temple of Janus on the Forum Romanum, in accordance with an old tradition that the building's doors were to be opened in times of war.[44] The siege continued, and many abandoned the city. Those who remained were reduced to foraging for herbs among the ruins and eating sausages made of dead mules.[45]

Twice more, Rome was besieged before the Byzantine general Narses (who replaced Belisarius) proclaimed victory. Rome was left a shell of its former self. The population had shrunk, probably from around the hundreds of thousands in the fifth century to well under a hundred thousand.[46] Buildings crumbled; shrubs and climbing plants flourished along the unkempt streets and abandoned lots. Yet the imperial administration refused to be daunted by the task of returning Rome to normalcy. Quite to the contrary, Justinian's Pragmatic Sanction in 554, concerning the newly conquered Italian territories, optimistically promulgated seventy-seven laws that would straighten out Italian affairs.[47] These confirmed all decrees made by Amalasuntha and her son Athalaric, nullified those made by Totila (the Ostrogothic king who had opposed Justinian), and attended to various issues of taxation, government, commerce, education, and other aspects of civil administration.

Urban life, so the Pragmatic Sanction decreed, would resume as normal. Civil and ecclesiastical administrators were to cooperate in maintaining lawful order: the task of overseeing weights and measures was entrusted jointly to the pope and senate.[48] Maintenance of public infrastructure (including specifically the Forum Romanum) was additionally spelled out as a desideratum.[49] Certainly Narses, who proudly celebrated a triumph in Rome in 554, embraced this ideology of restoration.[50] An inscription from the Ponte Salario, included in the Einsiedeln compilation, records its restoration by Narses "during the reign of our lord the most pious and always triumphant Justinian."[51]

The Pragmatic Sanction envisioned a separation of civil and military jurisdiction in Rome, but this system, if it ever took force on the ground, was short-lived. Lombard armies swept into northern Italy, and in the late 570s delegations of Romans went twice to Constantinople to request troops to protect Italy.[52] Emperor Maurice (582–602) united civil and military powers in the position of the exarch (governor) of Italy, based in Ravenna. By the late sixth century Rome had a dux (appointed from Constantinople), who answered to the exarch in Ravenna. Initially, this may have been envisioned as a military position, but the dux's authority quickly extended to include a range of civil matters. Judges (*iudices*) answered to the dux and carried out the day-to-day administrative business on the Forum. This system remained in place, more or less, for the next century and a half.

The Byzantine Forum Romanum

With the new administration came their saints. Four ecclesiastical foundations in and around the Forum Romanum may be attributed to the Byzantine administration: S. Maria Antiqua, S. Teodoro, the so-called Oratory of the Forty Martyrs, and SS. Sergio e Bacco.[53] When first established, these buildings likely served as the Christian face of the Byzantine administration: they provided the Christian foundations that updated Rome's decaying urban center and served the Byzantine administrators (whether individuals sent from Constantinople or, more likely, local Romans), who were tasked with governing Rome on behalf of the imperial administration in Constantinople.

My argument that Byzantine administrators, acting in an official capacity, were responsible for sponsoring these four dedications, is, admittedly, largely *ex silen-*

tio. As suggested by Robert Coates-Stephens, the absence of foundation notices in the serial biographies of the popes collectively known as the *Liber Pontificalis*, texts usually eager to credit popes with building activity in Rome, may indicate the lack of papal sponsors.[54] Furthermore, there is strong reason to believe that the Forum Romanum remained under the purview of the Byzantine administration throughout this period.[55] The most compelling reason, however, to attribute these foundations to Byzantine administrators is the similar nature of all four dedications. As we will see, all use Constantinopolitan saints to intervene in the Roman Forum. The individuals responsible for choosing their dedications were clearly aware of imperial politics in Constantinople and familiar with Rome and its imperial legacy. This bespeaks a calculated policy or, at the very least, a series of like-minded individuals in charge.

The earliest of these foundations was almost certainly S. Maria Antiqua, a church located inside a preexisting building at the foot of the Palatine Hill and connected, by a ramp, to the Palatine palaces above. Since this church was, for the most part, abandoned from the ninth century onward (but not destroyed), much of its early medieval decoration remains intact.[56] Excavations starting in 1901 revealed a wealth of frescoes, many Byzantine in style, some with Greek and others with Latin inscriptions. This material has led art historians and historians to question their assumptions about Rome's "Dark Ages." Yet copious as the evidence is, its interpretation has proved controversial.[57] S. Maria Antiqua is one of a kind, but is this a result of its chance survival, or was this building already unique when it was first constructed?

The earliest secure evidence for Christianity in this space is a fresco of Mary enthroned and dressed in the guise of a Byzantine empress (the so-called Maria Regina).[58] Maria Lidova has recently argued that this fresco may have been commissioned by Amalasuntha prior to the Gothic Wars.[59] Alternatively, it may have been executed in the years after the imperial conquest of Rome. In either case, there is no indication that when the fresco was added the building had been converted to a church. It may have served as part of the imperial complex, perhaps guarding the entrance to the palaces atop the Palatine—a suitable setting to invoke the protection of the Mother of God.[60] At some time in the later sixth century—that is, in the generations following the Byzantine conquest—the space appears to have been converted to a church.[61] The interior was divided into aisles separated by columns, and a new fresco of the Virgin flanked by two angels was painted over the Maria Regina.

Although veneration of the Virgin Mary was by no means restricted to Constantinople, she emerged in the sixth century as the city's special guardian.[62] Justinian's successor Emperor Justin II and his empress Sophia (r. 565–578) patronized two major Marian shrines in Constantinople: a church in the Blachernae neighborhood that held her robe and a church in Chalkoprateia (near the imperial palace) where her girdle was kept. In Ravenna the Chalcedonian bishop Ecclesius (r. 522–532) had built a Marian church after his visit to Constantinople; after the Byzantine conquest, the Arian baptistery was rededicated as a church for Mary (S. Maria in Cosmedin).[63] Analogously in Rome, we may imagine S. Maria Antiqua as offering a link to the heavens above by way of Constantinople.[64]

Soldier-Saints in the Forum

Encircling the Marian stronghold of S. Maria Antiqua were saintly bodyguards: the Forty Martyrs of Sebaste, St. Theodore, and Sts. Sergius and Bacchus. According to their *passiones* these were all soldiers of the imperial army, who, as Christians, refused to sacrifice to the pagan gods and were accordingly tortured and executed. These saints had never renounced their military careers per se, rendering them particularly protective guardians. The preference for soldier-saints on the Forum was similar to the situation in Ravenna, where, after the Byzantine conquest, numerous formerly Arian churches were rededicated to soldier-saints.[65] Noteworthy too is that the originally Greek *passiones* associated with these saints were all translated into Latin in this period.[66] The Byzantine administration, it seems, was likely involved in efforts to disseminate their legends and encourage devotion to these representatives of Byzantine power.

Right outside the main entrance to S. Maria Antiqua stood a small building (the so-called Oratory of the Forty Martyrs), whose apse fresco depicted the Forty Martyrs of Sebaste (Plate 3). Robert Coates-Stephens has recently argued that this building was first repurposed as a private funerary chapel but after the Byzantine conquest was transformed into a chapel for St. Andrew, decorated with scenes of the Forty Martyrs.[67] No traces of Andrew survive in the space, but later sources refer to such a chapel near S. Maria Antiqua.[68] The hypothesis is attractive because Andrew was Constantinople's favored apostle.[69] In any case, what we can be certain of is that the space showcased the Forty Martyrs: the apse fresco, dated to the seventh century, shows the martyrs standing semi-nude in a lake.[70]

According to their *passio* these were a group of forty Roman soldiers who had refused to sacrifice and were subsequently sentenced to freeze to death naked in an icy lake near Sebaste (in the Roman province of Lesser Armenia).[71] A warming hut was set up next to the lake to tempt them to apostatize; one of the forty succumbed to the temptation, but a Roman guard stepped in to take his place. The apse fresco depicts this event on the far right, against the backdrop of the motionless bodies and impassive faces of the nearly identical (but individually labeled) saints standing in the water. Since the building was located near to the *Lacus Iutur-*

nae, a water shrine associated with the Dioscuri (the mythical twin brothers Castor and Pollux), Gregor Kalas has argued that this fresco offered a "provocative juxtaposition" to pagan traditions: a Christian rejoinder to pagan healing and bathing for pleasure.[72] More than that, the Forty Martyrs were clearly seen as desirable patrons on their own terms. They are also depicted in a side chapel on the left aisle of S. Maria Antiqua, in what appears to have been a narrative cycle of their martyrdom, dated to the seventh century.[73]

The Forty Martyrs came to Rome charged with Constantinopolitan associations. The principal shrine for the saints was in Caesarea in Cappadocia, but Constantinople boasted numerous churches for them—and even their relics. Procopius tells us how masons conducting excavations for the construction of Hagia Eirene in Constantinople came across a chest containing relics, labeled as those of the Forty Martyrs. Their healing power was confirmed when the reliquary, brought to Justinian, cured his knee ailment.[74] Justinian's successors continued to promote the saints: Emperor Tiberius (r. 574–582) and his wife Anastasia began a church for them in Constantinople, dedicated in 589–590 by Emperor Maurice.[75] At least by the early ninth century there was a notarial office (*nome*) associated with this church in Constantinople.[76] We might wonder then if the so-called Oratory of the Forty Martyrs (whether or not it was dedicated to Andrew) might have served a similar purpose. Administrators must have conducted official business somewhere in close proximity to the imperial quarters, and where better than against the backdrop of forty named witnesses!

S. Teodoro

In the other direction from S. Maria Antiqua and the Forum Romanum, alongside the slope of the Palatine Hill, was a dedication to St. Theodore. A church, S. Teodoro, survives in situ, although only the apse, with a heavily restored late sixth-century mosaic, survives from its earliest phase as a Christian church (Plate 4).[77] We have already met St. Theodore in SS. Cosma e Damiano. Theodore was from Amaseia in Pontus, but was eventually buried in the nearby town of Euchaïta.[78] His *passio* proclaimed his steadfast commitment to Christianity. Theodore was a saint popular among Byzantine soldiers and had received the imperial stamp of approval from Justinian himself. Even before coming to the throne, the emperor had patronized a shrine for Theodore (in Rhesion, outside the walls of Constantinople).[79] In Ravenna, after the Byzantine conquest, another of the previously Arian churches in Ravenna was rededicated to St. Theodore.[80]

Given its convenient location near the Palatine Hill and the Forum Romanum, Theodore's shrine may have catered specifically to Byzantine soldiers stationed in

Figure 7. West end of Forum Romanum: Arch of Septimius Severus; Umbilicus Romae (site of SS. Sergio e Bacco), with Column of Phocas behind; Temple of Saturn. Photograph by author.

Rome or visiting the city. What is significant, however, is that the apse mosaic of S. Teodoro presents a portrait of harmonious concord between the patron saints of Rome and a patron saint of the Byzantine army. Peter and Paul introduce St. Theodore (and a second figure whose appearance dates to the later restorations and whose identity is disputed) to Christ himself.[81]

SS. Sergio e Bacco

Visitors approaching S. Maria Antiqua from the Tiber port would have passed by S. Teodoro on their way into the Forum; those descending from Rome's hills would have first encountered SS. Sergio e Bacco, a church dedicated to assertive saints stationed at the symbolic center of Rome (Figure 7). Nothing of the church survives today (it was torn down in the sixteenth century), but the location of this dedication and the stature of its saints call for closer examination.

Sergius and Bacchus were soldier-saints, martyrs of the imperial persecutions, who were said to have been buried in Resafa/Sergiopolis (in Syria). During a siege by the Persian king Khosrow I Anushirwan in 540, Sergius's relics were said to have miraculously defended the city.[82] The saints' reputation and relics spread throughout the late antique Mediterranean: Gregory (d. 594), bishop of Tours in southern Gaul, reports how a fellow bishop, familiar with Sergius's prowess, sought to obtain relics from a Syrian trader.[83]

Sergius and Bacchus were also saints whom Justinian had promoted as representatives of the empire's geographic and ecumenical aspirations. Justinian and Theodora, before ascending the throne, dedicated a church to the saints, still extant today (Küçük Ayasofya), in the palace of Hormisdas (named after a Persian prince who had fled to Constantinople in the fourth century), where the couple had resided before moving to the nearby Great Palace.[84] It was a lavish construction adorned with precious marbles and gold mosaic.

The church for Sergius and Bacchus was closely linked, architecturally and ideologically, to a slightly earlier enterprise of Justinian: a church dedicated to Sts. Peter and Paul, also located in the palace of Hormisdas. Together the two churches firmly asserted Constantinople as the imperial capital of an extensive empire. In the words of Procopius, "These two churches are so admirable that they manifestly form an adornment of the whole city, and not merely of the palace."[85]

Moreover, both churches fostered Justinian and Theodora's attempts to quell dissent and bolster their rule with the support of influential saints from East and West. The church of Peter and Paul was dedicated with relics of Peter, Paul, and Lawrence, sent from Rome by Pope Hormisdas (r. 514–523; his name bears no relationship to the Constantinopolitan palace).[86] Its dedication celebrated the end of the so-called Acacian Schism, a period of thirty-five years of strained relations between the sees of Rome and Constantinople after Pope Felix III (r. 483–492) had excommunicated the patriarch of Constantinople Acacius (r. 471–489) in 484 for promulgating the *Henotikon* (a document that sought doctrinal compromise by intentionally avoiding the controversial terms "person" of the Trinity and "nature" of Christ).

The dedication of the church for Sergius and Bacchus envisioned—rather too optimistically—a resolution for the much thornier issue of eastern opposition to the Council of Chalcedon. Although Justinian rigorously promoted Chalcedonian orthodoxy, his wife Theodora's charitable activities extended to non-Chalcedonian monks, who were even housed within the palace of Hormisdas.[87] The new church brought saints venerated by non-Chalcedonians into imperial quarters and included an inscription that celebrated the empress's charitable activities. Sergius and Bacchus were thereby mobilized as protectors of an imperial unity that stretched from Rome to the eastern frontier.

In Rome the new saints were positioned at the heart of the Forum Romanum, surrounded by older buildings and immediately adjacent to the Umbilicus Romae[88]—a complicated jumble of monuments at the end of the via Sacra that represented both the geographical center of Rome and Rome's centrality in the world (see Figure 7).[89] Early Roman legends associated the site with Rome's foundation. Emperor Augustus had embellished the area with a Golden Milestone, a symbolic marker from which all roads in the empire began. Constantinople, as we have already seen, had received its own symbolic milestone (the Milion on the Augustaion, not far from the palace of Hormisdas), but Rome had preserved its own.

The soldiers Sergius and Bacchus were well equipped for their new setting. Their *passio* maps neatly onto the historical topography of the Forum, providing a Christian commentary to Rome's pagan past. The oldest Latin version of their *passio* (a translation from the Greek that was very likely penned in Rome) describes their confrontation with the emperor as a triumph of Christian perseverance in the face of countless travails.[90] Sergius and Bacchus were officers in the imperial army. They were covert Christians until rivals jealous of the favor they received from the emperor Maximian accused them of being Christian. To test the accusation, Maximian undertakes a sacrifice at the shrine of Jupiter (*ad sacrarium magni Jovis*); Sergius and Bacchus remain outside praying to God, revealing their Christianity.[91] Enraged, the emperor has them stripped of their military vestments, dressed in women's garb, and dragged through the forum to the imperial palace.[92] After failing to convince them of the falsity of their beliefs (by comparing the Christian God, born out of wedlock, with the race of legitimately born pagan gods), Maximian has them sent to the province of Augusta Euphratensis, where, after enduring various tortures, they are martyred.

While the latter part of the *passio* is located in distinct locales in Syria, the Latin *passio*, following the Greek, leaves the initial location of Sergius's and Bacchus's accusation unspecified. The description is vague enough for it to refer to almost any major Roman city, but from the perspective of an inhabitant of Rome, it accorded remarkably well with the topography surrounding the church of SS. Sergio e Bacco. On the Capitoline Hill above the church stood the Temple of Jupiter, Best and Greatest (*aedes Iovis Optimi Maximi*), where the *passio*'s audience could have visualized Sergius and Bacchus declining to sacrifice.[93] Even closer was the temple of the god Saturn (see Figure 7), to whom Maximian refers when trying to convince the saints to convert.

Thereafter, when Sergius and Bacchus refuse to sacrifice, they are dragged "per medium forum" to the imperial *palatium*, again a description that could easily be mapped onto the Forum area, where the imperial residence was located on

Figure 8. Arch of Septimius Severus. Photographic print by John Henry Parker (d. 1884). American Academy in Rome, Photographic Archive: Library Collection, American Academy, LC.Italy.Rome.FoR.49a.

the Palatine Hill, on the other end of the Forum Romanum from the Capitoline. Christian audiences in Rome could have imagined Sergius and Bacchus dragged through the forum, chanting, "Though we walk through the valley of the shadow of death, we will fear no evil," transforming their humiliation into a Christian procession.[94]

Mapped onto the Forum Romanum, Sergius's and Bacchus's "procession" took on added significance as the church was located at a key junction of the via Sacra, the traditional route of imperial Roman triumphs. Immediately adjacent to SS. Sergio e Bacco, the Arch of Septimius Severus depicted scenes of imperial victory (Figure 8). Below the larger relief panels presenting a narrative of Severus's Parthian campaigns, smaller reliefs depict the emperor's triumphal procession to Rome, and there are reliefs of Roman soldiers with captives on the pedestals.[95]

The message of the saints' *passio* in this context is clear: Christian hymns are to supersede pagan rites. Appropriately, the church of SS. Sergio e Bacco was located just beyond the spot where Christian emperors halted, at the Senate house and Rostra, dispensing with the final climb to the Capitoline and the sacrifices at the temple of Jupiter Optimus Maximus with which the triumphal procession had once concluded.[96] Symbolically SS. Sergio e Bacco blocked the path to the temple of Jupiter, its Christian saints obstructing the pagan worship that they had once condemned. Text and church worked together to mark the Christian triumph over pagan traditions.

Phocas, Heraclius, and Imperial Intrigues

SS. Sergio e Bacco was positioned next to the path leading up toward the Capitoline Hill, but it also fronted the area by the Senate house where speeches were given, court cases adjudicated, and public and private business conducted. In 608 the Byzantine exarch of Ravenna Smaragdus updated this area by rededicating a monumental column to the Emperor Phocas (r. 602–610; see Figure 7).[97] Its inscription, facing the Senate house, celebrated Phocas as a pious and clement ruler who had brought peace and freedom to Italy; a statue of Phocas crowned the column.[98] Smaragdus's dedication emphasized the cooperation of the emperor and the Byzantine administration in a monumental form that hearkened back to Rome's older imperial monuments, as well as more recent Constantinopolitan dedications—such as a monumental column with an equestrian statue of Justinian that was set up in the Augustaion.[99] It was a gesture well received. Shortly thereafter Phocas gave permission to Pope Boniface IV (r. 608–615) to convert the Pantheon into a church (dedicated to Mary), demonstrating his imperial generosity to a city that had shown its respect for him.[100]

In contrast, in Constantinople, at least as described by Byzantine historians, Phocas was despised by all as a terrible tyrant, and in 610 he was deposed by Heraclius (r. 610–641). Heraclius's reign witnessed a series of reversals and victories of dramatic proportions. Jerusalem fell in 619 to the Persians, who took the True Cross in triumph to Ctesiphon. In Italy too Heraclius faced problems. The exarch Eleutherius proclaimed himself emperor in 619, although he was murdered by his own soldiers the next year before reaching Rome where he wanted to be crowned. Then in 626 Avar and Persian armies besieged Constantinople on land and by sea. Impressive Byzantine victories followed, and in 630 Heraclius could return the True Cross to Jerusalem—but soon thereafter the Byzantine army's defeat at the Battle of Yarmūk against the Arabs in 636 ended Byzantine rule in Syria-Palestine.

During this latter part of Heraclius's reign (quite possibly in the context or aftermath of his victories against the Persians), Pope Honorius (r. 625–638), the son of a Roman consul, intervened again in the western end of the Forum Romanum, dedicating the Senate house to a Constantinopolitan saint: Hadrian.[101] In contrast to the nearby column of Phocas, dedicated by the exarch, the new church of S. Adriano emphasized that the bishop of Rome too had a role to play vis-à-vis the emperor and the Byzantine administration in Rome.

Pope Honorius was eager to foster relations with the Byzantine administration, and his urban projects, as recorded in his papal biography, projected a sense of cooperation between Rome, Ravenna, and Constantinople (a policy similarly reflected in the pope's attempts to deal with ongoing dogmatic disputes).[102] He lavished attention on Roman dedications to the Constantinopolitan apostle Andrew and Ravenna's first bishop, St. Apollinaris.[103] Neither did he ignore Roman saints. Instead Honorius's program of patronage suggests a deliberate effort to mark Rome as a city in which the pope fostered the Christian sanctity nestled within it.[104]

S. Adriano: A Christian Official in the Senate House

In consecrating the Senate house as a church dedicated to St. Hadrian, Pope Honorius gave the building a new occupant appropriate to its senatorial past: an administrator-turned-martyr. It was a dedication that not only affirmed the role of Rome's senatorial elite in steering the empire but also implemented a Christian vision of government. Saintly protectors and ecclesiastical administrators would now replace or at least underpin the traditional forms of urban administration.

St. Hadrian was martyred in Nicomedia, but his *passio* relates that shortly thereafter his relics were brought to Constantinople (followed by his wife Natalia, who then died by the side of Hadrian's relics).[105] Hadrian's shrine was located on the outskirts of Constantinople in Argyropolis, a suburb of Constantinople across the Golden Horn.[106] Unlike the other saints we have met on the Forum, St. Hadrian, as far as we know, had no history of imperial patronage in Constantinople, nor did he have the charged militant connotations of Byzantine soldier-saints. He was an eastern provincial raised up from relative obscurity and placed center stage in Rome's most venerable governmental building.

The framing of Hadrian's *passio* in its new architectural setting affirmed both the continuity and the contrast between the old building and the new saint. Pope Honorius's conversion of the Senate house into a church essentially preserved its late antique, pre-Christian appearance.[107] (The church was subsequently significantly remodeled throughout the centuries. Its present appearance dates from 1936–1939 when the church was deconsecrated and "restored" to its pre-Christian state.[108]) The Senate house, as rebuilt under Emperor Diocletian (r. 284–305), was a tall hall with a relatively small footprint (25.2 m × 17.6 m; 31.6 m in height). Marble revetment adorned its walls and floors, and on either side of the hall were shallow steps that had provided seating for the senators (Plate 5).[109] Honorius's only substantial alteration of the building was to transform the speaker's podium into a presbytery and introduce a small apse into the back wall of the church.[110]

Presumably at this point the Senate house was no longer used for official meetings, although, as we shall see in Chapter 3, it was still possible to assemble some form of the Roman Senate in the early seventh century.[111] The building's new occupant, an official whose name evoked a Roman emperor renowned for his mercy, kept alive this senatorial past. At the same time his *passio* offered a radical Christian redefinition of "Romanness." The Latin *passio*, a translation from the Greek, told of how St. Hadrian, an administrator, converted to Christianity while watching the tortures endured by Christians who had refused to renounce their faith during the persecutions ordered by the Emperor Maximian in Nicomedia.[112] Hadrian's *passio* provides a commentary on the meaning of wealth, aristocracy, and loyalty—characteristics traditionally associated with Roman senators—offering its readers and listeners a narrative illustration of the Christian redefinition of these conventional Roman categories.

Rewards are a leitmotif of St. Hadrian's *passio*. When Hadrian first observes Christians suffering martyrdom, he asks them, "What is the recompense (*remuneratio*) which you expect from these tortures?"[113] Their biblical response is enigmatic: "For about that glory it is written: 'Eye hath not seen, nor ear heard, neither have entered into the heart of man, the things which the Lord hath prepared for them that love him.'"[114] Their response convinces him to convert and add his name to theirs.

Throughout the *passio* the definition of wealth (*divitiae*) constitutes a central theme.[115] When Hadrian's wife, Natalia, a covert Christian, learns of his conversion, she rushes to the prison and proclaims joyfully, "Blessed are you my lord Hadrian, since you have found the wealth which your parents did not give you"; she continues to discourse on this wealth, "which is lacking to those who possess much and abundant to those who are poor."[116] This inversion of traditional social classifications finds its most graphic expression in the scenes after Hadrian's martyrdom. Pious women spend their gold and precious gems to buy the bloodstained garments of the soldiers who had carried off the body of Hadrian to be (unsuccessfully) burned. Natalia herself wraps Hadrian's severed hand, which she has secretly hidden away, in precious purple cloth.[117]

The *passio* redefines the meaning of aristocracy along with that of wealth. It emphasizes Hadrian's aristocratic status, in contrast to that of the other Christians with whom he is martyred. Emperor Maximian encourages him to renounce

Christianity and accept the pagan gods once again, so that they may be favorable to him and honor him, reminding him, "For you are not similar to those with whom you are fettered. For you are the son of a well-born and important man; although you are young, nonetheless you are worthy of honors; but they [the other Christians] are country dwellers and the children of fools and paupers." To which Hadrian responds, "I am aware that you know my fatherland and family/race (*genus*) and even my forefathers; if, however, you became acquainted with the good birth (*natio*) and the wealth of those holy ones, or the fatherland which they are awaiting, immediately you would fall to their feet prostrate and would beg them to pray for you."[118] Thus, with Christianity, old classifications of nobility have been superseded by a new Christian community.

Loyalty is stressed as the key quality for this Christian community. The *passio* begins with scenes depicting the pagan community's lack of solidarity. Maximian offers a reward for those who inform on Christians, and as a result friends inform on friends, neighbors on neighbors, and relatives on relatives.[119] This fickle community is contrasted with the steadfast community of Christian martyrs with whom Hadrian is imprisoned.

The message of St. Hadrian's *passio*, by no means unusual for a hagiographical text, must have taken on particular resonance inside the Senate house. Given that the changes in the building, architectural as well as ornamental, were minimal, the setting was a reminder of the past, but also an explicit juxtaposition of old and new. The benches where Roman nobles had once (and still?) sat now accommodated a congregation defined foremost by their Christian ties. The extensive marble splendor, once celebrating the honor and prestige of the successful military and political administration of the Roman Empire, now provided adornment for the sanctuary of a saint who had renounced his administrative position for Christ. This radical transformation is aptly summed up by Hadrian's response to the emperor's query about his conversion: "I am not insane, O king; but rather from many insanities I return to sanity."[120]

S. Martina

Contemporaneous to the dedication of the Senate house (but not mentioned in the *Liber Pontificalis*) was very likely the Christian conversion of the adjacent Secretarium Senatus, a hall that had served as an annex to the Senate house.[121] This space was dedicated to St. Martina, whose legend told of her martyrdom in Rome on the first day of January during the reign of Emperor Alexander. Her colorful confrontation with the emperor, terrible torments, and many miracles are described in a *passio*, probably composed in Rome, which was originally written in Greek and subsequently translated into Latin.[122] What is intriguing about Martina's *passio* is that except for the name of the saint and her date of martyrdom, the text is an almost verbatim duplication of the Greek *passio* of St. Tatiana, a saint venerated by a Greek-speaking community in Rome on the Quirinal Hill.[123]

We might conjecture (since the dedication of the church is not mentioned in the *Liber Pontificalis*) that the Byzantine administration was responsible for the dedication to St. Martina, perhaps as a reciprocal gesture accompanying the dedication of the Senate house to St. Hadrian. In response to the pope's choice of a Constantinopolitan saint as the patron saint of the Senate house, the Byzantine administration chose a Roman noblewoman, of senatorial rank, martyred in Rome (but whose legend was conveniently available in Greek). Tellingly, Martina was also the name of Heraclius's niece, whom he married in 613–614 after the death of his first wife (despite the patriarch's protests that the marriage was incestuous) and who reigned briefly after Heraclius's death in 641. The empress cannot have been displeased to have a dedication to her name-saint in Rome.

Martina was the first female saint (other than the Virgin Mary) to receive a dedication on the Forum Romanum. Noteworthy is her reputation for destroying the pagan past, in which she vied with the most militant of soldier-saints. Amidst her trials Martina thrice causes temples to topple: first a temple of Apollo crumbles, causing the demon inside the statue of Apollo to lament Apollo's fate; then the temple of Artemis burns down, reducing its idol to ash; in a final climax, Martina destroys the idol of Zeus at a temple for the twelve gods. At her death, when she is at last decapitated, a voice from above welcomes her into heaven, while her executioners immediately fall over dead and the emperor dies a painful death. A final earthquake converts the crowds in attendance to Christianity. It is difficult to envision a more definitive overturning of the pagan past.

* * *

With St. Hadrian and St. Martina we come to the last of the saints whose arrival on the Forum Romanum registers the Byzantine administrative presence in this area. These were saints who would have been familiar to Byzantine administrators and, with the exception of St. Martina, the new dedications in Rome mimicked similar dedications in Constantinople. They were saints in the service of empire: saints whose legends reflected imperial ideals of Christian sanctity or who had been promoted by emperors in Constantinople. Once in Rome, however, these saints did not remain shadows of their Constantinopolitan cults, but rather took on lives of their own, infusing sites that bespoke the city's imperial and pagan past with their legends.

The earliest saints, Cosmas and Damian, brought to Rome at a time when the Forum's pagan past must still have seemed palpable, were healing saints whose violent martyrdom revealed the power of God to triumph over all adversities. After the devastating Gothic Wars the Virgin Mary arrived with her escort of soldier-saints. The Forty Martyrs of Sebaste stood firm in their icy lake. Theodore flanked the Palatine. Sergius and Bacchus celebrated the triumph of imperial Christianity at the foot of the Capitoline Hill. In the Senate house, the converted official Hadrian celebrated the redefinition of Roman values in Christian terms; adjacent to him, Martina extolled the violent overthrow of the old pagan order.

Altogether, these saints marked out the Forum Romanum as a site echoing with Christianity. The *passiones* of these saints (as is common for the hagiographical genre) resound with Christian hymns, usually from the Book of Psalms. At the beginning of Hadrian's *passio*, informants announce to the emperor that they have heard Christians singing hymns in a cave.[124] Imprisoned, Martina prays, "Keep me from the snares which they have laid for me, and the stumbling blocks of the workers of iniquity."[125] Theodore, undergoing torture, declares, "I will bless the Lord at all times: his praise shall continually be in my mouth."[126] Both Sergius and Bacchus (on their journey to Antioch) and Cosmas and Damian (as they are about to be thrown into the sea in chains) proclaim, "We have rejoiced in the way of thy testimonies, as much as in all riches."[127]

Above all the saints resort to the psalms to plead for God's assistance and to express their confidence in God's protection. St. Quirion, one of the Forty Martyrs of Sebaste, cries out as he freezes to death, "Help, Lord; for the godly man ceaseth";[128] dying, the Forty Martyrs chant, "Our soul is escaped as a bird out of the snare of the fowlers: the snare is broken, and we are escaped. Our help is in the name of the Lord, who made heaven and earth."[129] Early medieval readers and listeners would surely have been able to recite these same psalms, weaving themselves into the Christian history that stretched seamlessly from King David to Christ, to the martyrs of the imperial persecutions and to the present: the continual struggle against the forces of evil.

Beginning in the eighth century a procession in honor of the Virgin Mary knit churches along the via Sacra into the larger tapestry of a papal Rome.[130] At dawn on the Marian feast days the clergy would gather at the church of S. Adriano dressed in black, bearing candles and chanting as they awaited the arrival of the pope.[131] After prayers at the church, the group proceeded to S. Maria Maggiore on the Esquiline Hill, preceded by the stational crosses—a route that reversed that of the earlier imperial processions along the via Sacra and likewise evoked Sergius's and Bacchus's "procession."

Papal involvement in this space increased, but—with the exception of Pope Paul's (r. 757–767) dedication of a church to Peter and Paul along the via Sacra at the site where they had defeated Simon the Magician—no attempt was made to modify the distinctive set of Christian dedications that defined the Forum Romanum.[132] Woven into the fabric of Rome's monumental past, all were regarded as unquestionably Roman dedications. The restoration efforts of Pope Hadrian (r. 772–795) included SS. Cosma e Damiano, S. Maria Antiqua, S. Adriano, S. Martina, and SS. Sergio e Bacco.[133] In the atrium of S. Maria Antiqua, Pope Hadrian added a fresco of himself entreating the Virgin and Child; in attendance are Sts. Sergius and Bacchus and perhaps also St. Hadrian (Plate 6).[134] All the churches on the Forum are specifically enumerated as recipients of gifts from Pope Leo III (r. 795–816), who, so his biography reports, donated to "all holy churches of the saints in this nourishing Rome."[135] Meanwhile, throughout Rome representations and dedications to many of these saints proliferated.[136] Thus the saints who inhabited the Forum Romanum were dissociated from Constantinople and the Byzantine Empire even as they continued to impart a particular inflexion to the city of Rome: they were forceful saints who fearlessly overlaid its pagan past with Christian triumph.

CHAPTER 3

St. Caesarius on the Palatine: Enriching Rome by Imperial Orders

The Palatine Hill (*Palatium*) in Rome, more than any other site either in Rome or elsewhere in the Roman world, bespoke empire. Since Augustus this had been the primary residence of Roman emperors. When emperors built residences somewhere else (as they increasingly did in Late Antiquity), each new residence was referred to as a *palatium* for the eponymous hill that had given rise to the concept.

As in the Forum Romanum below, the Palatine Hill required a saint who could speak to his surroundings. Unlike the Forum, however, which was bustling with administrators and pedestrians passing through, the Palatine Hill was in essence a ceremonial space, rarely inhabited by its intended occupant: the emperor. Atop the hill in the imperial palaces, then, we find not a multitude of new saints, but a single saint to buttress the imperial majesty: St. Caesarius.

Caesarius came to Rome in the aftermath of the Justinianic conquest as an imperial saint. There on the Palatine he remained, but in the subsequent centuries his cult was reshaped to fit new understandings of the past. To explain Caesarius's presence in Rome a new legend developed, drawing on Constantinople's famed legacy of imperial relic translations and affirming the papacy's more assertive stance vis-à-vis the Byzantine emperor. By the ninth century, popes promoted the cult of Caesarius as a confident expression of a papal Rome, even as, on the ground, the Palatine Hill was occupied by Greek-speaking monks in contact with the Byzantine world outside of Rome.

A Maze of Imperial Palaces in Old Rome

Many of the ruins visible on the Palatine Hill today are substructures, concrete terraces built to allow construction atop the sloping hill (Map 5).[1] Disorienting

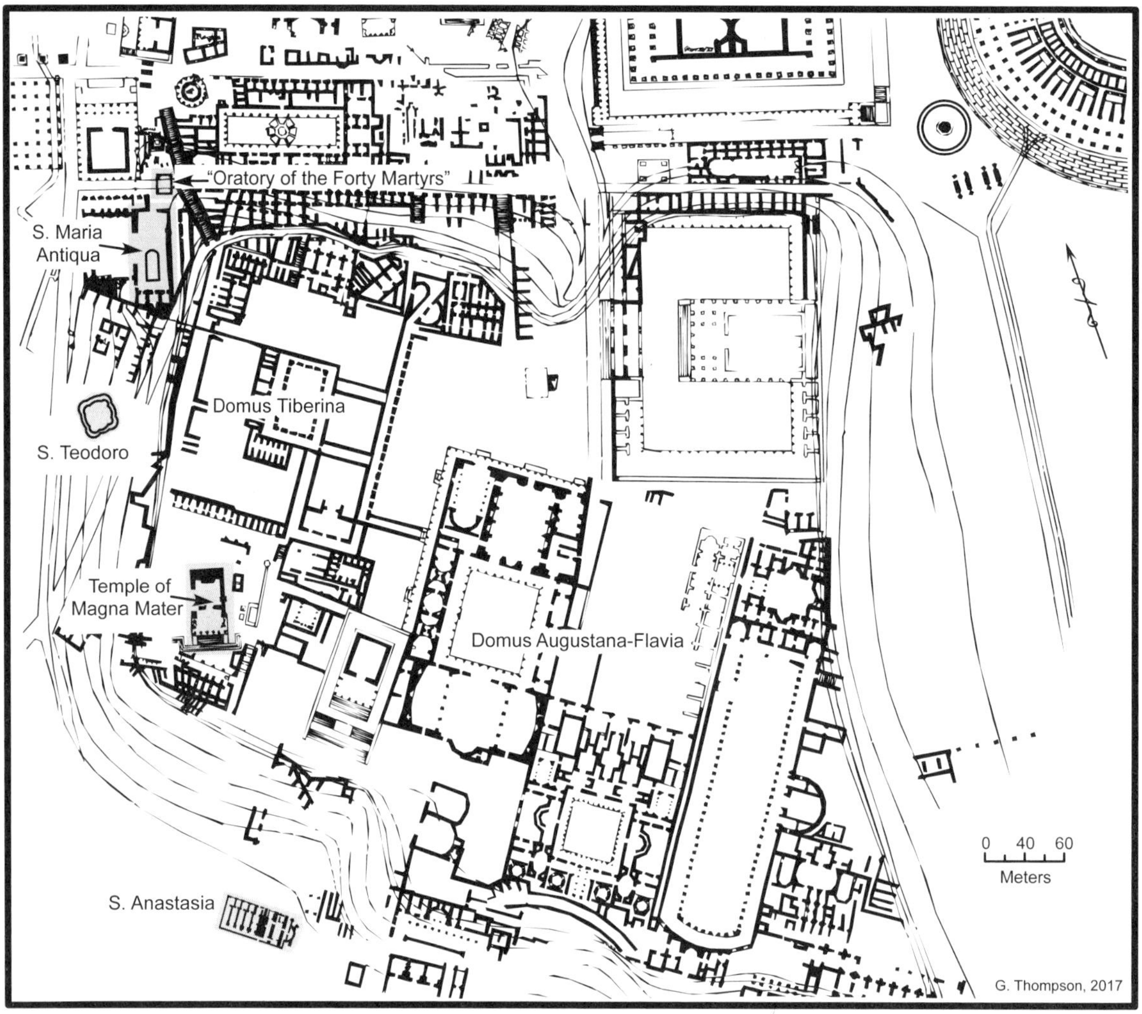

Map 5. Map of the early medieval Palatine Hill. Map created by Gordie Thompson.

the modern visitor even more is the chronological confusion of the visible sites—from Iron Age huts excavated by modern archaeologists to the Farnese gardens laid out in the sixteenth century. Centuries of occupation by notable medieval and early modern Roman families, compounded by early excavators' piecemeal search for imperial treasures and Rome's origins, have erased almost every trace of the Palatine's late antique and early medieval phases.[2]

Already in Late Antiquity, the Palatine Hill, accessed via steep streets, ramps, and staircases from the Forum Romanum below, must have housed a complicated array of buildings.[3] Atop the hill the sprawling Domus Augustana-Flavia occupied much of the available space. This vast imperial complex, with private quarters for the emperor and state rooms for him to receive visitors, was renovated and redecorated extensively over the centuries: polychrome marble, frescoes, and courtyards with bubbling fountains added to the luxury. From the lower levels of this residence the emperor could look out onto the Circus Maximus, where lavish shows exhibited his beneficence to the Roman people. At the foot of the hill adjacent to the Circus Maximus was a titular church, S. Anastasia, that likely served as the parish church for Palatine residents.[4] The space atop the hill, however, does not appear to have received a Christian dedication before the sixth century.

A New Palace for a New Rome

When Constantine founded Constantinople, the new Rome received an imperial palace modeled on the old: the Great Palace (Μέγα Παλάτιον/*Palatium Magnum*).[5] Except for some walls and substructures, little remains of this once grand palace; over time it ceased to be the official imperial residence, and it was damaged during the Fourth Crusade. The last Byzantine emperors never reoccupied the space. After the Turkish conquest, the ruins served as a quarry for new constructions, and the area was largely abandoned or built over. Excavations carried out in 1935–1938 and 1952–1954 discovered an apsed hall and courtyard with a sumptuous mosaic, but the imperial complex remains a maze poorly understood.

As in old Rome, Constantinople's palace was located on terraces on a sloping site, adjacent to the circus/hippodrome and to the Augustaion (Constantinople's analog of the Forum Romanum). Its lavish decorations evoked empire and sought to surpass the splendor of old Rome: in a poem in honor of Justin II's accession to the throne in 565, the Latin poet Corippus speaks of the "jewels which Roman power took in earlier times, which green Nereus and the land of India brought forth and which Caesar brought from the court of Memphis, which Cleopatra gave in supplication."[6] During ceremonial occasions the emperor received visitors seated on his throne in the Golden Hall (*Chrysotriklinos*), a magnificent octagonal room topped by a dome pierced with windows.[7] Throughout the centuries emperors eagerly renovated and enlarged the complex to retain and expand its imperial magnificence.

An Imperial Chapel on the Palatine Hill

Early medieval Rome could no longer boast such splendor, but the Palatine did retain its stately grandeur. When the Ostrogothic king Theoderic visited Rome in 500 he stayed on the Palatine and had restoration work carried out in the main palace.[8] Other buildings on the hill did not receive equal attention. Some areas, such as the Temple of the Magna Mater or sections of the Domus Tiberiana, were left to crumble—or were repurposed as burial sites.[9] After the Byzantine conquest this piecemeal approach to maintenance continued. The Domus Augustana-Flavia was kept in good condition, ready for the eventuality that an emperor might again deign to visit Rome. The dux responsible for the city likely occupied some part of the complex, and when in Rome exarchs from Ravenna presumably also stayed here.[10]

Although not physically present, Byzantine emperors retained a constant presence on the Palatine Hill. Imperial portraits were routinely sent to provinces, including Rome, on the accession of a new emperor. These images had a privileged status, sharing in many of the prerogatives of the emperor himself.[11] A document preserved with the correspondence of Pope Gregory the Great (r. 590–604) describes the arrival of such an image. The occasion was the accession of Emperor Phocas (r. 602–610), in whose honor, as we saw in Chapter 2, a monumental column would be erected on the Forum Romanum. The document recounts:

> The image of the above-named Augusti of Rome, Phocas and Leontia, arrived on the seventh day before the Kalends of May. And it was acclaimed in the Lateran in the basilica of Julius by the whole clergy and the senate: "Christ hear us! Long live Phocas Augustus and Leontia Augusta!" Then the most blessed and apostolic lord pope Gregory ordered that the image be placed in the oratory of the martyr St. Caesarius inside the palace (*intra palatio*).[12]

Both the senate and the clergy of Rome greeted the portraits of the new emperor and empress. Then the pope, as spiritual head of the Roman Church and as urban administrator, ensured that the portraits were properly stowed in the imperial chapel on the Palatine.

The chapel in question, the "oratory of the martyr St. Caesarius," must have been located somewhere within the Domus Augustana-Flavia, although its specific whereabouts are unknown.[13] As on the Forum below, Byzantine administrators likely established this chapel in the aftermath of the conquest, as they tried to regularize and modernize the city's aging infrastructure. After all, the Great Palace in Constantinople was fitted with Christian chapels; the original *palatium* too required a suitable Christian dedication.[14]

From Terracina to Rome: Along the Via Appia

The new saint bore a name that befitted his location: Caesar. Yet in other respects he was an unusual choice. For St. Caesarius was a saint neither from Rome nor from Constantinople; instead he was from a small town well known to Byzantine administrators: Terracina (Map 6).

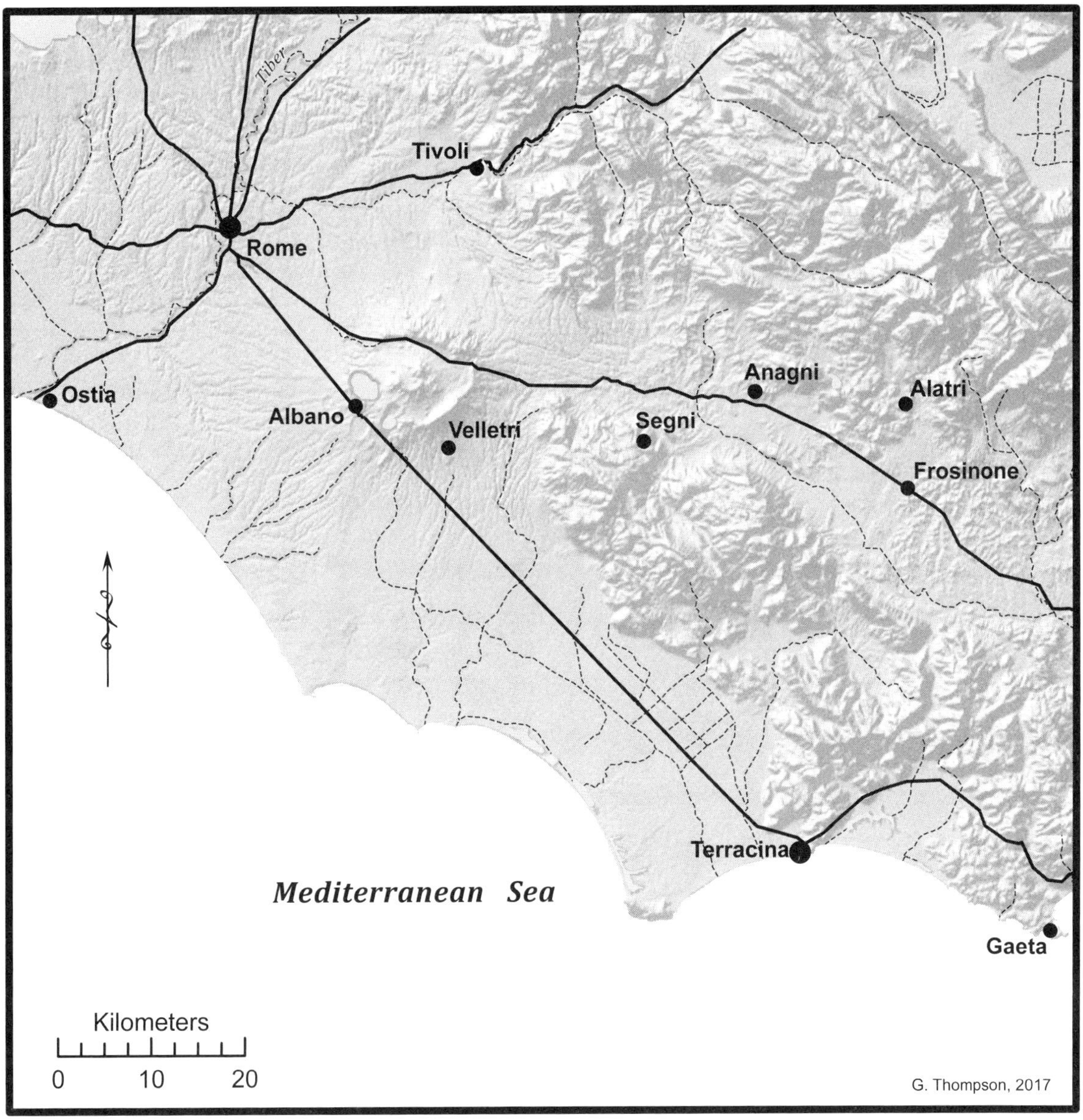

Map 6. Map of Rome and Terracina. Map created by Gordie Thompson.

The town of Terracina is nestled by the sea in front of the Volscian Hills, about seventy-five kilometers southeast of Rome along the via Appia. St. Paul (according to the Greek *Acts of Peter and Paul*) had stayed here for a short time, hosted by the deacon Caesarius, before continuing his journey north to Rome.[15] Terracina was a dramatically situated and strategically important site: here the narrow pass of Lautulae provided access from Rome to the rest of southern Italy. The pass was an engineering feat accomplished under Trajan that cut deep into the cliff to establish a secure route for the via Appia.[16] Maintaining the accessibility of the via Appia remained of concern to travelers and administrators in Late Antiquity as this was a route commonly traversed by travelers between Rome and Constantinople. Under Theoderic inscriptions were erected to commemorate the drainage of swamps that made the via Appia passable again.[17] During the Gothic Wars Terracina was a key port and garrison guarding the via Appia, and the town passed between Byzantine and Ostrogothic hands.[18] With the arrival of the Lombards in southern Italy in the later sixth century and the establishment of the Duchy of Benevento, Terracina continued to be a crucial link for defending Rome.

Imperial recognition of Terracina's significance survives in a curious bilingual inscription on a column reused as spolia in Terracina's medieval cathedral that fronts the ancient forum (Figure 9).[19] The column contains two inscriptions, one Greek, one Latin. Both, as Guillou has argued from epigraphic/paleographic criteria, date from the seventh or eighth century.[20] The upper inscription in Greek proclaims, "Many years to the orthodox and victorious emperors"—an acclamation customary in Byzantine ceremonies for imperial triumphs, largess distributed by the emperor, or other ceremonial events performed in his presence.[21] The lower inscription, in Latin, records, "This forum was embellished in the time of George, consul and dux."[22] This George, otherwise unknown, was presumably dux of Rome. This renovation attests to a concern for maintaining Terracina's urban infrastructure; moreover, the inscription's placement just below the imperial acclamation indicates that George was attentive to aligning his project of urban restoration with imperial control over Terracina.

In Rome, Byzantine administrators (like George but a few generations earlier) who were familiar with Terracina and its patron saint decided to dedicate the chapel on the Palatine Hill to Caesarius. This act may be regarded in part as a gesture acknowledging the town's importance. Caesarius, however, also had more to offer to the Palatine than his apposite name. His legend fit impeccably into the symbolism of the Palatine, offering a forceful Christian commentary on the meaning of the empire. In Caesarius the Byzantine administration found a saint capable of Christianizing Rome's imperial core.

Caesarius's *passio*, a Latin text, revolves around the good health or prosperity (*salus*) of the Roman Empire.[23] The legend presents Caesarius's martyrdom as proof that the well-being of the state rests more solidly on Christian foundations than on its pagan past. As such, Caesarius personified the consequences of Christianity for the empire, and his oratory on the Palatine served as a benchmark for the empire's Christianization.

Caesarius' *passio* is set in Terracina under the pagan emperor Claudius, who has commanded that customary sacrifices to the pagan gods should not cease. In Terracina, we are told, each year on the Kalends of January, a ceremony of self-

Figure 9. S. Cesareo, Terracina: column inscriptions. Photograph by author.

immolation occurred to assure the health of the empire (*pro salute reipublicae et principum et civium salubritate*).[24] A young man is pampered with material delights for a year and then obliged to plunge to his death from the city's cliffs. Thereafter his body is collected and burned and his ashes placed in the temple of Apollo. Indeed, the cliffs of Terracina, on which a Roman temple was located, still today offer a spectacular visual backdrop to the legend.

Caesarius, a deacon from Africa, arrives in Terracina and is shocked to learn of the ceremony. He protests: "Alas for a state and emperors who persuade by tortures and are fattened on the outpouring of blood."[25] He is duly arrested as a result of this public pronouncement. When interrogated, he refuses to sacrifice to the pagan gods, and subsequently his prayers cause the temple of Apollo to crumble, killing the pagan priest Firminus. Then Luxurius, the leading citizen, accuses Caesarius of homicide and destroying the ancient temple by casting magic spells. Caesarius wins approval from the people with this appeal: "Consider, brothers, whether it is just that a man should be feared more than God the creator of all things, and judge whether your city should be purified by the bloody death of men."[26] Christ's redemptive death, Caesarius argues, has proven the futility of such bloody sacrifices. Nevertheless Caesarius is martyred (together with the presbyter Julian), thrown into the sea tied up in a sack—although not before converting the consul and prophesying the death of Luxurius by a snake, a prediction promptly fulfilled in gruesome detail.

The figure of Caesarius the martyr likely developed out of earlier brief accounts found in the legends surrounding Peter and Paul and the martyrs Nereus and Achilleus.[27] As already noted, the Greek *Acts of Peter and Paul* mention a deacon Caesarius who hosts the apostle Paul in Terracina until he departs for Rome.[28] In the *passio* of Nereus and Achilleus, which contains the martyrdom of numerous saints, a deacon by the name of Caesarius is said to have buried the bodies of virgin martyrs in Terracina after he came across them unburied (his subsequent fate is not elaborated).[29]

From an undeveloped representative of early Christian piety, the figure of Caesarius is developed in his *passio* into a representative of how Christianity has—literally, in the form of the crumbling temple—overturned the pagan past. His *passio* presents an elaborate and gruesome panorama of the pagan ritual that, so its audience is led to believe, once underpinned the imperial administration. In contrast to this senseless and impious bloodshed, Caesarius's martyrdom truly works for the imperial *salus* by bearing witness to God's truth; commemoration of him offers a means to perpetuate that prosperity. Although the story remains anchored in Terracina, its geopolitical dimensions have expanded dramatically; Caesarius is no longer merely a deacon from Terracina, but instead has arrived from Africa. While the emperor himself does not appear in the story, the *passio* does accord a voice to the people of the town (*omnis populus*), who approve of Caesarius's words in a gesture of popular support that would have been welcome in an oratory that now housed the images of the emperors.

* * *

Caesarius offered a compelling narrative of Christian triumph for the Palatine, and so Byzantine administrators in the aftermath of the Justinianic conquest must have considered him a worthy addition to the imperial palaces. But that a saint from the small town of Terracina occupied such a central position on the Palatine Hill may still surprise—as it seems to have puzzled subsequent early medieval audiences. The result would be the formation of a new legend (that dates, I propose, to the early eighth century) recounting how, centuries earlier, a Christian emperor, with the assistance of a Roman bishop, had translated Caesarius's relics from Terracina to Rome.[30] To understand the formation of this legend we must first consider some of the developments that affected understandings of the Palatine's past: Constantinople's legacy of imperial relic translations, two memorable displays of imperial authority in mid-seventh-century Rome, and, in the late seventh century, expanding papal prerogatives on the Palatine.

Imperial Relics in Constantinople

During the reign of Emperor Heraclius the precious relic of the True Cross (recovered from the Persians in 629), as well as the relics of the Holy Lance and Sponge, were brought to Constantinople.[31] After Jerusalem fell to the Arabs in 637–638, the relics were permanently lodged within the Great Palace. There they joined an already impressive collection of imperial relics in the palace and, more generally, throughout the city of Constantinople.

By the time of Heraclius, Constantinople could already look back on a long history of relic translations orchestrated by its emperors.[32] Constantius II or, according to some traditions, Constantine himself, had brought the relics of Timothy, Andrew, and Luke to the city to be placed in Constantine's mausoleum.[33] From the late fourth century onward the practice of relic translation to Constantinople became well established. Under Theodosius I (r. 379–395), numerous relics, including the head of John the Baptist, were brought to Constantinople.[34] His successors Arcadius (r. 395–408) and Theodosius II (r. 408–450) acquired more relics, and relic translations undertaken by emperors or their family members into Constantinople became a recognized imperial paradigm—as shown, for example, on the "Trier Ivory," a Byzantine ivory casket that depicts an empress in front of a new but unfinished church, receiving a procession in which bishops transport a reliquary (Figure 10).[35]

Inside the Great Palace, a chapel housed the right arm of St. Stephen.[36] (The reception of these relics by Pulcheria Augusta, the influential sister of Emperor Theodosius II, is arguably the subject of the Trier Ivory.[37]) This chapel would come to hold an assortment of imperial paraphernalia and precious relics—such as the Gospel of Matthew copied by St. Barnabas, which the emperor Zeno (r. 474–491) had transported from the saint's tomb in Cyprus.[38] Constantinople could thus boast to be a veritable storehouse of relics, even a "new Jerusalem."[39]

Rome, in contrast to Constantinople, had no such rich tradition of imperial relics.[40] After all, initially Constantinople's many relic imports had been intended,

Figure 10. Trier Ivory, Trier Domschatz. Foto Marburg / Art Resource, NY.

at least in part, to compensate for the city's lack of "native" sanctity. Papal claims to Rome's primacy rested on the treasured relics of its apostle Peter, and Rome had many other martyrs that it could call its own.[41] For this reason the dismemberment of saints' bodies and translation of these relics had also been a less common practice in Rome than elsewhere in late antique Christendom. Refusing Empress Constantina's request for the relics of St. Paul, Gregory the Great famously intoned against such a sacrilegious treatment of relics, recalling stories of how attempts to translate relics had paralyzed their perpetrators.[42] Nevertheless successive Roman popes were not unwilling to accept relics from abroad, and as the practice of translating relics became increasingly common in both the Byzantine world and in western Europe, Rome could seem bereft of this form of imperial beneficence. Why had the great Christian emperors of the past showered relics on new, not old, Rome?

The Imperial Presence in Rome

Byzantine emperors did not lavish relics on Rome, but the city was by no means ignored. Two dramatic imperial encounters in the seventh century impressed Romans and lingered in the city's memory: the arrest and deportation of Pope Martin in 653 and Emperor Constans II's visit to Rome in 663.

The last years of the reign of Emperor Heraclius (d. 641) witnessed the Arab invasions that would dramatically reshape the geopolitical landscape of the eastern Mediterranean, causing Syria, Palestine, and Egypt to slip out of Byzantine control. As defeat followed defeat, many in the Byzantine world were convinced that something in the empire had gone awry. The question was what. And the answers proffered by Constans II (r. 641–668) and Patriarch Paul of Constantinople (r. 641–653) met with staunch resistance.

In 649 Pope Theodore (r. 642–649), born in Greece and the son of a bishop from Jerusalem, convened a church council, which was held after his death by his successor, Pope Martin (r. 649–655).[43] The council was largely organized by Greek-speaking monks and clerics, some of whom had arrived in Rome as refugees from regions in the eastern Mediterranean conquered by Arab armies (we will encounter such communities again in Chapter 5). The leading force behind the council was Maximus (the Confessor, ca. 580–662), a monk who had fled Constantinople after he was condemned for his opposition to Heraclius's religious policies.

After a sojourn in North Africa, Maximus arrived in Rome, where he continued to agitate against the "heresies" of monoenergism and monotheletism, which had found favor in Constantinople (and to which Pope Honorius had acquiesced and even, inadvertently it seems, helped develop). Only through a proper understanding of Christ's perfect humanity and perfect divinity, Maximus argued, could humans ever hope to ascend to God. Opposition to these pernicious doctrines was thus of the utmost importance for the preservation of a Christian Empire.

Maximus and his followers drew up the council acts in Greek and then translated them into Latin; at the council they were signed by the assembled bishops. Imperial edicts were anathematized, including the so-called *Typos* promulgated by Constans II in 648, which forbade further discussion of Christ's wills and energies, as well as Constantinopolitan patriarchs, including the patriarch Paul who had proposed the *Typos*. The emperor reacted swiftly against this challenge to his imperial authority. The exarch, Olympius, appointed by Constans, was ordered to arrest Pope Martin, as well as Maximus.

As recounted by the biography of Martin in the *Liber Pontificalis*, which portrays him as a heroic holy man who strove valiantly to uphold orthodoxy, the exarch Olympius attempted to carry out the imperial orders, but his efforts, first to arrest and then to assassinate the pope, were miraculously thwarted, and so he switched allegiance to him.[44] Emperor Constans promptly appointed a new exarch, Theodore Calliopas, who in 653 arrested the pope and brought him to Constantinople. (Meanwhile Olympius had marched with an army to Sicily, but died of disease in 652.) In Constantinople Martin was tried for treason and exiled to Cherson in the Crimea.[45] Maximus was likewise duly arrested, tried and exiled.

Roman (and Greek) tradition would eventually come to venerate Martin—and Maximus—as confessors, but in Rome, before Martin died in exile, a new pope, Eugene, was elected and confirmed by Constantinople. Normal relations resumed, leaving the doctrinal dispute unresolved until 680–681 when the Sixth Ecumenical Council in Constantinople rehabilitated the Lateran Council, vindicating Maximus the Confessor and Pope Martin I. An earlier expression of dissent, however, may perhaps be detected in a set of frescoes that were added to the church of S. Maria Antiqua, at the foot of the Palatine Hill, sometime after the Lateran Council and before the pontificate of Pope John VII (r. 705–707), when they were painted over.[46]

This fresco program included portraits of four leading Church fathers (Pope Leo I, Gregory of Nazianzus, Basil of Caesarea, and John Chrysostom), each holding scrolls with extracts, in Greek, from relevant texts of theirs that had been used in the Lateran Council (Plates 7 and 8). The S. Maria Antiqua frescoes (if indeed they were painted prior to the Sixth Ecumenical Council) would have been in defiance of the imperial position.[47] Presumably in this scenario a Greek-speaking faction that supported Maximus would have commissioned them. In any case, whatever their date—which may well have been after the Sixth Ecumenical Council—the frescoes certainly do demonstrate that the dramatic council was remembered and commemorated in Rome, in close proximity to the imperial palace.[48]

A decade after Pope Martin was arrested by the exarch, the Romans had another, even more unaccustomed, encounter with imperial authority. In 663, Emperor Constans II arrived in Rome, the first emperor to visit the city in almost two centuries.[49] Constans had traveled from Constantinople to Athens and then on to southern Italy, where he campaigned to strengthen the Byzantine provinces in southern Italy against the Lombard Duchy of Benevento. Given the dramatic losses of territory in the previous decades, retaining control over the grain-producing Italian provinces was a sensible priority for the Byzantine emperor.

Constans then traveled to Naples and continued north on the via Appia, passing through Terracina, to Rome. He was greeted by Pope Vitalian (r. 657–672) and his entourage at the sixth mile outside Rome—a ceremonial indication of the pope's due deference to the imperial majesty.[50] In turn, the emperor visited St. Peter's and presented a gift there, indicating his respect for St. Peter and his see. Later in his visit, the emperor also dined with the pope at the Lateran.

For twelve days, we may assume, the imperial palaces on the Palatine were once again inhabited by an emperor. Constans toured the city, but according to Pope Vitalian's biographer, this was no mere sightseeing: "he [Constans] dismantled all the city's bronze decorations; he removed the bronze tiles from the roof of the church of St. Mary *ad martyres* [that is, the Pantheon], and he sent them to the imperial city [Constantinople] with various other things he had dismantled."[51] It was imperial property that the emperor seized, presumably in part to pay his troops as he continued his military campaign in southern Italy against Lombard and Arab armies. Yet in the eyes of the pope's biographer (and presumably this sentiment was shared by others in Rome), it was unseemly for an emperor to dismantle Rome's urban infrastructure—although the pope, we should note, did not protest.

Constans II died in Syracuse in Sicily in 668, a few years after leaving Rome, murdered, so it was reported, by his bathing attendant. Constans' son Constantine IV (r. 652–685) assumed the purple in Constantinople and suppressed a revolt by the general Mezezius who laid claim to the throne from Sicily. Constantine IV probably did not personally participate in this Italian campaign; certainly neither he, nor any of his immediate successors, would again visit Rome.[52] Not until John VIII Palaiologos (r. 1425–1448) came to Rome to ask for military assistance against the Ottomans would another Byzantine emperor set foot in the city.

Constantine IV's reign saw Constantinople besieged by the Arabs (674–678) and Lombard advances in southern Italy, but also, most importantly from the perspective of the popes in Rome, the vindication of Pope Martin, Maximus, and the Lateran Council of 649. As mentioned, the Sixth Ecumenical Council, which met in Constantinople in 680–681 and was attended by papal delegates, drew up a decree confessing Christ's two wills and two energies/operations, one divine and one human, but perfectly united. Rome and Constantinople were thus again dogmatically aligned. Yet with hindsight, Pope Martin's "successful" defiance of imperial authority, as well as Constans II's "sack" of Rome—both inscribed into the institutional memory of the papacy, the *Liber Pontificalis*—had shifted the paradigms of imperial-papal relations.

Expanding Papal Prerogatives on the Palatine

Constantine IV was succeeded by his son Justinian II (r. 685–695 and 705–711). During the reign of this unpopular emperor the Palatine Hill became the site first of a contested papal election and then of an ambitious papal building project. In these events we can observe the increasing involvement of ecclesiastical administrators in imperial spaces on the Palatine Hill. Noticeable too is the shifting allegiance of both ecclesiastical and Byzantine administrators to the city of Rome and the papacy—and away from the emperor.

A contested papal election occurred in 687, and in response the Palatine chapel of St. Caesarius was mobilized as an alternative site of authority. Our source for this account is the *Liber Pontificalis*'s biography of the successful candidate, Sergius (r. 687–701), a text eager to legitimize his pontificate. After the election of two rival popes, both of whom were supported by rival factions and refused to give way, "the dignitaries of the judges, the army of the Roman soldiery, the majority (if it may be said) of the clergy and particularly of the priests, and a crowd of the citizens" decided on a third candidate: Sergius.[53] They brought him "into the oratory of Christ's martyr St. Caesarius, which is inside the imperial palace, and from there they led him to the Lateran *episcopium* with praise and acclamation."[54] (When Sergius and his faction arrived at the Lateran, one of his two rivals immediately accepted Sergius as the rightfully elected bishop.) With the Lateran, the usual site for episcopal elections, partially occupied by Sergius's rivals (as the preceding passage in the biography makes clear), the makeshift ceremony had used St. Caesarius' highly charged chapel as a substitute.

The biography also emphasizes the joint participation of both Rome's Byzantine and ecclesiastical administrators in electing the pope. Local Byzantine administrators in Rome initially supported the election of Sergius. Thereafter, when one of the two rival popes refused to give way and called on John the exarch of Ravenna for assistance, the exarch, so we are told, came to Rome, but found the city in support of Sergius. Accordingly, he too supported Sergius's election—although in an act much criticized by Sergius's biography, he demanded a payment of gold for his services.[55] Local politics, not the intervention of the exarch, had determined the selection of the pope.

As this account suggests, members of the Byzantine administration in Rome were liable to find more common ground with Roman ecclesiastical administrators than with the exarch, appointed from Constantinople. With the exception of the exarch, Byzantine personnel in Italy were generally recruited from the resident population.[56] Members of the same families (whether older senatorial families or more recent immigrants) might serve in both the Byzantine and ecclesiastical administration; indeed, the very same individual might pursue a career in both. Unsurprisingly, then, Byzantine administrators might feel greater allegiance to the pope in Rome than to the exarch in Ravenna or the emperor in Constantinople. This, we are told (again by the papal biography of Sergius), was the case later in Sergius's papacy when the pope refused to sign the acts of the Council in Trullo.

That council, held in 691–692 (and also known as the Quinisext Council) met in a domed hall ("trullus") inside the Great Palace in Constantinople to discuss a variety of ecclesiastical matters.[57] Among its many decrees, this council condemned certain ritual practices in Rome (such as fasting on the Saturdays of Lent). In response, Pope Sergius refused to receive the acts, preferring, so his biography claims, "to die sooner than consent to erroneous novelties."[58] Emperor Justinian II then sent an imperial official, Zacharias, to arrest the pope, but in the words of the same biography, "the hearts of the Ravennate soldiery were stirred up, along with those of the Pentapolitan duchy and the surrounding region, not to allow the pontiff of the apostolic see to go up to the imperial city [Constantinople]."[59]

Zacharias was reduced to cowering under the pope's bed to save himself.[60] What the final outcome of the altercation would have been is unclear, for shortly thereafter, Justinian II was deposed by a coup and exiled to Cherson, and Pope Sergius remained in office. By the time Justinian II regained the throne in 705, Sergius had died and been succeeded first by John VI (r. 701–705) and then by John VII (r. 705–707).

Pope John VII was intimately familiar with the Byzantine administration in Rome. His father Plato, for whom John erected an epitaph in 686, had served as a high-ranking official, the curator of the palace (*cura palatii*), responsible for the upkeep of the imperial palaces on the Palatine.[61] According to this epitaph Plato was of the highest senatorial rank (*vir illustris*) and had carried out repairs to the "ancient palace," including its "long stair" (one of the ramps leading down to the Forum Romanum).[62] The epitaph draws a parallel between these "ancient palaces of Rome (*prisca palatia Romae*)," restored by Plato, and the "divine palaces of the eternal king (*aeterni divina palatia regis*)," to which Plato, in dying, has now ascended, neatly juxtaposing Plato's concern for maintaining the Palatine as a representative site of the imperial presence with the heavenly court of God to which, in dying, Plato aspired.

On the ground John actively pursued this analogy between the earthly and the heavenly court of God. John's subsequent epitaph for his mother tells of how she devoted herself to charitable activities and encouraged her son to adopt a chaste Christian life.[63] John himself served as rector of the Appian way (*rector Appiae*), that is, as an administrator of papal properties, before becoming pope.[64] As pope, according to his biography in the *Liber Pontificalis*, John had the unprecedented idea of building an episcopal residence (*episcopium*) just up from the church of S. Maria Antiqua (which he also had redecorated).[65]

Nothing survives of his building project, but presumably the *episcopium* was located in the Domus Tiberiana up the hill from S. Maria Antiqua, accessed by means of the ramp from the church.[66] This palatial complex, now covered by the Farnese gardens, was adjacent to the Domus Augustana-Flavia with its chapel for St. Caesarius. Thus a former imperial residence was transformed into the bishop's residence—perhaps it was intended to replace the episcopal residence at the Lateran. We do not know, for John's pontificate lasted only two years and there is no evidence that any subsequent pope resided in this Palatine *episcopium*.

What does survive is much of John's fresco program in S. Maria Antiqua, including a portrait of himself (corroborating his biographer's claim that John had himself depicted in churches throughout the city).[67] The new frescoes in S. Maria Antiqua replaced many of the older images, including the earlier Church fathers with their scrolls.[68] The new frescoes, however, similarly hearkened back to the Lateran Council of 649. Again depicted were four Church fathers: Augustine, an unidentified figure, Gregory of Nazianzus, and Basil of Caesarea (replacing Leo, Gregory of Nazianzus, Basil, and John Chrysostom).[69] Below these were now four Roman popes: John VII himself, Leo, an unidentified pope, and Martin I, each labeled "Papa Romanus." Depicted at the top of the apse was the crucified Christ, adored by seraphs, angels, and the faithful (Plate 9). Arguably this scene transposes the iconography of the adoration of the lamb (whose depiction as a symbol for Christ had been prohibited by the Council in Trullo in 692), replacing the lamb with Christ.[70]

Deciphering the precise nuance of these frescoes has proven controversial.[71] Do John's frescoes indicate his consent to the acts of the Council in Trullo? Or should the depiction of Pope Martin be read as a symbol of papal resistance to imperial heresy? During John's papacy, Justinian II regained the throne in Constantinople, and Pope John was pressured by the emperor to convene a council and confirm the acts of the Council in Trullo that Sergius had rebuffed. The pope did not do so, but his decision to send back the acts without any emendations was criticized in his biography as a sign of his weakness.[72]

John's unusual decision to build an *episcopium* on the Palatine—like his decision to send back the acts unsigned and like the import of John's fresco program—has been variously interpreted as anything from an expression of submission to, or alliance with, the emperor to a calculated statement of Roman defiance.[73] It seems likely that such multivalent interpretations were intentional and represent John's attempt to balance rival factions in Rome. The Roman ecclesiastical administration prior to and including Pope John VII could not imagine Rome without an emperor, but popes could be and were interested in establishing more authoritative and prestigious positions for themselves and the city of Rome vis-à-vis this emperor. In this context of intensifying local sentiment that coalesced around the papacy, there developed a new explanation of how Rome had acquired Caesarius from Terracina.

Translating Sanctity to Rome

A Terracinan saint, an imperial chapel, Constantinople's legacy of imperial relic translations, and the increasing authority of the Roman bishop all fused to create a translation narrative that explained the dedication to Caesarius on the Palatine. This legend creatively builds on Caesarius's imperial pedigree, acquiring for Rome a legacy of imperial relic translations, but infusing it with a message of papal control—over Rome and even over the imperial family.

The *translatio*, a Latin text, is set in a fanciful past when the empire was ruled by the pious emperor Valentinian, who followed the commands of the Roman bishop, and the Roman Church was led by a most holy bishop, Damasus (r. 366–384).[74] The emperor Valentinian would seem to be a fusion of Valentinian I (r. 364–375), a contemporary of Damasus, and Valentinian III (r. 423–455), who had two daughters (as the text specifies) and was remembered favorably by the *Liber Pontificalis* for funding and encouraging church construction in Rome during the papacy of Pope Sixtus III (r. 432–440).[75] Pope Damasus, who was responsible for erecting epitaphs at the tombs of martyrs outside of Rome, was highly esteemed for his solicitude for saints' relics—a fitting protagonist for the story.

The opening section of the *translatio* reminds the reader of the imperial benefactions that Rome has received. We are told that Valentinian's wife Eudoxia was the daughter of Emperor Theodosius, who constructed the church of S. Paolo fuori le Mura, subsequently completed by Emperor Honorius. Eudoxia, the text recalls, constructed the basilica of S. Pietro in Vincoli.[76] Thus the new legend is embedded within, and made more plausible by, further memories of imperial beneficence.

After providing this brief background to the main characters of the legend, the story unfolds, revolving around the issue of papal versus imperial control over Roman property. Pope Damasus requests from the emperor a certain garden in which to build a basilica for St. Lawrence, and the emperor agrees (and the *Liber Pontificalis* tells us that Damasus was in fact responsible for the construction of a church for St. Lawrence). In the *translatio*, however, the emperor's daughter Galla (or Galla Placidia) refuses to acquiesce to her father's donation, for the garden is her playground. Galla attempts to prevent the church's foundation, but is suddenly possessed by an unclean spirit. She is brought to the relics of various saints in Rome to no avail, and finally the emperor decides to take her to St. Isidore on the island of Chios (in the Aegean sea, off the coast of Asia Minor), motivated by Isidore's reputation for curing the possessed.

The decision to travel to Chios is a convenient ploy to have the imperial family travel south along the via Appia and pass through Terracina. The proposed destination, however, is hardly far-fetched. By the later sixth century, St. Isidore's sanctuary on the island of Chios had gained widespread fame for its healing powers; Gregory of Tours refers to the curative powers of its well.[77]

As it turns out, the proposed journey and St. Isidore's assistance prove unnecessary. For, so the story continues, while on the journey south through Campania, the imperial entourage arrives at Terracina, where the town's bishop, Felix, directs the suffering girl to the relics of St. Caesarius and prays for her. Felix's intervention causes Caesarius to appear, and the saint cures Galla by pulling a snake out of her mouth—a tactic reminiscent of the incident in Caesarius's *passio* in which the saint prophesied that his persecutor would die from a snakebite.

The emperor is overjoyed at the news and immediately travels with a crowd to Terracina. He enters the church to find his daughter entirely healed. (One wonders whether this account might bear a distant echo of the imperial presence in Terracina commemorated on the column in Terracina's forum.) Thereupon the emperor honors the bishop Felix, giving many gifts to the church of Terracina, and, in an initiative distinctly less favorable to the town, has the relics of Caesarius and Julian transported to Rome. The relics, placed on the litter in which his daughter had been carried while ill, are transported on the shoulders of priests and followed by a crowd with candles chanting hymns and praise. Arriving in Rome the relics are brought, by the hands of Damasus himself, to an oratory in the *palatium*, located in the imperial bedchamber (*imperiale cubiculum*). In conclusion, the *translatio* assures that "even up to the present day, this place exhibits many miracles."[78]

The *translatio* provides Caesarius with imperial prestige suitable to his location on the Palatine. Rome is presented as a city that deserves—and receives—imperial patronage. Yet although framed against Constantinople's tradition of imperial relic translations and emphasizing imperial generosity to Rome, the *translatio* is careful to subordinate the emperor to bishops. Presiding over the initiative is the Roman pope Damasus and, to a lesser extent, the bishop of Terracina, Felix. In comparison, the emperor plays a minor role. Galla's illness is caused by her refusal to grant land for Damasus's church; the girl is cured by the intercession of Terracina's bishop Felix; and it is Damasus who brings the relics into the imperial oratory and dedicates the chapel. Imperial beneficence benefits Rome, but the key roles are played by bishops.

In Rome, we may imagine that the events narrated by the *translatio* were recalled each year during a procession, headed by the pope, that led to the chapel of St. Caesarius on the Palatine. At least by the late seventh century, each year on the feast day of Caesarius, the first of November, Romans would gather at SS. Cosma e Damiano on the Forum Romanum and from there, led by the pope, ceremoniously process to St. Caesarius on the Palatine.[79] The origins of this tradition are unknown, but whether it pre- or postdated the *translatio*, the two must have fused in significance to express the papal underpinnings of this imperial cult.

The Medieval Legacy: Caesarius as a Papal Saint and Greek-Speaking Monks on the Palatine

In the course of the next two centuries, as the Byzantine imperial presence in Rome faded or was actively erased by assertive popes, the papacy cultivated a closer relationship with the cult of St. Caesarius, both in Rome and in Terracina. Nevertheless, the oratory for St. Caesarius on the Palatine Hill developed a profile distinct from the papal web that would come to encompass much of the city. A monastery dedicated to Caesarius inhabited by Greek-speaking monks imbued the site with a spirit that hearkened to its patron saint, the Terracinan traveler.

In the early eighth century (in a process we explore further in the next chapter), successive Roman popes increasingly detached themselves from the emperor in Constantinople and laid claim to rule Rome and its environs, including Terracina. In the late eighth century, two letters from Pope Hadrian asking Charlemagne for help attest to the papacy's attempts to wrest control of Terracina from the Greeks and Lombards of southern Italy.[80] Meanwhile, in Rome, these same popes endeavored to style themselves legitimate rulers. Accordingly, the Lateran, the seat of the papacy, was outfitted with the architectural and ideological attributes of an imperial palace.

Pope Zacharias (r. 741–752), whom we encounter again in the next chapter, had a new *triclinium*, a reception hall, added to the Lateran. He may have been motivated by a Constantinopolitan precedent: not long before, under Emperor Justinian II, the Great Palace in Constantinople had received a new *triclinium*.[81] In 768, we also hear of an oratory dedicated to St. Caesarius at the Lateran complex—where the faction of one aspiring pope unsuccessfully tried to take refuge.[82] It is tempting to interpret the oratory for St. Caesarius at the Lateran as an attempt to transplant this key attribute of the Palatine's imperial palace to the palace of the popes. A century later, Pope Sergius II's (r. 844–847) gift of silk veils to the chapel, including two decorated with "Byzantine (*byzantina*)" (that is, Constantinopolitan) purple, reinforces the impression of the chapel's aspirations to an imperial pedigree.[83] Furthermore, a monastery dedicated to St. Caesarius at S. Paolo fuori le Mura (recorded in the extensive list of ecclesiastical institutions to which Pope Leo III gave gifts in 807), likewise suggests a papal interest in co-opting the cult of Caesarius.[84]

Not included as a beneficiary of Pope Leo III's generosity is the oratory to St. Caesarius on the Palatine Hill. Perhaps the chapel had fallen into disrepair and was abandoned, or as seems equally plausible, this was not a community in favor with Pope Leo III. This hypothesis is consistent with the evidence that twenty years later the Palatine Hill was occupied by a Greek-speaking monastic community, at least one member of whom was willing to assist a Frankish traveler in disobeying the pope by stealing relics from the catacombs.

In 827, Ratleig, the notary of Einhard (a prominent member of the Frankish elite who served as advisor to the Frankish emperor Charlemagne and his successor Louis the Pious), was in Rome attempting to acquire the relics of the Roman martyrs Marcellinus and Peter, which were buried outside Rome on the via Labicana.[85] As we have already seen in the introduction (and as will be discussed further in Chapter 7), the Carolingian elite eagerly embraced Roman relics as a form of portable sanctity that could fortify their communities. Although most notables likely obtained their relics directly from Roman popes, Ratleig decided to proceed by theft.

A *translatio* written by Einhard to commemorate the successful acquisition of relics narrates the events.[86] Ratleig, we are told, daringly attempts to acquire the relics of the Roman martyrs Marcellinus and Peter from the catacombs.[87] After successfully retrieving the body of St. Marcellinus from the crypt, the notary is reluctant to return north without the saint's companion and ponders how he may retrieve him. As a visitor to Rome, he has no acquaintances to help him. But in a fellow traveler he finds some consolation:

> For he realized that he could not find any Roman to help him in this affair, nor in fact was there [a Roman] to whom he dared reveal his secret thoughts. While wrestling with this worry in his heart, he happened to meet a foreign monk by the name of Basil who two years before had traveled from Constantinople to Rome. He resided in Rome with four of his students on the Palatine Hill in a house occupied by other Greeks. [Ratleig] went to him and revealed the [nature of the] anxiety troubling him. Then, encouraged by [the monk's] advice and confident of his prayers, he discovered such strength in his own heart that he was determined to attempt the deed as soon as he could, despite the danger to himself.[88]

And, Ratleig, his courage restored, plots another expedition to the Roman cemeteries, where he now successfully lays hands on the relics of Marcellinus's companion Peter as well. A Frankish notable and a Greek monk thus cooperate in sidestepping papal control over Rome's storehouse of relics.

By the mid-ninth century this monastery on the Palatine had developed a working relationship with Pope Leo IV (r. 847–855), as suggested by his gifts to the monastery.[89] Leo IV evidently sought to promote the papal associations of the cult of St. Caesarius. He converted his own house in Rome into a convent dedicated to the saints Symmetrius and Caesarius.[90] His biography also reports that he gave precious gifts to St. Caesarius's basilica in Terracina: "cloth decorated with a fourfold weave and with purple around it, with a gold-studded cross in the middle, with an inscription of the name of lord pope Leo IV."[91] Papal insignia are conspicuous on the gifts—at a time when Terracina had acquired further strategic importance. From the 840s onward, Arab raiders pillaged southern Italy, including, in 846, the environs of Rome.[92] Pope Leo's gifts made sure to remind Terracinans that he was their benefactor and protector.

Despite the rising tide of papal control, the medieval monastery for St. Caesarius on the Palatine Hill in Rome remained a world of its own, a hub for Greek-speaking travelers from the eastern Mediterranean and southern Italy.[93] In the 860s the Greek monk Blasios, born in Amorion in central Anatolia, spent eighteen years in the monastery before finding Roman politics too intricate for his liking.[94] The portrait of the monastery provided by the Greek *vita* of Blasios (which purports to have been written by one of Blasios's contemporaries, shortly after his death) is of a community that remained open to new travelers from the eastern Mediterranean, even as it was well integrated into a city whose religious life was now largely coordinated by the pope.

When Blasios arrives in Rome he finds a Greek-speaking monastery on the Palatine headed by the abbot Eustratios from Cyzicus (in Anatolia). The abbot allows Blasios to live in a cell at the monastery, but then, impressed by Blasios's fasting and prayer, convinces him to become a monk in the monastery. Blasios serves the monastery with dedication, engaged first in textile work and calligraphy and then as the monastery's librarian, canonarch, and sacristan. The impression is of an active and thriving community. Only because Blasios cannot find the solitude that he desires, we are told, does he leave.

More than a century later, the monastery was still attracting Greek-speaking travelers. As reported by his Greek *vita*, a vision enjoined Sabas the Younger (d. 990–991), a nomadic southern Italian monk born in Collesano in eastern Sicily, to seek out Rome for the final days of his life.[95] Sabas was a figure actively involved in the politics of the day, petitioning Emperor Otto II (r. 967–983) for the release of southern Italian hostages. In Rome he was received in the monastery of St. Caesarius, living just long enough to see the release of one of the young hostages for whom he had pleaded. The medieval monastery remained a hub facilitating Rome's contacts with the wider world, both to the south and the north.

* * *

By the time Sabas arrived on the Palatine Hill, any trace of the Byzantine administration that had first brought Caesarius to Rome was long gone. Still, amidst the fields, orchards, and ruins, the imperial resonance of Caesarius lingered on the Palatine, well into the Middle Ages.[96] In the mid-twelfth century Eugene III was elected pope at the monastery of Caesarius (now contained within the fortifications of the Frangipani family) and the twelfth-century guide to Rome's marvels, the *Mirabilia Urbis Romae*, describing the Palatine, puns that "where now St. Caesarius is, was once the augury-site of Caesar."[97]

CHAPTER 4

Miraculous Charity Along the Tiber's Banks

On the Forum Romanum and the Palatine Hill we encountered saints as forceful patrons of empire. Saints, however, offered much more concrete benefits than reinforcing imperial ideology. Above all, saints in Rome were venerated for the personal assistance, physical and spiritual, that they provided. In this chapter and the next, we move away from the center of Rome to investigate ecclesiastical foundations whose patron saints more clearly reflected the day-to-day needs and aspirations of their specific communities.

The low-lying area on the bank of the Tiber River, nestled against the Aventine, Palatine, and Capitoline Hills, was a natural place for traders and other frequent travelers to congregate. It was also conveniently close to the Forum with its administrative and commercial business. In the early Middle Ages, communities with ties to the wider Byzantine world were to be found in this Tiber neighborhood. This chapter focuses on the district's *diaconiae*, religious foundations whose members were committed to performing charitable works.

Beginning in the later seventh century, the Tiber neighborhood experienced the effects of Rome's shifting relationship vis-à-vis Constantinople and the papacy's increasing involvement in Rome's sacred and secular topography (examined in the previous chapter with respect to the Palatine). In this chapter we examine how this situation unfolded in the early eighth century as successive popes took steps to style themselves the rulers of Rome. The communities along the Tiber did not disappear, but instead took on new forms in what became known as the "Greek quarter."

Merchants Along the Tiber

The Tiber neighborhood that this chapter considers extended roughly from the base of the Aventine Hill to the bridge leading across to the Tiber island (Map 7).

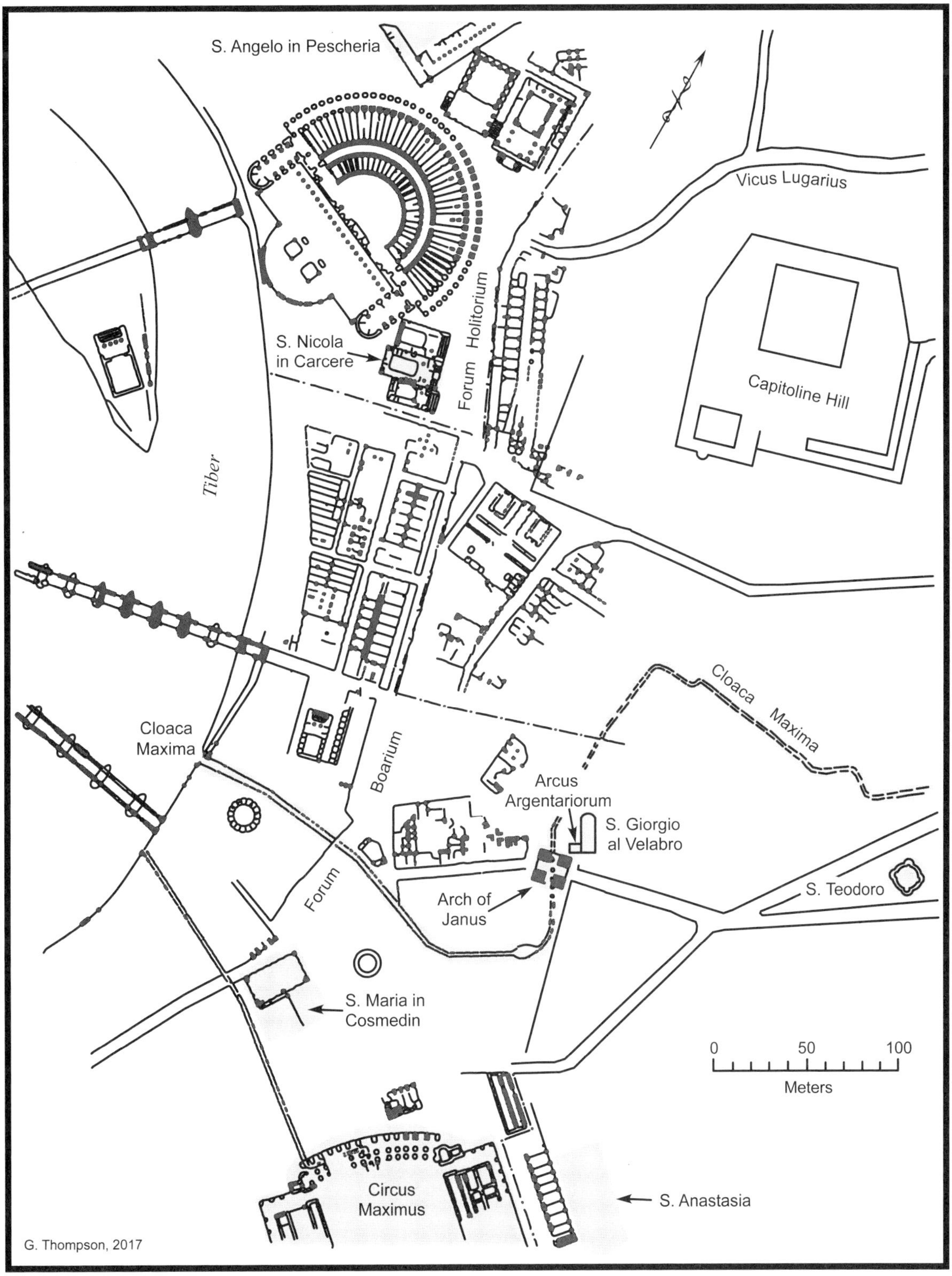

Map 7. Map of the early medieval Tiber Bend. Map created by Gordie Thompson.

Already in early Roman times, this area was a commercial district that housed the Forum Boarium, the "cattle market," and the Forum Holitorium, the "vegetable market."[1] These names remained even as the neighborhood became more affluent in the age of empire. The district was outfitted with sturdy infrastructure to serve its flourishing markets. Roads and storage facilities (*horrea*) allowed for the transport and storage of products, such as the free grain (*annona*) brought to Rome from across the Mediterranean that citizens of Rome expected from their government. An arch, the so-called Arcus Argentariorum, dedicated by money changers and merchants in honor of Emperor Septimius Severus (r. 193–211) and his family, attests to the confidence and prosperity of the neighborhood's residents.[2]

Snaking its way through this district was the so-called Great Sewer (Cloaca Maxima), the canal that extended from the Forum Romanum to the Tiber. This feat of Roman engineering helped drain these low-lying swampy, flood-prone regions. Nor was the neighborhood's densely built environment restricted to functional architecture. Smaller temples dedicated to a range of gods and goddesses abounded. Visually dominant was the imposing travertine theater of Marcellus: an inscription that records its restoration is included in the Einsiedeln compilation.[3]

In the early Middle Ages this was a residential neighborhood whose monumental heritage remained the backdrop for lively commercial exchanges. Perhaps it is not too far-fetched to imagine (along with the nineteenth-century historian of medieval Rome Gregorovius) fishermen advertising their Tiber wares piled high on reused travertine slabs.[4] In contrast with previous centuries, the volume of goods arriving in Rome had shrunk significantly by the seventh century.[5] And no longer (at least by the early seventh century, but likely earlier) did Roman citizens receive free grain, pork, or other handouts from the state.[6] Nevertheless, the abundance and variety of goods on sale must still have been impressive. Grain, primarily from North Africa and Sicily, continued to be transported to Rome. So were a range of other staples, as well as luxury goods like silks and spices. Merchants, arriving by sea, first docked at the seaside port of Portus and then ferried their goods up the Tiber, offloading at the quays alongside the Aventine Hill. In the Tiber district, traders selling their wares would have brushed shoulders with Byzantine envoys heading to the Forum Romanum and with other travelers from across the Mediterranean for whom this neighborhood served as a convenient point of entry into the city.

Diaconiae: Christian Charity by the Tiber

From an institutional and religious perspective, the distinguishing feature of the early medieval neighborhood was its *diaconiae*: religious foundations whose members dedicated themselves to performing charitable deeds, in particular provisioning travelers and the poor. These Christian communities, inspired by scriptural injunctions, confronted the demanding task of ministering to the poor in Rome. The assistance they provided was reminiscent of the *annona* (which may still have been doled out as the first *diaconiae* opened their doors), but whereas the distribution of the *annona* had been restricted to Rome's male citizens, *diaconiae* aspired to serve anyone in need.[7] *Diaconiae* were located throughout Rome (in the Introduction, we stopped at the *diaconia* dedicated to St. Eustachius on the Campus Martius, and many of the churches on the Forum were either founded as, or eventually became, *diaconiae*), but the Tiber district was especially well suited for these organizations. Many people seeking their charity surely lived in or passed through this neighborhood, and the necessary infrastructure was available for the *diaconiae* to carry out their work: the district had storage facilities and roads in close proximity to the ports where grain was unloaded.[8]

The *diaconiae* in Rome first appear in written (papal) sources only in the late seventh century. This means that little is known about the early configurations of these charitable institutions in Rome. But the sixth-century John of Ephesus's discussion of such organizations set up in other parts of the Byzantine Empire offers helpful information: in his Syriac biographies of contemporary saints, he tells of the many *diaconiae* (the Syriac text uses the Greek loanword from διακονία) that Paul of Antioch founded.[9] These *diaconiae* provided food, clothing, nourishment, and bathing facilities to the poor and to strangers in Constantinople, Chalcedon, Nicomedia, Cyzicus, Prusa (?),[10] and Heraclea. John of Ephesus also claims that many others imitated Paul, establishing additional *diaconiae*. His account gives the impression that these were low-profile private foundations, established and run by committed individuals, with little or no oversight by ecclesiastical or imperial officials.

In Italy the earliest evidence for *diaconiae* comes from the late sixth-century letters of Gregory the Great. These suggest the existence of *diaconiae* in Ravenna, Naples, and Pesaro—all cities with a strong Byzantine presence.[11] We may plausibly infer, then, that Rome's early *diaconiae*, which were all dedicated to saints from, or popular in, the eastern Mediterranean, were established in imitation of this latest brand of charitable organization fashionable across the Byzantine world.[12] Inhabitants of Rome, whether long-term residents or recent immigrants from Byzantine territories, gathered together to perform charitable deeds under the aegis of trusted heavenly patrons.

S. Maria in Cosmedin

One of Rome's earliest *diaconiae* was likely S. Maria in Cosmedin.[13] This church, today best known to tourists for the ancient sewer-drain cover, the *Bocca della Verità*, that sits in its portico, has been rebuilt, restored, and renovated many times over the centuries.[14] Little, then, can be concluded with certainty about its earliest Christian phase. Here I follow the interpretation of Krautheimer, Frankl, and Corbett, based, as they freely admit, on limited and inconclusive evidence.

In roughly the mid-sixth century (perhaps already during the reign of Amalasuntha, but more probably in the aftermath of the Gothic Wars), a preexisting portico was converted to create this *diaconia*.[15] This portico may once have been part of the administrative complex (*statio annonae*) that oversaw the distribution of free grain to Rome's citizens.[16] Presumably during or after the Gothic Wars the building was abandoned, and thus Rome's Byzantine administrators were willing to relinquish it to some individuals (perhaps affiliated with the administration) who wished to start up a charitable organization. Masons walled up and subdivided the space, creating a hall with small rooms (or perhaps aisles) on either side and galleries above. Liturgical furnishings and column capitals were imported,[17] but this was likely, for the most part, a rather unremarkable building—dramatically situated adjacent to an imposing Roman altar, formed of great tufa blocks and dedicated to Hercules.[18]

The construction technique and architectural style of this early *diaconia* suggest Constantinopolitan or southern Italian influence.[19] Most of all, the choice of dedication bespeaks a community that looked to Constantinople for inspiration. It was dedicated to the quintessential Byzantine protectress, the Virgin Mary, with a toponym "in Cosmedin," which evoked the Cosmidion in Constantinople, a renowned monastery dedicated to Cosmas and Damian.[20] This was a compelling dedication for a new *diaconia*.

The Constantinopolitan Cosmidion (Κοσμίδιον) was located in Blachernae, a northwestern suburb of Constantinople.[21] This monastery, renovated on the orders of Justinian after he was cured by Saints Cosmas and Damian, was a popular site of miraculous healing in Constantinople. As described in miracle stories, it was a grand complex where the monastery's trained personnel attended to the sick free of charge. The neighborhood of Blachernae also housed one of Constantinople's most illustrious Marian shrines (restored under Justin II), where miraculous healing likewise occurred. These two shrines appear to have shared the same bathing facilities and, more importantly from the perspective of those far from Constantinople but familiar with the region's distinctive reputation, the Virgin and the saints often cooperated in curing patients.

In the name "S. Maria in Cosmedin," we can thus identify the appropriation of two closely intertwined Constantinopolitan traditions of healing: the Virgin of Blachernae and Saints Cosmas and Damian. This, so it seems, was an effective collaboration. Naples also boasted a *diaconia* named S. Maria in Cosmedin; in Ravenna what had once been the Arian baptistery became the church of S. Maria in Cosmedin.[22] In Rome, as in Naples and Ravenna, a community sought to mimic two of Constantinople's most acclaimed healing shrines, creating a miniature Roman Blachernae.[23] A similar desire for an accomplished and formidable patron is evidenced by a second *diaconia* located in close vicinity to S. Maria in Cosmedin: S. Giorgio al Velabro.

S. Giorgio al Velabro

S. Giorgio al Velabro is located near the Palatine Hill at what was once a crossroads, which today is still marked by two arches, the quadrifrons Arch of Janus and, attached to the church itself, the Arcus Argentariorum. Running alongside the church (in part still visible today) is a section of the "Great Sewer," into which, according to the *passio* of St. Sebastian, Emperor Diocletian had the body of the martyr thrown.[24] S. Giorgio al Velabro, like S. Maria in Cosmedin, has been rebuilt and restored over the centuries, making its earliest Christian phase difficult to reconstruct with certainty.[25] Again, I follow Krautheimer's conclusions, supplemented by the more recent analyses of Castelli and Coates-Stephens.[26] Again, the archaeological evidence gives the impression of a fairly unassuming private foundation.

To create the *diaconia* its founders adapted a preexisting, probably private building. When these changes took place is unclear, although an interpolation in the *Liber Pontificalis*'s biography of Pope Leo II (r. 682–683), found only in later manuscripts, might indicate that this was a privately funded construction that took place during his pontificate.[27] The early *diaconia* consisted of an aisled basilica, slighter smaller in scale than the present church. The extent of modifications was dictated by the constraints of the building's location, and the *diaconia* continued to present clear indications of its humble beginnings. The building remained aligned relative to the preexisting streets; its façade with small rectangular windows was that typical of a private building.[28]

As its patron, this modest community chose the remarkable eastern soldier-saint and wonder-worker, St. George. Throughout the late antique Mediterranean world few saints enjoyed such widespread popularity as St. George. George's cult was initially centered around Lydda (Diospolis) in Palestine, where his tomb was venerated, but by the seventh century the saint was venerated throughout the eastern Mediterranean (including Constantinople), in Italy, and even in Gaul.[29]

In Rome the earliest attestation for the veneration of George is an inscription from the Porta Appia, one of the primary gates leading into Rome (Figure 11). Inscribed on the interior archway is a cross with a Greek inscription. Above the cross is the formula "God's Grace (ΘΕΟΥ ΧΑΡΙϹ)"; below is an invocation to

Figure 11. Porta Appia, inscription. Photograph by author.

St. George and St. Conon (a saint martyred in Pamphylia or, in other versions, Cyprus, particularly noted for his thaumaturgical powers over demons).[30] This inscription seems to date to the sixth century, perhaps as part of the restorations of the walls undertaken during or immediately after the Gothic Wars. According to this interpretation, the Byzantine military administration in Rome, as part of efforts to restore and defend the city, invoked the assistance of two eastern patrons, who together offered protection against natural and supernatural dangers.

Byzantine soldiers in Rome may also have had a hand in dedicating the new *diaconia* to George. George's cult was, however, by no means limited to soldiers. George's reputation for performing miracles made him an ideal saint for a community dedicated to carrying out charitable works; in Naples a *diaconia* was likewise dedicated to St. George.[31] Who, after all, could offer more hope of sustenance than a saint famed for achieving the impossible?

Reading the *Passio* of St. George at S. Giorgio

We cannot be sure with which of the many versions of George's *passio* the members of the Roman *diaconia* dedicated to him were familiar.[32] We can be sure, however, that in it George's miracles were presented as astonishing. Accordingly, we may conjecture that the message of George's miracles was further amplified by imperial monuments in the vicinity of the *diaconia*.

The *passio* of St. George was originally written in Greek, but it survives in countless versions—in Latin, as well as Coptic, Ethiopic, Armenian, and Arabic.[33] Although their multitude of differences have long confounded scholars trying to reconstruct the development of the legend, the texts are all permutations of the same basic narrative. In the context of his persecutions against Christians, the emperor of the Persians, Datianus, or, alternatively (as in the version hypothesized to have originated in Rome) a Roman emperor (such as Diocletian or Decius) calls together kings/procurators from throughout his realm. A soldier, George, a Cappadocian who is already a Christian but whose beliefs are unknown to others, decides to renounce his prestigious position in the military and distribute his goods to the poor. He proclaims himself a Christian to the court and subsequently undergoes countless tortures—all of which fail to kill him. Throughout, George performs miracles and converts many to Christianity, including, in many versions, the wife of the emperor.

More radical versions of the *passio* appear to have been fairly widespread throughout Late Antiquity and certainly circulated to Italy and Gaul at an early date. In these versions, George's powers are even more astonishing.[34] George is resurrected thrice during his seven years of torment, before he is at last martyred—although not without successfully petitioning God that a fire cremate the emperor along with his assembly and that all the prayers of those who honor his relics be granted.[35] During his trials George manages to survive a fatal potion prepared by a magician (thereby converting this eminent pagan), to cause bread to appear for the poor, and to cure animals and humans.[36] Perhaps most remarkably he resurrects the dust moldering in sarcophagi—equivalent, so it turns out, to five men, nine women, and three infants who had all been dead for hundreds of years.[37] Many of these miracles repeat, or even markedly exceed, those performed by Christ. George is a saint whose powers appear limitless.

Many versions (including the version that is plausibly from Rome) curtail the most dramatic events of George's legends; in particular, George is no longer resurrected from the dead.[38] Nonetheless, George remains a remarkable figure with capabilities few other saints could rival. George's youthful courage and valiant spirit were qualities that could appeal to audiences who wished to embrace a confident Christianity that could triumph over all misfortunes. To members of the *diaconia* George could offer an unsurpassable model of patience and fortitude in the face of hardship; to the *diaconia*'s clientele George's many miracles—in particular those that involved providing food for the poor and cures for the sick—could correspond to the types of assistance they wished to receive at the *diaconia*.

Furthermore, the *passio* of George is a spectacle, a litany of agonies that, judging from how these variants multiplied, fascinated many listeners. It enumerates

Figure 12. Arcus Argentariorum (attached to S. Giorgio). Scala / Art Resource, NY.

in graphic detail the countless gruesome tortures undergone by the saint: George is placed on a wheel of swords, molten iron is poured into him, he is sawn into pieces, and boiled—and yet the saint remains unharmed. Such vivid narration must have conjured a compelling portrait of the saint.

Many visitors to the *diaconia* (especially if they were travelers) would presumably have already heard about St. George; others might have learned about the remarkable saint from the *diaconia*'s members. At the *diaconia* this audience could also have found visual confirmation of St. George's power in the monuments that surrounded the building. Bits of the past could be reinterpreted with reference to St. George; in Italian, the sewage ditch next to the church would eventually become known as the "little stream (*la marrana*) of S. Giorgio."[39]

Directly adjacent to the church was the Arcus Argentariorum (Figure 12). This arch, as its inscription explains, was erected in honor of Emperor Septimius Severus (r. 193–211) and members of his family. It depicts imperial family members in relief pouring libations, along with scenes of cattle herding and the sacrificial procession.[40] Also adorning the arch are soldiers and their barbarian prisoners, as well as military insignia. For anyone who had recently heard or read George's *passio*

Figure 13. Arcus Argentariorum, reliefs. Photograph by author.

Figure 14. Arcus Argentariorum, reliefs. Photograph by author.

these could be viewed as scenes from the life of George. The scenes of sacrifice would, from this perspective, represent the many injunctions George had received to sacrifice (Figure 13); alternatively, the piles of fruit (a tripod with libations to the gods) could have been read as George's miraculous feeding of a poor widow; the scene with a bull (being led to sacrifice) could correspond to the scene in which a magician brought to compete with George cuts a bull in half. Meanwhile the soldiers and their barbarian prisoners could be reimagined as George in captivity; especially fitting for George is the Phrygian cap (worn by the prisoners) associated with "easterners" (Figure 14). In this interpretation the reliefs reinforced the legends associated with George.

A more literal-minded viewer might, of course, have read the inscription and identified these images as parts of a pagan monument. As such S. Giorgio would have juxtaposed Christian triumph to the decaying remnants of the pagan past. Eternal salvation (along with earthly charity) was to be found at the Christian *diaconia*, not through the failed sacrifices depicted on the nearby arch. Particularly noteworthy in this regard are the visual and textual erasures that mar the monument (which must have been carried out when Septimius Severus's son Caracalla became the sole ruler).[41] Members of the imperial family have been rubbed out in the reliefs and likewise their names removed from the dedicatory inscription: the futility of pagan sacrifice is thus confirmed in the monument itself.

Such viewers could also have taken confidence in the trajectory of Roman history presented by the nearby Arch of Janus. Today the Arch of Janus (a Renaissance name for the structure) is quite bare, but its many niches likely once contained statues. It has been argued to date from the early fourth century, perhaps dedicated in honor of Constantine or Constantius II (Figure 15).[42] As such, it would have showcased one of the early Christian emperors, thereby celebrating the conversion of the Roman Empire. Embedded in the monumental fabric of the city's imperial past, the cult of George had carved out a Christian identity that responded to Rome's pagan past.

Expanding Papal Prerogatives in Rome

In their early days, Rome's *diaconiae* were likely fairly improvised establishments, dictated by the needs and desires of their changing members and clientele. What defined and distinguished them was their compelling patron saints, not their constituents or their architecture. Accordingly, it is unsurprising that little trace remains of these private initiatives until they were co-opted by the papacy. As relations between the papacy and the emperor in Constantinople disintegrated

Figure 15. Arch of Janus. Photograph by author.

and Lombard kings threatened the city, successive popes expanded their involvement in the administration of the city, including its *diaconiae*. This was a new chapter in papal efforts to position themselves as religious experts in the sphere of "household management."[43]

It is in the late seventh century that Rome's *diaconiae* first appear in written sources, in papal biographies. Papal interest in Rome's *diaconiae* first manifested itself in the form of gifts. The biographies of Benedict II (r. 684–685), John V (r. 685–686), and Conon (r. 686–687) all report on papal donations to Rome's *diaconiae*.[44] Perhaps these donations were entirely motivated by a desire to support charitable organizations, but gifts then as now rarely come without strings attached. When we next hear of papal involvement in Rome's *diaconiae* in the early eighth century, the papal oversight implied in such generosity becomes clearer. To understand this situation, however, we must briefly consider some of the dramatic events through which Rome's popes acquired a more pronounced self-understanding of themselves as the principal rulers of Rome.[45]

As we saw in Chapter 3, Pope John VII (r. 705–707) had the novel idea of building an *episcopium* on the Palatine, perhaps implicitly putting forward a papal claim to imperial authority in Rome. Yet John also dutifully acknowledged the authority of the emperor, Justinian II. A few years later inhabitants of Rome (and Constantinople) might well have thought that the many squabbles between emperors and popes had finally been resolved: in 710–711, Pope Constantine (r. 708–715), summoned by Emperor Justinian II, visited Constantinople to discuss the unresolved canons of the Council in Trullo. The meeting, at least from the perspective of Constantine's official biographer, was a great success; the pope, sporting his usual camel-hair cap, was greeted at the seventh mile from Constantinople by the emperor, patriarch, and people of Constantinople and left only after the emperor had renewed all the Roman Church's privileges and implored the pope to pray for his sins.[46]

Yet shortly after the pope returned to Rome, Justinian II was murdered by his troops and a new emperor, Philippicus Bardanes (r. 711–713), took the throne. Philippicus Bardanes rejected the Sixth Ecumenical Council that had rehabilitated Pope Martin and Maximus the Confessor. Accordingly, again as reported by Constantine's biographer, "the Roman people had determined never to receive the name of the heretic emperor, his letters, or the gold coins with his image—so his image was not brought into church, nor was his name mentioned at the ceremonies of mass."[47] Thereafter violence broke out on the via Sacra as Romans (including the former dux, Christopher) refused to accept the new dux, Peter, appointed by the emperor. Relations between Rome and Constantinople had reached a new low.

Philippicus Bardanes was quickly deposed in Constantinople, but less than a decade later the streets of Rome again erupted in violent clashes between supporters of the pope (now Gregory II) and Byzantine administrators appointed from Constantinople (by Emperor Leo III).[48] At stake were increased taxes that the pope refused to pay, but shortly thereafter (or at least so claims the biography of Gregory II) heresy was added to the emperor's sins when Leo forbade the veneration of images of Christ, Mary, and the saints.[49] Compounding the administration's difficulties were the Lombard king Liutprand's aggressive campaigns to enlarge his Italian kingdom. Rome appeared threatened on all sides.

With hindsight, we can interpret Pope Gregory II (r. 715–731), and his successors, Pope Gregory III (r. 731–741) and Pope Zacharias (r. 741–752), as responsible for Rome's geopolitical realignment: a reorientation from the Mediterranean toward the North, with the papacy ruling over Rome and the surrounding territory. How aware these individuals were of the long-term repercussions of their decisions is, of course, impossible to determine. Yet as presented by their biographies in the *Liber Pontificalis*, these popes strove to establish the city of Rome as a bastion of orthodoxy overseen by the pope and, if necessary, disconnected from the emperor in Constantinople.

Gregory II (r. 715–731), especially as presented in the second, later recension of his biography, took steps to strengthen the city and knit together its religious institutions under papal supervision. His biography reports that he began the restoration of the Aurelian wall (although he did not make much progress), that he renovated deserted monasteries, repaired numerous churches, and donated generously to Rome's *diaconiae*.[50] Furthermore we are told that Gregory instituted stational masses for the Thursdays of Lent.[51] This decision integrated yet more churches throughout the city into papal ceremonies, including, eventually (perhaps only under one of Gregory II's successors), the *diaconia* of S. Giorgio.[52]

During the pontificate of Pope Gregory III (r. 731–741), Emperor Leo III (r. 717–741) redirected taxes from Sicily and Calabria (which had previously gone to Rome) to Constantinople and, so the *Liber Pontificalis* reports, continued to embrace iconoclastic policies. Nor did the Lombard problem disappear; quite to the contrary, in 739 Liutprand besieged Rome. Gregory III tried out different strategies to cope with these predicaments, holding a synod in 731 that upheld the veneration of sacred images and taking the unprecedented step, during Liutprand's siege of Rome, of sending an embassy to Charles Martel north of the Alps in a bid for Frankish assistance.[53] Even so, what his biography emphasizes most is the pope's extensive efforts to care for the city's religious infrastructure: the pope, we are told, beautified countless churches and renovated two smaller *diaconiae*.[54]

Pope Zacharias (r. 741–752) inherited this complex political situation, which became no less difficult when Constantine V (r. 741–775) succeeded his father Leo as emperor in Constantinople. Although Constantine V had a more concerted program of iconoclasm than his father, in Rome the more pressing issue remained the Lombards. Zacharias's biography presents him as an active spiritual leader and an effective ruler of Rome capable of tackling both of these challenges. Described in depth are Zacharias's embassies, in person, as the shepherd of his people, to plead with Liutprand. Later, Zacharias's powers of persuasion are so effective that Ratchis (the king of the Lombards who eventually succeeded Liutprand in 744) was not only converted by the pope but also decided to move with his family to Rome to spend the remainder of his life devoted to Christ.[55]

Zacharias's biography also details his attempts to demarcate (and expand) the role of the papacy and the city of Rome in the wider world. As already mentioned in Chapter 3, indicative of these ambitions were the improvements undertaken at the Lateran that drew on the iconography of imperial power, past and present, to foreground the temporal authority of the papacy. Zacharias had a new *triclinium*, a banqueting hall, constructed and decorated with "a representation of the world."[56] Such iconography was rich in ideological import; it bespoke authority over that which was represented. Even more momentous was Zacharias's miraculous discovery of St. George's head at the Lateran. This find appropriated for Rome the cult of a saint popular in Constantinople and asserted, none too subtly, papal control over the *diaconia* of S. Giorgio.

Zacharias's Miraculous Find and the Papal Appropriation of George

Immediately after describing the Lombard king Ratchis's striking decision to abdicate, move to Rome, and devote himself to Christ, the *Liber Pontificalis* reports:

> In his time our Lord God saw fit in this city of Rome to disclose a great treasure through this bountiful pontiff. In the venerable patriarchate the most holy pope discovered St. George the martyr's most holy head, stowed in a casket, in which he also found a note made out in Greek letters, indicating its identity. The most holy pope, altogether satisfied, immediately convened the people of this city of Rome, and caused it to be taken with hymns and spiritual chants to the venerable *diaconia* dedicated to him in this city of Rome, in the second region at the Velabrum; and there almighty God sees fit to work boundless miracles and benefits to the praise of his own name through this most holy martyr.[57]

Zacharias's discovery placed him in a venerable tradition of remarkable individuals allowed, through God's grace, to discover long-concealed relics. Empress Helena, mother of the first Christian emperor Constantine, had been guided to the discovery of the True Cross in Jerusalem (as mentioned in Chapter 1); in the late fourth century a vision guided Ambrose, bishop of Milan, to the bones of Milan's martyrs, Gervasius and Protasius.[58] More directly, Zacharias's find recalled a comparable event of fifty years earlier. Shortly after a Byzantine *spatharius* had failed in his mission to deport Pope Sergius I (r. 687–701) to Constantinople, this pope found fragments of the True Cross at St. Peter's.[59]

Like Sergius, who had discovered a relic closely associated with Constantinople, Zacharias too chanced on relics of a saint whose cult was prominent in Constantinople. The pope was undoubtedly aware of this connection; tellingly, the label through which the pope identified the new relic was written in Greek.[60] Constantinople possessed numerous churches dedicated to George, most notably a church dedicated to both St. Theodore of Sykeon (d. 613) and St. George, whose relics were believed to protect Constantinople.[61] Armed with George's head, Rome was now poised to become a new focal point in the saint's cult. Rome's usurpation of

George's cult was no trifling matter, especially at a time when Constantinople's orthodoxy was in question because of the emperor's iconoclastic policies. The message was clear: Constantinople was no longer an appropriate home for the saint; Rome offered him a safe haven.

Pope Zacharias had found the head of St. George at the Lateran, but after his discovery he convened the "people" of Rome and had the martyr's holy head taken with "hymns and spiritual chants" to S. Giorgio. This was no doubt a gesture of the papacy's goodwill and generosity; Zacharias was endowing the *diaconia* with a precious relic, and the procession emphasized the consensus and collaboration of the Roman population.[62] At the same time the gift made the *diaconia* more accountable to the pope and firmly knit it into an urban spiritual topography coordinated and supervised by the papacy.

Once a year, on the Thursday after Ash Wednesday, the pope would visit S. Giorgio to say mass.[63] The preceding day the pope would have visited S. Sabina; the subsequent day he would go to SS. Giovanni e Paolo; walking the streets, the papal entourage mapped out a papal city.[64] During the Thursday liturgy at S. Giorgio, the pope would read out a gospel text that integrated the cult of George into this papal vision of Rome.

A centurion comes to Christ at Capernaum and asks Christ to heal his servant, all the while professing himself unworthy to have Christ enter his house: "For I am a man under authority, having soldiers under me: and I say to this man, Go, and he goeth; and to another, Come, and he cometh; and to my servant, Do this, and he doeth it."[65] Christ praises the centurion's faith, and his servant is immediately healed. On the one hand, as a devout soldier, the centurion references St. George, reinforcing the message that soldiers too may be saved. Yet in its emphasis on Christ, the passage also reminds its listeners that all miracles, including those performed by George, are actualized by God.[66] Affirmed is the Christian hierarchy wherein miracle workers like George have a place but are subordinate to Christ—and thus also to Christ's vicar, the pope.

S. Nicola in Carcere

Was the *diaconia* of S. Giorgio as delighted to receive the gift of George's head as Pope Zacharias was to give it? We simply do not know, but clearly by the later eighth century *diaconiae* in Rome had become institutions overseen by the papacy.[67] Two formulas from the *Liber Diurnus Pontificum Romanorum*, a collection of formulas that date, for the most part, from the eighth century, address *diaconiae*. One describes the constitution of a *diaconia* by the pope; the other, the papal appointment of a steward (*dispensator*) in charge of the *diaconia*.[68]

There is a tantalizing possibility, however, that a *diaconia* could still remain outside of papal purview; there is circumstantial evidence for what was arguably a *diaconia* dedicated to St. Nicholas in the eighth century.[69]

At some point, three ancient temples, standing next to each other a few paces from the Tiber River, were repurposed for Christian use. A church was installed on the foundations of the middle temple, its walls incorporating the colonnades of the two adjoining temples. (Since the early 1930s the church has stood isolated, in between excavated remains of the two temples on either side.) The date and details of this ecclesiastical dedication are highly debatable since the church of S. Nicola in Carcere does not appear in written sources until the late eleventh century. Yet there are some indications that this was an ecclesiastical foundation, likely a *diaconia*, established in the eighth century (see Appendix 5). If so, this was a community that throughout the early Middle Ages declined—or was not offered—papal generosity. Moreover, this ecclesiastical dedication was, if not initially certainly later, dedicated to a "Greek" saint, Nicholas.

St. Nicholas was, like St. George, a remarkable wonder-working saint.[70] According to legend, he was the bishop of Myra (in Lycia in Asia Minor) in the time of Emperor Constantine. Nicholas's cult was known in seventh- to eighth-century Constantinople, and in Rome Theodotus's dedicatory inscription includes his name as one of the saints with whose relics he dedicated his new *diaconia* in 755.[71] Nicholas's astonishing miracles, in particular his reputation for protecting seafarers, made him a fitting saint for a *diaconia* located by the Tiber bend.[72] Another clientele in the neighborhood would also have appreciated his presence: prisoners. In the late eighth century a public prison, likely established by the Byzantine administration, was situated in the neighborhood: this appears to be the basis for the church's medieval toponym "in carcere."[73] The most widely circulating early medieval miracle story about Nicholas told of how the saint had rescued innocent men falsely condemned to death, and in the later Middle Ages, St. Nicholas is well attested as the patron saint of prisoners.[74] Although speculative, it is tempting to imagine a modest institution catering to prisoners with the support of a like-minded heavenly patron.[75]

Inside the medieval church of St. Nicholas, one of the columns bears two eighth-century Latin inscriptions (Figure 16).[76] These were likely carved in situ in the early *diaconia* (although it is also possible, in the scenario where the church was only built after the eighth century, that the column was already inscribed when it was brought into the church).[77] In either case the inscriptions evidence the continued role of private initiatives in supporting ecclesiastical institutions in the neighborhood.

The upper inscription, whose Latin poses some difficulties of interpretation, records the donation of gifts by a certain *maiordomus* Anastasius "to St. Anna,

Figure 16. S. Nicola in Carcere, column inscriptions. Photograph by author.

St. Simeon, and St. Lucy, for your feast days."[78] This is usually interpreted as referring to gifts to a church or chapel dedicated in honor of these saints, but we might also understand it to be a gift in honor of these saints to an unspecified church (such as a *diaconia* dedicated to Nicholas). The second inscription, near the base of the column, attests to the burial of Anastasius at the site.[79] Given their pairing, Simeon and Anna are presumably the individuals who, as described by the Gospel of Luke, first recognized Jesus as the messiah when he was brought to the temple in Jerusalem.[80] These are saints whose veneration is not well attested. In contrast, the cult of St. Lucy, martyred in Syracuse, was well known in eighth-century Rome; indeed two *diaconiae* were dedicated to her.[81] As *maiordomus*, Anastasius was a layman entrusted with overseeing an ecclesiastical "household."[82] We may imagine, then, that for reasons impossible to reconstruct, Anastasius cultivated a particular relationship with these three saints and, by being buried at the foot of the column, wished to remind the saints, in death, of the gifts he had given them during his life. Like other members of local ecclesiastical institutions throughout Rome, Anasastius trusted that, by seeking out the patronage of powerful saints and giving generously to his community, he would merit salvation after death.

Communities in Flux in Rome's "Greek Quarter"

Communities do not change overnight. In the Tiber district, gradual, uneven change resulted in an amalgamation of older traditions with newer paradigms. In the centuries that followed, this region retained the imprint of its imperial past, and private initiatives continued to play a prominent role in the area's religious infrastructure.[83] The evidence, as usual, is limited, but we may identify three characteristics of the neighborhood's distinctive profile: the prominent role of Roman duces in two of the neighborhood's *diaconiae*, the formation (or continuation) of the *schola Grecorum*, and the presence of a Greek-speaking community at S. Giorgio in the late ninth century. Greek influence, which had always been pervasive here, came to define this neighborhood as distinctive: this district became known as Rome's Greek quarter, as reflected in its tenth-century toponym, *ripa Greca*.[84]

As we have seen, the dux of Rome was a Byzantine administrator, responsible to the emperor in Constantinople, yet usually recruited from Rome's resident population. Accordingly, like other local Byzantine officials, the dux was liable to find more common ground with Romans in Rome than with the distant imperial administration in Constantinople. In the first half of the eighth century, as papal rule over Rome became a reality, the office of dux persisted, but his role and allegiance shifted.[85] When Pope Zacharias left Rome to negotiate with Liutprand, he entrusted the city, so his biography tells us, to the charge of the dux Stephen.[86] Lead seals bearing the phrase, in Greek, "Lord help your servant Stephen, patrician and dux of Rome," indicate that Stephen took his official position seriously, but this did not discourage him from working closely with the pope.[87]

In 755, in the Tiber district, an erstwhile dux, Theodotus, dedicated a new *diaconia*, eventually known as S. Angelo in Pescheria, for which he served as steward (*dispensator*). This was a position that allowed him to demonstrate his administrative skills and solicitude for the inhabitants of Rome.[88] Theodotus, as we saw in Chapter 1, was a member of the Roman elite who had served in both the Byzantine and the ecclesiastical administrations, and the dedicatory inscription of his new *diaconia* bespeaks Byzantine influence at ease in its Roman setting (see Figure 3).

Theodotus dedicated his new *diaconia* with an extensive collection of relics of Mediterranean saints (including the neighborhood's patrons, Cosmas and Damian, and George).[89] His choice of saints indicates the degree to which Theodotus felt at home in a world of "Byzantine" saints. At the same time his dedicatory inscription is in Latin, pride of place is given to St. Paul, and Theodotus refers to himself as the *primicerius sanctae sedis apostolicae*, the closest advisor to the pope: Theodotus evidently identified strongly with Rome as a city headed by the papacy.

In turn, our last surviving attestation of a dux as a military and civil administrator in Rome (throughout the Middle Ages the term would remain in use to refer to certain individuals' judicial authority) again served as a steward (*dispensator*) for a *diaconia* in the Tiber district. According to papal correspondence, Eustathius, a former dux (*quondam ducem*), was sent (in 756–757) by Pope Stephen II as the functionary to exercise papal authority in Ravenna: by this time, Ravenna, once the capital of the Byzantine exarchate, had been captured by the Lombards and had then passed into papal hands through the military assistance of the Franks.[90] Eustathius was also the *dispensator* of the Roman *diaconia* of S. Maria in Cosmedin and donated extensive properties to the holy queen of the heavens Mary, mother of God, for the *diaconia* to use "for the support of the poor of Christ."[91] These donations were recorded in a Latin commemorative plaque in two pieces that today is situated on either side of the entrance to the church (Figure 17).

There is nothing noticeably "Byzantine" about Eustathius's donation, but that Eustathius, who had once served in the Byzantine administrative post of dux, became the *dispensator* of a *diaconia* whose name was evocative of Constantinople, suggests a community that, at least to a certain extent, identified with—and strove to maintain a connection with—its "Greek" past. A similar impression, but from a papal perspective that was eager to cast this "Greek" heritage in a new light, is suggested by the subsequent restoration of S. Maria in Cosmedin under Pope Hadrian (r. 772–795). This renovation dramatically enlarged and remodeled the building; the nearby altar to Hercules was razed to the ground, some of its large tufa

Figure 17. S. Maria in Cosmedin, Eustathius's inscription. Photograph by author.

blocks were incorporated into the new walls of the *diaconia*, and a crypt for the church was hollowed out of the surviving temple podium.[92] In describing the construction project, Hadrian's biographer acknowledges the church's toponym—"the *diaconia* of the holy mother of God and ever-virgin Mary, which is called 'Cosmedin'"—but playing on the meaning of the Greek κόσμος, "good order," affirms that the pope's restoration made the *diaconia* truly "Cosmedin."[93] Constantinopolitan associations were to give way to papal associations—nevertheless it was a pun that required some knowledge of Greek.

At or in close proximity to the church of S. Maria in Cosmedin, was a community that would have understood the pun: the *schola Grecorum*.[94] This was an association of "Greeks" (what the precise criteria were for such an identification is unclear), united for mutual support and protection. Similar to the *scholae* of northerners, which were all located near the Vatican, the *schola Grecorum* might have provided assistance to "Greek" pilgrims and travelers.[95] By extension the term *schola*

Grecorum also appears to have been used to refer to the quarter around S. Maria in Cosmedin more generally.[96]

The origins of the *schola Grecorum* (first mentioned in itineraries in the Einsiedeln compilation) are unknown.[97] Sansterre (following Papencordt) has argued that the institution would have made little sense while Rome was still under Byzantine rule, in that the "Byzantines" would then have needed no separate association devoted to their interests.[98] His argument is by no means conclusive, given the many meanings that "Greek" might have had for contemporaries. However, we might imagine that a preexisting community in this area did decide to organize itself differently or at least designate itself differently in the altered political landscape of the late eighth century.

References to the *schola Grecorum* from the late ninth century indicate that by this time this was a community that operated in close cooperation with the papacy and was likely accountable in some way to the papal administration. In 896 when the east Frankish king, Arnulf of Carinthia, had taken control of Rome, the pope (according to a Frankish source, the Annals of Fulda) sent the senate of Rome and the *schola Grecorum* to greet the king and bring him to St. Peter's where he was crowned emperor.[99] During Otto III's time in Rome (r. 996–1002) we hear of

Figures 18 and 19. S. Giorgio al Velabro, epitaph of the archpriest John. Photograph by author.

Figure 20. S. Giorgio al Velabro, inscription fragments. Photograph by author.

the *schola Grecorum* chanting hymns during the yearly procession for the feast of the assumption of Mary.[100]

Fragmentary Greek inscriptions from the late ninth century attest to Greek speakers at another community in the Tiber neighborhood: at the *diaconia* of S. Giorgio. By this time the building had been remodeled under the directive of Pope Gregory IV (r. 827–844), giving it a more standard ecclesiastical appearance.[101] Nevertheless the church remained slightly irregular in shape and, to this day, has retained its distinctive juxtaposition with the Arcus Argentariorum.

One inscription that can be partially reconstructed is the epitaph of a certain archpriest John, born under Pope John VIII (r. 872–882).[102] Whether John was a priest serving S. Giorgio is not specified, but the extensive inscription indicates his close relationship with the church (Figures 18 and 19). One of the pieces (Figure 18), which formed part of an acrostic, tells how, as a child, John was educated in letters by his father, who seems (although the reading is uncertain) to have served as a sort of public teacher; his father is described as "rendering the bliss of learning to all."[103] His mother is described as a believer in God. The other piece (Figure 19), as interpreted by Batiffol, speaks of John's repentance (μετάνοια), of the tears he poured out, and of how he was humiliated by his errors and sullied by his faults but lifted up his eyes to God in his troubles and now asks for prayers to find mercy from God.[104]

Another Greek inscription, whose date is unclear, begins, "I write for you a just lamentation," continuing to speak of sorrow ("for there is nothing else than grief in life") and the law of God (Figure 20).[105] The rest of the text is fragmentary, but what is left indicates that this too was a commemorative inscription of some sort.

In hindsight this lament is poignantly fitting. S. Giorgio's later medieval community had little interest in preserving the memory of its earlier Greek community. These Greek inscriptions survived haphazardly, many trampled underfoot. A reused marble plaque on which the Greek word "BION" (life) can still be deciphered indicates the likely fate of other evidence of this community.[106] By the later eleventh century, S. Giorgio, like Rome's other *diaconiae*, had become a prestigious parish church assigned to a cardinal; long gone were any traces of the *diaconia*'s earlier charitable occupations.[107] What remained was the *diaconia*'s distinctive dedication to a remarkable miracle-working soldier-saint.

CHAPTER 5

Fashioning Saints for the Affluent on the Aventine Hill

Time seems to move slower in certain parts of Rome. Even today the Aventine Hill with its churches, gardens, and mansions, preserves a certain noble solitude. Its isolation from the bustling city below has characterized the area for more than two millennia.

The Aventine's apparent inertia, however, masks the radical, if sometimes subtle, shifts in sanctity that the region has undergone. This chapter explores the peculiar character of early medieval sanctity that developed on the Aventine Hill, focusing on the communities at two churches, located side by side, on the topmost ridge of the hill: S. Sabina and S. Bonifacio (today SS. Bonifacio e Alessio). Here we encounter "foreign" saints unique to Rome. Most of the saints discussed in previous chapters, such as Sts. Sergius and Bacchus or St. George, were well known throughout the early medieval Mediterranean. In contrast, early medieval visitors to Rome, whether from Italy, the eastern Mediterranean, or north of the Alps, were unlikely to have heard of Sts. Sabina and Serapia or St. Boniface of Tarsus before traveling to Rome. What comes into sharper focus on the Aventine, then, is how particular communities creatively adapted sanctity to suit their own purposes and their surroundings.

On the Aventine ridge affluent and cosmopolitan communities cultivated idiosyncratic saints whose cults reveal a dialogue concerned with the tensions between the local and universal dimensions of Christianity—was Christianity only a local phenomenon or did it create new bonds of interconnectivity across the inhabited world?—and, on a less theoretical level, how were the wealthy to achieve salvation? In addressing these questions, both communities, albeit in different ways, found the *foreignness* of their saints to their advantage—a subtlety that was often lost on later audiences.

Aristocratic Estates and Early Christian Communities on the Aventine

From the time of the Emperor Augustus (r. 27 B.C.–A.D. 14) onward, the Aventine Hill was dominated by large villas with extensive gardens.[1] This aristocratic character influenced the development of the Aventine's early Christian topography: a wealthy elite with far-flung connections across the Mediterranean world fostered Christianity on their private estates.

During classical antiquity the Aventine Hill housed a few prominent pagan temples, such as the Temple of Diana and the Temple of Juno Regina.[2] But for the most part, the hill, rising up steeply from the banks of the Tiber, was the domain of aristocratic dwellings. Some housed private cults, whose members were often knitted together by family ties; an Isis cult was located near the later site of S. Sabina, while a Mithraeum thrived immediately adjacent to what would become another early Christian church, S. Prisca.[3]

Christianity's appearance on the Aventine in the fourth century did not radically alter these preexisting patterns of family-based religiosity. As recent work, especially by Kimberly Bowes, has shown, aristocratic donors gave a particular inflection to the forms of Christianity that they sponsored.[4] In part, domestic aristocratic piety continued to flourish; in part, especially by the fifth century, wealthy donors supported the Church with pious donations that commemorated their generosity.

The late fourth-century letters of Jerome provide a glimpse of the mix of tradition and Christian innovation that characterized certain wealthy households throughout Rome, including on the Aventine. Marcella and her mother Albina, wealthy widows who had embraced Christian asceticism (and were patrons of Jerome), turned their household into a Christian haven. Jerome, in a letter written to honor the memory of Marcella after her death, portrays her as a noblewoman who, despite her illustrious lineage and enormous wealth, chose a path of chastity, charity, and humility that revolved around her home.[5] She and Albina surrounded themselves with religious advisors (both lay and clerical) and likely even had a private church on their Aventine estate furnished with relics toward which to direct their devotion (as did similar households throughout Rome).[6] Although they visited the shrines of Rome's martyrs, the women, with Jerome's encouragement, strove to avoid the public gaze.

The *Titulus Sabinae*: An Aristocratic Foundation

Albina and Marcella belonged to the illustrious Caeionii, one of the great families of late antique Rome. It was a member of such a clan, perhaps even one of the

Caeionii, who donated property on the ridge of the Aventine Hill to establish a new church, the *titulus Sabinae.*

In the early Middle Ages *tituli* were parish churches that served their local communities, but, as mentioned in Chapter 1, the term *titulus* initially referred to a legal agreement between private donors and the city's episcopate, recorded in the name of the resulting foundation. That is, a certain individual donated land (or money) to the Church of Rome and the resulting foundation bore his or her name. The foundation date of the *titulus Sabinae* is unknown, but by the time of the Roman Synod in 499, it was one of three *tituli* in the Aventine area, along with the *titulus Priscae* and the *titulus Fasciolae.*[7]

The "Sabinus/a" name is found among members of one branch of the Caeionii family (the Caeionii-Caecinae), so that it is tempting to speculate, following Julia Hillner, that it was a member of this clan who gave her name to the Aventine *titulus.*[8] Traditionally the Caeionii had participated in Rome's civic cults, but some were also members of private cults, such as those of Mithras, Isis, Vesta, and the Magna Mater.[9] By the early fifth century members of the Caeionii family, like so much of the Roman aristocracy, were turning to Christianity, and these conversions raised difficult questions about what Christians should do with their material riches.[10] Most spectacularly, a member of the Caeionii family, Melania the Younger, and her husband Pinianus sold off their vast estates spread across North Africa, Sicily, and Italy and retired to the Holy Land in a dramatic departure that caused chaos for their dependents.[11]

Such a spectacle of renunciation was not to everyone's taste, and members of the Caecinae branch of the family continued to reside on the Aventine into the sixth century.[12] We may then imagine Sabina as a wealthy Christian noblewoman who in the late fourth or early fifth century sought a middle path of Christian charity—not renouncing the secular world entirely, but seeking to support the Church by providing it with property on the Aventine Hill.

"Rich to the Poor": Monumentalizing S. Sabina

Initially the *titulus Sabinae*, like the nearby *titulus Priscae*, probably consisted of a private house used as a church. Only in the early to mid-fifth century was this residential structure replaced with the magnificent basilica that graces the site today (Figure 21).[13] Significantly modified over the centuries, the basilica was renovated in 1914–1919 by Antonio Muñoz in an attempt to re-create its late antique appearance.[14]

As is recorded in the extant monumental mosaic inscription, the basilica was the initiative of an Illyrian presbyter named Peter during the pontificate of Celestine

Figure 21. S. Sabina. Photograph by author.

I (r. 422–432) (Plate 10).[15] The new building was a grand basilica, spacious and ornately outfitted, its nave lined with Proconnesian marble columns. Exceptionally for the period, these reused columns were a matching set. In the midst of this splendor, Peter's dedicatory inscription tackled questions relevant to the Aventine's elite: Christianity's geographic and historic inclusivity and the renunciation of wealth necessary for Christian salvation.

The verse inscription in S. Sabina begins with the universal importance of the Roman bishop, Celestine, during whose episcopate the Illyrian presbyter Peter founded the church: "When Celestine held the apostolic summit and as first bishop was shining forth throughout the whole world (*in toto . . . orbe*), Peter, presbyter of the city [of Rome], of Illyrian descent (*Illyrica de gente*), founded this [church] which you admire."[16] Peter's deferential attitude to the Roman Church reflects contemporary politics; an imperial decree of Emperor Theodosius II in 421 had instructed that Illyrian councils should consult the archbishop of Constantinople, not the bishop in Rome, when resolving matters of canon law.[17] Clearly Peter, however, supported Roman involvement in the Illyrian Church and was keen to emphasize his attachment to Rome by means of his generosity.

The next lines of the dedicatory inscription tackle the vexed question of Christian wealth implicit in Peter's donation. The verses describe that Peter was "rich to the poor, but a poor man to himself, who fleeing the profits of this life deserves to hope in the future." The inscription emphasizes that geographic origins are no longer the criterion for belonging in the Christian community; it is Christian charity through which Peter is a member of the Church and can aspire to eternal salvation.

This message of a universal Christian community that transcended preexisting geographic, ethnic, or other social criteria is further reinforced by the figural imagery accompanying the inscription. On either side stand female figures with open books labeled, respectively, *ecclesia ex circumcisione* and *ecclesia ex gentibus*, representing Jews and gentiles, both permitted to hear God's message. This references the passage from Paul's epistle to the Galatians where Paul says that his own apostolic mission is to the gentiles, as Peter's is to the Jews.[18] Figures of Peter and Paul, once located above the representations of the *ecclesiae*, reinforced the import of this mosaic.[19] Through the efforts of Rome's patron saints Peter and Paul, Christian salvation had been offered to the entirety of humankind, whatever their descent.

To summarize: in its origins and subsequent transformation into a monumental basilica, the *titulus Sabinae* reflected certain forms of Christian philanthropy, which emerged in wealthy districts throughout late antique Rome. Private initiatives, whether by lay men and women or clerics, took center stage for this cosmopolitan elite as they strove for the salvation that they were convinced all Christians throughout the world could achieve. This legacy persisted in the subsequent centuries, in particular in the form of legends about *saint* Sabina—and Serapia—that attached themselves to the *titulus*.

Sabina Becomes a Saint

The Aventine, like the rest of Rome, suffered greatly from the sixth-century Gothic Wars. Yet although parts of the hill were abandoned or converted to agricultural use, nevertheless the hill remained a desirable neighborhood.[20] The *titulus Sabinae* continued to serve as an active parish, but as times changed, its community adjusted the past to the changing contours of early medieval Christianity.

"Sabina," as we have seen, was most plausibly the donor who had provided the *titulus* with property on the Aventine. Gradually, however, throughout Rome, many of the *tituli*'s donors metamorphosed into their communities' patron saints.[21] The designation *Sancta Sabina* is used unanimously by early medieval sources, and by the mid-seventh century, the feast of St. Sabina was celebrated at the church on August 29.[22]

None of these early sources referring to the church of *Sancta Sabina* elaborate on the identity of the *saint* Sabina, but the readings associated with her feast do suggest a profile of her—and of a community concerned with the proper Christian attitude toward material wealth. The reading for the feast of St. Sabina is a passage from the Gospel of Matthew on the nature of the kingdom of heaven as a treasure worth more than any other treasure.[23] Christ tells his disciples various parables, such as that of a merchant who found a costly pearl and went off and sold all that he had to buy it.[24] The different iterations all emphasize that worldly wealth is inferior to the treasure of heaven, a message appropriate to the concerns of an elite community wondering how best to dispose of its riches. The parables from Matthew conjure up the image of a saint reminiscent of the *titulus*'s aristocratic foundress Sabina, who had chosen to dedicate her fortune to the Christian community—and thus, implies the reading, had achieved eternal salvation. A similar thrust is found in the reading used for the papal liturgy that came to take place at S. Sabina each year on Ash Wednesday.[25] The reading, again from the Gospel of Matthew, reminds its listeners to store up treasure in heaven and not on earth: "For where your treasure is, there will your heart be also."[26]

This nebulous portrait of sanctity comes into sharp relief with the elaborate *passio* of Sabina (sometimes Savina) and Serapia (sometimes Seraphia), which probably developed gradually in the course of the sixth to eighth centuries.[27] The *passio* of Sabina and Serapia is set in the distant past of the Roman Empire (the emperor is not specified) in the *oppidum Vendinensium*—my best guess is that this obscure location was chosen by the author of the text to avoid situating the story in Rome, where there was no earlier attestation of these saints.[28]

The *passio* presents Sabina as a paragon of Christian charity. She is a wealthy woman from an illustrious family: "the wife of Valentinus and daughter of Herod, formerly responsible for the mines (?) (*metallarius*),[29] she had three times under the emperor Vespasian given games to the Romans in the city of Rome."[30] Her home is a haven of hospitality. Living with her is a virgin from Antioch named Serapia, who converts Sabina to Christianity. Then Serapia is arrested and executed, despite Sabina's efforts to protect her.[31]

After Serapia's martyrdom, Sabina continues to strive for the well-being of the Christian community. She collects Serapia's remains and deposits them in the funerary monument intended for her own remains—where she too is subsequently buried (by unnamed Christians) after her own martyrdom.[32] The language used to describe Serapia's relics corresponds with the readings associated with Sabina's feast and church. Serapia's body is described as a treasure (*thesaurum*) or costly pearl (*margaritam pretiosam*), as in Christ's parables to his disciples. Accordingly, Sabina's actions are portrayed as a fulfillment of Christ's injunction to prefer the treasure of heaven to that on earth.

Finally, while awaiting her own martyrdom, Sabina bides her time by performing charitable deeds: "And from that day forward she was unceasing in her many acts of mercy, trusting in the name of Christ and remaining in the faith which the holy virgin Serapia had bequeathed to her. Moreover, she busied herself every day by visiting the sick and imprisoned, offering them everything they needed in abundance."[33] Sabina's hospitality, generosity, and charitable deeds thus correspond to an idealized profile of the church's foundress and proffer a model life of Christian charity suitable for the wealthy elite.

However, such an interpretation does not suffice to explain the *passio*. Although it tackled the question of St. Sabina's identity, the *passio* presents much more than a justification of her sanctity. Its elaborate narrative, presenting side by side the life and death of St. Serapia—a name not found earlier in connection with the church—with that of St. Sabina, defies expectations and takes us to the heart of a cosmopolitan community on the late seventh-century Aventine.

Serapia: Sabina's Foreign Handmaiden

The *passio* begins by emphasizing the vast expanse of Christendom, united by shared experience: "Many throughout the world (*per orbem terrarum*) were undergoing martyrdom in the name of Christ."[34] It then introduces its protagonists living in the obscure town of *Vendinensium*: "There was in the *oppidum Vendinensium* a virgin, Serapia, an Antiochene citizen (*civis Antiochena*), [living] in the house of Sabina."[35] From its opening lines, then, the *passio* conjures up distant locations, calling attention to the geographic expanse of early Christianity.

The *passio* develops this theme through its attention to the Antiochene virgin Serapia. Not only is Serapia from the prominent Syrian city (and patriarchal see) of Antioch but also her very name—which evokes associations with the eastern mystery cult of Serapis or, in the form Seraphia, with the heavenly seraphim—further contributes to her distinctiveness. Moreover, Serapia is presented as being aware of her "foreign" status. When she prays to God, she refers to herself as his "foreign handmaiden" (*peregrinæ ancillæ tuæ Serapiæ*), a characterization Sabina does not use to refer to herself. Although a foreigner, Serapia is a virgin with impeccable Christian credentials who takes center stage in the *passio*. She is responsible for converting the aristocratic matron Sabina to Christianity, suffers terrible tortures, performs miracles, and is martyred. The *passio* thereby emphasizes to its listeners how much "foreigners" have contributed to Christianity.

This message resonates with the portrait of the Aventine community that emerges from a recently discovered fresco at the church of S. Sabina—the earliest indication that the cult of Sabina and Serapia had taken hold at the site. This fresco reveals a community that included Greek speakers who characterized themselves as Romans, but were aware of their diverse pasts and the interconnectedness of the wider Christian world: they were an audience who would have understood and appreciated the role of early champion of Christianity exemplified by this Antiochene virgin.

The fresco, discovered in 2010, is located in the narthex of the church next to the main door (Plate 11).[36] Latin inscriptions on the upper and side borders of the fresco date the image to the pontificate of Pope Constantine (r. 708–715) and explain that it was commissioned in fulfillment of a vow. At the fresco's edges are three donor figures, and in the center the Virgin and child are flanked by Peter, Paul, and two female saints. The female saints are not labeled, but given that the women are presented as a pair, it is reasonable to conclude that they represent Sabina and Serapia. Remarkably, the three donors depicted in the panel are also known from other contemporary sources.[37] This allows us to contextualize the fresco in the milieu of Rome's late seventh- to early eighth-century Greek-speaking ecclesiastical elite.

An inscription identifies the donor figures on the Virgin's right as the archpresbyter Theodore and the presbyter George.[38] The explicit reference to Constantine in the inscription that begins on the upper border suggests that the donor figure on the Virgin's left is Pope Constantine, a hypothesis confirmed by the pallium he wears.[39] According to his biography in the *Liber Pontificalis*, Pope Constantine was of Syrian descent (*natione Syrus*), an intriguing parallel with Serapia.[40]

Nor was Pope Constantine unusual in this respect; the *Liber Pontificalis* specifies that four other late seventh- to early eighth-century popes were of Syrian descent: John V (r. 685–686); Sergius I (r. 687–701), who is further specified to be from the region around Antioch; Sisinnius (r. 708); and Gregory III (r. 731–741).

All three of the fresco's donors appear to have been among the legates whom Pope Agatho sent to attend the Sixth Ecumenical Council in Constantinople in 680. This council (as we saw in Chapter 3) vindicated Maximus the Confessor and Pope Martin and their brand of Chalcedonian Christology, thereby condemning the "heresy" of monotheletism.[41] The council's proceedings were in the Greek language; in part, these legates must have been chosen for their linguistic abilities. More importantly, they must also have been regarded as worthy representatives of the Roman see's theological position, framed as correct adherence to the tenets of the Council of Chalcedon. This is corroborated by the fresco's iconography, which showcases the fundamental tenet of Chalcedonian Christology—that Christ has two coexisting natures, divine and human. Christ is seated on his mother's lap, as the product of her womb, while simultaneously set in an oval shield that emphasizes his divinity.[42] This is, again, an intriguing parallel with the passion of Sabina and Serapia, which likewise may be read in Chalcedonian-Christological terms: the passion depicts the more heavenly virgin Serapia, who leads a life of contemplative virginity, and the more earthly matron Sabina, an active woman in the world, as, despite their differences, an indivisible pair—just as Christ's heavenly and earthly natures, according to the Chalcedonian position, are perfectly joined in him but remain distinct. When Serapia is arrested, Sabina proclaims, "My daughter and my mistress, virgin Serapia, I ought either to live with you or die with you, let me not leave you."[43] Finally, after Sabina is martyred, her body is buried together with that of Serapia in the same tomb.

It is worth noting that at the Sixth Ecumenical Council, monotheletism was defended (according to the acts of the council) at long length and with great persistence by Macarius, patriarch of Antioch (in residence in Constantinople since his see was in Arab hands) and his followers.[44] When Macarius refused to be convinced by the conciliar proceedings, he was deposed and sent, at the conclusion of the council, to Rome, where he was relegated to a monastery; there, so we are told, Pope Benedict II (684–685) attempted, fruitlessly, to convince him to recant.[45] In contrast to this evident disunity of Christian doctrine, the *passio* of Sabina and Serapia proffers an idealized portrait of Mediterranean Christian unity: a narrative of an early Christian past in which eastern Antiochene traditions of Christianity and western Roman traditions are in harmonious alignment. This message of consensus was well suited for the papal legates to the Sixth Ecumenical Council, which claimed to speak for all of Christendom. It was especially appropriate on the Aventine given S. Sabina's neighbors: a Greek-speaking community that, I argue, initially consisted of or at least included refugees from a city not far from Antioch: the Anatolian city of Tarsus, the capital of the Roman province of Cilicia and the birthplace of St. Paul.

Cilician Refugees in Rome and on the Aventine

On the Aventine ridge, adjacent to S. Sabina, stands the church of SS. Bonifacio e Alessio. Its eventful medieval monastic history completely transformed the site, leaving no trace of the earliest ecclesiastical foundation at this location: a community dedicated exclusively to Boniface of Tarsus.[46] According to later, imaginative medieval traditions, the church of S. Bonifacio and also the tenth-century monastery were founded in the early Christian period.[47] However, the earliest secure written attestations of the community (as already in existence) date from the later eighth century.[48]

The dearth of evidence makes it impossible to determine the precise origins of the earliest ecclesiastical dedication on this site. However, on the basis of certain characteristics of the community—in particular, the community's unusual Greek *passio* of its patron saint, discussed in further depth in this chapter and in Appendix 6—I propose that Cilician refugees who arrived in Rome some time in the seventh or early eighth century first established a *diaconia* at this site. This admittedly speculative hypothesis is consistent with other evidence for similar refugee communities in Rome.

In the early seventh century Cilicia was invaded by Sasanian armies, who conquered major cities, including Tarsus.[49] Although reconquered by Byzantine armies, Cilicia was within decades the scene for further battles, as Arab armies swept in. Throughout the later seventh century Tarsus continued to be at the forefront of fighting. As a result, refugees fled the region, heading not only to Constantinople but also (at times motivated by their religious opposition to the "heresy" of monotheletism then in favor at the imperial court in Constantinople) to Rome, Sicily, and North Africa.[50]

In Rome, we have scattered evidence for the influence of such eastern émigrés. The most famous is without doubt Theodore, a native of Tarsus, who immigrated to Rome where he acquired a reputation for erudition in Greek and Latin and was eventually appointed archbishop of Canterbury by Pope Vitalian (r. 657–672).[51] There was a larger community of Cilicians at the monastery Ad Aquas Salvias (which we encountered in Chapter 1), southeast of S. Paolo fuori le Mura at the spot where St. Paul was believed to have been beheaded.[52] This monastic community (to which Theodore of Tarsus may have belonged during his time in Rome) is first attested at the Lateran Council in 649 as a well-established Greek-speaking community from Cilicia that was strongly opposed to monotheletism, a sentiment also shared by Theodore. At some time in the mid-seventh century this community was joined by refugees from the Jerusalem area, who brought with them the relic of the head of Anastasius the Persian, as well as his Greek *passio*, subsequently translated into Latin. By the late eighth century, the monastery, which had previously been referred to by various names, came to be known as "St. Anastasius ad Aquas Salvias," in honor of its cherished relic.[53]

Refugees also arrived in Rome from other parts of the eastern Mediterranean convulsed by the Arab conquests. Not far from S. Bonifacio, on the so-called Little Aventine—the spur rising behind the Aventine, away from the Tiber River—a community of Sabaite monks from the original monastery of Mar Saba outside Jerusalem or perhaps from the Sabaite community in North Africa had, by the later seventh century, established the monastery of S. Saba.[54] A member of this community, Leontius, also attended some of the sessions of the Sixth Ecumenical Council in Constantinople in 680.[55]

By analogy, we may postulate that sometime in the seventh or early eighth century, a group of eastern émigrés from Tarsus (or Greek-speaking Romans influenced by such émigrés) settled in the affluent and tranquil surroundings on the Aventine ridge. Their choice of this semi-rural location was likely influenced by the precious treasure they had brought with them: the corporeal relics of their patron saint, St. Boniface of Tarsus. As attested by pilgrimage itineraries to Rome, including the later eighth-century *Istae vero ecclesiae intus Romae habentur* (which survives in Carolingian manuscripts), this was "the basilica of St. Boniface, where he himself rests."[56] This was a bold claim for an eighth-century ecclesiastical foundation within Rome's walls and one that required some justification.[57] Pilgrims had typically visited the catacombs outside of the city to venerate corporeal relics, but only gradually, starting with Pope Paul I (r. 757–767), did large-scale relic translations into the city's churches become more frequent.[58]

On the Aventine the new community established a *diaconia* and dedicated itself to carrying out charitable works. Yet the *diaconia* never seems to have acquired the political importance of the monasteries of S. Saba or Ad Aquas Salvias. Moreover, I argue, unlike the refugees who settled at these monasteries, the *diaconia*'s members had not arrived in Rome with a *passio* of their patron saint, or perhaps the community found its rudimentary version insufficient. Inspired by older traditions of Cilician sanctity, their recent travels, and their new Aventine surroundings, the community crafted a Greek *passio* about their patron. This *passio* provided its members with a blueprint of the charitable life to which they had dedicated themselves and creatively refashioned the past to explain how the *diaconia* had acquired its remarkable relic.

Boniface of Tarsus: Charitable Works and Relics in an Interconnected Mediterranean World

The diversity of late antique and early medieval hagiography notwithstanding, the *passio* of Boniface of Tarsus is an unusual text.[59] As demonstrated by Pio Franchi De'Cavalieri, this *passio* was originally written in Greek (and shows similarities with other Byzantine hagiographical texts) and then translated into Latin, presumably to make the legend available to a wider audience in Rome.[60] The *passio* is set in the time of the imperial persecution of Christians (the Greek version does not mention a specific emperor; the Latin version situates the events in the reign of the emperors Diocletian and Maximian).[61] The *passio*'s protagonists are two Christians living in Rome: an exceedingly wealthy Roman noblewoman Aglaës (Ἀγλαΐς) and her head steward Boniface (Βονιφάτιος). The text specifies Aglaës's illustrious lineage: "the daughter [Latin: indeed] of Acacius, of the Clarus family [Latin: by family a Clarus], a former proconsul [he, not she]. She put on games (κάνδιδα/*candidam*) a third time [Latin: three times] in Rome"; the text then seems to suggest that she served as a prefect (? Greek) or perhaps that she also put on games "in the prefecture" (? Latin). And we are told that "she had under her seventy-three stewards for her property [Latin omits 'for her property']."[62]

The protagonists correspond well to the Aventine audience we may imagine for the *passio*. Aglaës is reminiscent of the wealthy elite who had once lived on the Aventine Hill and who had patronized churches such as S. Sabina. Indeed the *passio* even displays textual similarities with the *passio* of Sabina and Serapia, indicating that the two communities drew on each other's texts as they molded their stories about the early Christian past.[63] In contrast to Aglaës's decidedly Roman profile, Boniface's composite identity—a Roman by birth and a native of Tarsus by martyrdom—could have appealed to the *diaconia*'s members who had similarly complex identities. Boniface's travels across the Mediterranean would have struck a chord with their own experiences.

The narrative unfolds as a type of hagiographic romance between Aglaës and Boniface, in which carnal love is eventually transformed into Christian piety.[64] Aglaës and Boniface, although Christians, have an ongoing adulterous affair. Boniface is described as follows: "He was a drunkard and an adulterer and a lover of the things [Latin: sins] which the Lord God hates."[65] The *passio* tackles their moral quandary, a problem familiar to the Aventine and the wider Mediterranean world alike: how may wealthy—and even sinful—Christians hope to pass through the eye of the needle? The *passio*'s answer—through charitable works and the veneration of relics—affirmed the *diaconia*'s charitable mission and promoted its sacred treasure.

Already Boniface's name in Latin, "Lucky" (*bonum fatum* → Bonifatius, also easily interpreted, by a Latin-speaking audience, as *bonum facere*, "to do good deeds") suggests the *passio*'s didactic function: to remind its listeners of the salvific power of charitable works that can overcome personal moral failings. Boniface's luck, it turns out, may to some extent be imitated. Despite his sinful life, Boniface has three redeeming qualities, all characteristics that correspond to the responsibilities of a *diaconia*: hospitality, liberality, and compassion. The *passio* describes, "If ever he saw a foreigner or a traveler, he would immediately and eagerly urge him to be his guest and would minister (διηκόνει/*ministrabat*) to him. During the night he would wander the roads and byways [Latin: of the city] and give out necessities to the needy."[66] These qualities assure Boniface his salvation—and even a glorious martyrdom.

Aglaës too, despite her adulterous past, eventually gives away all her property and devotes herself to Christ, earning so much grace from God that she is able to expel demons and cure illnesses. She showcases how the wealthy can support the Christian Church through the appropriate use of their riches. After Boniface is martyred, Aglaës takes the initiative (convening "devout clerics [Latin: clerics and religious men]" to help her) in burying Boniface's body and building a fitting memorial for him.[67]

Good works pave the way for salvation, but they are not the exclusive path. The legend of Boniface has another thrust: the power of relics. This is an interest the *passio* of Boniface shares with some of the Byzantine legends to which it is related, but which also correlates specifically with the *diaconia*'s claim to possess the body of its patron saint. The *passio* presents a whole-hearted endorsement of relics as movable sanctity, arguing that Romans have much to gain from the geographic expanse of Christianity.

The *passio* recounts how, fearing the consequences of their sins, Aglaës summons Boniface and reminds him that they will have to answer to God for their adultery on the Day of Judgment. But, she says, she has heard that martyrs can provide support to them: "Now I have heard Christians saying that anyone who ministers to the saints who have struggled on account of Christ [Latin: the name of the Lord Jesus Christ] and undertaken battle on his behalf will be their partner on that terrible day of God's judgment."[68] Accordingly, to assure their salvation she wishes to acquire relics. Yet it would seem from the narrative that she believes their native city of Rome cannot furnish such treasures. Instead she proposes to Boniface a more complicated solution: to go to the distant East. This portrayal of Rome, a city so often celebrated for its profusion of early Christian martyrs, as a city lacking in sufficient "native" sanctity, would presumably have resonated with seventh- to eighth-century eastern émigrés' perception of Rome as a safe haven while the East had become the site of Christian martyrdom.

Aglaës implores Boniface: "Go therefore [Latin: to those regions] and bring relics [Latin adds: that is, the bodies] of holy martyrs to us, so that somehow [Latin adds: serving and] attending to them and [Latin: even] building houses of prayer in a manner worthy of their passions [Latin: them], we may be saved through them [Latin: through their sacred passions]—we and many others."[69] Boniface complies, taking with him twelve horsemen and three litters.[70] Days later he reaches Tarsus, but fulfills his commission differently than expected.[71] As soon as Boniface arrives in Tarsus, he sends his servants to look after the animals and find lodging, while he goes to observe the "athletes" of Christ undergoing martyrdom. He attends to them and asks them to pray for him, until his ministrations are interrupted by the arrival of pagan officials who interrogate and eventually execute him.

Meanwhile Boniface's servants roam the city looking for him, suspecting that, according to his usual habits, he is in some tavern or brothel. Finally, they discover his body and realize that he has been martyred. To complete Aglaës's commission, they then manage to bribe the guard (with 500 gold coins) to grant them his body and bring back his relics to Rome—a turn of events that displays a surprisingly positive attitude toward the sale and purchase of relics.[72] Meanwhile Aglaës, informed of Boniface's death in a dream, builds a sanctuary for his body and dedicates herself to honoring his relics at a site appropriate to the legend's setting during the imperial persecutions: outside the city's walls, and, according to the Latin translation, five stades (a little less than a kilometer) from the city of Rome on the via Latina. Thereby the *passio* provides a backstory for the relics of Boniface that the Aventine *diaconia* had presumably moved from outside the walls of Rome to the Aventine Hill. By so doing, the *diaconia*—as heir to this tradition of the empire-wide circulation (and sale) of relics—perpetuated the cult of Boniface, through whose relics Romans could continue to benefit.

Becoming Roman: The Medieval Afterlife of Sts. Sabina and Serapia and St. Boniface of Tarsus

Both the community at S. Sabina that embraced the *passio* of Sts. Sabina and Serapia and the community at S. Bonifacio that showcased its relics of Boniface of Tarsus appear to have taken pride in the "foreignness" of their saints. These were saints whose profiles not only reflected their Aventine setting but also corresponded and responded to particular circumstances of the late seventh to early eighth century: a

Figure 22. SS. Bonifacio e Alessio, *ciborium* fragment from S. Sabina. Photograph by author.

fragmenting Mediterranean, eastern émigrés moving to Rome, and a Roman elite clinging to the possibility of doctrinal unity across Christendom. Sts. Sabina and Serapia and St. Boniface were saints who bespoke a unified, interconnected Mediterranean Christianity and so were suitable patrons for a Mediterranean elite who professed to participate in shared Christian traditions. They were, in short, saints who represented what people in a particular time and place thought timeless, universal saints should look like—a parochial vision of universality.

As times changed, certain nuances of these saints, in particular their foreignness, lost their earlier resonance. Sts. Sabina and Serapia, as well as St. Boniface of Tarsus, would remain saints on the Aventine, but we can observe how, in the course of the ninth and tenth centuries, they were affected by shifting fashions of sanctity. Sts. Sabina and Serapia emerged as indisputably Roman saints, while St. Boniface's cult came to be overshadowed by that of a similar, but markedly more pious—and Roman—saint, St. Alexius.

By the ninth century the church of S. Sabina apparently claimed, as it still does today, to possess the relics of its patron saints. The earliest evidence of this claim is a small marble fragment of a *ciborium*, an altar canopy, that appears (on stylistic grounds) to date from the renovations of the church under Pope Eugene II (r. 824–827) (Figure 22).[73] Inscribed on this fragment are the words "[. . . and S]eraphia the martyr[s]"—surely referencing the presence, in the altar under the *ciborium*, of the relics of Serapia (and presumably also her companion Sabina).[74]

The presence of the saints' bodies in the altar of S. Sabina is likewise indicated by a later inscription (tenth or eleventh century) that further elaborates on Eugene's interventions at the church. It describes that Eugene had the relics of Alexander, Theodolus (*sic*), and Eventus—an early bishop of Rome and two of his clerics, all believed to have been martyred in Rome and buried on the via Nomentana—placed in the high altar next to the relics of Sabina and Serapia.[75] In distinguishing between these two groups of saints (Alexander, Theodolus, and Eventus whose relics are moved into the church, and Sabina and Serapia whose relics already rest beneath the altar), this intervention (whether undertaken by Eugene or only later credited to him) further strengthened the church's associations with Sabina and Serapia as its original, "native" saints. Neither this inscription nor any other surviving source indicates how or when the Aventine community obtained the relics of Sabina and Serapia. The implication is that these saints had been there from the time of the church's initial foundation. With their relics safely deposited under the church's altar, St. Sabina and St. Serapia had become unambiguously Roman martyrs.

Meanwhile, after a brief mention as the recipient of gifts from Pope Leo III (r. 795–816), the nearby *diaconia* dedicated to Boniface disappears from view for another century.[76] In the early tenth century (as recently argued by Santangeli Valenzani) restorations at the church were undertaken by the noblewoman Theodora, wife of Theophylact.[77] In 977 Pope Benedict VII (r. 974–983) granted the church to Sergius, formerly the metropolitan of Damascus, who had fled to Rome. A monastic community began to flourish on the site, hosting such luminaries as Adalbert, bishop of Prague, and Bruno of Querfurt, who later became a missionary bishop in eastern Prussia.[78] When he moved to Rome in the late tenth century, the emperor Otto III chose the Aventine for his residence and confirmed the extensive possessions of the monastery.[79] The monastery retained St. Boniface as one of its patron saints, but by this time he had been joined by a new addition, St. Alexius.[80] To this day the church retains its twin patrons, although with a distinct preference for Alexius.

St. Alexius bears a certain affinity to his predecessor at the site, St. Boniface, but he is a more overtly Roman (and respectable) saint. (Eventually Alexius's cult would have enormous medieval success throughout western Christendom, and his *passio* was translated at an early date into many vernacular languages.[81]) Alexius's Latin legend, like that of Boniface, is a translation from Greek.[82] It is set during the reign of the Christian emperors Arcadius and Honorius. Alexius, we are told, was the son of a wealthy and distinguished Roman nobleman, Euphemianus, and his wife, Aglaës (Ἀγλαΐς)—the same name as the female protagonist in the legend of Boniface, although this Aglaës does not share the other's dissolute life. Alexius wishes to embrace a chaste live, so rather than consummate the marriage that his parents have arranged for him (the wedding, according to some Greek and all Latin versions, takes place in the church of S. Bonifacio), Alexius leaves Rome and travels to the East—not, as Boniface had done, to search for relics, but rather to live as a beggar far from home.[83]

After living in poverty in Edessa, Alexius's ascetic practices eventually attract fame, and he flees again. Although he sets sail for Tarsus in Cilicia (where Boniface had been martyred), divine intervention leads the boat to the port of Rome instead.[84] There, hiding his true identity, he spends the rest of his life unrecognized as an impoverished beggar in his parents' household. Only after his death, guided by a voice that tells the Roman people to find the "man of God," is his secret revealed. Then, according to certain versions of the *passio*, his body is buried, with great honor, in the church of S. Bonifacio.[85] Thus the cult of St. Alexius tethered itself securely to the legacy of S. Bonifacio, even as it supplanted Boniface's cult.

* * *

As we have seen throughout the previous chapters, the early Middle Ages were both an exceptionally creative and decidedly formative period in the creation of Rome's sacred topography. The horizons of Roman sanctity stretched wide across the Mediterranean. The city was porous to eastern Mediterranean communities and their saints, eagerly soaking up—or inventing—saints from abroad. Byzantine administrators, ecclesiastical officials, eastern émigrés, and Roman aristocrats turned to saints from abroad to sanctify their Roman surroundings. In turn, these saints transformed their communities and the Roman past into which they entered: soldier-saints eradicated the pagan past on the Forum Romanum, a Terracinan deacon promoted a Christian framework of empire on the Palatine, a miracle worker provided charity at the Tiber bend, and cosmopolitan saints tended to the wealthy communities of the Aventine.

We could continue exploring Rome's remarkable ecosystem of sanctity with countless other examples, yet these should suffice to demonstrate both the diversity of the city's early medieval saints and their formative impact in building a new Christian city. We now turn away from the physical city to the idea of Rome that these saints helped craft. To do so we must examine the two interrelated groups that helped tether these saints collectively to Rome: popes and the Carolingian elite.

CHAPTER 6

Collectivities of Sanctity in Early Medieval Rome

Although the process by which saints arrived and were established in Rome was haphazard and unpredictable, many Romans and visitors to Rome must have been conscious of the ever-growing variety of saints whom they encountered throughout the city. Communities, on their own terms, venerated saints for the protection, healing, and patronage they offered—not primarily to embellish the city of Rome. Yet the potential of this accumulation of sanctity did not go unnoticed—in particular by the papacy.

As early medieval popes became ever more conscious of themselves as representatives of an institution responsible for Rome and its people, they also involved themselves more in the cults of Rome's saints, whether these saints had been martyred in Rome or farther afield. The most assiduously cultivated cult was that of St. Peter, the foundation stone of the Roman bishopric, but popes were well aware that there was more to the city's sanctity. In the previous chapters we encountered frequent examples of papal intervention in saints' cults: throughout the city popes built and refurbished churches, gave gifts, and integrated churches into the stational liturgy. Many of these papal efforts went hand in hand with other attempts at papal consolidation, such as the gradual replacement of a "civil" Byzantine administration with an ecclesiastical, papal administration and the papacy's attempts to imprint itself on the urban image of Rome. For example, Pope Zacharias's discovery of the head of St. George in the mid-eighth century (Chapter 4) and the donation of this precious relic to the *diaconia* of S. Giorgio al Velabro allowed the papacy to take on a larger role in the management of this and similar charitable organizations.

Alongside this micromanagement, there was also a papal interest in collectivities of sanctity—larger groupings of saints who offered sacred bulwarks for Rome and the papacy. Styling itself as guardian of all Christian sanctity, the papacy presented Rome as the home for all saints, whatever their origins. Threatened by neglect, indifference, or malevolent destruction elsewhere, the memory of such saints was to be secure in Rome. Rome was thus presented as a storehouse of Christian sanctity, and the specificity of the cult of saints lost importance as "the saints" became a collective entity whose members each reinforced each other and who could be venerated all together, most effectively when mediated by papal efforts.

This phenomenon is too large to be examined here in its entirety, and this chapter makes no attempt to be exhaustive.[1] Instead it focuses on select examples, primarily from some of the most prominent sites of papal influence throughout the city: the Lateran, St. Peter's, and S. Maria Antiqua. At such sites popes were particularly conscious of their role as guardians of the Church and were particularly attentive to the effective visual presentation of this message. I discuss these dedications in roughly chronological order: (1) the Lateran baptistery, where Pope John IV (r. 640–642) assembled the relics of saints he had rescued from barbarian attacks; (2) the All Saints' Oratory at St. Peter's, built by Pope Gregory III (r. 731–741); (3) a mid-eighth-century "panorama" of saints that adorns a wall in S. Maria Antiqua; and (4) the growing collection of relics housed at least from the time of Pope Leo III (r. 795–816) at the Lateran. These papal interventions demonstrate how, concurrent with the evolution of different neighborhoods throughout the city (discussed in the preceding four chapters), successive popes presented themselves as caretakers of the city's saints—as gardeners cultivating and taming Rome's thriving sacred ecosystem.

Chapels, frescoes, relic collections: each of these collectivities had its own logic. Furthermore, each of these sites had its own memories and resonances. Whereas at the Vatican the primary referent was, of course, the apostle Peter, the Lateran called to mind memories of the first Christian emperor Constantine, while S. Maria Antiqua was steeped in reminders of Rome's imperial legacy. Varied as they are, however, each of these examples expresses inflections and expressions of a growing papal desire to position Rome and specifically the papacy as the center of a "universal" and unified Church. The pervasive influence of such ideas is made clear by the undated legend of the Quattro Coronati, with which I begin and that lays out the dominant themes of this chapter: Rome as a home for all saints, the popes as guardians of the memory of saints, and the overarching unity of all saints.

Quattro Coronati: Pannonian Stonemasons and Roman Soldiers

The *passio* of the saints who came to be known as the *Quattuor (Quattro) Coronati* (a later designation not found in the earliest manuscripts) institutes, by a rather circuitous route, the veneration of a group of Diocletianic Pannonian martyrs in Rome.[2] The origins of this *passio* have been much discussed; the legend may contain an earlier core that was expanded on in Rome, or it may have been created ex nihilo in Rome.[3] These uncertainties notwithstanding, the *passio* must have been well established before the mid-ninth century when a fully-fledged cult for the saints, collectively known as the *Quattuor Coronati*, developed. Accordingly, the *passio* may be read as a paradigmatic early medieval example of Rome's ability to subsume saints into itself—in this case achieved through a remarkable substitution of saints orchestrated by papal authority.

The *passio* (with the exception of the final chapter) is set in Pannonia, where prisoners are forced to labor in a stone quarry. Five of them—Simpronianus, Claudius, Nicostratus, Castorius, and Simplicius—are skilled stonemasons and produce unrivaled works of art for Diocletian; their first product is an enormous statue of the sun on a chariot.[4] Yet artistic skill is not sufficient for the works they execute; only their faith in the Christian God enables them to produce such masterpieces. Four of the stonemasons are covert Christians; the fifth, Simplicius, converts when he discovers the secret of their talent; a bishop, Cyril of Antioch, likewise imprisoned in the quarries, baptizes him.[5] Diocletian is initially pleased with their work, but when they refuse to sculpt a porphyry statue of Asclepius (their earlier assignments apparently having caused them no qualms), they are put on trial and executed six days before the Ides of November (November 8); a certain Nicodemus, a Christian, buries their bodies. The *passio* is unusual for its extensive artistic dimension, offering a doctrine of Christian art and models of Christian artists. Unsurprisingly the saints were popular throughout the Middle Ages as the patron saints of craftsmen.

This self-contained narrative is then followed by an additional section, only loosely connected with the previous events. Leaving Sirmium, a city in Pannonia, Diocletian comes to Rome, where he has a statue made of Proconnesian marble, again of Asclepius, erected in the baths of Trajan (the origins of the statue are not specified). When four military adjuncts (*cornicularii*) refuse to make pagan sacrifices, they are quickly executed and their bodies thrown on the street. Then, however, St. Sebastian (a well-known Roman saint in the early Middle Ages) and the Roman bishop Militiades (r. 311–314) appear on the scene and, collecting the bodies of the martyrs, bury them on the via Labicana with other martyrs in a sand pit three miles from the city.[6] Thereupon,

> given that this had happened at the very same time, but two years later, that is, six days before the Ides of November, and since it was impossible to discover their names, the blessed bishop Militiades ordered that their commemorative anniversary should be celebrated under the names of the

> saints Claudius, Nicostratus, Simpronianus and Castorius [one ms. adds: and Simplicius].[7]

Thus the Pannonian saints, by papal fiat, are commemorated in Rome as a means of venerating the unknown soldier-saints who had been martyred on the same day (two years after the stonemasons). This is an odd turn of events, not least because there are five stonemasons in the story and only four soldiers. But the legend glosses over such practical problems and, more significantly, shows no hesitation in having Militiades conflate Pannonian artists and Roman soldiers. Neither their different professions nor their diverse geographical origins pose a problem in linking the saints; their martyrdom under Diocletian on the same day of the year provides sufficient connection.

What the text attempts to do, it seems, is put a legend regarding certain Pannonian martyrs to use in providing a narrative for a fairly homonymous set of Roman saints already venerated in Rome.[8] The *passio* appropriates the Pannonian stonemasons to make sense of these unknown Roman saints—turning to the motif of the vigilant papacy caring for the commemoration of Christian saints, whatever their terrestrial origins, and the ability of saints, whatever their site of martyrdom on earth, to stand in for each other as part of a collectivity of heavenly sanctity. In this way the legend both legitimizes a set of Roman saints of uncertain provenance and acquires for Rome another set of saints, artistic geniuses well suited to a city that prided itself on the splendor of its classical and Christian past.

Once the legend associated these Pannonian saints with Rome, Roman tradition came to naturalize these saints further, firmly embedding them into the city's topography, inside and outside the walls. The Pannonian/Roman saints were equated with the *Quattuor Coronati*, to whom an early Christian parish church (*titulus*), located on the north slope of the Caelian Hill, was dedicated.[9] Early medieval itineraries of Rome also recorded relics of the saints on the via Labicana.[10] In the mid-ninth century Pope Leo IV (r. 847–855) synthesized these intra- and extramural traditions by bringing the relics of many saints, including the Quattro Coronati (Claudius, Nicostratus, Simphronianus and Castorius—and Simplicius) from outside the city walls and assembling them in an annular crypt under the altar of the newly renovated church of SS. Quattro Coronati.[11] Inscriptions from the twelfth century attest to the continued veneration of their relics at the church.[12] With Pope Leo's translation, what had hitherto been a liturgical equation of saints developed into a physical collection of saints in Rome. Pannonian stonemasons fused with Roman soldiers had been fashioned into the Roman bulwark of what would become throughout the Middle Ages one of Rome's most impregnable papal fortresses.

* * *

The *passio* of the Quattro Coronati with its astonishing conflation of different saints is distinctive, and there are few legends that compare. Yet the phenomena it represents—the gathering of saints together in Rome under papal auspices and the possibility for saints to be equated—is by no means unique. It is a process that may be observed with particular clarity at sites that were cultivated as poles of papal authority. Indeed, the earliest surviving datable example of a papal chapel built explicitly to protect saints from abroad was located at the primary seat of the papacy, the Lateran.

Rescuing Dalmatian and Istrian Saints: The S. Venanzio Chapel at the Lateran

In the mid-seventh century a short-reigning pope from Dalmatia, John IV (r. 640–642), constructed a chapel adjacent to the Lateran baptistery and dedicated it to a group of saints whose relics he had brought from Dalmatia and Istria. To this day the so-called S. Venanzio chapel remains one of the best-preserved early medieval ensembles in Rome, with an extensive mosaic program that welcomes and naturalizes the new saints in Rome.[13] The primary motivation for building the chapel was that John IV had rescued the bones of his compatriots, including his father's namesake, St. Venantius. The chapel's spiritual and ideological connotations were, however, more far-reaching: the chapel enriched the sacred topography of the Lateran and expanded the prerogatives, and universalizing pretensions, of the papacy as caretaker of Christian sanctity.

Pope John IV took office in 640 as the Byzantine Empire appeared to be rapidly disintegrating. Damascus and Jerusalem had fallen to the Arabs; Alexandria looked to be next. Relations between Constantinople and Rome were strained. Prior to the consecration of Pope John IV's predecessor Pope Severinus (r. 640), the exarch of Ravenna, Isaac, had, so the *Liber Pontificalis* reports, "plundered" the Lateran, sending a portion of the wealth to the emperor Heraclius.[14] Pope John's successor Theodore (r. 642–649) would set in motion the Lateran Council of 649 that so forcefully opposed the "heresies" of monoenergism and monotheletism (and led to Pope Martin's arrest). In contrast to this drama, John IV's pontificate, as presented by his biography in the *Liber Pontificalis*, appears comparatively tranquil. John's salient achievement, we are told, was to take pity on the inhabitants, living and dead, of Dalmatia and Istria, regions that had seen Avar incursions in the early seventh century.[15]

The *Liber Pontificalis* reports:

> John IV, of Dalmatian origin (*natione Dalmata*), son of the *scholasticus* Venantius, held the see 1 year, 9 months, and 18 days. In his time he sent much money by the most holy and trustworthy abbot Martin throughout Dalmatia and Istria to ransom captives who had been captured by the heathens. He built a church for the blessed martyrs Venantius, Anastasius, Maurus and many other martyrs whose relics he had ordered to be brought from Dalmatia and Istria; he deposited them in that church close to the Lateran Font and the oratory of St. John the Evangelist.[16]

Judging from John's Dalmatian origins and the correspondence between his father's name and one of the saints (Venantius), John's decision to "rescue" saints from Dalmatia and Istria was personally motivated. Bringing the relics of his father's namesake to safety was a gesture of filial piety; according to his biography, the relic translation was closely linked with charity toward the region's residents.[17] Concurrently, in placing these relics in a chapel "close to the Lateran Font and the oratory of St. John the Evangelist," John was making an ambitious statement about Rome's suitability as a home for endangered saints and the Roman bishop's right to decree the veneration of saints in Rome.

The placement of the chapel at the Lateran baptistery augmented the sanctity of what was, by the seventh century, a site emblematic of papal authority and prestige. According to the *Liber Pontificalis*, the first Christian emperor, Constantine, had lavished precious gifts on the baptistery, including a font and column both made of porphyry, the imperial stone.[18] In addition, the baptistery boasted three chapels, built and lavishly decorated in the mid-fifth century by Pope Hilarius (r. 461–468) and, dedicated to St. John the Baptist, the Holy Cross, and St. John the Evangelist.[19]

Each of these dedications affirmed one of the phases of Christ's mission on earth, contributing to the rich symbolism of the site. John the Baptist reminded viewers of Christ's incarnation on earth as a man; the Holy Cross celebrated Christ's death and resurrection; and John the Evangelist, as a "pillar" of the early Church (in the words of St. Paul) who spread the message of Christ, reflected the continuation of the Church after Christ's death. These chapels surrounded the newly baptized with a synopsis of church history, presenting Rome as the "orthodox" capital, the first and foremost of the apostolic sees—as Pope Hilarius strove to convince his correspondents throughout his pontificate.[20]

These chapels quickly became established markers of papal primacy in Rome. When the aspiring pope Symmachus (r. 498–514) was excluded from the Lateran by his rival Lawrence, he took refuge at Rome's alternate pole of spiritual power, St. Peter's.[21] But an attempt to build up St. Peter's as a worthy seat of the papacy also required expanding its facilities, so Symmachus constructed, adjacent to St. Peter's baptistery, oratories dedicated to St. John the Baptist, the Holy Cross, and St. John the Evangelist.[22] So necessary had the presence of these chapels become for papal legitimacy that Pope Symmachus could not do without them.

In dedicating a new chapel at the Lateran baptistery in the mid-seventh century, then, Pope John IV selected a site that bespoke papal authority and the history of the Christian Church from Christ's appearance on earth to the early apostles. His chapel, which is markedly larger than Hilarius's chapels, ambitiously built on these traditions with a collectivity of saints—and Roman bishops—that reflected the subsequent phase of Christian history: that of the post-apostolic Church that had expanded into the wider world, but that was resolutely held in place by the Roman papacy. This message was proclaimed by the elaborate mosaics that survive to this day, perpetuating the presence of Dalmatian and Istrian saints at the Lateran (Plates 12–14).[23]

The shimmering gold mosaic program in the S. Venanzio chapel presents the saints whom John had rescued as they are brought into Christ's heavenly presence. Depictions of Jerusalem and Bethlehem in the upper left and right corners of the apsidal arch situate us within the timeless sphere of the eternal Church.[24] At the top of the apse is Christ, his hand outstretched in a gesture of blessing. He is flanked by two archangels and surrounded by wispy clouds that set him apart from the figures who stand on the green earth below (Plate 12). Beneath Christ stands the Virgin Mary, her hands outstretched in prayer as she petitions Christ on behalf of the figures who surround her. Peter and Paul flank the Virgin; then come St. John the Baptist and St. John the Evangelist, the patron saints of the Lateran Baptistery. Next are two bishops, labeled Venantius and Domnius, Dalmatian saints. At the far ends of the apse are two Roman bishops, unlabeled, without halos; presumably they represent Pope John himself and his successor Theodore, who probably completed the chapel.

On walls adjacent to the apse, the succession of saints continues (Plates 13 and 14). In contrast to the *Liber Pontificalis*'s report that mentions only three saints by name, a much larger—and more heterogeneous—group of saints is included in the mosaic: another bishop (Maurus) but also a layman dressed in gold cloth (Anastasius, according to his legend a wealthy fuller of cloth), a deacon (Septimius), a priest in a black robe (Asterius), and officials (Antiochianus, Gaianus, Paulinianus, and Tellius, according to legend members of Diocletian's bodyguard who refused to arrest Christians).[25] Again, as in the apse, the figures are individually distinguishable by their physical appearance, dress, and names, while their halos make clear that they are saints who have warranted their places in this heavenly sphere. A dedicatory inscription below the apse commemorates Pope John's pious vow fulfilled by dedicating the church and proclaims the salvific power this impressive assembly of saints will provide to all who penitently pour forth their prayers to Christ in heaven.[26]

Thus a group of Dalmatian and Istrian saints had found a home at the Lateran through the charity of the Roman bishop. In turn, they would reward the Roman people by acting as intercessors with the heavens above. The mosaic celebrates the saints whose relics, to this day, form the invisible cynosure of the chapel. Their corporeal presence renders the mosaic's depiction of the eternal heavenly Jerusalem more tangible on earth. In 1962–1964 the relics were examined, revealing about a half-kilo of small bones, human and animal, as well as dust and two unidentifiable Byzantine coins—all contained within a lead casket (in which they were placed in 1698), inside a small sarcophagus within the altar. Whole bodies, it seems, were not brought from Dalmatia/Istria to Rome, but bodily remains were.[27] The physical transfer of such a quantity of relics had an air of finality, rendering their burial sites in Dalmatia and Istria obsolete. These saints had not come to Rome for a visit: they were here to stay. Henceforth their cult was to be mediated through Rome, by the papacy—an expansion of papal power justified in John's biography by the threat to the saints and their memory.

What distinguished the S. Venanzio chapel from earlier papal dedications to saints from abroad (such as, for example, SS. Cosma e Damiano, with its very similar mosaic composition), was not only its placement adjacent to the Lateran baptistery, the impressive panorama of saints that it assembled, and the significant quantity of relics that were physically transported to Rome but also, more subtly, the papal prerogatives it implied: the power to discern and authenticate sanctity. Archaeological evidence from Salona in Dalmatia attests to the veneration of some of these saints before that city's abandonment in the seventh century.[28] In Rome, however, there is no evidence that these saints were known prior to John IV's initiative, and indeed, to this day, they have remained rather obscure saints.[29] The chapel's audience is expected to have full confidence in Pope John IV's affirmation of the sanctity of these otherwise unknown individuals. Welcomed and naturalized in Rome by the pope, these saints have taken their rightful place in the history of the Christian Church, attending to the ever-growing collectivity of Christians in Rome for whose salvation the Lateran Baptistery provided.

All the Saints at St. Peter's

The most sacred site in Rome, as late antique and early medieval audiences would have concurred, was St. Peter's. Although the Lateran was the papal residence and the site of papal administration, it was St. Peter's that could claim the bones of Peter himself as its foundation. We should not be surprised then, that it was here that the most ambitious of early medieval papal collectivities was dedicated: an oratory for the liturgical commemoration of Christ, the Virgin, the apostles, and all the martyrs and confessors. In dedicating this prominently positioned oratory, Pope Gregory III (r. 731–741) responded to what he perceived as the threat to Christian saints from Byzantine iconoclasm. In its implications, however, this oratory far exceeded the challenges posed by the immediate circumstances by endowing Rome with a microcosm of Christian sanctity's universality. Most remarkably, this universality was achieved not by specificity, but, in contrast to the examples we have seen so far, by appealing to a nameless collective.

The pontificate of Pope Gregory III, together with those of his predecessors and successors, was, as we saw in Chapter 4, a pivotal period in the papacy's conception of itself as responsible for Rome as a city and as a Church. Papal claims to be guardians of a universal Church and curators of the city's sanctity expressed themselves in lavish gifts to ecclesiastical institutions and in construction projects throughout the city. Among Pope Gregory III's initiatives was a new chapel at St. Peter's. His biography in the *Liber Pontificalis* describes:

> He built an oratory within the same basilica [St. Peter's], close to the principal arch, on the men's side; in it, to honor the Savior and his holy mother, he placed in safety relics of the holy apostles and all the holy martyrs and confessors, perfect and righteous, resting in peace throughout the world.[30]

The chapel survived until it was demolished under Pope Julius II (r. 1503–1513) in preparation for the new St. Peter's. As confirmed by later sources it was located inside the main apse of St. Peter's basilica, at the base of the south side of the triumphal arch (Map 8).[31] Its prominence in the basilica may be appreciated from a fifteenth-century manuscript illumination depicting the coronation of Charlemagne (a subject that certainly benefited from the oratory's universalizing implications), which shows the chapel in the background (Figure 23).

The chapel, in close proximity to the tomb of Peter, occupied a charged position in what was an extremely coveted space. Early Christian graffiti attest to the veneration, even earlier than the third century, accorded to what was believed to be the tomb of St. Peter, and the construction of the Constantinian basilica further increased its renown both in Rome and farther afield. Initially St. Peter's was a church whose connotations were more imperial than papal, but throughout Late Antiquity, as successive popes associated themselves more firmly with Peter, they also co-opted the space as their own.[32] As mentioned earlier, Pope Symmachus (r. 498–514) outfitted the Vatican baptistery with oratories that mimicked those at the Lateran. Pope Gregory the Great (r. 590–640), attentive to the social ramifications of the cult of saints, had the basilica remodeled to facilitate pilgrimage to the relics of Peter (without, however, allowing pilgrims to access the relics themselves).[33] Whenever a pope celebrated mass at the main altar, he stood directly

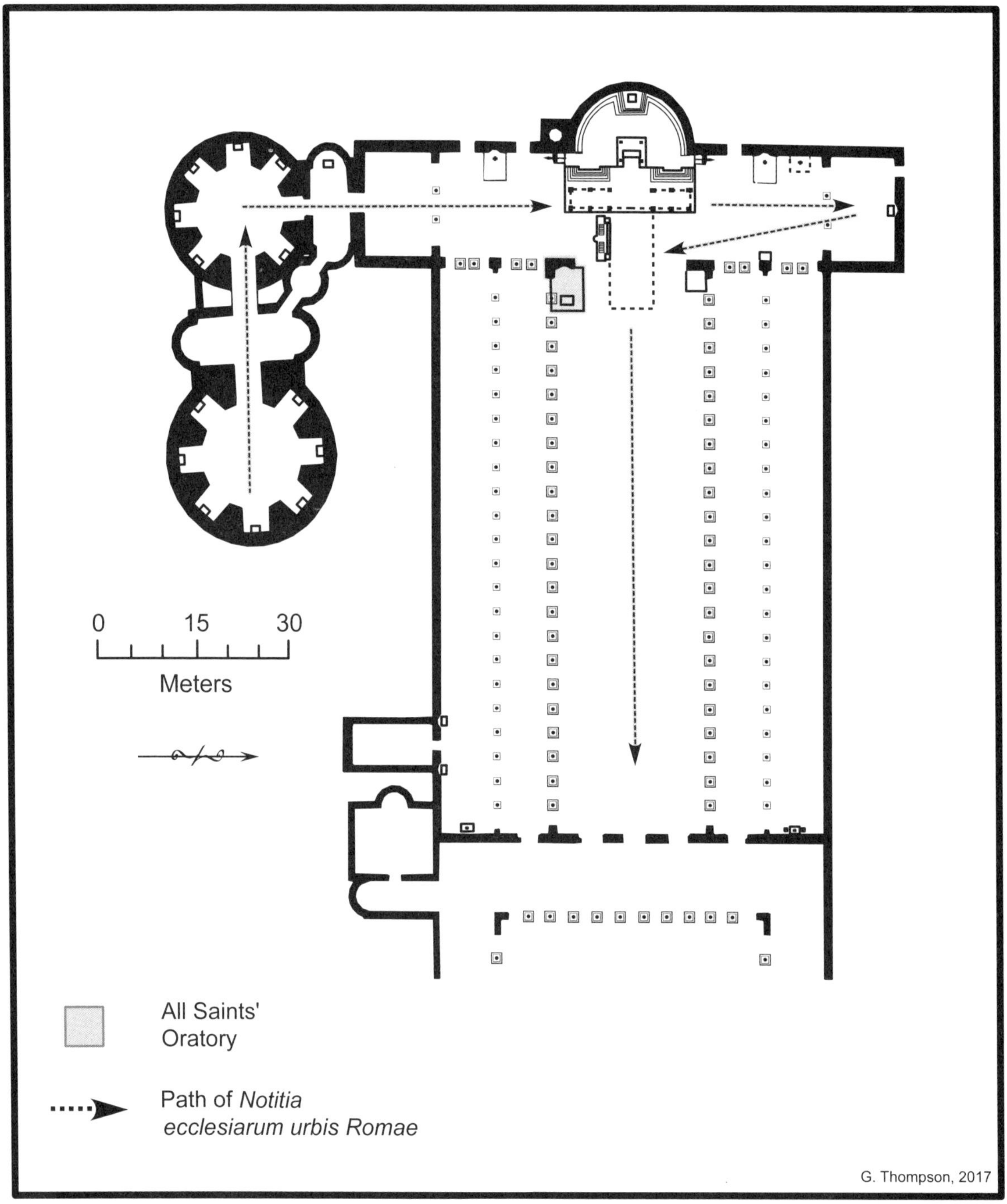

Map 8. Plan of early medieval St. Peter's. Plan created by Gordie Thompson.

Figure 23. Coronation of Charlemagne in *Les grandes chroniques de France* (Paris, BnF, Département des manuscrits, français 6465, f. 89v). Courtesy of the Bibliothèque nationale de France.

above the tomb of St. Peter. Tellingly, from the late fifth century onward (and continuing all the way until the tenth century) almost every pope was buried at St. Peter's.[34] St. Peter's was transformed into a symbolic site of papal power, a stage on which popes strove to style themselves as leaders of a universal Church.

By the eighth century successive dedications, burials, and donations had transformed the interior of St. Peter's into a dense web of Christian memory.[35] We can appreciate this rich tangle of sacred sites by turning to an early medieval itinerary of Rome, the *Notitia ecclesiarum urbis Romae*, which circulated in the Carolingian world.[36] This document's description of St. Peter's, which dates to the mid- to late eighth century (that is, shortly after Gregory III's dedication), takes its reader on an emotionally charged whirlwind tour of the church's sanctity.

The route begins with the chapels adjacent to the basilica. Entered first is the chapel dedicated foremost to St. Andrew, Constantinople's apostle; the veneration of Peter's brother provides an overture preparing the visitor for the first of the apostles, St. Peter himself.[37] Inside this oratory the visitor also found altars for a variety of Roman and Italian saints (St. Lawrence, St. Vitus, St. Cassian, St. Apollinaris, St. Sossius) and the apostle Thomas.[38] From here St. Martin, one of the very few saints from Gaul whose cult is well attested in early medieval Rome, guided the pilgrim onward. In the next chapel, which would be dedicated to Petronilla in the mid-eighth century by Gregory III's successors (see the later discussion), were altars dedicated to Mary, Christ the Savior, and the soldier-saint Theodore.[39]

At last the pilgrim prepared to enter into the apse and advance toward the tomb of St. Peter, a path watched over both by the archetypal soldier-saint, the archangel Michael, and, not least, a Roman pope, Leo the Great.[40] The visit reached its climax at the crypt and *confessio*, from which the pilgrim leaves "having poured out tears of penance."[41] On the other side of the apse remained such highlights as, at least according to the *Notitia*, an altar in the wall for another soldier-saint, the popular St. George. Heading out of the church the pilgrim was invited to kiss the crib of Christ, joyfully climb onto the bed of Gregory the Great, and visit numerous shrines for Mary. In an itinerary less than a half-kilometer long—especially short when contrasted to the long treks along the extramural roads required by the rest of the *Notitia*—the pilgrim had encountered countless treasures of Christendom.

In dedicating the All Saints' Oratory, Pope Gregory III drew on and strengthened the universalizing pretensions of St. Peter's many altars. Yet such an ambitious undertaking required justification, and although the *Liber Pontificalis* does not specifically mention the cause, its impetus would have been clear enough to contemporaries. For throughout his papacy Pope Gregory took a determined stance against what was seen in Rome as the Byzantine heresy of iconoclasm.[42]

Most pointedly, Gregory held a synod (on November 1, 731) excommunicating anyone who "should remove, destroy and profane or blaspheme against this veneration of sacred images."[43] Correspondingly, Rome's churches were bedecked with numerous new icons of Mary, Christ, apostles, and saints. The oratory in St. Peter's was the crowning gesture of Pope Gregory's efforts. For not only was the chapel dedicated to Christ, Mary, the apostles, and all the saints but it also actively propagated their appropriate veneration.

Immediately after describing Gregory's oratory, the *Liber Pontificalis* proceeds to record how, in conjunction with the dedication, the pope instituted liturgical arrangements for the commemoration of all the saints. These provisions were agreed on by a council on April 12, 732, and then inscribed on marble tablets (fragments of which still survive) and placed in the new oratory.[44] Their public display (which corresponds to similar practices known from Constantinople) projected papal authority that could be readily appreciated, even by the illiterate. Those who did read the text were treated to a carefully crafted message of papal authority.

The text is dated (as Hubert Mordek has pointed out) according to the fifteen-year indiction cycle used in the Byzantine world but, contrary to customary practice, is not dated according to the Byzantine emperor.[45] It presents Gregory III as orchestrating the council; Gregory's close bond with the chapel was further reinforced when he was buried in this chapel on his death in 741 and a fourth tablet was added with prayers for his soul.[46] Yet Gregory's initiative is also framed in the language of consensus. Almost a third of the text is taken up with the subscriptions of the many bishops, archpresbyters, presbyters, archdeacons, and deacons who participated in the council. In contrast to the universal nature of the saints commemorated by the council, however, the council's attendees were resolutely Roman; all the bishops are from around Rome, and the lower-ranking ecclesiastics are without exception from Rome.[47] Thus it is very explicitly *Roman* consensus that legitimizes these decrees, a decision-making process that accords with the message of Rome's responsibility for providing for the proper commemoration of Christian sanctity.

At the heart of the decree are the provisions for the liturgical commemoration of the saints at Gregory III's oratory.[48] From the tablets we learn that the three monasteries adjacent to St. Peter's, which were already responsible for saying vespers at the *confessio* of St. Peter's, are henceforth to follow the conclusion of these vespers by singing three psalms and some of the gospels at the newly built oratory. Thereafter the priest to whom the duty falls that week for saying mass at the tomb of St. Peter's is to hold a second mass at this oratory in honor of Christ, the Mother of God, and the holy apostles, martyrs, and confessors whose feast day it is.[49] Spelled out are the prayers that are to be said by the presiding priest. Invoking Christ, Mary, and the totality of apostles and saints to whom the oratory was dedicated, these prayers beg for protection and deliverance from danger. Having received a safe haven, these saints now guarantee the security of their new home—the basilica of St. Peter's, and their protector, the pope.

Neither the *Liber Pontificalis* nor the tablets with their detailed instructions specify what we might expect to be a crucial piece of information necessary for this daily commemoration to take place: who are the saints who make up this universal collective? The prayers on the tablets invoke the saints obliquely with the words: "and especially celebrating the feast day/birthday (*diem natalicium*) of all your martyrs and confessors, perfect and just, whose solemnity is celebrated today in the presence of your glory."[50] It is unclear whether the presiding priest would ever have specified more precisely who these saints were. Even if he did, the wording of the decree meant that this set of saints could change over time. Conversely, by not naming any specific saints, the decree avoids omitting any saint from potential commemoration. Anonymity is used in the service of universality. The papacy serves as the authoritative spokesman for the bond between the saints in heaven and their celebration at St. Peter's.

A Panorama of Saints in S. Maria Antiqua

St. Peter's and the Lateran: these are the two poles of Christian sanctity that were (and still are) most readily associated with the papacy in Rome. At other sites where the papacy's presence was less firmly entrenched, early medieval popes proceeded differently. As we have seen in Chapter 3, attempts to redefine Rome in papal terms were especially delicate around the Palatine Hill because of its formidable imperial associations. When Pope John VII (r. 705–707) had the church of S. Maria Antiqua redecorated (in conjunction with adding an episcopal residence above the church), his fresco program prominently included Roman bishops (including himself). Yet his critics in Rome contended that he did not stand up forcefully enough to the emperor in Constantinople. We can observe the continued care with which a subsequent early medieval pope (perhaps Pope Paul I) approached the church in an impressive fresco of saints added to S. Maria Antiqua in the mid-eighth century. While unflinchingly emphasizing the primacy of Rome, this collectivity of sanctity, unlike Pope Gregory III's oratory at St. Peter's, dresses Rome's privileged position in a portrait of the harmonious consensus of eastern and western traditions of sanctity.

Located on the left aisle of S. Maria Antiqua (next to the entrance to the vestibule) the large fresco depicts Christ enthroned between what were once at least twenty-two saints, all meticulously labeled in Greek (Plate 15).[51] To the left of a door are two additional figures; the fresco may also have extended further (along the wall separating the church from the vestibule).[52] An altar was located in front of the fresco, allowing for the celebration of mass against the backdrop of these saints.[53]

The "panorama of saints" (as I henceforth refer to it) was part of a more extensive program that redecorated the nave of S. Maria Antiqua to narrate the history of the Church from the creation of the world to the present. The conventional dating of this decorative program is to the time of Pope Paul I (r. 757–767), who appears on the main apse (labeled in Latin), standing adjacent to a large figure of

Christ, but the attribution of the nave's frescoes to his pontificate is not conclusive.[54] Yet we may confidently interpret the fresco program as a papal project, whether by Paul or by one of his predecessors or successors.

The fresco cycle begins to the left of S. Maria Antiqua's main entrance (immediately above the panorama of saints) and continues on the opposite side of the church; the cycle presents Old and New Testament scenes (labeled in Latin).[55] Its concluding scene is the panorama of saints: an assembly of Church fathers and other key (male) figures of the post-apostolic Church gathered in Christ's heavenly presence. Against a deep red background (in contrast to the generally blue and yellow hues of the Old Testament scenes above) stand, on either side of a bearded imperial Christ, the male saints. Christ sits enthroned on a bejeweled chair wearing purple robes, his right hand raised in blessing. All the saints, who are of uniform height, stand on either side of him, facing the viewer in identical poses.[56] Behind them, a dark blue band slightly below the level of their faces focuses attention on their haloed heads; these halos correspond in color to the gospel books that most of the figures clutch in their hands. The message is one of concord and uniformity.

A closer look, however, reveals substantial, if subtle, diversity among the saints. Care was taken to depict the features of each saint appropriately. The saints are individualized; some are young, some old with white hair and wrinkled brows. Likewise, attention was given to their dress.[57] Most are dressed as ecclesiastics, but a few (such as St. Clement) wear the classical costume of a tunic covered by a mantle known as a pallium (not to be confused with the ecclesiastical pallium, a scarf worn around the shoulders, which St. Clement also wears) and have bare feet. Two (Sts. Sergius and Bacchus) are dressed in the garb of Byzantine military officials, wearing the chlamys pinned on their right shoulder.

Almost all the figures wear the ecclesiastical pallium, but here too the style varies (Plate 16). Some of the saints wear this scarf draped around their shoulders; others have it wrapped more tightly around their neck.[58] The crosses that decorate their pallia are also subtly different (Figure 24). Whereas the five figures to Christ's right—all Romans—wear pallia decorated with simple bar-shaped crosses, the nine figures to Christ's left, "easterners," wear pallia with two types of more ornate crosses. These cross shapes clearly follow contemporary styles or conventions; for example, a seventh-century mosaic in Rome at S. Agnese fuori le Mura depicts Roman popes with the same bar-shaped cross (Plate 1), whereas a ca. seventh-century icon at Mt. Sinai depicting the eastern Church fathers Athanasius and Basil (both also present in the S. Maria Antiqua fresco) has examples of the latter two types of crosses (Plate 17).[59]

Assembled here, as their clothing indicates, is not an indistinguishable mass of saints, but instead a carefully depicted selection of saints—bishops, priests, monks, and lay officials—from Rome and the Byzantine Mediterranean. Tidily

Figure 24. S. Maria Antiqua, panorama of saints, crosses. Left: "Roman" cross. Center and right: "Greek" crosses.

written inscriptions (placed beside the saints' halos) identify the figures more precisely. It is significant that these captions are written in Greek (in contrast to the Latin inscriptions that label the narrative scenes located immediately above), a linguistic choice that hearkens back to S. Maria Antiqua's traditions of sanctity and acknowledges Greek as a language of the Church still relevant for Rome. Similarly, a number of the saints depicted in the fresco had been previously depicted in the church, thus presenting a message of continuity with the past—even as the fresco maneuvers these saints into new constellations.

The panorama of saints is organized hierarchically. Closest to Christ are the most distinguished clerics. Romans are generally on his right, and "Greek"—that is, Greek-speaking Church fathers—are on Christ's left. Pride of place is given to Rome's clerics, but as co-participants in this larger Church. Immediately to the right of Christ are four Roman popes and two Roman presbyters, all saints characterized by their involvement in the Christian conversion of Rome and the empire and including two popes (St. Leo and St. Sylvester) strongly associated with securing the Roman see's claims to primacy within the Church and vis-à-vis the emperor.[60]

Analogously positioned, to Christ's left, are the "Greek" saints: two Constantinopolitan archbishops, followed by bishops from throughout the Byzantine Mediterranean (Asia Minor, North Africa, Cyprus, and southern Italy). These are all well-known Church fathers, some of whom had been previously depicted elsewhere within S. Maria Antiqua.[61] More subtly, a number of these saints (in particular John Chrysostom, Gregory of Nazianzus, Cyril of Alexandria, and Athanasius of Alexandria) were known for their resistance to imperial policies: a message particularly appropriate in mid-eighth-century Rome as papal opposition to Byzantine iconoclasm continued.[62]

Farther afield, on the "Roman" side, the succession of saints continues in an unexpected and telling fashion: next to the Roman clerics appear two representatives of eastern monasticism, Euthymius and Sabas, both known for their involvement in imperial politics. At the far end, flanking a Roman bishop labeled Gregory are two young men dressed in military attire: the soldier-saints Sergius and Bacchus.[63] This placement succinctly encapsulates the overarching thrust of the fresco: the Roman Church buttressed by, and itself buttressing, Christian saints from throughout the Mediterranean.

Inside a church that had been appropriated by the papacy but that still remained attached to the traditions of the Byzantine Empire, this fresco presented a vision of what it meant to belong to that world. It proffered a vision of a community headed by an imperial Christ and anchored in the Mediterranean world of the Roman Empire, but resolutely led by ecclesiastics and held together by Rome and the papacy: a universal Roman Church.

A Storehouse of Relics at the Lateran

What is *not* present in S. Maria Antiqua's panorama of sanctity is any indication of the direction in which the papacy's allegiances were shifting. By the mid-eighth century when this fresco was designed, Frankish and Roman visitors and diplomats were shuttling across the Alps, successive Roman popes were cultivating their contacts with the nascent Carolingian dynasty, and papal Rome was on its way to becoming the primary ecclesiastical reference point for western Europe. Pope Paul I's predecessor, his brother Stephen II (r. 752–757), had made the unprecedented decision, in 753, to undertake a journey across the Alps to the Frankish king Pippin, requesting military assistance against the Lombards. This new political and spiritual alliance was expressed at St. Peter's by the dedication of a chapel for St. Petronilla, requested by Pippin, promised by Pope Stephen, and carried out by Pope Paul.[64]

What Frankish audiences wanted and expected from Rome shaped not only to whom new chapels in Rome were dedicated but also how the papacy cultivated Rome's sacred topography. This is especially apparent in its growing participation in the Carolingian vogue for carefully authenticated bodily relics. Although the cult of relics was by no means new in early medieval Rome, only in the later eighth century did it become a craze. Relics were translated en masse from the catacombs to churches within the walls, and the papacy began collecting what would become one of medieval Europe's most cherished relic collections: the so-called holy of holies, the sancta sanctorum.

The term "sancta sanctorum" is a later medieval designation for a collection of relics that dates back at least to the time of Pope Leo III (r. 795–816).[65] It is a collection of more than a hundred relics, most labeled with "authentics," that is, labels that identify a relic by the name of the relevant saint or holy object, as a means of vouching for and authenticating the relic. The relics were located inside a cypress chest inscribed with the name of Pope Leo III; this, in turn, at least by the later eleventh century, was kept in the pope's private oratory dedicated to St. Lawrence at the Lateran palace.[66] In the early twentieth century its contents were made available for scholarly study; because of scholarly rivalries, they have been carefully cataloged only recently.[67]

The collection's contents were modified and rearranged throughout the Middle Ages, meaning that the choice and arrangement of the relics cannot be interpreted as Leo's initiative.[68] Caution is also needed in using the authentics to trace the origins of the collection, because the date of relic authentics does not necessarily indicate the date of their acquisition by the papacy. Relics dated to the early Middle Ages may only have been placed in the chest (complete with earlier authentics) significantly later. Likewise, relics previously acquired may have been relabeled at a later date. These caveats notwithstanding, the relics and their authentics, when cautiously examined, can provide some tantalizing indications of the accumulation of sanctity at the Lateran and of how the papacy in the later Middle Ages built on its earlier traditions. Even as the early medieval popes turned to face toward the north, they continued to draw on the eastern Mediterranean's vast reservoir of sanctity as a foundation for their claims to primacy. Yet from a later medieval perspective, these "Greek" saints became a more unusual part of the collection.

All in all there are about eighty-eight authentics dating from the seventh to ninth centuries.[69] Of these, by far the largest proportion (roughly two-thirds) are relics associated with the Holy Land, either related to Christ, the Virgin Mary, or to places in the Old or New Testament. Of the thirty labels that mention saints, there are a few Old Testament figures, a handful of New Testament figures, and a slightly larger number of Roman saints.[70] Often, especially with less commonly found names, it can be impossible to determine to which saint these laconic tags refer. However, we can say with certainty that the largest proportion of the saints (roughly twelve of thirty) are those associated with the eastern Mediterranean.[71] Similar to the patterns of sanctity presented in the previous chapters, these eastern saints are for the most part martyrs of the imperial persecutions—indeed, the collection includes numerous saints discussed in previous chapters.

As we would expect, the Lateran relic collection comprised many saints whose cults are attested in early medieval Rome. Included were relics of the physician-saints Cosmas and Damian (their authentic written in a seventh- to late eighth-century hand), as well as the soldier-saints Sergius and Bacchus (their authentic labeled in an early eighth-century hand).[72] A number of saints associated with the early medieval Lateran were also found in the chest. There are relics of George (labeled in a ninth-century hand), whose head Pope Zacharias had discovered in

Plate 1. S. Agnese, apse mosaic. Courtesy of the Bibliotheca Hertziana, Max-Planck-Institut für Kunstgeschichte, Rome. Photographer: Arnaldo Vescovo.

Plate 2. S. Maria Antiqua, Theodotus chapel, fresco. Courtesy of the Ministero dei Beni e delle Attività Culturali e del Turismo, Soprintendenza Speciale per il Colosseo, il Museo Nazionale Romano e l'Area archeologica di Roma.

Plate 3. Oratory of the Forty Martyrs, apse fresco. Courtesy of the Ministero dei Beni e delle Attività Culturali e del Turismo, Soprintendenza Speciale per il Colosseo, il Museo Nazionale Romano e l'Area archeologica di Roma.

Plate 4. S. Teodoro, apse mosaic (heavily restored). Scala / Art Resource, NY.

Plate 5. Reconstruction of the interior of the Senate house. UCLA Digital Forum. Copyright © 2017 by Frischer Consulting, Inc., with all rights reserved.

Plate 6. S. Maria Antiqua, fresco with Pope Hadrian. Scala / Art Resource, NY.

Plates 7 and 8. S. Maria Antiqua, frescoes of church fathers with scrolls. Courtesy of the Ministero dei Beni e delle Attività Culturali e del Turismo, Soprintendenza Speciale per il Colosseo, il Museo Nazionale Romano e l'Area archeologica di Roma.

Plate 9. S. Maria Antiqua, apse fresco. Courtesy of the Ministero dei Beni e delle Attività Culturali e del Turismo, Soprintendenza Speciale per il Colosseo, il Museo Nazionale Romano e l'Area archeologica di Roma.

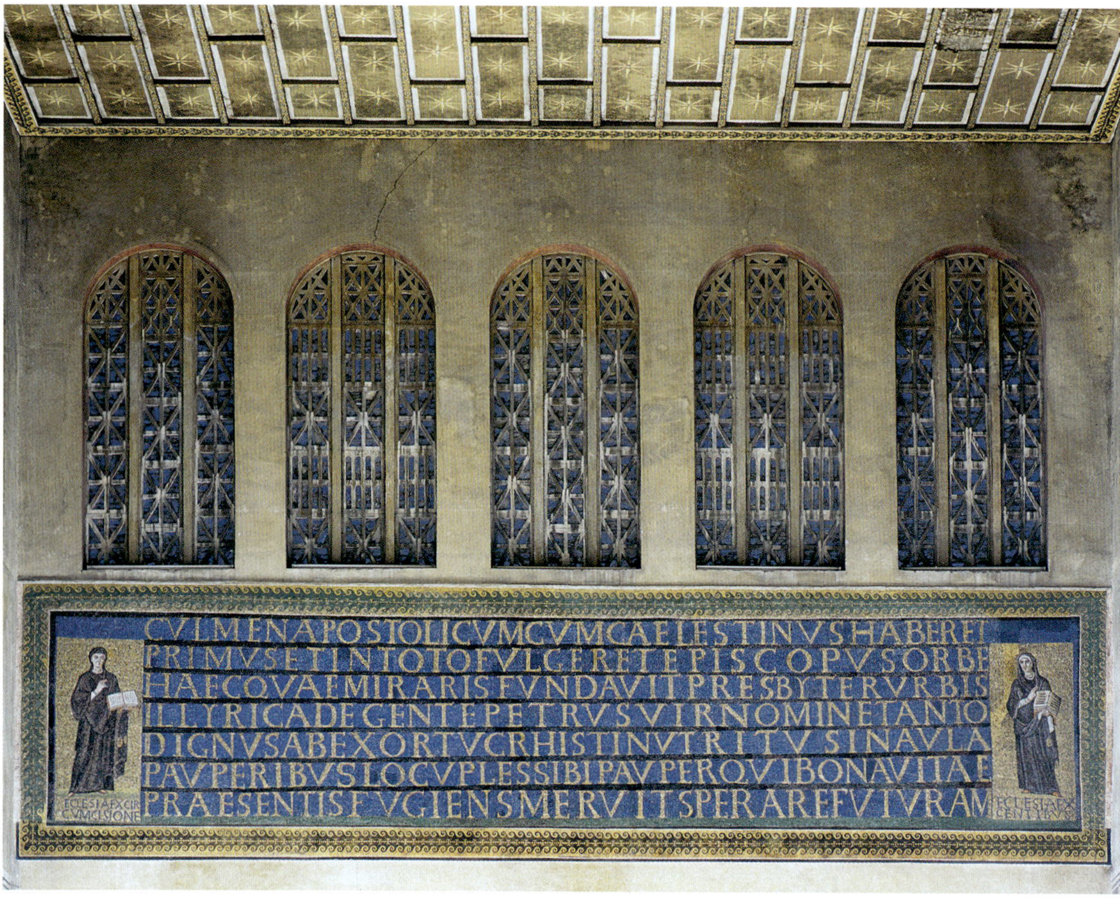

Plate 10. S. Sabina, dedicatory inscription. Courtesy of the Bibliotheca Hertziana, Max-Planck-Institut für Kunstgeschichte, Rome. Photographer: Arnaldo Vescovo.

Plate 11. S. Sabina, donor portrait (narthex). Courtesy of the Polo Museale del Lazio, Archivio fotografico.

Plate 12. S. Venanzio chapel, apse mosaic. Andrea Jemolo / Scala / Art Resource, NY.

Plate 13. S. Venanzio chapel, mosaic to the left of the apse. Andrea Jemolo / Scala / Art Resource, NY.

Plate 14. S. Venanzio chapel, mosaic to the right of the apse. Andrea Jemolo / Scala / Art Resource, NY.

Plate 15. S. Maria Antiqua, panorama of saints (fresco, left aisle). Courtesy of the Ministero dei Beni e delle Attività Culturali e del Turismo, Soprintendenza Speciale per il Colosseo, il Museo Nazionale Romano e l'Area archeologica di Roma.

Plate 16. S. Maria Antiqua, panorama of saints (fresco, left aisle), detail. Left: Sylvester (ecclesiastical pallium around shoulders); Right: Basil (ecclesiastical pallium wrapped around neck). Courtesy of the Ministero dei Beni e delle Attività Culturali e del Turismo, Soprintendenza Speciale per il Colosseo, il Museo Nazionale Romano e l'Area archeologica di Roma.

Plate 17. Mt. Sinai icon, Sts. Athanasius and Basil. By permission of Saint Catherine's Monastery, Sinai, Egypt. Photograph courtesy of Kurt Weitzmann Archive, Department of Art and Archaeology, Princeton University.

Plate 18. S. Prassede, triumphal arch mosaic. Scala / Ministero per i Beni e le Attività culturali / Art Resource, NY.

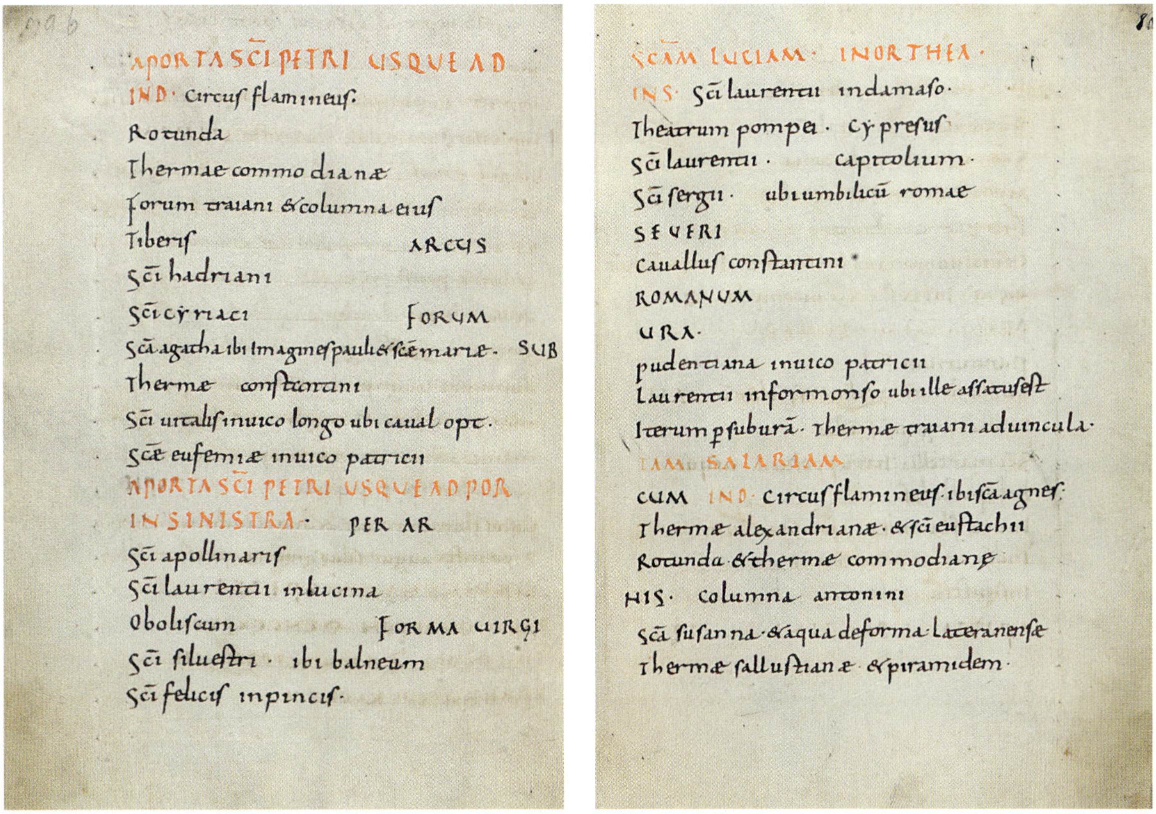

A PORTA SCI PETRI USQUE AD
IND· circus flamineus.
Rotunda
Thermae commodianae
Forum traiani & columna eius
Tiberis ARCUS
Sci hadriani
Sci cyriaci FORUM
Sca agatha ibi imagines pauli & scae mariae· SUB
Therme constantini
Sci uitalis in uico longo ubi caual opt.
Scae eufemiae in uico patricii
A PORTA SCI PETRI USQUE AD POR
IN SINISTRA· PER AR
Sci apollinaris
Sci laurentii in lucina
Obolisccum FORMA UIRGI
Sci siluestri · ibi balneum
Sci felicis in pincis·

SCAM LUCIAM· IN ORTHEA·
INS· Sci laurentii in damaso·
Theatrum pompei · Cypresus
Sci laurentii · capitolium·
Sci sergii · ubi umbilicu romae
SEVERI
Caballus constantini
ROMANUM
URA·
pudentiana in uico patricii
Laurentii in formonso ubi ille assatus est
Iterum p suburā· Therme traiani ad uincula·
TAM SALARIAM
CUM IND circus flamineus· ibi sca agnes.
Therme alexandrianae· & sci eustachii
Rotunda & therme commodiane
HIS· columna antonini
Sca susanna· & aqua de forma lateranense
Therme sallustianae & piramidem·

Plate 19. Einsiedeln Itinerary no. 1: Codex Einsidlensis 326, ff. 79v–80r. Virtual Manuscript Library of Switzerland (www.e-codices.unifr.ch/en/list/one/sbe/0326) with permission of the Stiftsbibliothek, Einsiedeln.

Plate 20. Church of St. George, Reichenau-Oberzell, fresco. Erich Lessing / Art Resource, NY.

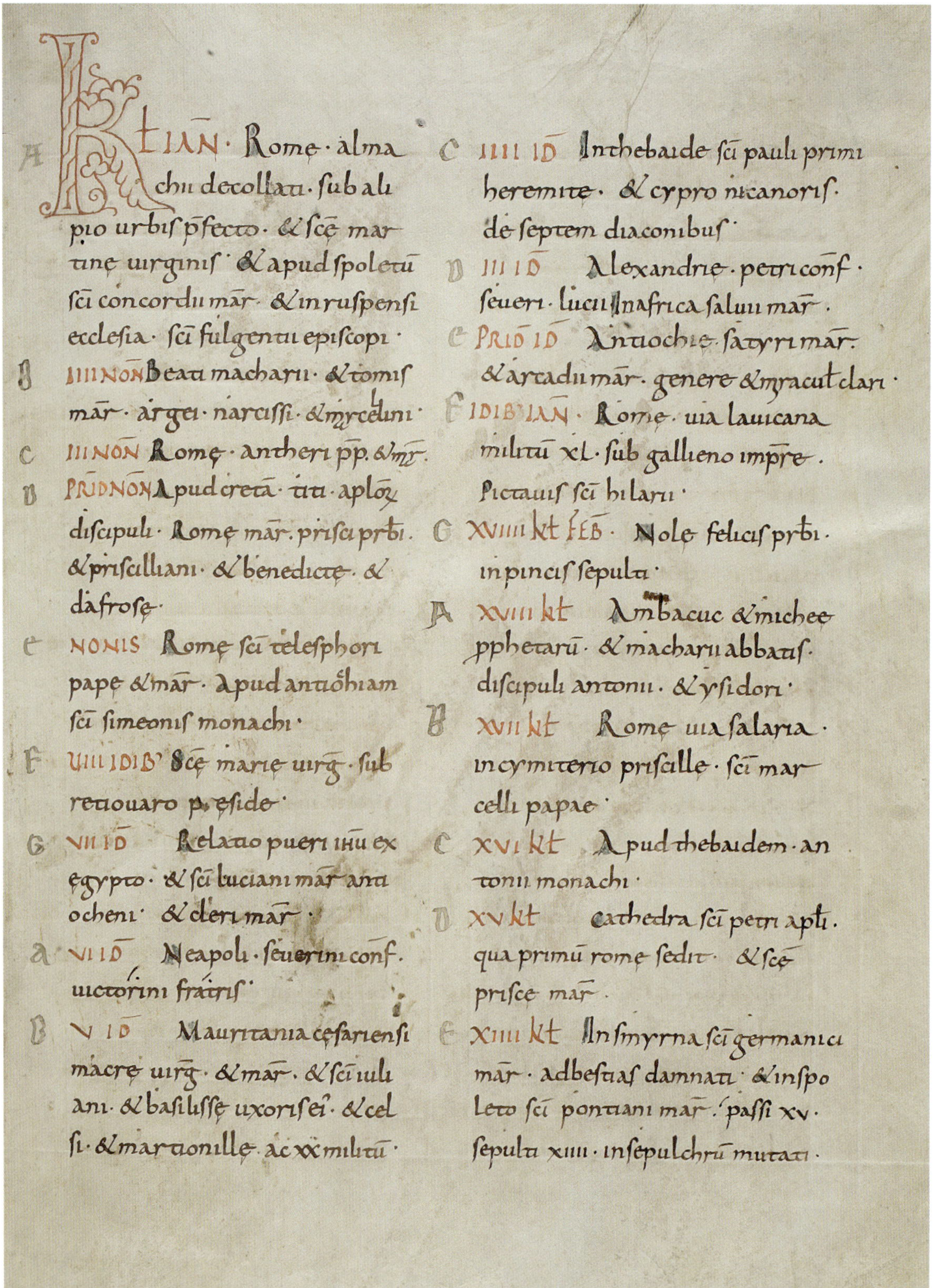

Plate 21. Roman Martyrology: St. Gallen, Stiftsbibliothek, Cod. Sang. 454, p. 3. Virtual Manuscript Library of Switzerland (www.e-codices.unifr.ch/en/list/one/csg/0454) with permission of the Stiftsbibliothek, St. Gallen.

the Lateran in the eighth century, and of the protomartyr Stephen, an extremely popular saint, for whom there was also a chapel at the Lateran.[73] The relic labeled "Domninus" may refer to the bishop of Dalmatia portrayed in the S. Venanzio chapel at the Lateran baptistery.[74] Furthermore the collection contained relics of the Emperor Constantine, whose cult is not otherwise attested in early medieval Rome, but who was closely associated with the Lateran.[75]

The authentics and arrangement of the relics also give some indications as to the history of the collection. Some of the relic authentics were written in the same hands; later, many relics were grouped together into different reliquaries inside the chest.[76] These clusters give a sense of the logic by which saints were organized—whether this categorization took place at the Lateran or elsewhere. Relics whose authentics are written in the same hand must have been in some way associated with each other, either because they had been acquired together or because they were perceived to "fit" together. In contrast, although the groupings of relics into reliquaries do not necessarily reflect early medieval attitudes toward relic collecting, they can indicate how later papal organizers of the collection tried to make sense of its diversity.

Most conspicuous in the labeling of seventh- to ninth-century relics is a distinction between two categories: Holy Land relics and those of other saints. Relics whose authentics are written in the same hand usually consist of groups of relics from the Holy Land. Such groups likely originated as collections gathered by pilgrims to the Holy Land that were subsequently labeled together.[77] When another saint's relics (not from the Holy Land) were included in such collections, they were likely relics added to the collection when it arrived in Rome.[78] Only one set of relic authentics written in a single early medieval hand (dated to the late seventh to early eighth century) comprises non-Holy-Land saints. These are a diverse group, including the seventh-century Aldegund, the foundress of the abbey of Maubeuge (present-day northern France).[79] Most of the saints labeled in early medieval hands, however, have no corresponding authentics written in the same hand. This suggests that in general in the early Middle Ages most saints' relics were acquired individually as representatives of their distinctive cults, not as larger groups.

Later regroupings of relics exhibit much more of an attempt to organize relics by type. Again, most common are groups of Holy Land relics. One round wooden reliquary contained a selection of eight Holy Land relics (with relic authentics dated to the eighth or ninth century), as well as the relics of one Roman martyr, Hermes (labeled in a tenth-century hand).[80] A second, identically shaped reliquary contained a group of eastern saints, almost all labeled in Greek: Sisinnius, Pantaleon, and Isidore (all labeled in Greek, in the same hand, undated); Nicholas (labeled in an eighth-century Greek hand); and the Old Testament prophet Amos (labeled in Latin in a seventh- to eighth-century hand).[81] These were all fairly common

Byzantine saints, many of whom were associated with healing (both Nicholas and Pantaleon are among the saints' relics with which Theodotus dedicated his new *diaconia* in the mid-eighth century).[82] Similarly, another reliquary (a copper casket) contained teeth of two "Greek" saints, together with other precious treasures.[83]

In contrast to these small select groups of relics, a larger grouping (whose location in the chest is unclear) contained a wider assortment of relics, primarily of saints with eastern pedigrees.[84] Packaged together when the casket was opened in the twentieth century were fourteen authentics, all but one in Latin, most dating from the ninth century or earlier.[85] Included was one Old Testament prophet (Isaac), one archangel (Michael), one apostle (Andrew), various saints of the imperial persecutions (such as Cosmas and Damian, Lucy, Lawrence, and George), as well as confessors, such as a hermit (Arsenius, a Roman aristocrat who fled to Alexandria in the time of Arcadius and Honorius), Domninus (?bishop of Salona), and Emperor Constantine.

Although the fit was not perfect, clearly the person who grouped these relics had tried to match together similar saints. Previous groupings (as attested by the relic labels written in the same hand) were disrupted in the process; the new group included the relics of Isaac, Cosmas and Damian, and Michael, but the relics of Aldegund, initially part of the same group, were placed in a different group.[86] Similarly, although the relics of Lucy were included in this group, those of the Holy Land (labeled in the same seventh- to eighth-century hand as that of Lucy) were placed in a different group.[87]

These later regroupings suggest the degree to which, from a later medieval perspective, eastern saints had become a distinctive feature of the collection. Their relics represented a sustained spiritual contact with the eastern Mediterranean that was increasingly uncommon in the Middle Ages. Yet even as the patterns of sanctity shifted throughout the centuries, the contents of the sancta sanctorum ensured that the papal edifice of the Middle Ages continued to rest on its Mediterranean foundations. Of course, limited access to the collection meant that only a select audience, if any, would have been aware of this heritage. Unlike other relic collections, such as at the S. Venanzio chapel, whose contents were visually proclaimed, an extensive catalog of the papal relic collection was never promulgated before the twentieth century. Judging from the later evidence, most popes were themselves not fully informed of the specific contents of the chest: the relic collection remembered a past of which individual popes were only dimly aware. Nonetheless, by means of their careful labels, the collection continued, internally, to secure proof of the collection's authenticity—and thus its efficacy.

Nor should we presume that the lack of disclosure of the collection's contents in any way inhibited the perceived significance of the papal relic chest. Any list of the relics rendered it finite, exchanging its marvelous secrecy for dry specificity.

As with the All Saints' Oratory, anonymity assured that nothing was lacking. What precisely the chest contained was less important than its very presence as a papal reservoir of sanctity at the Lateran.

* * *

Wherever and whenever saints had died, their status granted them special access to divine grace that transcended the historical and geographical dimensions of their lives. In this chapter we have seen the attempt, by successive popes, to anchor saints more firmly on earth, or rather, more specifically, in Rome.

Heavenly Jerusalem, so ninth-century visitors to Rome's churches might have concluded, was closer than ever before.[88] Depictions of the bejeweled cities of Jerusalem and Bethlehem were to be found on the apsidal mosaics of late antique/early medieval churches throughout Rome, including at SS. Cosma e Damiano on the Forum Romanum, and at S. Venanzio at the Lateran.[89] These walled cities were often depicted as roughly circular, corresponding more to Rome's fortifications than the square Jerusalem described by the Apocalypse of John.[90] The implication was made explicit in a mosaic commissioned by Pope Paschal (r. 817–824) for the triumphal arch of S. Prassede (Plate 18).[91] Here a multitude of saints are welcomed into a heavenly city already populated by Christ and the apostles. The depiction references the large numbers of saints' relics, transferred from the catacombs, with which Paschal dedicated the church, proclaiming Rome as the heavenly Jerusalem.

Whether threatened by barbarian invasions (as with the Dalmatian and Istrian saints gathered into the S. Venanzio chapel), oblivion (as with the Roman soldier-saints conflated with Pannonian artisans), or destruction (as in Byzantine iconoclasm), all saints were assured a warm welcome in Rome. As a heavenly collective at home in Rome, these saints needed not be enumerated specifically (nor were they in the All Saints' Oratory) or known to a wider public (nor were they in the swelling and potentially limitless collection of relics stockpiled at the Lateran). Rome, buttressed by all the saints, could stand in for all of Christendom.

CHAPTER 7

Carolingian Romes Outside of Rome

To be the repository of all saints, Rome needed an audience who recognized it as such. And it was only the determined and textually prolific nature of these communities—in the Carolingian and post-Carolingian world—that so successfully valorized the emerging idea of a universalizing Christian Rome. These communities and their relationship to Rome are the subject of Chapters 7 and 8. This chapter discusses the appropriation of Rome and its saints in monasteries north of the Alps. We return to the Einsiedeln compilation, around which I constructed the walk through Rome in Chapter 1, and examine the Carolingian afterlife of some of the saints we encountered in Chapters 2 through 4. Chapter 8 then turns to one particularly influential attempt to create a comprehensive calendar of Roman saints. Together, these chapters present a snippet of a much larger story.

Carolingian rulers, ecclesiastics, writers, and thinkers interacted with a Rome that took on multiple guises: as a city of martyrs and monuments, as the seat of the papacy, and as a model for empire.[1] Their interest in Rome and the papacy often followed earlier Merovingian precedents, cultivated not least by Rome's ecclesiastical administration. For example, Pope Gregory the Great (r. 590–604) had sent the Merovingian king Childebert filings of Peter's chains inside a key, explaining that the relic, worn around the king's neck, could protect him from all evils.[2] But the Carolingian engagement with Rome also took on new forms. At least according to the account crafted by later Carolingian sources, Pippin, before deposing the last Merovingian king, sent legates to Pope Zacharias in 751 to ask whether it was right that he who did not have royal power should be called king.[3] Papal approval provided one form of legitimation for the Carolingian dynasty's claims to power. It was, in turn, with Pippin's permission that Fulrad (whom we met in the Introduction) journeyed to Rome to acquire relics of Roman saints: Rome was a pilgrimage location whose spiritual benefits could be disconnected from the city and brought back home.

Roman materials of various sorts interested Charlemagne. From Pope Hadrian (r. 772–795) he requested an authentic Roman sacramentary; performing the liturgy the "Roman" way became, in the Carolingian Empire, a recurrent strain in the "rhetoric of reform" (to follow Yitzhak Hen's words).[4] According to the biography of Charlemagne written by his advisor Einhard, the emperor had columns and marbles imported from Rome (and Ravenna) for a church he had built at his new capital of Aachen.[5] The stones of antiquity, as well as Roman models, both literary and architectural, were to conjure up a "second Rome."[6] Rome opened up wider horizons, geographically and intellectually; for instance it was when Einhard's notary Ratleig visited Rome to acquire relics that he encountered the Greek monk Basil on the Palatine (see Chapter 2).

Charlemagne's successor Louis the Pious (814–840) continued to draw on Roman precedents, both imperial and Christian, as part of his attempt to unify the empire. And even in the later ninth century, as claimants to the throne jostled for power and local concerns came to the fore, Rome continued to fascinate, and Roman Christianity continued to be showcased as the paradigmatic form of Christianity.[7] Crucial to this enterprise were the great monasteries of the Carolingian world. These monasteries were "powerhouses of prayer" (in Mayke de Jong's words), whose churches, fortified with relics, and whose monks, supplied with authoritative texts to guide their prayers, were to serve as a steadfast network holding together the Christian realm.[8] This chapter focuses on four examples of the engagement with Rome that took place at prominent monasteries in the Carolingian world: Fulda, Weissenburg, Prüm, and Reichenau. Carolingian intellectuals at these monasteries promoted an expansive view of "Rome," which included as Roman the physical city, both classical and Christian; its imperial past and papal present; and saints martyred in locations outside of Rome whose cults were found in the city. I begin with an ambitious attempt to encapsulate "all" of Rome before turning to examples of the piecemeal appropriation of specific saints.

Compiling a Rome for the Soul in Fulda: The Einsiedeln Compilation

Early medieval Rome had much to offer. It was hard to describe this complexity, yet we owe much of what we know about the early medieval city to northern visitors who tried to do just that. Particularly noteworthy was the attempt of an anonymous ninth-century compiler in the monastery of Fulda. The result was the Einsiedeln compilation (Codex Einsidlensis 326, ff. 67–97), a collection of materials that aimed to capture Rome on the page for the spiritual benefit of its readers.

In the mid-eighth century, Sturm, a disciple of the renowned monk and bishop Boniface (who was called Wynfrith before he assumed his new name in Rome on the feast day of St. Boniface of Tarsus), founded the monastery of Fulda (in Hesse, Germany).[9] Already at its foundation it was a monastery linked to Rome. Boniface, whose missionary efforts and martyrdom (in 754) in the German regions of the Frankish kingdom earned him near-apostolic status, had acquired for the monastery before his death a special exemption from Pope Zacharias, placing it directly under the papal see (rather than under the local bishop). The monastery's close ties to Rome continued in the subsequent decades as the monastery grew in wealth and prestige, becoming, by the turn of the ninth century, one of the leading monastic centers of the Carolingian Empire.

The ninth-century monastery of Fulda was an aspiring "Rome." In 819 a grand new church was consecrated that architecturally evoked St. Peter's. Its altar, centered in the transept right in front of the apse and directly above the tomb of Boniface (buried at Fulda after his death), mimicked the placement of the altar in St. Peter's directly above St. Peter's tomb.[10] In the 830s Fulda's abbot, the learned Hrabanus Maurus (whose explanation for the significance of Rome's Capitolium was cited in Chapter 1), purchased the relics of more than forty Roman saints from a notorious Roman relic dealer, the deacon Deusdona. Most of the relics (which derived primarily from catacombs along the via Appia, the via Labicana, and the via Pinciana-Salaria)[11] were deposited in two precious reliquaries in the main church of Fulda. Others were distributed to churches associated with the monastery and its dependents.[12] Paintings and inscriptions celebrated the relics, and the monastery recorded the miracles they performed.[13] The monastery's own illustrious past was thus bolstered by, and brought closer to, that of Rome.

The ninth-century monastery also possessed an active scriptorium and a well-stocked library whose collection ranged from Christian classics to more unusual classical Roman texts.[14] Included therein were hagiographical texts and martyrologies: the monastery was thus well equipped to research the saints it acquired.

It was in this context that a ninth-century compiler at the monastery gathered together earlier documents, many of which must have been written or brought back by visitors to Rome as early as the mid- to late eighth century, and copied them out into a neatly written, handy little volume (18 × 12.5 cm): the Einsiedeln compilation.[15] This manuscript offered a guide to Rome for armchair readers north of the Alps who had never visited the city of Rome and probably never would.[16] Readers far from Rome were invited to conjure up a Rome of the mind—an imaginative exercise that, if done properly, was for the benefit of their soul.

* * *

As it survives today, the compilation begins with transcriptions of inscriptions from all over Rome, each labeled in red with its location.[17] The inscriptions range widely in date and location and include both pagan and Christian inscriptions. Many were easily visible monumental inscriptions, such as the mosaic inscription from St. Peter's basilica, but others were more unusual and obscure, such as the epitaph of a certain Gaius Dillius Vocula.[18]

The so-called itineraries follow: they crisscross the city of Rome, visiting most of the city's neighborhoods.[19] Our walk through intramural Rome in Chapter 1 was guided by these itineraries and the sites they mention. Laid out over a two-page spread, each of these itineraries begins with a title, in red capital letters, that sets out the route (Plate 19). These routes usually lead from one of the city's gates to another or from a gate to the center of the city, although some include sites, primarily martyr shrines (and aqueducts), located outside the walls. The manuscript then lays out the sites located along each route, with their names located on the left, right, or even the center of the page to designate where the sites are located with respect to the path. A range of sites are included: roughly half of the entries are for churches and other Christian sites, but monuments from classical antiquity are also cited frequently. What should be emphasized is that these itineraries list only the names—that is, the patron saints—of ecclesiastical dedications. There is no indication as to which of these saints are Roman martyrs and which are saints from abroad: all the ecclesiastical dedications are presented on equal footing as part of the topography of the city.

The next section in the manuscript is a statistical inventory of Rome's wall, tallying its architectural features (towers, gates, windows, etc.) from gate to gate and concluding with a total count of each of these features (cited at the beginning of our walk through Rome).[20] Then, on the back of this page, begins a description of the liturgy on the Thursday, Friday, and Saturday of Holy Week at the Lateran, as conducted by the bishop of Rome (whose procession to "Jerusalem" we accompanied at the end of Chapter 1).[21] The description is by no means comprehensive; it is from the perspective of an outsider remarking on what struck him as most unusual and interesting. Lastly, the Einsiedeln compilation includes a poetry collection, with a range of Roman, late antique, and Carolingian verse.[22]

Altogether the compilation conveys an idea of Rome that is both more and less than the city. On the one hand it has shrunk Rome into a set of words and numbers. The living, breathing complexity is gone. Rome has become static; changes to the urban fabric are no longer recorded. At the same time, the compilation conveys a Rome that is more than the physical city. We are presented with an idea of Rome that exceeds the city itself. This is best appreciated by the materials in the compilation that are not specifically about the city.

Among the inscriptions are a handful of transcriptions not from Rome, but from Pavia.[23] These include imperial titulature from an Augustan triumphal arch and a Christian inscription, in Greek, from a church dedicated to St. Peter. Caesar Augustus and St. Peter: these are the quintessential marks of "Romanness."

The idea of Rome expands when we move into the poetry collection. Here we see a slippage from Rome to Romanness—classical and Christian culture more broadly conceived; this heritage, as the poems demonstrate, has not ceased, but actively continues. "Rome" emerges as a flexible resource that is more than a physical landscape. It is both the living present and the past of a city from which empire and Christianity emanated, and this idea of Rome may be appreciated, imitated, and even appropriated far away from the city.

The pieces in the poetry collection were not selected to form a unified corpus. What we should imagine, I suggest, is that our compiler, having finished copying out the other documents, still had space in the quire (and then added on some additional quires as poems he was copying did not quite fit on the available pages).[24] He included various verses that struck him as useful and interesting addenda to the Roman materials. The result is an eclectic assortment that ranges freely in date from classical antiquity to contemporary ninth-century verse. The manuscript makes no note of the authors of these poems and presents all on equal footing. Leitmotifs include conflict, especially the tension between classical learning and Christian salvation, and reflections on the working and fate of the Christian soul.

The first verses in the poetry collection are a mathematical puzzle, evocative of the earlier wall description with its extensive numerical statistics.[25] The verses tackle the task of defending a city (or rather, of avoiding that burdensome task). A group of white and black soldiers come together under one roof and dispute who should be responsible for the night watch. Clever reasoning allows the commander of the white soldiers to avoid assigning any of his men to that duty. Such puzzles were in vogue among the Carolingian elite as pedagogically useful for sharpening that most rational part of the soul, the mind.

The next poem in the collection continues the theme of conflict with a short poem listing the labors of Hercules (by the fourth-century poet Ausonius).[26] Hercules was an ambivalent figure in the Carolingian imagination, symptomatic of the contrasting and not necessarily compatible natures of classical and Christian thought.[27]

The latent Christian implications that can lurk beneath the veneer of pagan antiquity are made clearer by the subsequent piece. This is the "Conflict of Spring and Winter" by the eighth-century Carolingian court poet and scholar Alcuin, a classicizing poem rich in Christian theological implications.[28] It presents a dialogue between winter and spring presided over by two of Virgil's shepherds, young Daphnis and old Palaemon. Severe winter greedily seeks to prevent the advent of the cuckoo, the harbinger of spring; at the end of the poem Daphnis and Palaemon, supported by a "crowd of pious shepherds," intervene to welcome the cuckoo, who is Christ himself.[29]

Greed, epitomized by winter, is one of the vices that lead the soul away from Christ. The following couplet (without a title) warns of another: "Nothing is more just than envy, which straightaway gnaws on its own creator and torments the soul."[30] The verses continue, "You Tityrus, reclining under the trusted/faithful covering of Christ," which plays on a line from Virgil's *Eclogues* (1.1): "You Tityrus, reclining under the covering of the wide-spreading beech tree."[31] The text proceeds to exhort the reader to the study of the divine scriptures as that which is most beneficial to the soul.

Discussion of the soul continues with a few lines (not in verse and not attributed) from Isidore's *Etymologies*, explaining the different terms (soul, will, mind, memory, reason, spirit, and sense) used to refer to the soul according to its different functions.[32] A pithy two-line epigram follows: "You will deceive others with your words and mild looks / but to me you will be known as a dissembler."[33]

Then comes the longest of the poems included in the manuscript, the *Tituli Historiarum* (by the late fourth-century Prudentius): forty-nine verses of Christian history that were likely originally intended as captions for the image cycle of a basilica.[34] Each of these verses is labeled in red by its subject (similar in format to the labels that accompany the inscriptions earlier in the manuscript). The verses begin with the fall of Adam and Eve; summarize key scenes of the Old and New Testaments; and conclude with the martyrdom of Stephen, two scenes from the life of Peter, the conversion of Paul, and the apocalypse of John. The saints, above all Peter and Paul, are the prelude to the end of times.

Fittingly for a compilation that begins with inscriptions, the poem collection ends with two epitaphs: one of Gerold, the brother-in-law of Charlemagne, who died in 799, and one of Bernald, a bishop who died in 844.[35] Both epitaphs are from Reichenau, like Fulda a key monastic center of the Carolingian Empire (see the later discussion). Both memorialize the Christian virtues of the deceased in classical meters: dactylic hexameter for Gerold, who had contributed generously to the monastery and was "slain on behalf of the true peace of the Church at the hands of the Pannonians,"[36] and elegiac couplets for Bernald, "whose modest life ornamented his noble birth."[37] Bernald's epitaph reminds us of the rewards that await the pious for their merits;[38] in dying, Gerold—in the classical tradition of astral immortality—"gave his soul to the stars."[39] These two epitaphs suggest that a synthesis of classical learning and Christian piety is indeed possible: classical Rome is a resource that may be successfully put to use in building a new Christian Empire.

* * *

The various components of this compilation each contribute to a storehouse of materials that construct a "Rome" for the reader; that is, Rome as a resource that may be profitably recalled by those acquainted with it. To understand this process—the construction of a Rome of the mind—we turn to a widely circulating treatise on the nature of the soul by Alcuin, whose poem "Conflict of Winter and Spring" is included in the Einsiedeln compilation as we just saw.[40] In his treatise on the soul, Alcuin reflects on how the soul constructs memories: this description neatly parallels the Einsiedeln compilation.

The soul (*anima*), so Alcuin explains, quickly fashions mental images for itself of everything that the bodily senses, like messengers (*nuntios*), bring to it.[41] These it stashes away in the treasury of its memory (*in suae thesauro memoriae*). Thus anyone who sees Rome creates a Rome in his mind. Then when he hears or remembers Rome, immediately his mind runs to that memory that he has formed of it, and he recalls the Rome that he had stashed away.

What if someone has never been to Rome? Can he still have an image of it? Alcuin proceeds to explain how we can have images of places (in this case, Jerusalem) in our mind, even if we have never been there: things read or heard can also create images in the mind.[42] And, clever as the mind is, it will form these images appropriate to the type of thing imagined; thus, in creating an image of Jerusalem, the mind will imagine there to be walls and houses and streets, as it knows exist in other cities.[43] Once such images are formed, when the mind hears or sees or smells or tastes something that it had previously registered, it can conjure up again the image of the thing in its mind.[44] But always only one image at a time: "For when I think of Jerusalem I cannot in the same moment think of Rome."[45]

For those who cannot visit Rome, the Einsiedeln compilation conjures up with words the sights, smells, and concepts that belong to the city, which are, literally, brought to the reader by messengers from the city. Moreover, the poems in the compilation offer reflections on the soul and its path to salvation, thus supplementing the storehouse of materials with good advice for rendering Rome beneficial for the soul.

As Alcuin makes clear in his treatise, the "treasury"—that is the soul—has a very precise purpose: to attain knowledge of God. In constructing images for itself the mind must always strive for this purpose and seek out the wisdom that is to be found in Christian truths, not in "Virgilian lies."[46] The reward of this pursuit is the immorality enjoyed by the saints: the *anima*, "if it had remained in that state of nobility, such as it was founded by the Creator, it would, in all ways, be immortal, just as are the souls of the saints."[47]

Alcuin concludes, "For the kingdom of God is not so much in words, but rather in the power of the Holy Spirit and the perfect brilliance of holy merits."[48] So, too, the Einsiedeln compilation, in concluding with the epitaphs of Gerold and

Bernald, reminds its readers that Christian salvation is not to be found in words alone, but in the meritorious actions of laymen and clerics. Rome is but an entry point into the heavens above, where the saints—with whom Rome is filled—enjoy blissful immortality.

Transplanting Rome Saint by Saint

The Einsiedeln compilation is a unique document. It exists in a single manuscript and is the only surviving attempt to encapsulate the physical city in words. This was, we may conclude, an endeavor too ambitious in scope. Rome, in its entirety, could not be captured on the page, nor easily conjured up again. More successful, as we shall see, were efforts to transplant Rome piece by piece, saint by saint. The examples that follow demonstrate how specific saints from abroad venerated in central areas of Rome—on the Forum Romanum, the Palatine Hill, and the Tiber bend (all neighborhoods visited by the itineraries in the Einsiedeln compilation and investigated in previous chapters)—contributed to Rome's profile of sanctity north of the Alps. Like the anonymous compiler at Fulda, the Carolingian elite responsible for appropriating these saints took an expansive view of Rome as a resource that could be mobilized for the spiritual benefit of communities north of the Alps.

Sts. Sergius and Bacchus: Soldier-Saints for the "White Castle"

At the Weissenburg monastery (today located in the town of Wissembourg, France), relics of Sergius and Bacchus, translated from the city of Rome in the 840s, linked the monastery to the heavens above. This monastery, whose name "White Castle" is taken from the region's white limestone, is located at a pass (the so-called Wissembourg Gap) leading out of the Rhine Valley into what is now northeastern France.[49] It is on a strip of land to the west of the Rhine that has often been claimed by rulers on either side of the river. Many battles throughout the centuries have taken place here. The early history of the monastery is unknown; its location, more so than a prominent individual, seems to have provided the main impetus for its foundation. By the eighth century a church had been built in honor of the Roman apostles, Peter and Paul. Whatever its more immediate geographical and political affiliations, then, this was a monastery that looked toward Rome.

Starting in the later eighth century the monastery became more tightly associated with the Carolingian dynasty. Accordingly, as Charlemagne's heirs squabbled over the empire, control over Weissenburg too became a point of contention. In 839 Emperor Louis the Pious (r. 814–840), having regained authority in the area, appointed as abbot of the monastery one of his supporters, Otgar, archbishop of Mainz (r. 826–847).[50] Otgar was part of a group of notables whose territorial ambitions extended to both sides of the Rhine; Weissenburg thus provided him a useful stronghold in the region. Otgar immediately set about fortifying the monastery, militarily and spiritually. To do so he endowed it with relics from Rome. And who better than the soldiers Sergius and Bacchus!

Sts. Sergius and Bacchus, as we saw in Chapter 2, were saints with a reputation for defending cities. A church to them was dedicated on the Forum Romanum at the end of the via Sacra. By the ninth century there were also at least two monasteries in Rome dedicated to the saints, one near the Lateran and the other in the Subura (between the Viminal and Esquiline Hills).[51] Otgar presumably acquired his relics not from any of these ecclesiastical dedications, but rather, as in other contemporary examples, directly from the pope.

Verses composed for the tomb of Sergius by Hrabanus Maurus, abbot of Fulda (who like Otgar supported Louis the Pious and idealized Rome), celebrated the new martyrs:

> The greatest honor on earth is for those sacred martyrs,
> who merited to die for the name of Christ.
> Distinguished among them, the blessed Sergius rejoices, who
> with his brother Bacchus suffered harsh tortures.
> From the city of Romulus, the bishop Otgar both
> did bring, and placed great Sergius here.[52]

Above the *confessio* of the tomb the verses continued, emphasizing the assistance the martyrs could provide:

> Whoever wishes, solemnly intoning, to obtain gifts,
> as a suppliant let him appeal here to the aid and assistance of the martyrs.[53]

Through the terrible tortures and martyrdom they endured, Sergius and Bacchus had earned themselves a place in heaven. Lest anyone doubt that they were powerful intercessors, their Roman provenance added further assurance of their efficacy.

Sergius and Bacchus came to Weissenburg from Rome, but their eastern origins were not forgotten. The translation of their relics was accompanied by their Latin *passio*, which, as we have seen, narrates the vicissitudes of the martyrs from their initial accusation in front of the emperor to their deaths in Syria.[54] A ninth-century hymn from Weissenburg engages with this tradition by describing the saints in markedly military language and by a highly self-conscious use of Greek.[55] It refers to Sergius and Bacchus as "comrades by the crown" (i.e., of martyrdom) and as "athletes" who have "conquered the arms of the savage enemy of old and of the world [*cosmi* < Greek κόσμος] by the contest of the flesh"; Christ is a "radiant soldier"; a "troop [*tacma* < Greek τάγμα] of heavenly Jerusalem above" praises him.[56]

By their martyrdom, the hymn describes, the saints have "departed from the enclosure of their flesh to above the stars," where they serve as protectors of Weissenburg.[57] Correspondingly, urban imagery figures prominently in the hymn, tying Weissenburg firmly to the heavenly city above:

> And so you who attend to the prayer of the age,
> we beseech: favor us with your rewards,
> so that illnesses [*nosos* < Greek νόσος] are not able to harm these
> your citizens.
>
> This your place [*topus* < Greek τόπος] is called the White
> City, decorated with sacred treasures;
> sacred ashes adorn it:
> your holy bodies [*somata* < Greek σῶμα].
> . . .
> Ask these comrades of the cross of Christ,
> who accompanied the lamb of God the Father,
> that we may merit the heavenly city's
> enclosure to enter.[58]

The heavenly Jerusalem is also mentioned by name earlier in the hymn. Noticeably omitted, but lurking in the shadows of the hymn's highly classicizing language, is that other city, somewhere between heaven and earth, that had provided Weissenburg with these saints: Rome.[59]

In the eleventh or twelfth century a brief account of the monastery and its history was appended to the saint's *passio*.[60] This text reiterates how the construction of Weissenburg as a heavenly city had been mediated through Rome. First, the saints are martyred.

> Then that most noble of cities and mistress of the world, Rome, obtained their venerable relics (*exuvias*), which afterwards were translated to Gaul by Otgar, the venerable bishop of Mainz and were entrusted to a most worthy burial in the "Leucopolitan city" [Greek for "white city"], which is called "Wizenburch." Here without doubt each awaits the fulfillment of his

> brother and the day of the great resurrection when the glorious resurrection will take place, which is the perfection of the blessedness of the bodies in which they triumphed.[61]

Centuries later, the account still remembers the city of Rome as the source of the saints' corporeal relics. Rome, however, is important only as a mediator of the relics. What matters most is that now it is the city of Weissenburg that will see the full bodily resurrection of the saints on the day of the last judgment.

In subsequent centuries, Sergius and Bacchus were further incorporated into the liturgical life of their new home and their veneration continued: in 1284 a new church was dedicated with relics of the saints; a tympanum depicted Sergius and Bacchus alongside Saints Benedict, Peter, and Paul; and a bell cast in 1466 was inscribed with the names of Peter, Paul, Sergius, and Bacchus.[62] So closely associated with Weissenburg were these saints that in 1354 the monastery supplied Emperor Charles IV with relics of Sergius and Bacchus for the cathedral of Prague. From Rome, the cult of Sergius and Bacchus radiated out through medieval Europe.

St. Caesarius: A Roman Triumph for November in Prüm

Next we turn to the monastery of Prüm (today in Germany near the border with Belgium and Luxemburg), where a calendar celebrated Rome's most imperial saint: St. Caesarius. As we saw in Chapter 3, an oratory dedicated to St. Caesarius, a deacon martyred in Terracina, was located in the imperial palaces on the Palatine, and in the course of the eighth century, additional dedications to him sprang up throughout the city.

In the Carolingian world Caesarius was among the ranks of saints regularly venerated in the course of the liturgical year.[63] In general, Caesarius remained most closely associated with Terracina, where, according to his well-known *passio*, he was martyred. However, we do also find a tradition—at some of the Carolingian monasteries that most intensively cultivated the idea of Rome—that presents him first and foremost as a Roman saint.[64] The entry, "At Rome [the commemorative feast day] of Caesarius," is found in calendars from Fulda and Reichenau (a monastery discussed in more depth later).[65] The association of Caesarius with Rome is evoked with particular elegance in a calendar from the monastery of Prüm.

Prüm, like Fulda and Reichenau, was fostered by the Carolingian dynasty as one of the principal monasteries that was to buttress their Christian kingdom.[66] Under the influence of the first Carolingian king Pippin (r. 751–768), the monastery was founded anew and its church dedicated to Christ the Savior, a dedication that evoked the Lateran basilica in Rome. Under Abbot Marcward (r. 829–53) and supported by the patronage of Emperor Lothar I (the eldest son of Louis the Pious), who gave lavishly to the monastery and retired there in 855, Roman sanctity came ever more to the fore.

Marcward traveled to Rome (ca. 844) and requested Roman relics, presenting the pope with a letter from Emperor Lothar specifying that "he [the Pope] ought to give him [Marcward] the body of some extremely illustrious martyr of distinguished fame, about whose passion and veneration none of the faithful would be in doubt."[67] Pope Sergius (r. 844–847) granted him relics of the Roman martyrs Chrysanthus and Daria and also provided him with a copy of the saints' *passio*.

An eagerness to promote Roman sanctity in Prüm is also evident in a martyrology, a calendar of saints, composed by Wandalbert (d. ca. 870), a monk in Prüm.[68] Wandalbert wrote this text at the request of Abbot Marcward and dedicated it to Emperor Lothar in 848. The martyrology is in verse, but closely follows earlier Latin martyrologies, above all that of Florus of Lyons (ca. 825–840), which included large numbers of saints from Rome.[69] At times, however, Wandalbert's martyrology even goes beyond that of Florus in associating saints with Rome. This is evident in the case of St. Caesarius. Florus presented Caesarius as a Terracinan saint (including a brief excerpt from his *passio*), but Wandalbert's martyrology jubilantly proclaims:

> Caesarius with his first appearance marks out November,
> and in his splendid triumph Rome delights.[70]

St. George: Roman Veneration Conquers Frankish Doubts in Reichenau

Our final example takes us to the monastery island of Reichenau (in Lake Constance in southern Germany), where the reception of the relics of St. George from Rome was inflected by their Roman cult. Although the veneration of George north of the Alps long predated Pope Zacharias's miraculous discovery of the head of St. George in Rome (discussed in Chapter 4), George's Roman prestige gave new impetus—and credibility—to his cult.

Unsurprisingly, given the extraordinary nature of George's *passio*, not all readers were equally convinced that it was a trustworthy narrative. The great scholar of hagiography, Hippolyte Delehaye (1859–1941), likened the early *passio* to "a sort of Monte Testaccio, formed by debris from every source and without cohesion," and certainly some members of the Carolingian elite shared the sentiment.[71] Circulating widely in early medieval Francia and northern Italy was the *Decretum Gelasianum de libris recipiendis et non recipiendis*, a handbook of orthodox Christian literature (which purports to have been written by Pope Gelasius, r. 492–496, but which was certainly a later composition).[72] With regard to "the deeds of the holy martyrs" (*gesta sanctorum martyrum*), the *Decretum* warns against those "[written] by infidels and idiots" providing unreliable narratives.[73] Specifically enumerated as an example of such a text is the *passio Georgii*.

The *Decretum*'s critique, it should be stressed, targets the *passio*, not the cult, of St. George, yet it must have made some scholars pause. In addition, there were various accounts of St. George in circulation that disagreed not only in the narrative they offered but also, more distressing from a liturgical perspective, in the date of George's martyrdom.[74] According to many versions of the martyrology ascribed to Jerome (held in high esteem by Carolingian scholars), George's feast was to be celebrated on April 25.[75] However, many other texts (including the widespread Roman sacramentary, the *Hadrianum*) placed it on April 23—and there was even another tradition, found in certain versions of George's *passio*, that placed it on April 24.[76]

One scholar who wrestled with these divergent traditions was the learned Notker the Stammerer (d. 912), a monk at the intellectual powerhouse of St. Gall. In his martyrology, Notker includes two entries for St. George: one on April 23 and the other on April 25. On April 23 he provides a very brief summary of George's *passio* and concludes (following verbatim the text of Ado's martyrology, discussed in Chapter 8) that "although the deeds of his martyrdom are reckoned among the apocryphal writings, nevertheless the Church of God venerably honors his illustrious martyrdom among the crowns of martyrs."[77] On April 25, a second entry for George reads as follows:

> In Persia [the feast day] of St. George the martyr, according to the calendar of the most learned Jerome. His passion is celebrated among the Romans and nearly all others on the 9th day before the Kalends of May (April 23), as was noted above. On that account, I thought this should be pointed out so that our patriarch [archbishop] Hatto of Mainz—who, in this very year from the incarnation of Christ, brought to Alemannia, to his new monastery, his [George's] head and a certain other limb with many other great relics of saints, all granted to him by Pope Formosus—might act cautiously in fixing his feast day, that is, of St. George, since many others have been accustomed to celebrate his birthday on this day.[78]

Notker indicates that he is aware of the various problems associated with George's cult but, careful scholar that he is, presents the evidence and urges caution, rather than ironing out all the difficulties. On April 23 he reminds his readers that George's *passio* is suspect, yet, based on tradition, accepts the veneration of George as a saint. Then on April 25 he emphasizes that this (not the Roman date of April 23) is the date that the "most learned" Jerome (and many others) regarded as the correct feast day of St. George. Notker does not resolve the discrepancy in dates, instead urging Archbishop Hatto of Mainz (ca. 850–913) to be careful in deciding when to celebrate the feast of St. George.

The impetus for this discussion, as Notker explains, was the translation of the precious relic of George's head and other limbs of the saint from Rome to a new dedication in Alemannia—the newly built Oberzell church on the monastery island of Reichenau (about forty-five kilometers from St. Gall). As mentioned earlier, Reichenau, which had close ties with the nearby monastery of St. Gall, was another of the foremost imperial monastic centers of the Carolingian Empire. By the time of Archbishop Hatto, the island of Reichenau already boasted two splendid churches: a Marian church (Mittelzell) and a church for Peter and Paul on the far end of the island (Niederzell). Hatto made use of his visit to Rome to acquire relics for a third church.

Hatto was a supporter of Arnulf of Carinthia, one of the claimants to power in the fragmenting Carolingian Empire of the late ninth century.[79] Hatto accompanied Arnulf to Rome in 896 (the occasion on which, as mentioned in Chapter 4, the pope sent the senate and the *schola Grecorum* of Rome to meet the king). Arnulf was crowned emperor by Pope Formosus (r. 891–896), and Abbot Hatto returned from the expedition with the relics of George as a gift from the pope. With these the abbot dedicated Reichenau's new church to St. George. Relics from Rome added further prestige and protection to the illustrious monastery of Reichenau.

The community took pride in its new patron saint, freshly arrived from Rome. Still—as Notker's contemporaneous chiding remarks reminded them—George was a thorny saint to handle. Hatto's response? To steer clear of awkward questions of George's miraculous powers and to emphasize Roman tradition as the authority legitimizing George.

The new church was decorated with paintings in the tenth century, including, in the nave, an elaborate cycle of miracles. These depict not, as one might expect, miracles performed by George, but rather those performed by Christ: there are eight scenes in which Christ cures the blind, lame, and possessed or resurrects the dead (Plate 20).[80] The emphasis is on Christ as a wonder-worker, avoiding any suggestion that St. George's miracles might have exceeded those of Christ and reminding viewers that all miracles, even those performed by saints, occur through the will of Christ.

At the same time the community proudly celebrated its new patron. A new copy of Jerome's abbreviated martyrology produced in Reichenau in the late ninth or early tenth century singled out, in majuscules, the feast of St. George as one of the five feast days of greatest importance to the monastery.[81] This was to be celebrated, according

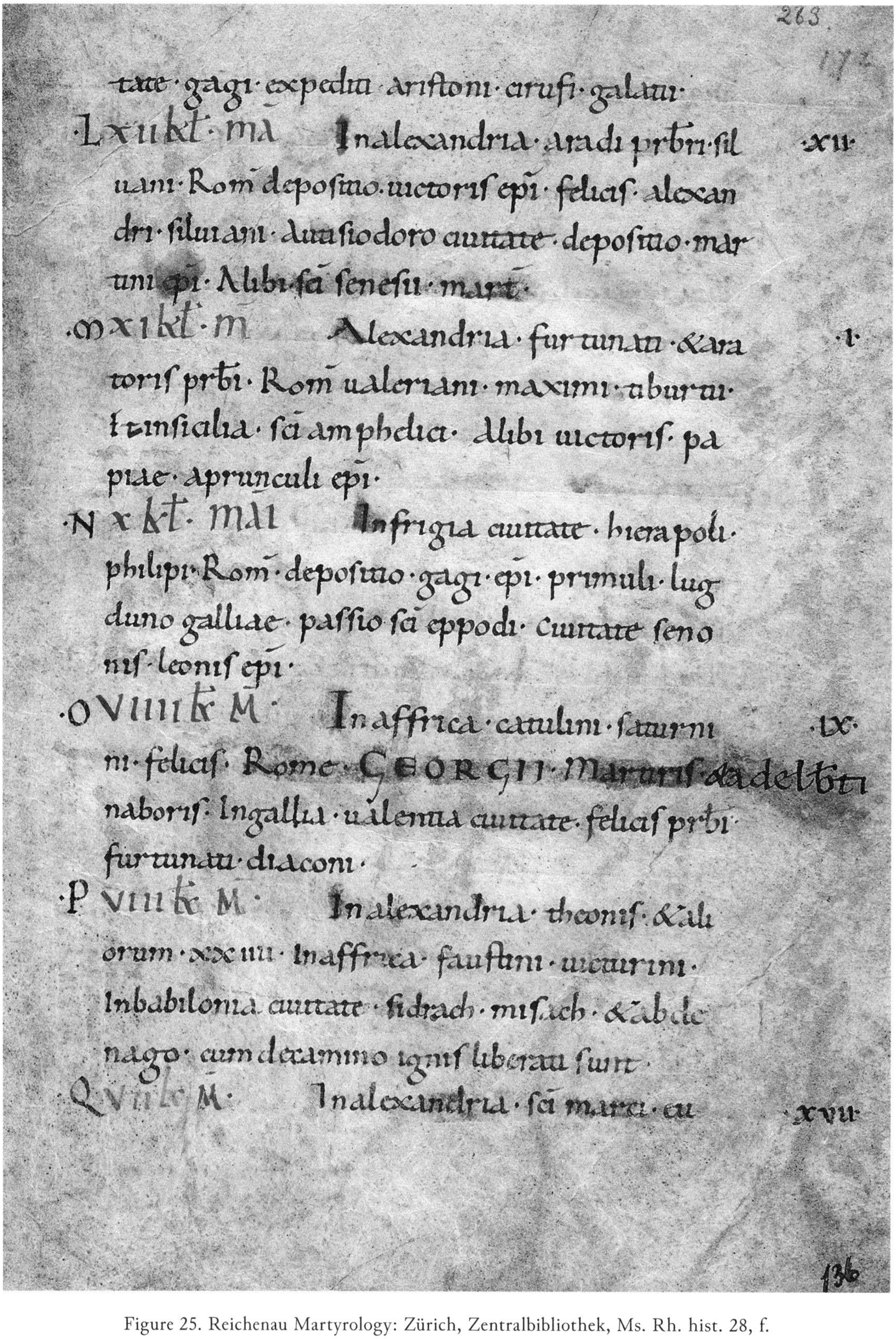

tate · gagi · expediti · aristoni · crusi · galatii ·
·L xii kl · ma In alexandria · aradi prbri · sil ·xii·
uani · Rom depositio · uictoris epi · felicis · alexan
dri · siluani · Autisiodoro ciuitate · depositio · mar
tini epi · Alibi · sci senesii · mart ·
·M xi kl · m Alexandria · furtunati · & ara ·i·
toris prbi · Rom ualeriani · maximi · tiburtii ·
& in sicilia · sci amphelici · Alibi uictoris · pa
piae · apruncul[i] epi ·
·N x kl · mai In frigia ciuitate · hierapoli ·
philipi · Rom · depositio · gagi · epi · primuli · lug
duno galliae · passio sci eppodi · ciuitate seno
nis · leonis epi ·
·O viiii kl M · In affrica · catulini · saturni ·ix·
ni · felicis · Rome · GEORGII Martiris & adelberti
naboris · In gallia · ualentia ciuitate · felicis prbi
furtunati · diaconi ·
·P viii kl M · In alexandria · theonis · & ali
orum · xxiiii · In affrica · faustini · uictorini ·
In babilonia ciuitate · sidrach · misach · & abde
nago · cum de camino ignis liberati sunt ·
Q vii kl M · In alexandria · sci marci · eu ·xvii·

Figure 25. Reichenau Martyrology: Zürich, Zentralbibliothek, Ms. Rh. hist. 28, f. 136r. Courtesy of the Zentralbibliothek Zürich.

to Roman tradition, on April 23, noted in an unambiguous entry for the feast: "in Rome, of GEORGE the Martyr"—*Rome · GEORGII · Martiris* (Figure 25).[82] St. George had been reconfigured as a Roman saint.

* * *

In Chapter 6 we considered how papal efforts built up the idea of Rome as a heavenly Jerusalem, a home for all saints whatever their origins. In this chapter we have seen how monasteries throughout the Carolingian world actively participated in similar ideas of Rome by translating relics from Rome and by crafting texts that documented Rome and its sanctity.

Rome, from these Carolingian perspectives, was a resource, a quarry from which new landscapes were built. It was neither finite nor immutable. Appropriation of Rome was shaped by the concerns and the preoccupations of distinct individuals or communities, and it would be a mistake to equate the different examples of engagement with Rome just presented. There was no consensus. Nevertheless, the varied visions of Rome that emerged magnified Rome—for contemporaries and for later generations who inherited and refashioned the Carolingian legacy.

CHAPTER 8

A Universalizing Rome Through the Lens of Ado of Vienne

This chapter focuses on Ado of Vienne's mid-ninth-century martyrology, which can stand in both as a representative example and as a convenient endpoint in our survey of the growth and codification of the idea of Rome as a storehouse of sanctity. Two closely interrelated themes encountered in Chapter 7 stand out here: the extent to which the Romanization of saints from abroad was the result of their Carolingian reception and how this Carolingian appropriation shaped, and often magnified, Roman sanctity. As we shall see, this was the result, above all, of the rewriting but also the standardization of texts, as well as the force of portable sanctity: relics.

Ado and His Roman Martyrology

Ado (d. 875) was a Frankish aristocrat, monk and eventually, beginning in 860, bishop of Vienne in Provence, where the powerful count Gerhard maintained control throughout the successive reigns of Lothar, Charles the Bald, and Lothar II. Ado maneuvered in this complex world, turning again and again to the papacy in Rome as a source of temporal legitimacy and spiritual authority.[1] Against this backdrop Ado also undertook to construct a "complete" martyrology: a calendar of saints' feasts that would have an entry for every day.[2]

Among Louis the Pious's reforms of 817 that sought to standardize the diverse monastic practices of the vast empire was a decree prescribing the daily reading of martyrologies in monasteries.[3] Each day all monasteries would commemorate in unison the feast of that day's saint, thereby knitting together these distant communities in joint prayer. The genre of martyrologies was by no means new to the Carolingian period; already in circulation was a martyrology falsely ascribed to Jerome, filled with laconic notices of an enormous number of saints, and Bede's martyrology (before 735), containing fewer saints but accompanied by more extensive historical notices regarding these saints.[4] The Carolingian interest in a comprehensive and uniform commemoration of Christian sanctity, however, gave rise to a number of ninth-century rewritings that were ever more encyclopedic in their approach to Christian sanctity.[5] The most ambitious was that of Ado of Vienne.

In the preface to the second recension of his martyrology, completed ca. 865 (perhaps in response to critiques of his first edition), Ado explains the purpose of his text and his methods in accomplishing it:

> Lest you think that I labored on this work in vain or accomplished an unnecessary task, I will briefly reveal to you the reason for the work. Foremost was the command and order of holy men to fill in those days which were marked down without the name of any martyr in that martyrology, which grew by the zeal of the venerable Florus on the basis of the work done by the master Bede. Then, the *passiones* [which I had] collected from all over [to fulfill this task] kindled in me the resolve that I should transcribe not only the days' neglected feasts, but also, more extensively and a bit more clearly, [the feasts] of other [days] which were recorded throughout the year, as a service to the weaker brothers and those less able to read and for the glory of the omnipotent God, so that they [the brothers] should have a short reading for the commemoration of the martyrs and [find] in this book that which others seek out with much labor from many books.[6]

As Ado describes, his martyrology was modeled on that of his predecessor Florus of Lyon (ca. 825–840), but it significantly expanded the text. In the first edition alone, Ado added almost 200 new entries and modified almost 200 more.[7] In his expanded martyrology, every day of the year boasts a saint; indeed, most days have multiple saints with notices that incorporate substantial excerpts from the saints' *passiones*. The result was the most extensive and expansive martyrology to date.

In addition to adding new entries to Florus' martyrology, Ado achieved his desired result of a martyrology without empty days by modifying many of Florus's dates for the commemoration of saints' feasts.[8] In his preface, Ado credits these changes to a "venerable and ancient martyrology," a remarkable document that takes us to the heart of a compelling Carolingian image of Rome:

> In order that the feast days of martyrs should be recorded most accurately (since, as is known, these days tend to be confused in calendars), I had recourse for my work to a venerable and very ancient martyrology (*venerabile et perantiquum martyrologium*) sent from the city of Rome by the Roman pope to a certain holy bishop in Aquilea and afterwards loaned to

> me by a certain devout monk for a few days. And since I had transcribed it with diligent care while I was in Ravenna, I thought it best to place it at the beginning of this work.[9]

As promised, Ado supplies, as a preface to his own martyrology, the text of this other martyrology, by means of which, so he claims, he was able to achieve his desired result of a more complete and more definitive martyrology (Plate 21).[10] This "Roman Martyrology" (as the text calls itself, and as I refer to it hereafter) is a martyrology for the entire year with succinct notices that record the names, places, and dates of saints or groups of saints.[11] A typical entry is that for the Kalends of April (April 1): "At Rome, [commemorative feast] of Theodora, sister of the martyr Hermes, martyred under Aurelian, buried on the via Salaria."[12] Its extreme brevity notwithstanding, this Roman Martyrology serves as the backbone for Ado's own martyrology, corroborating its dates and other questionable "historicizing" snippets of information.

Ado claims a prestigious pedigree for the Roman Martyrology; it is, he tells us, a "venerable and very ancient martyrology," emanating from the city of Rome, authorized by the pope himself, and transcribed in Ado's own hand. As meticulously demonstrated by the philologist Henri Quentin in the early twentieth century, however, this martyrology is not what it purports to be.[13] A careful analysis of the text (which in manuscripts is always found alongside Ado's martyrology) revealed that the Roman Martyrology is *not* an ancient Roman document, but rather Ado's fabrication, constructed to justify the editorial decisions, particularly the choice of dates, he made in his own martyrology.

Yet the Roman Martyrology should not be disregarded as a useless "fake." Instead, this document can provide insight into the making of the idea and ideal of a Christian Rome. As we shall see, Ado did not callously or ignorantly construct his Roman Martyrology. Ado was also the author of a universal chronicle: a history of the world in six ages from the creation of the world to 870, based on Bede's chronicle, but also incorporating a variety of early Christian, late antique, and Frankish sources.[14] Ado put this knowledge to use in composing the Roman Martyrology. Accordingly we may read this work as a learned ninth-century attempt to reconstruct the cult of saints as venerated in late antique Rome.

Ado's Sources: Building Rome from a Carolingian Perspective

To construct his Roman Martyrology and expand the number of saints found in Florus's martyrology, Ado drew on a variety of sources, in particular the Bible and a selection of hagiographical texts.[15] His technique was guided by two principles that were generally characteristic of the Carolingians and their relationship to Rome: a confidence in the written word and an attentiveness to saints' names, relics, and Roman topography as convincing evidence regarding their cults. The result was a portrait of Christian sanctity rooted in biblical and Roman history, but filtered through the Carolingian historical imagination—and often shifted around a bit to fill in empty days.

In forging their empire, both Charlemagne and his successor, Louis the Pious, had championed a reform (*correctio*) of Christian society.[16] Among the lasting effects of this program, the so-called Carolingian Renaissance, was the production of more standardized, "correct" texts. For "correct" texts were seen as the means to achieving "correct" religious observance—"correct" as measured against a rather elusive "Roman" norm. Correcting texts involved not only the standardization of grammar, orthography, and script but also an attentiveness to establishing consistent and definitive texts. This interest in collecting, comparing, and standardizing texts is most apparent with respect to the Bible, which was increasingly copied as a single volume with uniform texts arranged in an established order. Yet the same impulse extended to a much wider genre of texts. Although one should not overemphasize the degree of uniformity achieved, increasingly stable texts began to circulate, in turn bolstering confidence in the written word. Ado's project drew on this Carolingian legacy of the authoritative text.

Many of the new names added by Ado to the Roman Martyrology derive from the Old and New Testaments. Although earlier martyrologies had included key figures from these texts, Ado significantly widened the selection. A favorable mention of an individual in the Bible, however brief, was sufficient proof of his or her sanctity; so, for example, Ado includes the centurion Cornelius in Caesarea, whose conversion by Christ is described in the Acts of the Apostles, and Joanna, the wife of Chuza, manager of Herod's household, who is mentioned among the women cured by Christ.[17] Furthermore, Ado was generally content to locate these individuals where the Bible had mentioned them; for example, Cornelius's feast is located "at Caesarea." Not uncommonly, as in the case of Cornelius, Ado renders these individuals bishops of their city before their death.

Ado followed a similar method in exploiting patristic sources, above all Eusebius/Rufinus's ecclesiastical history and Jerome's *De viris illustribus*. Also available to Ado was the *Liber Pontificalis*, a text that circulated widely in the Carolingian world and whose lives, in tallying the extensive constructions and restorations undertaken by successive popes, presented ever-grander portraits of Rome as a sacred city filled with a great diversity of saints.[18] Because Bede and Florus had already made good use of versions of the *Liber Pontificalis*, both to include notices for Roman popes and feasts celebrated in Rome, this text provided Ado with little new material for his Roman Martyrology.[19] Nonetheless, in expanding the notices for Roman popes in his own martyrology (especially in the second recension), Ado frequently had recourse to the *Liber Pontificalis*. Furthermore, in accepting Rome and the papacy as arbitrators of Christian sanctity, Ado's Roman Martyrology was generally indebted to the vision of papal Rome proffered by the *Liber Pontificalis*.

In addition to these biblical and ecclesiastical writings, equally important to Ado's project were hagiographical texts. In particular, as demonstrated by Quentin, Ado clearly had access to one or more passionaries, that is, collected volumes of hagiographical texts. These provided him with the *passiones* of about 90 different saints.[20] Such passionaries reflected the particular Carolingian interest in collecting and standardizing saints' legends. Before the eighth century these legends generally circulated individually or in smaller collections; there was no official collection, whether in Rome or elsewhere. Starting in the later eighth and early ninth centuries, however, Carolingian scribes increasingly began to gather saints' legends under one cover. Many of these Frankish passionaries collected materials from Rome (often termed, misleadingly, by later scholars, the *gesta martyrum*).[21] In addition to forming the beginnings of a corpus of Roman hagiography, this process of transmission was influential in establishing more standardized versions of saints' *passiones*.

The passionary (or passionaries) Ado used closely resembles many of the earliest surviving Frankish passionaries.[22] Available to Ado was material associated with Roman saints in the broadest sense, ranging from Rome's well-known martyrs, such as Cecilia and Sebastian, to the Latin translations of Greek *passiones* of saints venerated in Rome, such as Cosmas and Damian or the Forty Martyrs of Sebaste. Ado treated these texts as authoritative, that is, as faithfully reflecting early Christian traditions. Thus, as with biblical sources, he felt confident in mining these *passiones* to extract as many names of saints as possible—each of whom he allotted a feast day. Furthermore, as Ado describes in the preface to his martyrology (cited earlier), the notices of his martyrology also included lengthy excerpts from these saints' *passiones*.

In working with his different sources Ado was often confronted by discrepancies and contradictions. Since he was unwilling to disregard the testimony of sources that he considered authoritative, he attempted to resolve these difficulties by reinterpreting them, guided, above all, by two key, if sometimes contested, features of Carolingian piety: names and relics.

In her work on Jerome's martyrology, Felice Lifshitz demonstrated the emergence, especially from the late eighth century onward, of a Carolingian-specific "name-centered piety"—a belief that the very names of saints, almost as if a form of contact relic, provided access to a saint.[23] Accordingly, there was an increasing enthusiasm for recording and reciting saints' names, for example in litanies of saints' names, a genre that proliferated throughout the later eighth and ninth centuries.

Alongside (and potentially in competition with) this veneration of saints through their names, veneration of relics gained in popularity throughout the later eighth and ninth centuries. As we saw in Chapter 7, Carolingians were keen to take advantage of the portable nature of this form of sanctity, embracing relics as a means of cementing bonds between individuals and communities. Particularly reliable in this regard were *Roman* relics, because their authenticity and efficacy were assured by early Christian tradition and papal approval. In their eager acquisition of Roman relics for monasteries and churches back home, Frankish luminaries reinforced the image of Rome as a source of relics.

In constructing the Roman Martyrology, Ado was attentive to both names and relics as the means of synthesizing his sources. This is exemplified by the case of the martyr Gorgonius. Ado's source, Florus, had included a notice for a certain Gorgonius at Rome, without further details, on September 9. Ado was unfamiliar with this tradition, but knew of the Nicomedian martyrs, Gorgonius, Dorotheus, and Peter, mentioned in Eusebius/Rufinus's *Ecclesiastical History*. Given their identical names, Ado felt justified in identifying Florus's Gorgonius as the Nicomedian martyr of the same name. But how to explain the discrepancy in locations? The logical solution for Ado was a translation of relics. Thus, on September 9, the Roman Martyrology announces, "At Nicomedia, Dorotheus and Gorgonius martyrs, of whom one, that is Gorgonius, was translated to Rome."[24] A translation of relics readily explained how a saint once associated with Nicomedia had been co-opted by Rome.

Alongside names and relics, Ado was also interested in ecclesiastical dedications in Rome as a reliable source regarding saints' cults. In contrast to the extensive selection of hagiographical texts available to him, however, Ado does not seem to have used many sources on Roman topography. There is no evidence that he used the Einsiedeln compilation, whose detailed itineraries through Rome enumerate many of Rome's churches, nor any other such detailed guide to Rome; instead his information generally derives from earlier martyrologies, combined with vague reports about the city. Likewise, Ado does not seem to have made use of sacramentaries, again extracting information about where saints' feasts were celebrated primarily from earlier martyrologies.

Nonetheless, throughout his martyrology, Roman topography does appear as a basis for Ado's synthesis of his materials. For example, Florus's martyrology, based on the Gregorian sacramentary, had included a notice for the feast day of St. John the Apostle at his church in Rome at the Porta Latina; meanwhile, Bede's chronicle told of John the Apostle's submersion in boiling oil, but had not specified where this occurred.[25] Ado connected the dots, and his notice in the Roman Martyrology reads, "St. John the Apostle, who at the Porta Latina was cast into a jar of boiling oil," while his own martyrology narrates the story at greater length.[26] In this way Ado recast his sources to foreground Rome as a city of churches, relics, and feasts, safeguarded by Roman popes: a matrix of ecclesiastical precedents for western Christendom.

The Result: A Universalizing Rome

What we have in the Roman Martyrology, then, is a well-researched guide to the cult of saints in late antique Rome based on biblical, ecclesiastical, and hagiographical sources, but refracted through a particular Carolingian approach to saints' cults, focused primarily on names and relics and, to a lesser degree, on ecclesiastical dedications in Rome. The result is a universalizing portrait of Rome that resembles, but far magnifies the Rome that we have seen developing in previous chapters. The Roman Church is presented as a reference point for the commemoration of a diverse panoply of sanctity centered in Rome but extending across the Mediterranean world and even stretching its tentacles farther afield. Ado's conception of Rome derives from these papal efforts to consolidate the city's sanctity, but he has transformed this Rome from city to idea. Rome is a storehouse of universal sanctity, a portable resource that can be transferred away from the city to new locations.

In total, the Roman Martyrology contains about 600 saints, groups of saints, or other liturgical feasts. Most of these notices are associated with a specific location, none of which rivals Rome. Saints or feasts are associated with Rome more than 100 times in the martyrology—and many more saints are associated with specific streets or cemeteries in Rome, without mention of the city itself.[27] Yet alongside Rome, a myriad of distant regions and cities fill the martyrology. Prominent are the apostolic sees of Alexandria (mentioned twenty-six times) and Antioch (mentioned twenty-three times). Repeated mentions are also made of Nicomedia (thirteen mentions), the capital of the East before Constantinople; "Africa" (thirteen mentions); the holy city of Jerusalem (eight mentions); and Constantinople (six mentions).

As these cursory statistics suggest, the Roman Martyrology presents a Mediterranean portrait of sanctity; roughly 50 saints are associated, respectively, with cities in the regions of Italy (excluding Rome), Africa, Asia Minor, and the Levant; roughly 25 are associated with Greece.[28] The ancient and late antique centers of these regions recur most frequently; in addition to the cities just mentioned, saints are repeatedly associated in Italy with Ravenna, Milan, and Aquileia; in Africa with Carthage; in Greece with Athens, Thessaloniki, and Corinth; and in the East with Constantinople, Smyrna, Caesarea in Cappadocia, and Caesarea in Palestine.[29]

While by far the majority of saints in the Roman Martyrology are associated with locations around the Mediterranean, its reach also extends farther afield; in the East as far as Armenia and Persia (mentioned six times); in the West, to Spain (at least six mentions in different locations), southern France, and a sprinkling of more distant northern locations, such as an entry for St. Afra in Raetia or for the bishop St. Patrick, "who first preached among the Scots."[30] Most notices are for saints from apostolic or imperial times, but, as the example of Patrick demonstrates, the Roman Martyrology presents a Church that is continually growing and that can also continue to grow—thereby justifying the inclusion of more contemporary and northern/western saints in the expanded martyrology to which Ado attached his own name.

Codifying Christian Sanctity: Ado's Martyrology and the Romanization of Saints

Armed with the authority of the Roman Martyrology, Ado could construct his own martyrology with confidence and poise. In contrast to the extreme brevity of the Roman Martyrology, Ado's martyrology contains extensive excerpts from saints' *passiones* and supplementary explanations regarding their cults. By gathering together his sources, filling in "empty" days, and resolving inconsistencies, Ado aimed to create a definitive martyrology: accurate in that it was based on Roman tradition and complete in that it included saints for every day of the year. We can watch this process and trace its results by returning once more to the saints discussed in the previous chapters, focusing on Ado's attempts to establish a single, definitive interpretation of their cults. Ado's approach to these saints varied, depending on what information he had at hand and the degree to which they had become associated with Rome. In general, however, we may characterize his as a "maximizing" view of Rome that eliminated discrepancies, but not saints.

Most of the saints we encountered in the preceding chapters were already included, albeit usually with only very brief notices, in Ado's template, Florus's martyrology. These were fairly straightforward saints for Ado to work with. When Ado had available to him a saint's *passio*, he was able to expand his martyrology with additional information about the saint, but he retained (or only slightly modified) the basic coordinates provided by Florus. The Roman Martyrology includes the feasts of the child martyr Vitus, the soldier-saint Theodore, and the soldier-saints Sergius and Bacchus on the same dates as recorded in Florus's martyrology, but Ado's martyrology also supplements Florus's laconic notices for these saints with excerpts from their *passiones* describing their martyrdom and the subsequent fate of their relics.[31] Similarly, the Roman Martyrology includes the feast of the Forty Martyrs of Sebaste—although shifted two days later than in Florus's martyrology (to fill in an "empty" day)—and Ado's martyrology contains an excerpt from the saints' *passio*.[32] With little difficulty Ado was thus able to render his martyrology more complete.

A subtle (and perhaps unintentional) change can be detected in Ado's treatment of the Terracinan martyr, St. Caesarius. Bede's martyrology (725–731) contained a notice for St. Caesarius, including a short excerpt from his *passio* telling how Caesarius, coming to Terracina, had protested the worship of idols in public, had caused a temple to crumble, and had been martyred.[33] Bede's excerpt was copied by Florus and then by Ado (from Florus).[34] The Roman Martyrology, in contrast, announces, "At Rome [the feast] of Caesarius the deacon," thereby associating Caesarius's cult with Rome—a tradition that, as discussed in Chapter 7, is found in other Carolingian martyrologies.[35]

Ado's impulse to associate saints with Rome is more clearly evident in his treatment of the Quattro Coronati. Here, addition and omission of material render the saints more Roman. Florus's martyrology (following Bede) announced November 8 as the feast, at Rome, of the Quattro Coronati, namely, as Florus specifies, Claudius, Nicostratus, Simpronianus, Castorius, and Simplicius (how five saints can be the "Four Crowned Ones" is not explained).[36] Available to Ado was the *passio* that told of Claudius, Nicostratus, Simpronianus, Castorius, and Simplicius as stonemasons, martyred in Pannonia, who were subsequently venerated in Rome by papal fiat as a way of commemorating the unknown soldier-saints who were martyred in Rome two years after the deaths of the stonemasons (see Chapter 6). Selectively using this *passio*—and legitimizing his new version by means of the Roman Martyrology—Ado, in his martyrology, includes two sets of Roman saints on November 8: at Rome, the feast of Claudius, Nicostratus, Simpronianus, Castorius, and Simplicius, stonemasons martyred under Diocletian, and, on the same day, the feast of the Quattro Coronati, soldiers who refused to sacrifice and were subsequently buried on the via Labicana next to the five stonemasons.[37] For each group of saints Ado includes an excerpt from the *passio*, but omits any mention of Pannonia. Ado's account instead implies that all nine saints were martyred and commemorated in Rome.

When Ado knew of an ecclesiastical dedication for a saint in Rome he might mention it in his martyrology or use it to extrapolate further conclusions about a saint's cult. Ado's entry for the physician-saints from Aegeae, Cosmas and Damian (whose feast Florus had included but without further comment), includes a lengthy excerpt from the saints' *passio* chronicling their martyrdom and the burial of their bodies not far from Aegeae. Then Ado concludes the entry with this comment: "Rome still solemnly keeps the memory of the two brothers Cosmas and Damian in a shining temple built in their name."[38]

Ado was likewise familiar with the nearby church for St. Hadrian on the Forum Romanum, which he mentions as the starting point for processions on Marian feast days.[39] Because of this church Ado felt justified in inferring the translation of Hadrian's relics to Rome. Florus had included a brief notice for Hadrian, but Ado had access to Hadrian's *passio*, which told of the translation of Hadrian's relics from Nicomedia to Constantinople.[40] Ado added an excerpt from this *passio* to his martyrology and furthermore explains, "Not long thereafter the body of the blessed Hadrian was translated again to Rome and there was also furnished with an honorable church."[41] This attempt to connect all information regarding Hadrian's cult is carried further in a later version of Ado's martyrology (likely completed after Ado's death). An alternative tradition, found in Jerome's martyrology, recorded the date of Hadrian's *passio* as March 4; the revision of Ado's martyrology incorporates this date as that of Hadrian's death, but retains the notice for Hadrian on September 8, interpreting this as the date of the feast commemorating Hadrian's burial in Rome, rather than his death.[42] Thus all traditions regarding Hadrian are subsumed into one version, focused on Rome.

Roman tradition could also serve as a way for Ado to bolster the authority of his martyrology, as apparent in his treatment of St. George. Ado had available Florus's martyrology's brief entry for George, the *Decretum Gelasianum*'s condemnation of the *passio* of George as apocryphal, and the story of Pope Zacharias's miraculous discovery of the head of St. George in the Lateran, as recounted by the *Liber Pontificalis*.[43] Evidently the *Liber Pontificalis* provided the clinching piece of evidence for Ado: the Roman Martyrology contains a notice for George without further comment, and Ado's own martyrology clarifies that "although the deeds of his martyrdom are reckoned among the apocryphal writings, nevertheless the Church of God venerably honors his illustrious martyrdom among the crowns of martyrs" (a verdict repeated verbatim by Notker in his martyrology, as we saw in Chapter 7).[44] The second recension of Ado's martyrology (carried out by Ado himself, to be distinguished from the later version probably carried out after Ado's death) further clarifies this statement by including, on March 15, the *Liber Pontificalis*'s account of Pope Zacharias's discovery of the head of St. George: "At Rome, Zacharias the pope; he presided over Rome for ten years. In his patriarchate he found the head of St. George kept safe in a casket in which he also found a note; this was made out in Greek letters. He [Zacharias] was buried in the church of St. Peter the Apostle."[45] Roman tradition trumped any doubts the *Decretum Gelasianum* raised about the legitimacy of George's cult.

In these examples Ado based his entries on Florus's martyrology. When Ado encountered "new old saints"—that is, saints of the imperial persecution not included in Florus's martyrology—he was able to proceed more freely in interpreting a saint's cult—but was also more obliged to justify his decisions by means of the Roman Martyrology. For example, he added certain saints to the Roman Martyrology and, in turn, to his own martyrology without further ado. On January 1, the Roman Martyrology announces the feast of the Roman martyr St. Martina (not included in Florus's martyrology), and Ado's martyrology includes Martina's feast and an excerpt from her *passio*.[46]

More imaginative is Ado's treatment of saints who were more tangentially related to Rome. In such cases, Ado proceeded, by the logic of names, relics, and Rome-centered piety, to introduce a new saint into his martyrology. A good example of this approach is the cult of St. Boniface of Tarsus, a saint unknown to Florus but whose *passio* was available to Ado. The Roman Martyrology includes a notice for Boniface on June 5: "[Commemorative feast] of Boniface the martyr. Martyred in Tarsus on the 14th day in the month of May. Buried in Rome on the Nones of June [June 5]."[47] Ado's own martyrology correspondingly includes Boniface's feast on June 5 and provides a lengthy extract from Boniface's *passio*. Behind this seemingly simple entry we can identify a number of bold editorial decisions made by Ado.

In choosing June 5 as Boniface's feast date, Ado privileges the date of Boniface's burial in Rome over that of his martyrdom in Tarsus. Thus the location of Boniface's relics, in Rome, takes precedence over the event of Boniface's martyrdom in Tarsus. Moreover, although the choice of June 5 as Boniface's feast day has parallels in other sources, as Quentin suggests, it likely also derives from the presence of the more well-known, homonymous, missionizing St. Boniface on the same day.[48] By the logic of "name-centered piety" this was an appropriate day for the feast of St. Boniface of Tarsus. A later revision of Ado's martyrology (likely completed after Ado's death) further neatens and clarifies this situation by providing a brief notice for Boniface on May 14 that refers the reader to the notice on June 5.[49] This later version also clarifies the status of June 5 by changing the notice from "natale sancti Bonifacii" (birthday, that is, martyrdom of St. Boniface) to the vaguer, more accurate, "festivitas sancti Bonifacii" (feast of St. Boniface).[50]

Reorienting the cult of Sabina and Serapia to Rome required still more heavy-handed textual intervention. Florus's martyrology (following Roman liturgical sources) contained a brief notice for St. Sabina, "virgin and martyr," on the Aventine on August 29, but did not include Serapia.[51] Ado, however, had available the *passio* of Sts. Sabina and Serapia.[52] This *passio*, as we saw in Chapter 5, tells of both Serapia and Sabina and plays out in the *oppidum Vendinensium*; it is there, at the *arcus Faustini*, that Sabina is buried. The *passio* makes no mention of Rome nor of the Aventine and furthermore presents Sabina as a matron, not a virgin. To resolve these contradictions Ado intrepidly melded his sources together, linking the saints firmly to Rome. The Roman Martyrology includes two notices for these saints, both situated in Rome: on August 29, "At Rome, at the *arcus Faustini*, [commemorative feast] of Sabina the martyr," and on September 3, "At Rome, [commemorative feast] of Serapia the virgin, martyred four days before the Kalends of August [July 29], buried on the day before the Kalends of August [July 31], but the memory of whose passion is more celebrated three days before the Nones of September [Sept. 3]."[53] Ado's martyrology contains extended entries for both these saints, based on their *passiones*.[54] The result is two neatly ordered entries for two Roman saints.

In this way, throughout his martyrology Ado attempted to fit together all the information available to him into a Rome-centered vision of Christian sanctity. In merging his sources to create a comprehensive guide to Christian sanctity, Ado's portrait of Rome's saints is a fully formed and timeless universalizing Rome. Christian Rome, we are led to believe, had always venerated saints from around the Mediterranean. Missing are the complexities and idiosyncrasies that accompanied the development of these cults in Rome. Absent is any sense of the particular communities that had promoted these cults in Rome, such as the *diaconia* of S. Giorgio al Velabro, whose promotion of George predated Pope Zacharias's cooption of the cult, or the Greek-speaking community on the Aventine that had proudly showcased its relics of St. Boniface. Absent too are the many phases that accompanied these cults' progressive Romanization; from Ado's martyrology we would never know that the *passiones* of Cosmas and Damian, Sergius and Bacchus, Hadrian, George, and Boniface were composed in Greek and only subsequently translated into Latin. In creating a universal Christian city, Ado flattened the history of late antique and early medieval Rome, absorbing saints and legends with complex backstories into an orderly, ageless, and easily transportable portrait of universal sanctity.

All the Saints at Home in Rome

Ado's most decisive—and most audacious—revision was his entry for November 1. In addition to listing the feast of St. Caesarius on this day, Florus's martyrology had also included an entry for a "Feast of All Saints." In accordance with its universalizing aspirations, Ado's martyrology likewise includes this entry for the universal collectivity of saints. Ado records the dedication of the Pantheon in Rome to the Virgin Mary and all the saints, closely following Florus's text, as can be observed by the italics that here indicate the additions made by Ado to the text of Florus:

> The Feast of All Saints. For on the request of Pope Boniface the Emperor Phocas ordered that in the old temple which was called the Pantheon—*and*

> *which was first constructed by Domitian*—the filth of idolatry be swept away and a church of the blessed and ever virgin Mary and all the martyrs be made, so that where once was held the cult of all, not gods, but demons, there from then on would be instituted the commemoration of all saints.[55]

Not content with this description, however, Ado adds to it, supplementing Florus with a more explicit correlation between the construction of a Roman church dedicated to all the saints and the Carolingian origins of the feast for all the saints (again italics here indicate Ado's additions to the text of Florus):

> *which from that time onwards, on the Kalends of November, in the city* Rome, *was celebrated and* common to all. *But also in Gaul, since Pope Gregory urged for its sacred commemoration, the most pious emperor Louis, with the agreement of all the bishops of his kingdom and Empire, established that the feast of all saints be solemnly commemorated on the above-named day, yearly in perpetuity. And, just as though it was a sacred decree, the whole Church undertook [it] with reverent love.*[56]

There is no contemporary evidence to support Ado's explanation for the Roman origins of the yearly Feast of All Saints. To the contrary, it seems that the feast on November 1 was unknown in early ninth-century Rome but was celebrated and promoted by prominent Carolingian ecclesiastics as early as the late eighth century.[57] By associating the feast with the dedication of the Pantheon to all the saints, Florus of Lyon had infused it with an aura of Roman, and imperial, legitimacy; Ado sought to make this relationship more precise. The Feast of All Saints, based on his interpretation, was a long revered Roman feast and so, it must have been, Ado reasons, on the urging of the Roman pontiff, Pope Gregory IV (r. 827–844), and by agreement of the Frankish emperor, Louis the Pious, that the feast came to be celebrated throughout the Carolingian world. The collective commemoration of all Christian sanctity thus had its origins in papal Rome—and by celebrating the date the Carolingian Empire had successfully taken up the mantle of Christian Rome.

* * *

Ado is an example of the Carolingian inventiveness that constructed a comprehensive vision of a universalizing Christian Rome, an idea of Rome that far surpassed the city itself and could be mobilized in new settings far from it. Ado's was a maximizing vision of Rome, but, as we have seen, his codification of Roman sanctity followed the lead of a variety of Carolingian cultural phenomena: the widespread diffusion of the *Liber Pontificalis*; the compilation (and correction) of martyrologies; collections of saints' legends, litanies, and other hagiographical and ecclesiastical sources; an interest in Roman topography; and, above all, a relic- and name-centered piety that eagerly associated saints with Rome. Furthermore, not only did Ado's project draw on and resemble those of his Carolingian contemporaries but his martyrology would also have a lasting legacy in shaping the Western canon of saints.

Ado's martyrology proved to be a highly serviceable document in rendering Roman sanctity an available resource for later audiences throughout western Christendom. It was widely copied, adjusted, and abbreviated; in particular, it served as the basis for Usuard's shorter martyrology, a standard of sorts throughout the Middle Ages.[58] In the late sixteenth century Ado and his Roman Martyrology received renewed and enthusiastic attention as part of the Counter-Reformation efforts to establish an authoritative martyrology for the Catholic Church, spearheaded by Cardinal Baronio. Cardinal Baronio, more famous for his history of the Catholic Church, the *Annales Ecclesiastici*—which sought to demonstrate that despite centuries of change, the Church was nonetheless *semper eadem*, true to its origins—mined historical sources, including Ado's martyrology, in an attempt to resolve discrepancies and establish a single definitive martyrology.[59] Baronio placed great faith in Ado's martyrology; so, on November 1, the new *Martyrologium romanum* follows Ado's interpretation for the Feast of All Saints:

> The feast of all saints, which—once the temple of the Pantheon had been dedicated in honor of the blessed mother of God virgin Mary and the holy martyrs—Pope Boniface IV instituted to be celebrated and common to all, yearly, in the city of Rome. But later Gregory IV also decreed the same feast, which was still celebrated in various ways by different churches, to be solemnly observed in honor of all the saints by the universal Church in perpetuity.[60]

Eliminated are references to emperors: both Phocas and Louis the Pious have disappeared from the text. But the new *Martyrologium romanum* has retained the Roman origins of the feast; it repeats the very phrase introduced by Ado, that Pope Boniface had made the feast "celebrated and common to all" (*celebris et generalis*) in Rome, as well as Ado's explanation that Pope Gregory IV had then decreed its perpetual commemoration by all.

Baronio regretted, however, not having access, among his sources, to the Roman Martyrology, mentioned by Ado in the preface to his text. Accordingly, it was with much fanfare that this text was published by the great Jesuit scholar Heribert Rosweyde, whose work in gathering and editing hagiographical texts would give birth to the encyclopedic task of collecting all texts related to the saints, the *Acta Sanctorum*.[61] Rosweyde's edition of the Roman Martyrology, the *Vetus Romanum Martyrologium*, as he calls it, proudly proclaims in its dedication to Pope Paul V (r. 1605–1621):

> It returns to Rome, MOST HOLY FATHER, that which was once conceived at Rome, which once set out from Rome, which pined for Rome the seat of its origin, that is, the ANCIENT ROMAN MARTYROLOGY, which your predecessors, having collected with great care in the city and written out with unique faith, sent out to the dioceses of the Roman world for the greatest benefit.[62]

And so, we have come full circle as the Roman Martyrology, the idea of Rome as shaped by Ado and his contemporaries, came "home" to Rome, participating, in turn, in new visions of a Christian Rome.

Epilogue

The story of early medieval Rome is the story of a city that enchanted the minds of men and women throughout Christendom. Christian Rome emerged as the embodiment, on earth, of the eternal and universal Church in the heavens above. This story of early medieval Rome was also the story of its many neighborhoods, whose communities, in dialogue with a wider world beyond Rome, built up the city's distinctive repertoire of "universal" sanctity.

This was the story of many stories: the stories of saints whose lives transpired across the Mediterranean and the stories of communities in Rome who made these saints present in the city. On the Forum Romanum administrators who recognized the authority of the emperor in Constantinople dedicated a string of new ecclesiastical foundations. Saints venerated in Constantinople, whose cults stood for imperial unity, modernized the administrative center of Rome. On the Palatine Hill an imperial saint was placed in the imperial palaces.

In more peripheral areas of Rome, at the Tiber bend and on the Aventine Hill, urban aristocrats took the lead in establishing new dedications. These were, for the most part, fairly unassuming private foundations whose dedications reflected their communities' Mediterranean horizons. Immigrants who settled in Rome continued to venerate saints with whom they were familiar; long-term residents sought out new saints from abroad whose patronage offered hope of succor. Some communities chose as their patrons well-known saints with wonder-working powers (such as St. George); others venerated more unusual saints (such as the adulterer-turned-martyr St. Boniface). Even as Rome became progressively more disconnected from the Mediterranean world that had given rise to its cosmopolitan sanctity, these saints left their lasting imprint on the city. Forgotten or erased were the individuals and communities who had brought this diverse sanctity to Rome, but the saints themselves continued to be assiduously cultivated.

* * *

This city of saints was built onto and into the city's past. As we have seen again and again throughout the preceding chapters, the city's pasts remained on view in early medieval Rome. Every time members of the *diaconia* dedicated to St. George walked to the Tiber, they passed by scenes of libation and barbarian prisoners on the adjacent arch. Farther down the Tiber were partially worked marble blocks, brought to Rome from afar in centuries past, but never put to use for new constructions.[1] From atop the Aventine, the Palatine, or the Capitoline, the vista of a dense urban jungle presented itself.

As radically different as the new Christian Rome was, its reference point did not change. Previous centuries—and millennia—had shaped Rome. Volcanic eruptions beginning about two and half million years ago produced a tuff plateau onto which the city would one day be built. Early settlers had found the S-bend of the Tiber that widens and divides around the Tiber island a convenient place to ford the river. The nearby hills were easy to defend; the low-lying plain in between provided an open space to meet, trade, and deliberate. Then Rome expanded and the wealth from distant locations flowed in, monumentalizing the city. Rome became a city of immigrants, an imperial capital, full of unparalleled luxury and desperate poverty side by side. The world was to be found in Rome: "Whatever one does not see here neither did nor does exist," wrote the mid-second-century Greek aristocrat Aelius Aristides in his oration *To Rome*.[2]

The early medieval city remained rooted in this past. The Christian city developed alternate poles on either end: the Vatican and the Lateran. In the later fourth and fifth centuries, the catacombs, the new focus of veneration outside the walls, seemed set to turn the city inside out. This was not to be. Instead, by and large, the much-reduced population maintained the form of the imperial Rome that had preceded it. The Aurelian walls remained intact; the streets deteriorated, but were not abandoned. Neighborhoods contracted and became more rural; temples and baths were left to disintegrate or were dismantled for new projects. Local churches became the nodal points for these more isolated communities. But still the Forum remained a site of public gatherings, the Palatine's imperial rank was not forgotten, the Tiber bend bustled with activity, and the Aventine took pride in its serene isolation. And, most importantly for the history of Rome, despite all the localizing tendencies, these districts made up one city, unified by liturgical processions and by the city's unforgettable name.

More remarkable than the continuity of spaces and the idea of the city was the continuity of the new stories that were grafted onto Christian Rome. In becoming Christian, the city acquired new heroes—above all, Peter and Paul. Through relics, images, and ecclesiastical dedications the stories of its saints were embedded into Rome, bathing the city in blood and victorious redemption. Yet these were stories that remained rooted in Rome's imperial patrimony. Rome's imperial machinery and succession of emperors were presented as a necessary stage on which the city's rise to Christian glory was played out.

Thus the Christian city emerged out of and into the many "Romes" that had preceded it. It took the same shape as what had come before, even as it gave this past new meanings. Out of the monumental remains and lingering imperial associations emerged a new vision for the future, a heavenly city populated with an ever-growing collectivity of Christians. Responsible for this vision were the individuals and communities in Rome who crafted stories about the past and clung to them. Many of these stories were about Romans and Rome. Saints from abroad, as this book has argued, added breadth to these heavenly horizons.

In building a new Rome, these saints from abroad ensured that the expansive geographical imagination that had once characterized imperial Rome became a feature of its Christian instantiation. Whereas a visitor could once have identified the origins of the marble quarried in distant locations as symptomatic of the city's imperial reach, now it was the city's saints who bespoke the far-reaching tentacles of the Christian city. These saints had infused Rome with an inbuilt universality that, when mobilized, whether by ambitious popes or creative thinkers like Ado of Vienne, could be endlessly expanded.

* * *

Ado's portrait of late antique Rome was based on sources but also on his own imagination. The exercise of interpreting the past is always an imaginative one—and I too am conscious that my imagination has contributed to reconstructing early medieval Rome. Perhaps this is the greatest continuity of Rome: its persistent ability to fascinate, its beguiling allure that cannot help but conjure up new stories. Such stories are grounded in the physical city but will always be much more expansive and far-reaching than what was—or could ever be—built in stone.

APPENDIX 1

Saints from Abroad Venerated in Rome, ca. 500–800

Included in this list are saints whose presence in Rome is attested, in the form of ecclesiastical dedications, fresco evidence, or relics, from ca. 500–800. I include all saints who were associated, by their liturgical commemoration, with locations outside Rome. I include saints whose presence is attested earlier than 500 if there is evidence for their continued veneration. Saints are included in the approximate order of their appearance in Rome, although given the extremely fragmentary nature of the evidence, this is no more than a rough and largely speculative ordering. Relics with authentics from the sancta sanctorum are included according to the date of their relic authentics, although as discussed in Chapter 6, these authentics do not necessarily prove that the relics were in Rome at that time. *Diaconiae* are dated to roughly the mid-seventh century (see further Chapter 4). Pictorial cycles including Old and New Testament figures do not warrant the inclusion of these figures; however, when there is evidence for their specific veneration (such as icons or relics), such individuals are included.

This is a conservative list. Only evidence from Rome is included. Names of saints (in particular from frescoes and relic authentics) whose reconstruction is highly speculative, or whose identity is unclear, are not included. Also not included as evidence for the veneration of a saint is Jerome's *Martyrology*, since there is no clear evidence to suggest that this highly problematic text represents a list of saints venerated in Rome.[1] Similarly, the circulation or translation of hagiographical material regarding a saint is not admitted as evidence unless there is very good reason to situate this activity in Rome.[2] More problematic evidence, such as later legends that record the arrival of relics in Rome, is also omitted.

Saint	*Site of Martyrdom (for confessors, site most associated with saint's life)*	*Early Evidence for Veneration in Rome*	*Discussion in Text*
Cyprian	Carthage	*Depositio martyrum* (354); *De locis sanctis martyrum* (mid-7th century); 7th- or 8th-century relic authentic in sancta sanctorum	
Perpetua and Felicity	Carthage	*Depositio martyrum* (354)	
Nereus and Achilleus	Terracina	Pope Damasus (d. 384) epigram; *diaconia*	mentioned in Ch. 1
Clement	Cherson (Crimea)	church at least by late 4th century; association with Cherson later	
Gervasius, Protasius, Vitalis	Milan	Pope Innocent (d. 417) dedicates church (LP)	
Stephen	Jerusalem	frequently attested at least from mid-5th century onward	mentioned in Ch. 1
John the Evangelist	Ephesus	Pope Hilarius (d. 468) dedicates oratory at Lateran (LP)	mentioned in Ch. 6
John the Baptist	Palestine	Pope Hilarius (d. 468) dedicates oratory at Lateran (LP)	mentioned in Ch. 6
Andrew	Patras; cult in Constantinople	Pope Simplicius (d. 483) dedicates church (LP); frequently attested thereafter	mentioned in Ch. 1
Nicander	Campania	Pope Gelasius (d. 496) dedicates church (LP); Theodotus's dedicatory inscription (755)	
Martin	Tours	Pope Symmachus (d. 514) dedicates church (LP); *diaconiae*; monastery prior to late 7th century	mentioned in Ch. 6
Apollinaris	Ravenna	Pope Symmachus (d. 514) dedicates oratory (LP); Pope Honorius (d. 638) dedicates church (LP)	mentioned in Ch. 1
Agatha	Catania	Pope Symmachus (d. 514) dedicates church (LP); *diaconia*	
Cassian	Imola (near Ravenna)	Pope Symmachus (d. 514) dedicates altar (LP)	
Sossius	Misenum (Bay of Naples)	Pope Symmachus (d. 514) dedicates oratory (LP)	
Thomas	Edessa	Pope Symmachus (d. 514) dedicates oratory (LP)	

Cosmas and Damian	Aegeae (Cilicia)	Pope Symmachus (d. 514) dedicates oratory (LP); Pope Felix IV (d. 530) dedicates church (LP)	discussion in Ch. 2
Theodore	Euchaïta (Pontus)	early 6th-century mosaic in SS. Cosma e Damiano; *diaconia*	discussion in Ch.2
George	Lydda/Diospolis (Palestine)	6th-century Porta Appia inscription; *diaconia*	discussion in Ch. 4
Conon	Pamphylia or Cyprus	6th-century Porta Appia inscription	mentioned in Ch. 4
James and Philip, apostles	Jerusalem; Hierapolis (Phrygia)	Pope Pelagius I (d. 561) begins church (LP)	
Seven Maccabean brothers	Antioch (Syria)	Pope Pelagius I (d. 561) or Pope Pelagius II (d. 590) places relics in S. Pietro in Vincoli; 7th-century fresco in S. Maria Antiqua	
Chrysogonus	Aquileia	*titulus* dedicated to saint before synod of 599	mentioned in Ch. 1
Anastasia	Sirmium (Pannonia) or Palmaria (island just off the Ligurian coast)	Palmarian saint associated with Chyrsogonus; *titulus* dedicated to saint prior to 8th century, probably much earlier	mentioned in Ch. 1
Menas	Phrygia; Alexandrian cult	church by the time of Gregory the Great (d. 604)	
Leucius	Brindisi	monastery by the time of Gregory the Great (d. 604)	
Januarius	Benevento	oratory by the time of Gregory the Great (d. 604)	
Lucy	Syracuse	monastery by the time of Gregory the Great (d. 604); Pope Honorius (d. 638) dedicates church (LP); *diaconia*; 7th- or 8th-century relic authentic in sancta sanctorum; 8th- century inscription in S. Nicola in Carcere	mentioned in Ch. 4
Caesarius	Terracina	oratory on Palatine Hill by the time of Gregory the Great (d. 604)	discussion in Ch. 3
Severinus	Noricum	Pope Gregory the Great (d. 604) dedicates church with relics	

(*continued*)

Saint	*Site of Martyrdom (for confessors, site most associated with saint's life)*	*Early Evidence for Veneration in Rome*	*Discussion in Text*
Demetrius	Thessaloniki	late 6th- to mid-7th-century fresco in S. Maria Antiqua	
Forty Martyrs of Sebaste	Sebaste (Lesser Armenia)	7th-century fresco in Oratory of the Forty Martyrs; mid-7th- to 8th-century fresco in S. Maria Antiqua	discussion in Ch. 2
John Chrysostom	Pontus; archbishop of Constantinople	late 7th-century apse fresco in S. Maria Antiqua; mid-8th-century panorama fresco in S. Maria Antiqua	mentioned in Chs. 2 and 6
Gregory	Nazianzus (Cappadocia)	late 7th-century apse fresco in S. Maria Antiqua; mid-8th-century panorama fresco in S. Maria Antiqua; church in Catalogue of 807 (LP)	mentioned in Chs. 2 and 6
Basil	Caesarea in Cappadocia	late 7th-century apse fresco in S. Maria Antiqua; mid-8th-century panorama fresco in S. Maria Antiqua	mentioned in Chs. 2 and 6
Euphemia	Chalcedon	church prior to Pope Sergius (d. 701) (LP)	
Hadrian	Nicomedia	Pope Honorius (d. 638) dedicates church (LP)	discussion in Ch. 2
Quattro Coronati (Simpronianus, Claudius, Nicostratus, Castorius, Simplicius)	Sirmium (Pannonia)	Pope Honorius (d. 638) dedicates church (LP); earlier evidence for veneration of similarly named saints	discussion in Ch. 6
Venantius, Domnius, Maurus, Anastasius, Septimius, Asterius, Antiochianus, Gaianus, Paulinianus, Tellius	Dalmatia and Istria	Pope John IV (d. 642) dedicates church (LP)	discussion in Ch. 6
Vincent	Saragossa	feast in *Capitulare Evangeliorum* (Π)	
Elisha (Eliseus)	Sebastia (Palestine)	feast in *Capitulare Evangeliorum* (Π)	

Timothy	Ephesus	feast in *Capitulare Evangeliorum* (Π)	
Euplus	Catania	Pope Theodore (d. 649) dedicates oratory (LP); Theodotus's dedicatory inscription (755)	
Anastasius	Persia	monastery in *De locis sanctis martyrum* (mid-7th century)	mentioned in Chs. 1 and 5
Quirinus/Cyrinus	Sesica (Dalmatia)	*Notitia*; *De locis sanctis martyrum* (mid-7th century)	
Sabas	Kidron Valley (Palestine)	monastery founded in mid-7th century; mid-8th-century panorama fresco in S. Maria Antiqua	mentioned in Chs. 5 and 6
Vitus	Lucania	*diaconia*; monastery prior to Pope Stephen III (d. 762) (LP)	mentioned in Introduction and Ch. 1
Sergius and Bacchus	Resafa/Sergiopolis (Syria)	*diaconiae*; Pope Gregory III (d. 741) restores *diaconia* by St. Peter's (LP); 8th-century relic authentic in sancta sanctorum	discussion in Ch. 2
Boniface	Tarsus	*diaconia*; William of Malmesbury's *Gesta regum anglorum* (based on later 7th-century model); *Istae vero ecclesiae* (late 8th century)	discussion in Ch. 5
Erasmus	Formia	monastery by the time of Pope Adeodatus (d. 676); early 8th-century frescos in S. Maria in Via Lata; Theodotus's dedicatory inscription (755); mid-8th-century panorama fresco in S. Maria Antiqua	mentioned in Ch. 1
Cyrus and John	Canopus; cult in Menouthis (near Alexandria)	early 8th-century frescoes in S. Maria Antiqua; Latin translation of Sophronius's *Miracles* (as early as the late 7th century)	
Sabina and Serapia	*oppidum Vendinensium* (location uncertain)	fresco from time of Pope Constantine (r. 708–715)	discussion in Ch. 5
Augustine	Hippo	early 8th-century fresco in apse of S. Maria Antiqua	mentioned in Ch. 3

(continued)

Saint	Site of Martyrdom (for confessors, site most associated with saint's life)	Early Evidence for Veneration in Rome	Discussion in Text
Martin	Cherson (Crimea)	early 8th-century fresco in apse of S. Maria Antiqua	mentioned in Ch. 3
Celsus	Milan	early 8th-century fresco in Chapel of Physicians in S. Maria Antiqua; Theodotus's dedicatory inscription (755)	
Dometius	Phrygia or Syria	early 8th-century fresco in Chapel of Physicians in S. Maria Antiqua; Theodotus's dedicatory inscription (755)	
Pantaleon (Panteleemon)	Nicomedia	early 8th-century fresco in Chapel of Physicians in S. Maria Antiqua; Theodotus's dedicatory inscription (755)	
Procopius	Caesarea in Palestine	early 8th-century fresco in Chapel of Physicians in S. Maria Antiqua; Theodotus's dedicatory inscription (755)	
Anne (mother of Mary); Elizabeth (mother of John the Baptist)		8th-century fresco in S. Maria Antiqua; Theodotus's dedicatory inscription (755)	
Barbara	Nicomedia	8th-century fresco in S. Maria Antiqua	
Amos (prophet)	Palestine	7th- or 8th-century century relic authentic in sancta sanctorum	mentioned in Ch. 6
Constantine	cult in Constantinople	7th- or 8th-century century relic authentic in sancta sanctorum	mentioned in Ch. 6
Martha	Bethany (Palestine)	7th- or 8th-century century relic authentic in sancta sanctorum	
Isaac	Palestine	7th- or 8th-century century relic authentic in sancta sanctorum	
Aldigund	Maubeuge (northern France)	7th- or 8th-century century relic authentic in sancta sanctorum	mentioned in Ch. 6

Michael the archangel	archangel	7th- or 8th-century century relic authentic in sancta sanctorum; Theodotus's dedicatory inscription (755)	mentioned in Ch. 1
Cornelius the Centurion	Caesarea in Palestine	8th-century century relic authentic in sancta sanctorum	
Arsenius	Constantinople	8th-century century relic authentic in sancta sanctorum	
Gabriel the archangel	archangel	Theodotus's dedicatory inscription (755)	
Twelve Apostles (Peter, Paul, Andrew, James, John, Thomas, James, Philip, Bartholomew, Matthew, Simon, Thaddeus)		Theodotus's dedicatory inscription (755); included in *communicantes* prayer in the Roman canon of the mass	
Donatus	Arezzo	Theodotus's dedicatory inscription (755); Pope Leo III (d. 816) dedicates monastery (LP)	
Nicholas	Myra (Lycia)	Theodotus's dedicatory inscription (755); mid-8th-century panorama fresco in S. Maria Antiqua; 8th-century relic authentic in sancta sanctorum; *diaconia*	discussion in Ch. 4
Christopher	Antioch (Syria)	Theodotus's dedicatory inscription (755)	
Anthimius, Leontius, Euprepius (companions/relatives of Cosmas and Damian)	Aegeae (Cilicia)	Theodotus's dedicatory inscription (755)	
Antipa	Pergamon	Theodotus's dedicatory inscription (755)	
Athanasia, Theoctiste, Eudoxia (Christian martyrs whom Cyrus and John support)	Canopus; cult in Menouthis (near Alexandria)	Theodotus's dedicatory inscription (755)	
Dionysius	Paris	Pope Stephen II (d. 757) brings back relics from Francia	
Quiricus and Julitta	Tarsus	mid-8th-century frescoes in Theodotus Chapel in S. Maria Antiqua	mentioned in Ch. 1

(*continued*)

Saint	*Site of Martyrdom (for confessors, site most associated with saint's life)*	*Early Evidence for Veneration in Rome*	*Discussion in Text*
Peter	Alexandria	mid-8th-century panorama fresco in S. Maria Antiqua	
Cyril	Alexandria	mid-8th-century panorama fresco in S. Maria Antiqua	mentioned in Ch. 6
Epiphanius	Constantia/ Salamis (Cyprus)	mid-8th-century panorama fresco in S. Maria Antiqua	
Athanasius	Alexandria	mid-8th-century panorama fresco in S. Maria Antiqua	mentioned in Ch. 6
Euthymius	Palestine	mid-8th-century panorama fresco in S. Maria Antiqua	mentioned in Ch. 6
Mammes	Caesarea in Cappadocia	mid-8th-century panorama fresco in S. Maria Antiqua	
Simeon and Anna (Luke 2:25–36)	Jerusalem	8th-century inscription in S. Nicola in Carcere	mentioned in Ch. 4
Isidore	Chios	monastery and/or church before late 8th century (LP and Einsiedeln compilation)	
Peregrinus	Auxerre	*xenodochium* before late 8th century (LP)	
Aquila and Prisca	Ephesus	earlier *titulus* associated with saints before late 8th century (LP)	

Sources for this list:

evidence for the **foundation of ecclesiastical dedications** in Rome usually derives from the *Liber Pontificalis*;

for **monasteries**: Ferrari, *Early Roman Monasteries*;

for **ecclesiastical dedications** in Rome more generally: Hülsen, *Chiese*; Armellini and Cecchelli, *Chiese*; Michael Jost, *Die Patrozinien der Kirchen der Stadt Rom vom Anfang bis in das 10. Jahrhundert* (Neuried: Ars Una, 2000);

for **itineraries**: *CTCR* 2, eds. Valentini and Zucchetti; for the itineraries in the Einsiedeln compilation see Walser, *Die Einsiedler Inschriftensammlung*;

for **frescoes in S. Maria Antiqua**: Rushforth, "The Church of S. Maria Antiqua"; for the panorama of saints, here the "panorama fresco," see Chapter 6;

for **frescoes** elsewhere in Rome: Lesley Jessop, "Pictorial Cycles of Non-Biblical Saints: The Seventh- and Eighth-Century Mural Cycles in Rome and Contexts for Their Use," *PBSR* 67 (1999): 233–79;

for **liturgical commemoration** in mid-7th-century Rome as attested by the earliest version of the ***Capitulare Evangeliorum*** (a list of gospel readings for the liturgical year): ed. Klauser, *Das römische Capitulare Evangeliorum*, 13–46;

for the **sancta sanctorum relic authentics**: Galland and Vezin, *Les authentiques de reliques*;

for **Theodotus's dedicatory inscription**: see Appendix 2;

for many of these saints see also, with caution: Donckel, "Außerrömische Heilige in Rom."

APPENDIX 2

Theodotus and S. Angelo in Pescheria

Theodotus is known from three sources:

***Liber Pontificalis*, 97.2, ed. Duchesne, 1: 486, lines 7–9:**

Hic namque beatissimus vir, defuncto eius genitore atque parvulus suae nobilissimae genetrici relictus, studiose a proprio thio Theodoto dudum consule et duce, postmodum vero primicerio sanctae nostrae ecclesiae, post antedictae suae genetricis obitum nutritus atque educatus est.

An inscription in the Theodotus chapel in S. Maria Antiqua (by 752); transcription in Rushforth, "The Church of S. Maria Antiqua," 43:

+[t]HEODOTVS PRIM(iceri)O DEFENSORVM / ET D[isp]ENSATORE S(an)C(ta)E D(e)I / GENETR[ic]IS SENPERQVE / BIRGO MARIA QVI APPELLATVR / ANTIQ<u>A

Dedicatory inscription of the *diaconia* of S. Angelo in Pescheria (Figure 3):[1]

[+] Haec sunt nomina s(an)c(t)orum c(orp)orum
beneficia hic requiescunt. Idest
D(omi)ni et Salvatori n(ostri) Ih(es)u Chr(ist)i, s(an)c(t)ae quae
eius genetricis Mariae Dominae n(ostrae),
s(an)c(t)i Michael et Gabriel archangeli,
s(an)c(t)i Petri, s(an)c(t)i Pauli, s(an)c(t)i Andreae,
s(an)c(t)i Iaccobi, s(an)c(t)i Iohanni, s(an)c(t)i Thomae,
s(an)c(t)i Iaccobi, s(an)c(t)i Philippi, s(an)c(t)i Bartholomei,
s(an)c(t)i Matthei, s(an)c(t)i Simonis, s(an)c(t)i Thaddei,
s(an)c(t)i Iohanni baptistae, s(an)c(t)i Selbestri,
s(an)c(t)i Stephani, s(an)c(t)i Zini, s(an)c(t)i Laurentii,

s(an)c(t)i Cesarii, s(an)c(t)i Nicandri, s(an)c(t)i Celsi,
s(an)c(t)i Eupli, s(an)c(t)i Petri, s(an)c(t)i Marcellini,
s(an)c(t)i Balentini, s(an)c(t)i Donati, s(an)c(t)i Nicolai,
s(an)c(t)i Pancratii, s(an)c(t)i Anastasii, s(an)c(t)i Iuda,
s(an)c(t)i Theodori, s(an)c(t)i Georgii, s(an)c(t)i Christophori,
s(an)c(t)i Alexandri, s(an)c(t)i Erasmi, s(an)c(t)i Thothaelii,
s(an)c(t)i Abbaquiri, s(an)c(t)i Iohanni, s(an)c(t)i Dometii,
s(an)c(t)i Procopii, s(an)c(t)i Pantaleoni, s(an)c(t)i Nicasi,
s(an)c(t)i Cosmae, s(an)c(t)i Damiani, s(an)c(t)i Anthimii,
s(an)c(t)i Leontii, s(an)c(t)i Euprepii, s(an)c(t)i Antipae,
s(an)c(t)a Anna, s(an)c(t)a Elisabet, s(an)c(t)a Euphumia,
s(an)c(t)a Sophia, s(an)c(t)a Thecla, s(an)c(t)a Petronella,
s(an)c(t)a Theodotae, s(an)c(t)a Theopisti, s(an)c(t)a Aurea,
s(an)c(t)a Athanasia, s(an)c(t)a Theoctisti, s(an)c(t)a Eudoxia.
+Est enim dedicatio ecclesie istius,
at nomen beati Pauli apostoli calend(as)
iunias, per indictione octaba, anno
ab initio mundi sex milia ducentos
sexxaginta tres, temporibus domni
Stephani iunioris papae. Theodotus,
holim dux, nunc primicerius s(an)c(t)ae sedis
apostolicae et pater uius ben(edictae) diac(oniae), a solo
edificavit pro intercessionem animae sua[e]
et remedium omnium peccatorum.

APPENDIX 3

The *Translatio* of St. Caesarius from Terracina to Rome

The story of Caesarius's *translatio* from Terracina to Rome is found in two different versions, one freestanding, the other appearing as part of the *vita* of Pope Damasus. Certain manuscripts include, after the *passio* of Caesarius, the freestanding *translatio*, conventionally titled the *Sanatio Gallae et translatio S. Caesarii Romam* (BHL 1517–18): AASS Nov. I: 126B–129C. The other version of the *translatio* is found in one version of the *vita* of Damasus (BHL 2087). Another version of Damasus's *vita* (BHL 2086) does *not* have the *translatio* but does have a shorter story that tells of his construction of a church for St. Lawrence and the illness of the emperor's daughter. A third version of Damasus's *vita* (BHL 2088) does not have any part of the story. For all three versions, see *S. Damasi papæ opera quæ extant et vita ex codicibus MSS*, ed. M. Sarazanius (Paris: Billaine, 1672): 15–20 (BHL 2086), 21–42 (BHL 2087), 42–57 (BHL 2088).

Both versions of the *translatio* are difficult to date and undoubtedly considerably postdate the late fourth or early fifth century, in which the events they purport to relate are set.

Duchesne argued that the legend developed in the sixth century.[1] He bases his claim on the fact that by the ninth century the term *palatium* came to refer to the Lateran; therefore, the legend's description that the relics were brought "intro Romanum palatium, in optimo loco, imperiali cubiculo" must date to an earlier time when the term *palatium* was in use for the palaces on the Palatine. As Duchesne himself points out, however, the monastery on the Palatine continued to be referred to as "in Palatio," and the twelfth-century *Mirabilia Urbis Romae* speaks of the imperial palaces that existed on the Palatine.

Duchesne does not spell out his other arguments, and in light of recent research, the tendency of earlier scholars (such as Duchesne) to date legends exhibiting "Greek" influence to the sixth century is no longer convincing. In the *translatio* narrative the new church is dedicated with relics of its patron saint; such an emphasis on relics as necessary for an ecclesiastical dedication only gradually became the norm in Rome in the sixth to seventh centuries.[2]

It is also unclear whether the *translatio* narrative developed initially as part of Damasus's *vita* or whether it arose in the context of Caesarius on the Palatine; both texts are full of anachronisms and implausibilities. The editors of the text in the *Acta Sanctorum* (C. de Smedt, G. van Hooff, and J. de Backer) argued, based on the greater number of historical errors in the *translatio* than in Damasus's *vita*, that the *vita* was written first.[3]

Given that both texts include details not necessary for the logic of their narratives, I suggest that both represent a fusion of two legends: Damasus's construction of a church for St. Lawrence accomplished through an imperial cure and the cure of an imperial daughter by Caesarius, which gave rise to the translation of the relics of Caesarius to Rome. As discussed by Claudia Rapp, the paradigm of a cure of an imperial family member is commonly found in the legendary lives of late antique bishops.[4] In support of this theory, one of the lives of Damasus (BHL 2086) tells of how Damasus's construction of St. Lawrence was temporarily impeded by the emperor's daughter, who was then seized by an unclean spirit—yet how she was cured is not precisely specified; meanwhile in the extended versions (BHL 2087 and BHL 1517) the legend inexplicably jumps from the construction of S. Lorenzo to Caesarius and the dedication of the oratory on the Palatine, without specifying the completion of S. Lorenzo.

Although a sixth-century origin (as favored by Duchesne) or a significantly later date cannot be excluded, as I suggest in Chapter 3, various events that occurred in the seventh century help make sense of the development of the *translatio* narrative: thus, I suggest that the formation of the legend in its present form took place around the early eighth century.

Finally, it is worth emphasizing that the legend is found almost exclusively in Roman manuscripts from the eleventh century onward—neither version of the legend had a prominent afterlife outside of Rome. What we have here is a legend for Roman consumption that developed in Rome and stayed in Rome; the fame of Caesarius would continue to spread abroad, but the story of his translation to Rome did not.

APPENDIX 4

The Spread of St. George's Cult

Pilgrim accounts, from the first half of the sixth century onward, include George's tomb in Lydda (Diospolis) in Palestine as a noteworthy site where miracles were known to occur.[1] Some of these reports were by Latin travelers and must have helped spread news of the saint across the Mediterranean.

Ecclesiastical dedications to St. George sprang up rapidly throughout the Eastern Mediterranean.[2] By the fifth century at the latest, Constantinople housed one church (ἐν τῷ Ξηροκέρκῳ) dedicated to St. George; by the fifteenth century the number had increased to at least eight.[3] By the sixth century the cult of George had spread to the West.[4] By the mid-sixth century there was a church for George in Mainz, for which Venantius Fortunatus composed a poem celebrating George as a saint "whose great honor is spread throughout this world."[5] His verses stress that although the church in Mainz is far from George's burial site in the East, George "offers his assistance here under the western meridian."[6] Gregory of Tours also included George in his late sixth-century *Glory of the Martyrs*.[7] In Italy early dedications to George include a church in Sicily (mentioned in a letter by Gregory the Great).[8]

APPENDIX 5

An Early Medieval *Diaconia* Dedicated to St. Nicholas?

The earliest surviving written attestations of a church dedicated to Nicholas at the Tiber bend date from the time of Pope Urban II (r. 1088–1099). They are an inscription in the church that details the gifts given by the presbyter Romanus to the church during the papacy of Urban II,[1] and the *Liber Pontificalis*'s biography of Urban II, which describes the pope dying in a house "apud sanctum Nicolaum in Carcere": LP 160, ed. Duchesne, 2: 294.

However, evidence, recently reexamined by Andreina Palombi, suggests a significantly earlier date for the church.[2] Particularly significant are (1) the construction technique of the church's foundation that arguably dates to around the mid-eighth to the ninth century and (2) two inscriptions on a column, dated by paleographers to the eighth century (Figure 16). Arguably, this column might have been moved into the church at a later date.[3] Even so, as discussed by Campese Simone, the upper inscription's reference to vineyards "in portu," a phrasing that is similarly found in the inscription (dated to the mid-eighth century) detailing Eusthathius's donations to S. Maria in Cosmedin, suggests that the column inscription refers to the neighborhood, and thus the column was not brought from far away.[4]

The primary reason to suppose that this ecclesiastical dedication was a *diaconia* is that it eventually became one of the churches of the cardinal-deacons (*cardinales diaconi*).[5] Its status as such is documented under Pope Gelasius II (r. 1118–1119): LP 162, ed. Duchesne, 2: 313. The reason many scholars have been reluctant to include it among Rome's early *diaconiae* is that it is not on the extensive list of ecclesiastical foundations that received gifts from Pope Leo III (r. 795–816). However, only if we assume that this list was complete does its omission pose a problem.

Finally, the dedication to St. Nicholas must be addressed. Older scholarship tended to assume that the church was always dedicated to St. Nicholas.[6] More recently, some alternatives have been raised. The upper column inscription has been construed to suggest a church dedicated to Sts. Anna, Simeon, and Lucy or to St. Mary.[7] In 1970 Proja claimed that, according to medieval and Renaissance sources, the church was originally dedicated to Christ the Savior (S. Salvatore); however, this claim is, to my knowledge, unsubstantiated.[8] According to Proja the church was probably only dedicated to St. Nicholas in the time of Pope Urban II (who had the relics of St. Nicholas translated from Myra to Bari in 1087). However, there is no mention of this dedication in the *Liber Pontificalis*'s biography of Urban II or any other source. In 1128, under Pope Honorius II, the church was renovated and reconsecrated (again to St. Nicholas).

More plausible, to my mind, is that this ecclesiastical foundation was dedicated to St. Nicholas at its initial foundation. (In this scenario we might imagine that there was increased interest in the church after Urban II's translation of Nicholas's relics to Bari.) There is other evidence for the veneration of St. Nicholas in eighth-century Rome: he is included in the panorama of saints in S. Maria Antiqua (see Chapter 6) and in Theodotus's dedicatory inscription (see Appendix 2). Furthermore, oratories dedicated to St. Nicholas are mentioned in the *Liber Pontificalis*'s biography of Leo IV (r. 847–855): LP 105.27 and 44, ed. Duchesne, 2: 112 and 116. When these oratories were initially founded is unclear.

APPENDIX 6

The *Passio* of St. Boniface of Tarsus

As convincingly demonstrated by Pio Franchi De'Cavalieri, the *passio* of Boniface was originally written in Greek.[1] Although the Greek text contains Latinisms, they are all terms usual in Greek. In contrast, the Latin text is full of Graecisms that are otherwise difficult to explain. The *passio* also displays similarities (both in its motifs and its specific language) to other Byzantine hagiographical texts. Accordingly, it must have been written in a location where Byzantine cultural influence was strong.

Franchi De'Cavalieri argued, however, that the *passio* of Boniface was not composed in Rome for the following reasons: (1) it would not have made sense to *compose* a Greek text in Rome during the sixth or seventh century because it would have had few readers there (although he freely admits that Greek monks in Rome translated texts into Greek); (2) a Roman writer would never have made the main protagonist go off to Tarsus in search of martyrs, given that Rome had so many; (3) a Roman writer would not have imagined traveling east by land (rather than by sea); (4) the writer imagines the distance between Rome and Tarsus to be much shorter than it is; (5) no specific details about Roman topography are given; and (6) the Greek text describes Aglaës burying Boniface outside the walls—if the text had been written in Rome it would have mentioned the dedication on the Aventine, rather than have the body of the saint placed outside the walls of Rome. As Franchi De'Cavalieri points out, however, the legend also gives no specifics about Tarsus.

In light of recent decades of scholarship that have demonstrated the vigor of Rome's early medieval Greek-speaking communities, his conclusion is ripe for re-evaluation. There is, to my mind, no reason that a Greek-speaking community in Rome (likely armed with earlier memories and perhaps even a rudimentary *passio* of the saint) could not have composed the Greek *passio* in Rome.

I do not find Franchi De'Cavalieri's specific arguments convincing for the following reasons:

1. Greek-speakers were certainly present in seventh-century Rome; and, as suggested by the evidence of other eastern cults in Rome, as well as the very circulation of Boniface's *passio*, there was an audience for Greek hagiographical texts.
2. From a seventh-century standpoint, it was not absurd to imagine Tarsus and the Levant as a place of Christian persecutions.

3–4. Throughout antiquity the via Egnatia and other Balkan land (or land/sea) routes were used by travelers between Italy and Asia Minor; McCormick estimates that the different land routes ceased to be used ca. 550–650 (as the Byzantine imperial administration lost control of the area).[2] More importantly, whether writing in Rome or elsewhere, the author(s) are clearly not interested in describing details of the journey (the party sets off by land and then arrives).

5. Since the *passio* gives no specific details about Rome *or* Tarsus that would prove the author's familiarity with either city, it seems more accurate to conclude that the author was uninterested in providing more verisimilar descriptions of the cities, which could easily have been included even without direct knowledge.
6. Given that the text is set in the time of the imperial persecutions it makes sense to have Boniface buried outside the walls of Rome (most hagiographical legends of Roman martyrs have them buried outside the city). Furthermore, it seems to me unlikely that a newly founded early medieval religious establishment would have claimed to be built on the site of a martyrial tomb within the city (from a Roman perspective, a rare occurrence) for which there were no preexisting traditions, while the claim to continue or revive the legacy of a preexisting martyrial tradition from outside Rome's walls at a new site inside the city would have seemed more reasonable.

Franchi De'Cavalieri also suggested that the Latin translation was modified to make it more compatible with the Roman context. This translation was produced at some time before the ninth century (the date of the earliest manuscripts).[3] Duchesne pointed out the following differences between the Greek and Latin text: (1) only in the Latin version is it specified that Boniface's martyrdom occurred under the Diocletianic persecutions; (2) in Greek the burial of the martyr takes places fifty stades from Rome; in the Latin, the distance is given as five stades; (3) in Greek the name of the street on which Boniface is buried is not specified; in Latin it is the via Latina; and (4) at least one Latin manuscript (the sixteenth-century Vat. lat. 6075) modifies "ædificans ei domum" to "donec ædificaret domum," after describing Boniface's burial on the via Latina, thus perhaps suggesting that Aglaës subsequently built another memorial (i.e., on the Aventine) for Boniface.[4] Other than the change in distance, which would seem to be a simple confusion, I agree that the changes stem from a desire to add specificity to the text; however, except for no. 4, I do not see how they could have served to situate the legend at the Aventine *diaconia.*

Furthermore there is no evidence, to my knowledge, for any ecclesiastical dedications to this saint (or other forms of veneration) earlier than the *diaconia* in Rome.[5] This again suggests that, at least in its early medieval form, the cult of Boniface—and more specifically the early medieval *passio* of Boniface—may be closely associated with the Aventine community in Rome. It would also explain certain textual similarities between the *passio* of Boniface and that of Sabina and Serapia.[6]

Above all, I suggest that the contextualization of this text in Rome finds justification in its ability to make sense of much about the *passio*'s puzzling narrative. Read as a reflection of the Aventine *diaconia*, the *passio*'s anomalies reveal themselves as the contemporary concerns of a very particular Greek-speaking community perched on the Aventine Hill.

From Rome the *passio* of Boniface could have been transmitted to other locations in the Byzantine Mediterranean. An early ninth-century marble calendar from Naples includes Boniface.[7] Boniface's subsequent veneration in the Byzantine Empire is well attested, although no churches in Constantinople appear to have been dedicated to him.[8]

Abbreviations

AASS	*Acta Sanctorum*. Edited by the Bollandists. Antwerp; Tongerlo; Brussels, 1643–1940.
AB	*Analecta Bollandiana*
ActaIRNorv	*Acta ad archaeologiam et artium historiam pertinentia*, Institutum Romanum Norvegiae
ASRSP	*Archivio della Società romana di storia patria*
BHG	*Bibliotheca hagiographica graeca*, 3rd ed. Edited by François Halkin. Brussels: Société des Bollandistes, 1957; repr. 1969.
BHG Auct	*Bibliotheca hagiographica graeca. 4: Auctarium*. Edited by François Halkin. Brussels: Société des Bollandistes, 1969.
BHG NovAuct	*Bibliotheca hagiographica graeca. 5: Novum auctarium*. Edited by François Halkin. Brussels: Société des Bollandistes, 1984.
BHL	*Bibliotheca hagiographica latina antiquae et mediae aetatis*. Brussels: Société des Bollandistes, 1898–1911; new suppl. 1986.
Brill's New Pauly Online	*Brill's New Pauly*. Edited by Hubert Cancik, Helmuth Schneider, and Manfred Landfester. English translation edited by Christine F. Salazar and Francis G. Gentry. Online Edition. Brill, 2006–. referenceworks.brillonline.com/browse/brill-s-new-pauly.
BS	*Bibliotheca Sanctorum*. Rome: Istituto Giovanni XXIII nella Pontificia Università lateranense, 1961–1970.
BZ	*Byzantinische Zeitschrift*
CBCR	Krautheimer, Richard. *Corpus Basilicarum Christianarum Romae: The Early Christian Basilicas of Rome (IV–IX Cent.)*. 5 vols. Vatican City: Pontificio Istituto di archeologia cristiana, 1937–1977.
CCCM	Corpus christianorum: continuatio mediaevalis. Turnhout: Brepols, 1971–.

CCSL	Corpus christianorum: series latina. Turnhout: Brepols, 1953–.
CIL	*Corpus inscriptionum latinarum.* Berlin, 1862–.
CSEL	Corpus scriptorum ecclesiasticorum latinorum. Vienna, 1866–1913.
CTCR	*Codice topografico della città di Roma.* Edited by Roberto Valentini and Giuseppe Zucchetti. 4 vols. Fonti per la storia d'Italia 81, 88, 90, 91. Rome: Tipografia del Senato, 1940–1953.
DOP	*Dumbarton Oaks Papers*
EI^2	*Encyclopaedia of Islam*, 2nd ed. Online Edition. Brill, 2012. referenceworks.brillonline.com/browse/encyclopaedia-of-islam-2/.
EME	*Early Medieval Europe*
ICUR	*Inscriptiones christianae urbis Romae septimo saeculo antiquiores.* Edited by Giovanni Battista de Rossi. Rome, 1857–1888.
ILCV	*Inscriptiones latinae christianae veteres.* Edited by Ernst Diehl. 3 vols. Berlin: Weidmann, 1961.
Janin	Janin, Raymond. *Le siège de Constantinople et le patriarcat œcuménique. Tome III: Les églises et les monastères.* La géographie ecclésiastique de l'Empire byzantin 1. Paris: l'Institut français d'études byzantines, 1953.
Lampe	Lampe, G. W. H. *A Patristic Greek Lexicon.* 20th ed. Oxford: Clarendon Press, 2007.
Lewis and Short	Lewis, Charlton Thomas, and Charles Short. *A Latin Dictionary Founded on Andrews' Edition of Freund's Latin Dictionary.* Revised ed. Oxford: Oxford University Press, 2002.
LexMa	*Lexikon des Mittelalters & International Encyclopaedia for the Middle Ages.* Munich: Brepols, 1977–1995; Online, 2004–. www.brepols.net/Pages/BrowseBySeries.aspx?TreeSeries=LEXMA-O.
LP	*Le Liber Pontificalis.* Edited by Louis Duchesne. 3 vols. Paris: E. Thorin, 1886–1892; repr. Paris: de Boccard, 1955; vol. 3 with additions and corrections edited by Cyrille Vogel, 1957. Translated by Raymond Davis, *The Book of Pontiffs*, 3rd ed. (Liverpool: Liverpool University Press, 2010); *The Lives of the Eighth-Century Popes*, 2nd ed. (2007); *The Lives of the Ninth-Century Popes* (1995).

LTUR	*Lexicon topographicum urbis Romae*. Edited by Eva Margareta Steinby. 6 vols. Rome: Edizioni Quasar, 1993–2000.	
LTUR Suburbium	*Lexicon topographicum urbis Romae: Suburbium*. Edited by Adriano La Regina, Vincenzo Fiocchi Nicolai, Maria Grazia Granino Cecere, and Zaccaria Mari. 4 vols. Rome: Edizioni Quasar, 2001–2008.	
MEFR	*Mélanges d'archéologie et d'histoire*, École française de Rome	
MEFRA	*Mélanges de l'École française de Rome: Antiquité*	
MEFRM	*Mélanges de l'École française de Rome: Moyen Âge, Temps modernes* (1971–1988); *Mélanges de l'École française de Rome: Moyen Âge* (1989–)	
MGH	*Monumenta Germaniae Historica*	
	AA	*Auctores antiquissimi*. Berlin, 1877–1919.
	Capit.	*Capitularia regum Francorum*. Hannover, 1883–1897.
	DD O III	*Die Urkunden Otto des III.* Hannover, 1893.
	Epp.	*Epistolae*. Hannover, 1892–1939.
	Poetae	*Poetae Latini medii aevi*. Hannover, 1881–1899.
	SS	*Scriptores*. Hannover, 1826–1924.
	SS rer. Ger.	*Scriptores rerum Germanicarum in usum scholarum separatim editi*. Hannover, 1871–1987.
	SS rer. Lang.	*Scriptores rerum Langobardicarum et Italicarum*. Hannover, 1878.
	SS rer. Merov.	*Scriptores rerum Merovingicarum*. Hannover, 1884.
Mombritius	*Sanctuarium seu Vitae Sanctorum*. Edited by Boninus Mombritius. Milan, 1475; Paris: Fontemoing, 1910; repr. Hildesheim: Olms, 1978.	
NPNF	*A Select Library of Nicene and Post-Nicene Fathers of the Christian Church*, 2nd ser. Edited by Philip Schaff and Henry Wace. New York: Christian Literature Company, 1890–1900.	
ODB	*The Oxford Dictionary of Byzantium*. Edited by Alexander Kazhdan et al. Online Edition. Oxford, 2005. DOI: 10.1093/acref/9780195046526.001.0001.	
PBSR	*Papers of the British School at Rome*	

PG	*Patrologiae cursus completus: series graeca*. Edited by J.-P. Migne. Paris, 1857–1866.
PL	*Patrologiae cursus completus: series latina*. Edited by J.-P. Migne. Paris, 1844–1880.
PLRE	*The Prosopography of the Later Roman Empire*. Edited by A. H. M. Jones, J. R. Martindale, and J. Morris. 3 vols. in 4. Cambridge, 1971–1992.
RACr	*Rivista di archeologia cristiana*
RendPontAcc	*Atti della Pontificia Accademia romana di archeologia. Rendiconti*
RQ	*Römische Quartalschrift für christliche Altertumskunde und für Kirchengeschichte*
Settimane	Settimane di studio del Centro italiano di studi sull'alto medioevo
ThLL	*Thesaurus linguae latinae*. Leipzig: Teubner, 1900–.

Notes

Introduction

1. *Translatio sancti Viti martyris* (BHL 8718–19), 2, ed. I. Schmale-Ott (with German translation), 32–34: "Hic cum magno desiderio aestuaret, qualiter beatissimis martyribus honorem debitum impendere potuisset, non est contentus eorum sola corpora amplecti, quibus sedulum exhibebat officium, sed praefatum principem adiit petivitque, ut eum Romam ire permitteret atque inde sanctorum corpora ad praefatum monasterium aliqua, sicut cupidus erat, transferre potuisset." Regarding Fulrad, see Alain Stoclet, *Autour de Fulrad de Saint-Denis (v. 710–784)* (Geneva: Droz, 1993).

2. *Translatio sancti Viti martyris*, Preface, ed. Schmale-Ott, 30: "Nam postquam nostris meritis in hoc caliginoso carcere decidimus, nec deserentes te deseruisti, sed stellas, quae nobis in nocte iter agentibus viam ostenderent, misisti. Ante oculos namque habemus, nisi forte mortali somno obdormiverimus, Abel, Seth, Enoch, Noe, Abraham caeterosque patriarchas, prophetas, apostolos, martyres, confessores, virgines, viduas atque laudabiles monachos." Regarding the text see Hedwig Röckelein, *Reliquientranslationen nach Sachsen im 9. Jahrhundert: Über Kommunikation, Mobilität und Öffentlichkeit im Frühmittelalter* (Stuttgart: Thorbecke, 2002), 100–108.

3. Julia M. H. Smith, "Old Saints, New Cults: Roman Relics in Carolingian Francia," in *Early Medieval Rome and the Christian West: Essays in Honour of Donald A. Bullough*, ed. J. M. H. Smith (Leiden: Brill, 2000), 317–39.

4. *Orbis*, designed by Walter Scheidel and Elijah Meeks (2012; orbis.stanford.edu/), calculates a 52.9-day journey in the ancient world; medieval itineraries suggest 6–11+ weeks: Debra J. Birch, *Pilgrimage to Rome in the Middle Ages: Continuity and Change* (Woodbridge: Boydell Press, 1998), 60.

5. The foundational study remains that of Percy Ernst Schramm, *Kaiser, Rom und Renovatio: Studien und Texte zur Geschichte des römischen Erneuerungsgedankens vom Ende des karolingischen Reiches biz zum Investiturstreit* (Leipzig: B. G. Teubner, 1929). See further Chapter 7.

6. Unsurpassed in its breadth remains Ferdinand Gregorovius's magisterial *Geschichte der Stadt Rom im Mittelalter vom V. bis zum XVI. Jahrhundert* (1859–1872), edited by W. Kampf, 4 vols. (Munich: C. H. Beck, 1978; first edition 1953–1957); trans. A. Hamilton, *History of the City of Rome in the Middle Ages*, 8 vols. (London: Bell, 1894–1902). A prodigious historiography surrounds the "rise" of Christian Rome. In the following notes I cite only some of the studies most salient for my work.

7. For an introduction to Rome in the early Middle Ages see especially Paolo Delogu, "Il passaggio dall'antichità al medioevo," in *Storia di Roma dall'antichità a oggi. 2. Roma medievale*, ed. A. Vauchez (Rome: Laterza, 2001), 3–40. The most detailed narrative remains Ottorino Bertolini, *Roma di fronte a Bisanzio e ai Longobardi* (Bologna: L. Cappelli, 1941); for a thematic

introduction still helpful is Peter Llewellyn, *Rome in the Dark Ages* (New York: Praeger, 1971). For medieval Rome see now Chris Wickham, *Medieval Rome: Stability and Crisis of a City, 900–1150* (Oxford: Oxford University Press, 2015).

8. For the sake of clarity I too use the anachronistic term "Byzantine" to refer to the Roman world from the time of Justinian onward, so as to distinguish it from the Roman Empire of classical antiquity (a distinction ideologically important to contemporaries in the Latin West), although this empire based in Constantinople continued to see itself as the continuation of the Roman Empire.

9. Especially significant are the Crypta Balbi excavations: Lucia Saguì, "Roma e il Mediterraneo: la circolazione delle merci," in Maria Stella Arena et al., eds., *Roma dall'antichità al medioevo: archeologia e storia nel Museo Nazionale Romano Crypta Balbi* (Milan: Electa, 2001), 62–68.

10. Raymond Van Dam, *Rome and Constantinople: Rewriting Roman History during Late Antiquity* (Waco, TX: Baylor University Press, 2010), 9 n. 5 and 49–50 n. 5; Riccardo Santangeli Valenzani, "Strutture demografiche, economiche e sociali," in Roberto Meneghini and Riccardo Santangeli Valenzani, *Roma nell'altomedioevo: topografia e urbanistica della città dal V al X secolo* (Rome: Istituto poligrafico e Zecca dello Stato, 2004), 21–24.

11. Meneghini and Santangeli Valenzani, *Roma nell'altomedioevo*, provide the most up-to-date overview of the early medieval city; for monuments prior to the mid-sixth century see also Andrea Carandini and Paolo Carafa, eds., *Atlante di Roma antica: biografia e ritratti della città* (Milan: Electa, 2012).

12. For the institutional history of the early medieval papacy see Thomas F. X. Noble, *The Republic of St. Peter: The Birth of the Papal State, 680–825* (Philadelphia: University of Pennsylvania Press, 1984). Regarding papal ideologies see Claudio Azzara, *L'ideologia del potere regio nel papato altomedievale: secoli VI–VIII* (Spoleto: Centro italiano di studi sull'alto medioevo, 1997); Franz Alto Bauer, *Das Bild der Stadt Rom im Frühmittelalter: Papststiftungen im Spiegel des Liber Pontificalis von Gregor dem Dritten bis zu Leo dem Dritten* (Wiesbaden: L. Reichert, 2004).

13. Discussions of Byzantine cultural influence on Rome include Cyril Mango, "La culture grecque et l'Occident au VIIIe siècle," in *I problemi dell'Occidente nel secolo VIII*, Settimane 20 (Spoleto: La sede del Centro, 1973), 693–721; Filippo Burgarella, "Presenze greche a Roma: aspetti culturali e religiosi," in *Roma fra Oriente e Occidente*, Settimane 49 (Spoleto: La sede del Centro, 2002), 943–98. See also, with caution, Andrew J. Ekonomou, *Byzantine Rome and the Greek Popes: Eastern Influences on Rome and the Papacy from Gregory the Great to Zacharias, A.D. 590–752* (Lanham, MD: Lexington Books, 2007).

14. Some attempts have been made to catalog these saints, but not to explain them: Emil Donckel, "Außerrömische Heilige in Rom von den Anfängen unter Liberius bis Leo IV. (847): ein Beitrag zur Entwicklung des stadtrömischen Festkalenders" (PhD diss., Hermann, 1938); Michel Andrieu, "Chronique d'archéologie chrétienne: Les églises de Rome au Moyen-Âge," *Revue des sciences religieuses* 9 (1929): 540–74 (who provides a chronological list of churches by saint). A good introduction is provided by Letizia Pani Ermini, "Spazio cristiano e culto dei santi orientali a Roma," in *Oriente cristiano e santità: figure e storia di santi tra Bisanzio e l'Occidente*, ed. S. Gentile (Milan: Centro Tibaldi, 1998): 85–92. See also, with caution, the Appendix "Di alcuni aspetti della vita religiosa e civile di Roma nell'alto medievo," in Carlo Cecchelli, "Continuità storica di Roma antica nell'alto medioevo," in *La città nell'alto medioevo*, Settimane 6 (Spoleto: La sede del Centro, 1959), 89–149 at 134–49.

15. See, for example, G. W. Bowersock, Peter Brown, and Oleg Grabar, *Late Antiquity: A Guide to the Postclassical World* (Cambridge, MA: Belknap Press, 1999).

16. Maria Fabricius Hansen, *The Eloquence of Appropriation: Prolegomena to an Understanding of Spolia in Early Christian Rome* (Rome: L'Erma di Bretschneider, 2003).

17. Recent work, especially Kate Cooper and Julia Hillner, eds., *Religion, Dynasty, and Patronage in Early Christian Rome, 300–900* (Cambridge: Cambridge University Press, 2007), has done much to dispel this myth for the period before 600, but a pope-centered paradigm remains strong for the sixth to ninth centuries.

18. *Translatio sancti Viti martyris*, 5, ed. Schmale-Ott, 48.

19. For this phrasing and conceptualization of Rome, see Peter Brown, *The Rise of Western Christendom: Triumph and Diversity, A.D. 200–1000* (Malden, MA: Blackwell, 1995). For Rome as the Church, see especially Judith Herrin, *The Formation of Christendom* (Princeton, NJ: Princeton University Press, 1987).

20. The literature is vast. Seminal remains Peter Brown, *The Cult of the Saints: Its Rise and Function in Latin Christianity* (Chicago: University of Chicago Press, 1981). For the Middle Ages one place to begin is Robert Bartlett, *Why Can the Dead Do Such Great Things? Saints and Worshippers from the Martyrs to the Reformation* (Princeton, NJ: Princeton University Press, 2013).

21. Gregory the Great, *Dialogues*, 1.12.4, ed. A. de Vogüé, 2: 116: "Vitae namque uera aestimatio in uirtute est operum, non in ostensione signorum."

22. Sofia Boesch Gajano, "La proposta agiografica dei 'Dialogi' di Gregorio Magno," *Studi medievali*, 3rd ser., 21 (1980): 623–64; Conrad Leyser, "The Temptations of Cult: Roman Martyr Piety in the Age of Gregory the Great," *EME* 9.3 (2000): 289–307. For an overview of Latin *passiones* written in Italy see Cécile Lanéry, "Hagiographie d'Italie (300–550). I. Les Passions latines composées en Italie," in *Hagiographies: histoire internationale de la littérature hagiographique latine et vernaculaire en Occident des origines à 1550*, vol. 5 (Turnhout: Brepols, 2010), 15–369.

23. Matthew J. Dal Santo, *Debating the Saints' Cults in the Age of Gregory the Great* (Oxford: Oxford University Press, 2012); for Gregory's pastoral theology more generally, see George E. Demacopoulos, *Gregory the Great: Ascetic, Pastor, and First Man of Rome* (South Bend, IN: University of Notre Dame Press, 2015).

24. For the connectivity of the early medieval Mediterranean see Michael McCormick, *Origins of the European Economy: Communications and Commerce, A.D. 300–900* (Cambridge: Cambridge University Press, 2001); Jonathan P. Conant, "Europe and the African Cult of Saints, circa 350–900: An Essay in Mediterranean Communications," *Speculum* 55 (2010): 1–46.

25. For an introduction see Chris Wickham, *Framing the Early Middle Ages: Europe and the Mediterranean, 400–800* (Oxford: Oxford University Press, 2005).

26. See recently, Ralf Behrwald and Christian Witschel, eds., *Rom in der Spätantike: historische Erinnerung im städtischen Raum* (Stuttgart: Franz Steiner Verlag, 2012).

27. Richard Krautheimer, *Rome, Profile of a City, 312–1308* (Princeton, NJ: Princeton University Press, 1980); for revisions to Krautheimer's assessment of church building in early medieval Rome see Robert Coates-Stephens, "Dark Age Architecture in Rome," *PBSR* 65 (1997): 177–232. For an insightful critique of Krautheimer's iconographical approach to churches as too limited for understanding their religious significance, see Caroline Goodson, *The Rome of Pope Paschal I: Papal Power, Urban Renovation, Church Rebuilding and Relic Translation, 817–824* (Cambridge: Cambridge University Press, 2010), esp. 81–92.

28. Albert Dufourcq, *Étude sur les Gesta martyrum romains* (Paris: Fontemoig, 1900); Louis Duchesne, in successive articles, all titled "Notes sur la topographie de Rome au Moyen-Âge," published in the *MEFR* between 1886 and 1915. Not all take a topographical approach, but many do, in particular no. 7 ("Aventin") in vol. 10 (1890): 225–50.

29. Recent scholarship has done much to unpack Carolingian ideas of Rome, emphasizing that Carolingian interactions with Rome should often be seen as processes of active appropriation, not passive reception. See especially Smith, ed., *Early Medieval Rome*; and Claudia Bolgia, Rosamond McKitterick, and John Osborne, eds., *Rome Across Time and Space: Cultural*

Transmissions and the Exchange of Ideas, c. *500–1400* (Cambridge: Cambridge University Press, 2011).

30. My understanding of saints as participants in urban settings draws on scholarship that has conceptualized the space of cities in active terms, theorized saints' cults as social constructs, and studied the interaction of topography and historical memory. Particularly influential to my thinking on these subjects are Michel de Certeau, *The Practice of Everyday Life,* trans. S. Rendall (Berkeley: University of California Press, 1984); Hedwig Röckelein, "'Die Hüllen der Heiligen': zur Materialität des hagiographischen Mediums," in *Reliquiare im Mittelalter,* eds. B. Reudenbach and G. Toussaint (Berlin: Akademie Verlag, 2005), 75–88; and Pierre Nora, "Between Memory and History: Les Lieux de Mémoire," *Representations* 26, Special Issue: Memory and Counter-Memory (Spring 1989): 7–24.

Chapter 1. A City of Saints

1. My walk takes its inspiration from the walks in Diane G. Favro, *The Urban Image of Augustan Rome* (Cambridge: Cambridge University Press, 1996).

2. The bibliography on the Einsiedeln compilation is vast. Seminal studies include Christian Hülsen, *La pianta di Roma dell'anonimo einsidlense* (Rome: E. Loescher, 1907); Heinrich Jordan, *Topographie der Stadt Rom im Alterthum* (Berlin: Weidmann, 1871); and Rodolfo Lanciani, *L'itinerario di Einsiedeln e l'ordine di Benedetto Canonico* (Rome: Tipografia della R. Accademia dei Lincei, 1891). Recently, Caroline Goodson has used the itineraries in the Einsiedeln compilation to imagine the architectural diversity that remained on view in early ninth-century Rome: Goodson, *Rome of Pope Paschal I,* 44–80. I am also grateful to Caroline Goodson for sharing with me her unpublished presentations, "The Attitudes of the Carolingians Towards the Remnants of the Late Antique Past, Taking Rome as a Case Study" and "Strategies of Power in Early Medieval Rome." For additional bibliography see below, esp. nn. 5, 7, 98 and Chapter 7.

3. Baudouin de Gaiffier, "La lecture des passions des martyrs à Rome avant le IXe siècle," *AB* 87 (1969): 63–78.

4. Pio Franchi De'Cavalieri, "S. Martina," *RQ* 17 (1903): 222–36. See also Chapter 2.

5. The itineraries contained in the ninth-century Einsiedeln compilation appear to have been compiled during the pontificate of Pope Paul I (757–767): Donatella Bellardini and Paolo Delogu, "*Liber Pontificalis* e altre fonti: la topografia di Roma nell'VIII secolo," in *Atti del Colloquio internazionale: il Liber Pontificalis e la storia materiale (Roma, 21–22 febbraio 2002),* ed. H. Geertman (Assen, the Netherlands: Koninklijke Van Gorcum, 2003), 205–23. The liturgical description found in the manuscript arguably dates to around the first half of the eighth century: see n. 98. Fulrad and his relative, discussed in the Introduction, acquired their Roman relics between 751 and 777.

6. Hendrik W. Dey, *The Aurelian Wall and the Refashioning of Imperial Rome, A.D. 271–855* (Cambridge: Cambridge University Press, 2011).

7. As tallied by the so-called wall description in the Einsiedeln compilation: Codex Einsidlensis 326, f. 86r, ed. G. Walser, 158: "Sunt simul turres CCCLXXXIII propugnacula VII XX posternae V necessariae CXVI fen(estrae) maior(es) forins(ecus) II LXVI." (The section-by-section statistics provided by the wall description do not add up to this total count.)

8. This inscription is included in the Einsiedeln compilation: Codex Einsidlensis 326, f. 70r, ed. Walser, 27, no. 21; discussion, 80–81. I give here the reconstructed version of the original inscription based on the Einsiedeln's transcription: CIL VI 1402. Expanded, the inscription reads, "C(aio) Dillio A(uli) f(ilio) Ser(gia tribu) Voculae trib(uno) milit(um) leg(ionis) I IIII-viro viarum curandar(um) q(uaestori) provinc(iae) Ponti et Bithyniae trib(uno) pl(ebis)

pr(aetori) leg(ato) in Germania leg(ionis) XXII Primigeniae Helvia T(iti) f(ilia) Procula uxor fecit"; "For Gaius Dillius Vocula, son of Aulus, from the Sergian tribe, military tribune in the first legion, member of the collegium of four for the upkeep of the streets, quaestor of the province of Pontus and Bithynia, tribune of the people, praetor, legate of the 22nd legion Primigenia in Germany; his wife Helvia Procula, daughter of Titus had [this] erected."

9. Again, this inscription is recorded in the Einsiedeln compilation: Codex Einsidlensis 326, f. 74r, ed. Walser, 43, no. 46: "Imp(erator) caesar M(arcus) aurelius antonius aug(ustus) germanicus sarmatic(us) hos lapides constitui iussit p(ro)p(ter) controversias quae inter mercatores et mancipes ortae erant uti fine(m) demonstrarent vectigali foriculari et ansarii p(ro) mercaliu(m) secundu(m) vetere(m) lege(m) semel dumtaxat exigundo." Cf. CIL VI 1016a and 31227 for surviving fragments of such customs inscriptions.

10. For Fulrad, see the Introduction. Regarding pilgrimages to early medieval Rome see, with further bibliography, Letizia Pani Ermini, ed., *Christiana loca: lo spazio cristiano nella Roma del primo millennio*, 2 vols. (Rome: Fratelli Palombi, 2000–2001).

11. Such itineraries survive in Carolingian manuscripts: they include the *De locis sanctis martyrum quae sunt foris civitatem Romae* and the *Notitia ecclesiarum urbis Romae* (containing, contrary to what its title suggests, primarily extramural sites), in *CTCR* 2: 72–99 (*Notitia*), 106–18 (*De locis*).

12. For an overview of Rome's extramural Christian topography see Louis Reekmans, "L'implantation monumentale chrétienne dans le paysage urbain de Rome de 300 à 850," in *Actes du XIe Congrès international d'archéologie chrétienne: Lyon, Vienne, Grenoble, Genève et Aoste (21–28 Septembre 1986)*, eds. N. Duval et al. (Rome: École française de Rome, 1989), 861–915 at 902–15; and Pani Ermini, *Christiana loca*, especially Philippe Pergola, "Dai cimiteri ai santuari martiriali (IV-VIII secolo)," 1: 99–105 and Vincenzo Fiocchi Nicolai, "Sacra martyrum loca circuire," 1: 221–30.

13. Hugo Brandenburg, "S. Petri Basilica, Coemeterium, Episcopia, Cubicula, Habitacula, Porticus, Fons, Atrium," LTUR Suburbium 1: 185–95; Roberto Meneghini, "Il Vaticano," in Meneghini and Santangeli Valenzani, *Roma nell'altomedioevo*, 217–21.

14. See Chapter 6.

15. Codex Einsidlensis 326, f. 68v, ed. Walser, 21, no. 10; discussion 70–71: "Iustitiae sedis, fidei domus, aula pudoris / haec est quam cernis, pietas quam possidet omnis, / quae patris et fili virtutibus inclyta gaudet / auctoremq(ue) suum genitoris laudibus aequat." My translation is based on Richard Krautheimer, "A Note on the Inscription in the Apse of Old St. Peter's," *DOP* 41, Studies on Art and Archeology in Honor of Ernst Kitzinger on His Seventy-Fifth Birthday (1987): 317–20 at 317.

16. Maureen C. Miller, "The Sources of Textiles and Vestments in Early Medieval Rome," in *Rome and Religion in the Medieval World: Studies in Honor of Thomas F. X. Noble*, eds. V. L. Garver and O. M. Phelan (Farnham: Ashgate, 2014), 83–100.

17. Marios Costambeys and Conrad Leyser, "To Be the Neighbour of St Stephen: Patronage, Martyr Cult, and Roman Monasteries, *c*.600–*c*.900," in Cooper and Hillner, *Religion, Dynasty, and Patronage*, 262–87.

18. Riccardo Santangeli Valenzani, "Hosting Foreigners in Early Medieval Rome: From *Xenodochia* to *Scholae Peregrinorum*," in *England and Rome in the Early Middle Ages: Pilgrimage, Art, and Politics*, ed. F. Tinti (Turnhout: Brepols, 2014), 69–88; Myla Perraymond, "Le scholae peregrinorum nel borgo di San Pietro," *Romanobarbarica* 4 (1979): 183–200.

19. Roberto Luciani, "Le chiese mariane," in Pani Ermini, *Christiana loca*, 1: 131–45.

20. For Rome's Greek-speaking monasteries see Jean-Marie Sansterre, *Les moines grecs et orientaux à Rome aux époques byzantine et carolingienne: milieu du VIème s.–fin du IXème s.* (Brussels: Palais des Académies, 1983). More generally regarding Roman monasteries, see Guy Ferrari,

Early Roman Monasteries: Notes for the History of the Monasteries and Convents at Rome from the V through the X Century (Vatican City: Pontificio Istituto di archeologia cristiana, 1957).

21. Palmira Maria Barbini, "S. Agnetis Basilica, Coemeterium," LTUR Suburbium 1: 33–36.

22. Damasus, epigram no. 37, ed. A. Ferrua, *Epigrammata Damasiana*, 175–78: "SPONTE TRVCIS CALCASSE MINAS RABIEMQ(ue) TYRANNI." The Einsiedeln compilation includes Damasan inscriptions, although not this one.

23. *Passio* of Agnes (BHL 156): PL 17: 735A–742D. Regarding the development of this *passio* see Cécile Lanéry, "La légende de sainte Agnès: quelques réflexions sur la genèse d'un dossier hagiographique (IVe–VIe s.)," *MEFRM* 126.1 (2014): 17–26.

24. *De locis*, eds. Valentini and Zucchetti, *CTCR* 2: 109: "Inde haud procul in meridiem monasterium est Aquae Salviae, ubi caput sancti Anastasi est, et locus ubi decollatus est Paulus." Carmela Vircillo Franklin, *The Latin Dossier of Anastasius the Persian: Hagiographic Translations and Transformations* (Toronto: Pontifical Institute of Mediaeval Studies, 2004).

25. The exorcism is described in the so-called Roman Miracle, written in Greek and then translated into Latin: see Franklin, *Latin Dossier*, 126–51. I am grateful to Julia M. H. Smith for sharing her forthcoming article regarding this exorcism: "Cursing and Curing, or the Practice of Christianity in Eighth-Century Rome," *Italy and Medieval Europe: Papers for Chris Wickham on the Occasion of his 65th Birthday*, eds. R. Balzaretti, J. Barrow and P. Skinner (Oxford: Oxford University Press, forthcoming).

26. John Osborne, "The Roman Catacombs in the Middle Ages," *PBSR* 53 (1985): 278–328.

27. Patrick J. Geary, *Furta Sacra: Thefts of Relics in the Central Middle Ages* (Princeton, NJ: Princeton University Press, 1978).

28. Flavia De Rubeis, "Epigrafi a Roma dall'età classica all'alto medioevo," in Arena et al., *Roma dall'antichità al medioevo*, 104–21 at 116, no. 5.3: "Ego Rapulus humil[i]s et indignus monachus." De Rubeis dates the inscription to the seventh or eighth century.

29. *Notitia*, eds. Valentini and Zucchetti, *CTCR* 2: 92–93: "Deinde ambulas ad sanctum Pancratium . . . et in illa ecclesia intrabis longe sub terra et invenies Ardhimium martirem, et in altero loco sanctum Paulinum martirem, et in altero antro sanctam Sobiam martirem et duae filiae eius Agapite et Pistis martires."

30. See Chapter 8, n. 24.

31. Ambrose, *De virginibus*, 1.2.5–9, ed. E. Cazzaniga, 3–6.

32. For this practice see Martin Heinzelmann, *Translationsberichte und andere Quellen des Reliquienkultes* (Turnhout: Brepols, 1979), 84 n. 169.

33. For an introduction to some of the many traditions about Peter and Paul, see David L. Eastman, *The Ancient Martyrdom Accounts of Peter and Paul* (Atlanta: SBL Press, 2015).

34. Damasus, epigram no. 20, ed. Ferrua, *Epigrammata Damasiana*, 142: "Discipulos Oriens misit, quod sponte fatemur; / sanguinis ob meritum (Christ)umq(ue) per astra secuti / aetherios petiere sinus regnaque piorum: / Roma suos potius meruit defendere cives"; Marianne Sághy, trans., "Martyr Cult and Collective Identity in Fourth-Century Rome," in *Identity and Alterity in Hagiography and the Cult of Saints*, eds. A. Marinkovic and T. Vedriš (Zagreb: Hagiotheca, 2010), 17–34 at 31. This inscription, which was located at S. Sebastiano on the via Appia, is included in the Einsiedeln compilation: Codex Einsidlensis 326, f. 78v, ed. Walser, 61, no. 75; discussion, 132. Damasus's epigrams for St. Saturninus, from Carthage (no. 46), and St. Hermes, from Greece (no. 48), likewise describe the saints as acquiring Roman "citizenship" through their martyrdom in Rome. For discussion see Sághy, "Martyr Cult," 31–34; Pierre-Yves Fux, "Les patries des martyrs: doctrine et métaphores chez les poètes Damase, Ambroise, Paulin de Nola et Prudence," in *Mauritius und die thebäische Legion: Akten des internationalen Kolloquiums,*

Freiburg, Saint-Maurice, Martigny, 17–20 September 2003, ed. O. Wermelinger (Fribourg: Academic Press Fribourg, 2005), 365–75.

35. This story is found in various versions; for example, *Passio sanctorum apostolorum Petri et Pauli* (BHL 6657–59), 66, eds. R. Lipsius and M. Bonnet, *Acta apostolorum apocrypha*, 1: 118–77, here 175. Eastman, *Ancient Martyrdom Accounts*, provides a translation, 229–69, and discussion of the text, 221–27.

36. Leo the Great, Sermon 82.6, ed. A. Chavasse, CCL 138A, 508–18, here 516–17: "beatorum martyrum milia . . . apostolicorum aemula triumphorum, urbem nostram purpuratis lateque rutilantibus agminibus [populis: β] ambierunt, et quasi ex multarum honore gemmarum conserto [uno: add. B] diademate coronarunt"; trans. C. L. Feltoe, in NPNF, 2nd ser., 12: 196 (modified).

37. Unless otherwise noted, the descriptions of saints that follow are derived from the martyrology of Bede (before 735) and/or Florus (ca. 825–840): Geneviève Renaud and Jacques Dubois, *Edition pratique des martyrologues de Bède, de l'Anonyme lyonnais et de Florus* (Paris: Centre national de la recherche scientifique, 1976).

38. Abbreviated mention of this legend is already found in the *Liber Pontificalis*'s Life of Sylvester: LP 34.2, ed. Duchesne, 1: 170. The widely circulating *Actus Silvestri* (usually thought to date to around the second half of the fifth century) remains without a reliable edition. See the older edition in Mombritius, 2: 508–31, and the work of Wilhelm Pohlkamp (who is working on an edition); particularly helpful is his article, "Kaiser Konstantin, der heidnische und der christliche Kult in den Actus Silvestri," *Frühmittelalterliche Studien* 18 (1984): 357–400.

39. For the figure of Lucina, see Kate Cooper, "The Martyr, the *Matrona* and the Bishop: The Matron Lucina and the Politics of Martyr Cult in Fifth- and Sixth-Century Rome," *EME* 8.3 (1999): 297–317.

40. Prudentius, *Crowns of Martyrdom*, no. 2, lines 401–4, ed. and trans. J. H. Thomson, 132.

41. Gregorovius, *Geschichte der Stadt Rom*, 1.1, ed. Kampf, 1: 6; trans. Hamilton, 1: 10.

42. The mausoleum contained the remains of Hadrian, as well as later emperors and other members of the imperial family. Numerous inscriptions from the mausoleum are included in the Einsiedeln compilation: Codex Einsidlensis 326, ff. 76r–77r, ed. Walser, 51–55, nos. 56–66; discussion 116–25.

43. Rev. 12:7–9. Ado of Vienne's Martyrology (see Chapter 8), of which there is reason to be skeptical, reports that an oratory to Michael was dedicated by a certain Pope Boniface: Ado, Sept. 29, eds. J. Dubois and G. Renaud, 336. This is generally believed to be Pope Boniface IV (d. 615), but there is no clear evidence.

44. Gregory of Tours (d. 594) describes such serpents (*serpentes*) and a dragon (*draco*) floating by prior to an outbreak of the plague under Pope Gregory the Great: *Historiae*, 10.1, eds. B. Krusch and W. Levison, MGH SS rer. Merov. 1.1: 477.

45. Lucrezia Spera, "Trasformazioni e riassetti del tessuto urbano nel Campo Marzio centrale tra tarda antichità e medioevo," *MEFRM* 126.1 (2014): 47–74.

46. This cypress "Cypresus" in the vicinity of the Crypta Balbi appears in two of the itineraries in the Einsiedeln compilation: Itineraries no. 1 and no. 8 (as numbered by Walser).

47. Riccardo Santangeli Valenzani, *Edilizia residenziale in Italia nell'altomedioevo* (Rome: Carocci, 2011), 91–98.

48. Agnes's *passio*, cited in n. 23, describes her torments as occurring in an unspecified "theatrum," but the church's location suggests that at an early date the tradition developed that Agnes was martyred in the piazza (the ancient Stadium Domitiani, which an itinerary in the Einsiedeln compilation appears to identify as the Circus Flaminius): Mariano Armellini and Carlo Cecchelli, *Le chiese di Roma dal sec. IV al XIX*, 2nd ed., 2 vols. (Rome: N. Ruffolo, 1942), 1:

469–70; Alan Thacker, "The Origin and Early Development of Rome's Intramural Cults: A Context for the Cult of Sant'Agnese in Agone," *MEFRM* 126.1 (2014): 137–146.

49. The church appears as "Sci Laurentii in Damaso," in the Einsiedeln Itinerary no. 1 and Itinerary no. 8. See further Christian Hülsen, *Le chiese di Roma nel medio evo, cataloghi ed appunti* (Firenze: L. S. Olschki, 1927), 284.

50. The "thermae Alexandrianae" (Einsiedeln Itinerary no. 2), whose ruins remained visible into the sixteenth century: see Walser, 167.

51. Throughout the Einsiedeln compilation, both imperial baths ("thermae") and palaces ("palatia") are generic designations for ancient ruins: Walser, 160. Christian attitudes to bathing were complex, but ascetics adverse to it could cite Jerome's letter to the monk Heliodorus that "he who has bathed once in Christ has no need to bathe again": *Epistulae*, Ep. 14.10, ed. I. Hilberg, 1: 44–62, here 60, "sed qui in Christo semel lotus est, non illi necesse est iterum lauare."

52. Hendrik W. Dey, "*Diaconiae*, *Xenodochia*, *Hospitalia* and Monasteries: 'Social Security' and the Meaning of Monasticism in Early Medieval Rome," *EME* 16.4 (2008): 398–422. The foundational work on Rome's *diaconiae* remains Ottorino Bertolini, "Per la storia delle diaconie romane nell'alto medioevo sino alla fine del secolo VIII," *ASRSP* 70 (1947): 1–145; for a more recent overview see Ugo Falesiedi, *Le diaconie: i servizi assistenziali nella Chiesa antica* (Rome: Istituto Patristico Augustinianum, 1995). See further Chapter 4.

53. This is most clearly the case for S. Maria in via Lata, which was built right into a *horreum* (a storage facility).

54. Roberto Meneghini, "Acquedotti," in Meneghini and Santangeli Valenzani, *Roma nell'altomedioevo*, 65–70.

55. *Passio* of Eustachius, Greek (BHG 641), Latin (BHL 2760): AASS Sept. VI: 123A–137B. Hippolyte Delehaye, "La légende de Saint Eustache," *Bulletin de la Classe des lettres et des sciences morales et politiques*, 5th ser., 5 (Brussels: Académie royale de Belgique, 1919): 175–210.

56. This was likely a fairly recent construction in the mid-eighth century. The earliest surviving attestations of this church are the Einsiedeln compilation and the *Liber Pontificalis*'s Life of Hadrian (r. 772–795), which describes the church as already in existence: LP 97.61, ed. Duchesne, 1: 504.

57. Deborah Mauskopf Deliyannis, *Ravenna in Late Antiquity* (Cambridge: Cambridge University Press, 2010), 38.

58. I follow the version of Apollinaris's *passio* summarized by Agnellus, *Liber pontificalis ecclesiae Ravennatis*, 1, ed. D. M. Deliyannis, 148–49; trans. D. M. Deliyannis, *The Book of Pontiffs of the Church of Ravenna* (Washington, DC: Catholic University Press, 2004), 102–4, but not including the anomalies particular to Agnellus's version.

59. LP 72.4, ed. Duchesne, 1: 323.

60. CIL VI 896.

61. Gerhard Wolf, "Icons and Sites: Cult Images of the Virgin in Mediaeval Rome," in *Images of the Mother of God: Perceptions of the Theotokos in Byzantium*, ed. M. Vassilaki (Aldershot: Ashgate, 2005), 23–49 at 28–31.

62. LP 69, ed. Duchesne, 1: 317.

63. See Chapter 3.

64. See Chapter 8.

65. As recounted in the *Actus Silvestri*, see n. 38.

66. In the mid-ninth century the *Liber Pontificalis* reports that Pope Leo IV halted at the church of S. Lucia in Orphea on the Esquiline Hill to expel a serpent: "qui basiliscus grece, latine regulus dicitur": LP 105.18, ed. Duchesne, 2: 110.

67. *Passio* of Susanna (BHL 7937): AASS Aug. II: 361F–362F. Scholars generally agree that the earliest remains of the present church date only from the restorations of Pope Leo III

(r. 795–816): Margherita Cecchelli, "Santa Susanna," in Arena et al., *Roma dall'antichità al medioevo*, 641–43.

68. For a general introduction see Victor Saxer, "La chiesa di Roma dal V al X secolo: amministrazione centrale e organizzazione territoriale," in *Roma nell'alto medioevo*, Settimane 48 (Spoleto: La sede del Centro, 2001), 493–632 at 553–71 and 605–14; and Federico Guidobaldi, "L'inserimento delle chiese titolari di Roma nel tessuto urbano preesistente: osservazioni ed implicazioni," in *Quaeritur inventus colitur: miscellanea in onore di Padre U. M. Fasola* (Vatican City: Pontificio Istituto di archeologia cristiana, 1989), 381–96. Regarding the dedications of the *tituli* see Alan T. Thacker, "Martyr Cult within the Walls: Saints and Relics in the Roman *Tituli* of the Fourth to Seventh Centuries," in *Text, Image, Interpretation: Studies in Anglo-Saxon Literature and Its Insular Context in Honour of Éamonn Ó Carragáin*, eds. A. J. Minnis and J. Roberts (Turnhout: Brepols, 2007), 32–70.

69. Antoine Chavasse, "L'organisation stationnale du carême romain, avant le VIIIe siècle: une organisation 'pastorale'," *Revue des sciences religieuses* 56 (1982): 17–32; Victor Saxer, "L'utilisation par la liturgie de l'espace urbain et suburbain: l'exemple de Rome dans l'Antiquité et le Haut Moyen Âge," in N. Duval et al., *Actes du XIe Congrès*, 917–1033.

70. The *Liber Pontificalis* (LP 6.2, ed. Duchesne, 1: 126) claims that in the early second century Pope Evaristus had organized the system of *tituli*; however, later papal biographies also record the foundation of *tituli*.

71. Julia Hillner, "Families, Patronage, and the Titular Churches of Rome, *c.*300–*c.*600," in Cooper and Hillner, *Religion, Dynasty, and Patronage*, 225–61; Kimberly Diane Bowes, *Private Worship, Public Values, and Religious Change in Late Antiquity* (Cambridge: Cambridge University Press, 2008), 65–71.

72. Foundational is Johann Peter Kirsch, *Die römischen Titelkirchen im Altertum* (Paderborn: F. Schöningh, 1918).

73. It was founded in the mid-fifth century by Pope Sixtus III (r. 432–440): Margherita Cecchelli, "S. Maria Maior," LTUR 3: 217–18.

74. Dale Kinney, "The *Praesepia* in S. Maria in Trastevere and S. Maria Maggiore," in *Marmoribus vestita: miscellanea in onore di Federico Guidobaldi*, eds. O. Brandt and P. Pergola (Vatican City: Pontificio Istituto di archeologia cristiana, 2011), 777–95.

75. For S. Prassede and its restoration in the early ninth century under Pope Paschal, see Goodson, *Rome of Pope Paschal*.

76. *Passio* of Vitus (BHL 8711): AASS Jun. II: 1020E–1026E.

77. *Passio* of Vitus: *clementia* (§10); *virtus* (5, 7, 9, 15, 17); *pietas* (8); *sanctus* (1, 10, 13). Arch of Galienus (*Porta Esquilina*): CIL VI 1106: "GALLIENO · CLEMENTISSIMO · PRINCIPI · CVIVS · INVICTA · VIRTUS · SOLA · PIETATE · SVPERATA · EST · ET · SALONINAE · SANCTISSIMAE · AVG(ustae) / AVRELIVS · VICTOR · V(ir) · E(gregius) · DICATISSIMVS · NVMINI · MAIESTATIQUE · EORVM."

78. Almost all the itineraries in the Einsiedeln compilation begin, end, or pass through the Forum Romanum.

79. Hrabanus Maurus, *De rerum naturis (De universo libri)*, 14.10, PL 111: 9–779, here 387: "Capitolium Romae vocatum, quod fuerit Romanae urbis et religionis caput summum"; cited and translated by Jason Moralee, "A Hill of Many Names: The Capitolium from Late Antiquity to the Middle Ages," *ActaIRNorv* 26 (2013): 47–70 at 58.

80. Codex Einsidlensis 326, ff. 73r–v, includes five inscriptions from the Capitoline Hill: ed. Walser, 39–41, nos. 38–40, 42–43; discussion, 97–103. Many of the itineraries in the Einsiedeln compilation note the *Capitolium*, but none specifies sites on top of it.

81. The Basilica Aemilia/Basilica Pauli shows evidence of such reuse: Heinrich Bauer, "Basilica Paul(l)i," LTUR 1: 183–87.

82. CBCR 1: 64–74 (R. Krautheimer, with W. Frankl, "S. Angelo in Pescheria"); Coates-Stephens, "Dark Age Architecture," 198–99. The *diaconia*'s inscription (see Appendix 2) dates the dedication to "the first of June, in the eighth indiction, in the year 6263 from the creation of the world, in the reign of Pope Stephen the younger," that is, A.D. 755.

83. The precise interpretation of this chapel and the family members depicted in it has been much debated: Hans Belting, "Eine Privatkapelle im frühmittelalterlichen Rom," *DOP* 41, Studies on Art and Archeology in Honor of Ernst Kitzinger on His Seventy-Fifth Birthday (1987): 55–69; Arno Rettner, "Dreimal Theodotus? Stifterbild und Grabstiftung in der Theodotus-Kapelle von Santa Maria Antiqua in Rom," in *Für irdischen Ruhm und himmlischen Lohn: Stifter und Auftraggeber in der mittelalterlichen Kunst*, eds. H.-R. Meier et al. (Berlin: Dietrich Reimer, 1995), 31–46; Natalia Teteriatnikov, "For Whom Is Theodotus Praying? An Interpretation of the Program of the Private Chapel in S. Maria Antiqua," *Cahiers archéologiques: fin de l'Antiquité et Moyen Âge* 41 (1993): 37–46.

84. Teteriatnikov, "For Whom Is Theodotus Praying?," 39–40.

85. *Passio* of Chrysogonus and Anastasia (BHL 1795 + 118 + 8093 + 401), ed. Delehaye, in his *Étude sur le légendier romain: les saints de novembre et de décembre* (Brussels: Société des Bollandistes, 1936), 220–49, see also discussion at 151–70; Lanéry, "Hagiographie," 45–60.

86. Roberto Santangeli Valenzani, "Celio," in Meneghini and Santangeli Valenzani, *Roma nell'altomedioevo*, 151–55.

87. Ferrari, *Early Roman Monasteries*, 138–51.

88. Sansterre, *Moines grecs*, especially 1: 35–36.

89. *Passio* of Erasmus (BHL 2578): AASS Jun. I: 211A–219F.

90. Sansterre, *Moines grecs*, 1: 152, suggests that Erasmus's travels may have added to his appeal as a patron saint for a community that included Greek-speaking immigrants to Rome.

91. This so-called Quo Vadis scene is found in many versions of Peter's martyrdom, such as in the *Passio sanctorum apostolorum Petri et Pauli*, 61, eds. Lipsius and Bonnet, *Acta apostolorum apocrypha*, 1: 171.

92. *Passio* of Nereus and Achilleus (BHL 6058–59, 6061–64, 6066): AASS Maii III: 6E–13B.

93. None of the itineraries in the Einsiedeln compilation proceed up the Aventine Hill; however, the compilation does include an inscription from S. Sabina (on the Aventine), f. 71r, ed. Walser, 31, no. 25; discussion, 84.

94. Spoliation of older monuments appears to have been officially regulated during the Ostrogothic period (fifth/sixth century). There is, however, little evidence for the situation in the subsequent period. From at least the mid-ninth century onward, ownership of these previously public buildings appears to have passed into private hands. See Roberto Meneghini, "Monumenti come cave," in Meneghini and Santangeli Valenzani, *Roma nell'altomedioevo*, 70–72. For the Colosseum, see Rossella Rea, "Il Colosseo: destrutturazione e riuso tra IV e VIII secolo," *MEFRM* 111 (1999): 183–95.

95. Roberto Meneghini, "Sepolture Urbane," in Meneghini and Santangeli Valenzani, *Roma nell'altomedioevo*, 103–25, at 16, site no. 6 (for the Colosseum).

96. Margherita Cecchelli, "S. Salvator, Basilica," LTUR 4: 230–33; Carlo Pietrangeli, ed., *San Giovanni in Laterano* (Firenze: Nardini Editore, 1990).

97. LP 93.1, ed. Duchesne, 1: 426. Zacharias was the last of Rome's popes described as such. For Zacharias, see further Chapter 4.

98. Here I follow the liturgical description found in the Einsiedeln compilation: Codex Einsidlensis 326, ff. 86v–88v, conventionally referred to as the Ordo Romanus XXIII; ed. M. Andrieu, in *Les ordines romani du Haut Moyen Âge*, 3: 269–73; translation and discussion in Clyde Brockett, "Processing from Lateran to Hierusalem and Back: A Unique Ritual for the Cross Relic," in *Cantus Planus*, ed. R. Klugseder (Purkersdorf: Hollinek, 2012), 78–83. As demonstrated by Andrieu (*Les ordines romani,* 266), the vocabulary used indicates that the

author of this description came from north of the Alps. Antoine Chavasse, *Le Sacramentaire Gélasien, Vaticanus reginensis 316: Sacramentaire presbytéral en usage dans les titres romains au VII*[e] *siècle* (Tournai: Desclée, 1958), 88, suggests that Andrieu's dating of this document to the first half of the eighth century may be slightly too late. For the ceremony see also Sible de Blaauw, *Cultus et decor: liturgia e architettura nella Roma tardoantica e medievale. Basilica Salvatoris, Sanctae Mariae, Sancti Petri* (Vatican City: Biblioteca Apostolica Vaticana, 1994), 1: 186–95.

99. This gemmed golden cross disappeared in 1945, but was examined by scholars before that and was judged to date from around the sixth to eighth centuries: Erik Thunø, *Image and Relic: Mediating the Sacred in Early Medieval Rome* (Rome: Erma di Bretschneider, 2002), 17–23, Pl. IV, Figs. 2 and 8.

100. Ordo Romanus XXIII, 12: "Et, dum perveniunt ad Hierusalem," ed. Andrieu, 3: 271.

101. Sible de Blaauw, "Jerusalem and the Cult of the Cross," in *Pratum Romanum: Richard Krautheimer zum 100. Geburtstag*, ed. R. L. Colella (Wiesbaden: Reichert, 1997), 55–73.

Chapter 2. Imperial Saints Triumphant in the Forum Romanum

1. Gilbert J. Gorski and James E. Packer, *The Roman Forum: A Reconstruction and Architectural Guide* (New York: Cambridge University Press, 2015), and Dunia Filippi, "Regione VIII. *Forum Romanum Magnum*," in Carandini and Carafa, *Atlante di Roma antica*, 1: 143–206, provide introductions to the Forum in Classical Antiquity. For the late antique period see Gregor Kalas, *The Restoration of the Roman Forum in Late Antiquity: Transforming Public Space* (Austin: University of Texas Press, 2015). I am grateful to Gregor Kalas for sharing with me his unpublished dissertation, "Sacred Image/Urban Space: Image, Installations, and Rituals in the Early Medieval Roman Forum" (PhD diss., Bryn Mawr College, 1999).

2. Michael McCormick, *Eternal Victory: Triumphal Rulership in Late Antiquity, Byzantium, and the Early Medieval West* (Cambridge: Cambridge University Press, 1990), 84–91, 267–84.

3. Diane G. Favro, "Moving Events: Curating the Memory of the Roman Triumph," in *Memoria Romana: Memory in Rome and Rome in Memory*, ed. K. Galinsky (Ann Arbor: University of Michigan Press for the American Academy in Rome, 2014), 85–102.

4. For excavations prior to 1945 see Giuseppe Lugli, *Roma antica: il centro monumentale* (Rome: G. Bardi, 1946).

5. My analysis of the Byzantine Forum is indebted to Robert Coates-Stephens, "The Forum Romanum in the Byzantine Period," in Brandt and Pergola, *Marmoribus vestita*, 385–408; idem., "Byzantine Building Patronage in Post-Reconquest Rome," in *Les cités de l'Italie tardo-antique, IV*[e]*–VI*[e] *siècle: institutions, économie, société, culture et religion*, eds. M. Ghilardi et al. (Rome: École française de Rome, 2006), 149–66; Franz Alto Bauer, *Stadt, Platz und Denkmal in der Spätantike: Untersuchungen zur Ausstattung des öffentlichen Raums in den spätantiken Städten Rom, Konstantinopel und Ephesos* (Mainz am Rhein: P. von Zabern, 1996), 7–79, 100–124.

6. Lucy Grig and Gavin Kelly, eds., *Two Romes: Rome and Constantinople in Late Antiquity* (Oxford: Oxford University Press, 2012), especially Ch. 1, "Introduction: From Rome to Constantinople," 3–30; Van Dam, *Rome and Constantinople*.

7. Bryan Ward-Perkins, "Old and New Rome Compared: The Rise of Constantinople," in Grig and Kelly, *Two Romes*, 53–78; Sarah E. Bassett, *The Urban Image of Late Antique Constantinople* (Cambridge: Cambridge University Press, 2004); Cyril A. Mango, *Le développement urbain de Constantinople, IV*[e]*–VII*[e] *siècles* (Paris: De Boccard, 1985).

8. Wolfgang Müller-Wiener et al., *Bildlexikon zur Topographie Istanbuls: Byzantion-Konstantinopolis-Istanbul bis zum Beginn des 17. Jahrhunderts* (Tübingen: E. Wasmuth, 1977), 216–18; Cyril A. Mango, *The Brazen House: A Study of the Vestibule of the Imperial Palace of Constantinople* (Copenhagen: Munksgaard, 1959), 47–48.

9. See further Chapter 3.

10. Filippo Carlà, "Milan, Ravenna, Rome: Some Reflections on the Cult of the Saints and on Civic Politics in Late Antique Italy," *Rivista di storia e letteratura religiosa* 46 (2010): 197–272.

11. George E. Demacopoulos, *The Invention of Peter: Apostolic Discourse and Papal Authority in Late Antiquity* (Philadelphia: University of Pennsylvania Press, 2013).

12. Andrew Gillett, "Rome, Ravenna and the Last Western Emperors," *PBSR* 69 (2001): 131–67.

13. Kalas, *Restoration*, 9, counts 101 surviving inscriptions, most of which would have accompanied imperial portraits.

14. Carlos Machado, "Between Memory and Oblivion: The End of the Roman *Domus*," in Behrwald and Witschel, *Rom in der Spätantike*, 111–38.

15. Described by an anonymous chronicler: *Excerpta Valesiana*, 65–67, eds. J. Moreau and V. Velkow, 19–20. For discussion see Massimiliano Vitiello, "Teoderico a Roma: politica, amministrazione e propaganda nell' 'adventus' dell'anno 500 (Considerazioni sull' 'Anonimo Valesiano II')," *Historia: Zeitschrift für Alte Geschichte* 53.1 (2004): 73–120; Jonathan J. Arnold, *Theoderic and the Roman Imperial Restoration* (Cambridge: Cambridge University Press, 2014), 201–29.

16. Richard Westall, "Theodoric Patron of the Churches of Rome?," *ActaIRNorv* 27 (2014): 119–37; Paola Guerrini, "Theodericus rex nelle testimonianze epigrafiche," *Temporis signa: archeologia della tarda antichità e del medioevo* 6 (2011): 133–74; Ludovico Gatto, "Ancora sull'edilizia e l'urbanistica nella Roma di Teodorico," *Romanobarbarica* 12.3 (1992–1993): 311–80; Giuseppina Della Valle, "Teodorico e Roma," *Rendiconti della Accademia di archeologia, lettere e belle arti di Napoli* 34 (1959): 119–76.

17. CBCR 1: 137–43 (R. Krautheimer, "SS. Cosma e Damiano"), here 138.

18. Pope Simplicius (r. 468–483) dedicated S. Stefano Rotondo. For an overview of ecclesiastical dedications see Reekmans, "L'implantation monumentale."

19. I am grateful for clarification by Gregor Kalas on this point.

20. For example, the *Passio sanctorum apostolorum Petri et Pauli*, 56, eds. Lipsius and Bonnet, *Acta apostolorum apocrypha*, 1: 167. For a translation of this *passio* and other legends of Peter and Paul see Eastman, *Ancient Martyrdom Accounts*; topographical resonances of the legend in the Forum are discussed in Kalas, *Restoration*, 161–65.

21. As in the *Passio sanctorum apostolorum Petri et Pauli*. The differing versions are discussed in Erik Inglis, "On Storied Ground: Finding Apostolic Presence in the Streets and Springs of Medieval Rome" (forthcoming). I am grateful to Erik Inglis for sharing his unpublished article with me.

22. LP 56.2, ed. Duchesne, 1: 279: "Hic fecit basilicam sanctorum Cosmae et Damiani in urbe Roma, in loco qui appellatur via Sacra, iuxta templum urbis Romae."

23. *Codex Justinianus* 1.5.12.17, ed. P. Krueger, 54: "de severitate nonnihil eis remittere decrevimus et foederatos eos fieri honoribusque decorari permittimus, quemadmodum nobis visum fuerit"; trans. Alexander Alexandrovich Vasiliev, *Justin the First: An Introduction to the Epoch of Justinian the Great* (Cambridge, MA: Harvard University Press, 1950), 247, modified by Geoffrey B. Greatrex, "Justin I and the Arians," *Studia Patristica* 34 (2001): 73–81 at 79. As Greatrex describes, the following year an exception was again made for the Arian Goths.

24. Phil Booth, "Orthodox and Heretic in the Early Byzantine Cult(s) of Saints Cosmas and Damian," in *An Age of Saints? Power, Conflict and Dissent in Early Medieval Christianity*, eds. P. Sarris et al. (Leiden: Brill, 2011), 114–28, argues that the sixth-century miracle stories associated with Constantinople's Cosmidion (dedicated to Cosmas and Damian) portray

the saints as "theologically multivalent": these saints provided healing to all visitors, even "heretics."

25. In Rome an oratory in S. Maria Maggiore, established by Pope Symmachus (r. 498–514), was dedicated to the saints: LP 53.9, ed. Duchesne, 1: 262. For their earliest dedications in Constantinople, see Janin, 294–300, no. 3 and no. 6. For other dedications see Pierre Maraval, *Lieux saints et pèlerinages d'Orient: histoire et géographie des origines à la conquête arabe* (Paris: Cerf, 1985), 352, 354, 403; Ludwig Deubner, *Kosmas und Damian* (Leipzig: B. G. Teubner, 1907), 71–83.

26. Procopius, *Buildings*, 1.6.5–8. The specific date of restoration is unknown.

27. M. Perraymond, "Linee di diffusione del culto dei Santi Anargiri attraverso le testimonianze monumentali ed epigrafiche del VI secolo," in *Acta XIII Congressus internationalis archaeologiae christianae (Split-Poreč 25 settembre–1 ottobre 1994)* (Vatican City: Pontificio Istituto di archeologia christiana, 1998), 673–87.

28. Wendy Mayer, "Antioch and the Intersection Between Religious Factionalism, Place and Power," in *The Power of Religion in Late Antiquity*, eds. A. Cain and N. Lenski (Aldershot: Ashgate, 2009), 357–67.

29. Cyrrhus: Procopius, *Buildings*, 2.11; Pamphylia: Procopius, *Buildings*, 5.9.37; Gerasa: Maraval, *Lieux saints*, 330.

30. In the sixth-century Basilica Euphrasiana in Poreč the saints appear on an apse mosaic in a side aisle: Ann Bennett Terry and Henry Maguire, *Dynamic Splendor: The Wall Mosaics in the Cathedral of Eufrasius at Poreč* (University Park: Pennsylvania State University Press, 2007), 2: 164–71 and figs. 59–60. For Ravenna see Deliyannis, *Ravenna*, 194, 253–54.

31. Cf. Beat Brenk, "Zur Einführung des Kultes der heiligen Kosmas und Damian in Rom," *Theologische Zeitschrift* 62.2 (2006): 303–20.

32. CBCR 1: 137–43 (R. Krautheimer, "SS. Cosma e Damiano"); Roberta Budriesi, *La basilica dei SS. Cosma e Damiano a Roma* (Bologna: R. Pàtron, 1968); Gabriella Flaccomio, ed., *Il "tempio di Romolo" al foro romano*, Quaderni dell'Istituto di storia dell'architettura 26, fasc. 157–62 (Rome: Multigrafica Editrice, 1981); Kalas, *Restoration*, 62–68. Regarding the medieval church see Peter Cornelius Claussen, *Die Kirchen der Stadt Rom im Mittelalter 1050–1300, 1. A–F* (Stuttgart: Franz Steiner, 2002), 360–85.

33. The twelfth-century *Mirabilia Urbis Romae* describes this as the vestibule of the "templum Asili": 24, eds. Valentini and Zucchetti, *CTCR* 3: 3–65, here 57.

34. This now-lost inscription is known only from two varying sixteenth-century transcriptions: Kalas, *Restoration*, 63–64.

35. This observation is made by Brenk, "Zur Einführung," 312. The mosaic has been much restored over the centuries: Guglielmo Matthiae, *SS. Cosma e Damiano e S. Teodoro* (Rome: Danesi, 1948). For discussion of the mosaic see Erik Thunø, *The Apse Mosaic in Early Medieval Rome: Time, Network, and Repetition* (New York: Cambridge University Press, 2015), esp. 13–15, 40–41.

36. Erik Thunø, "Inscription and Divine Presence: Golden Letters in the Early Medieval Apse Mosaic," *Word & Image: A Journal of Verbal/Visual Enquiry* 27.3 (2011): 279–91 with a transcription and translation of the SS. Cosma e Damiano inscription by Karl F. Morrison, 289–90, which I have modified here.

37. Sible de Blaauw, "L'altare nelle chiese di Roma come centro di culto e della committenza papale," in *Roma nell'alto medioevo*, Settimane 48, 969–89 at 982.

38. *Passio* of Cosmas and Damian, Greek (BHG 378–79), Latin (BHL 1967–70). The manuscript tradition of the Latin *passio* (a translation and extension of an earlier Greek version) is complex and has not been sufficiently studied; for the Greek texts see Deubner, *Kosmas und Damian*. The earliest version of the text known in the West seems to have been the so-called Arabic version (this is the version I cite later): BHL 1967: AASS Sept. VII: 471B–473C (Mombritius, 1:

374–76); Albert Siegmund, *Die Überlieferung der griechischen christlichen Literatur in der lateinischen Kirche bis zum zwölften Jahrhundert* (Munich-Pasing: Filser Verlag, 1949), 216–17, based on the conclusions of Deubner.

39. *Passio*, 1, AASS Sept. VII: 471B: "Tempore Diocletiani & Maximiani imperatorum, sedente Clinio [Lysio] pro tribunali in civitate Ægæa, quidam ex ejus officio dixerunt ei: Sunt hic quidam Christiani industrii artis medicæ: qui circueuntes civitates & vicos, varios infirmos & spiritibus inmundis vexatos sanant in nomine ejus, qui dicitur Christus: & multa signa facientes, non permittunt homines templorum sacrificiis deos adorare." (Note that Latin texts typically refer to Aegeae in Cilicia as Aegaea.)

40. *Passio*, 8, AASS Sept. VII: 472B–C: "libera nos ab insurgentibus in nos; ne quando dicant, qui te non noverunt: Ubi est Deus eorum? Ita autem eis orantibus, statim terræmotus factus est magnus: & flamma exiliens conbussit multitudinem gentilium astantium. Martyres autem intacti exierunt ab igne, ita ut nec capillus eorum tactus esset ab igne: & sic steterunt in conspectu omnium."

41. *Passio* of Theodore, Greek (BHG 1761), Latin (BHL 8077–78). Theodore's Latin *passio* is a translation from the Greek. My summary follows BHL 8077 (according to Siegmund, the earlier of the two Latin versions, likely translated in Rome): AASS Nov. IV: 29F–39D; Siegmund, *Überlieferung*, 252.

42. Gianluca Pilara, *La città di Roma fra chiesa e impero durante il conflitto gotico-bizantino* (Rome: Aracne, 2006).

43. Procopius, *Gothic Wars*, 1.22.

44. Ibid., 1.25.

45. Ibid., 2.3.

46. Santangeli Valenzani, "Strutture," in Meneghini and Santangeli Valenzani, *Roma nell'altomedioevo*, 23.

47. *Novellae*, App. 7, eds. R. Schoell and W. Kroll, Corpus Iuris Civilis 3 (Berlin: Weidmann, 1928), 779–802.

48. *Novellae*, App. 7.19, eds. Schoell and Kroll, 801.

49. *Novellae*, App. 7.25, eds. Schoell and Kroll, 802: "Ut fabricae publicae serventur. Consuetudines etiam et privilegia Romanae civitatis vel publicarum fabricarum reparationi vel alveo Tiberino vel foro aut portui Romano sive reparationi formarum concessa servari praecipimus, ita videlicet, ut ex isdem tantummodo titulis, ex quibus delegata fuerunt, praestentur."

50. Agathias, *Histories*, 2.7, trans. J. D. Frendo, 43.

51. Codex Einsidlensis 326, ff. 67r–v, ed. Walser, 15, nos. 1–2: "Imperante d(omino) n(ostro) piissimo ac triumphali semper Iustiniano," discussion, 64–65.

52. Bernard Bavant, "Le duché byzantin de Rome: origine, durée et extension géographique," *MEFRM* 91.1 (1979): 41–88 at 47–49.

53. Archaeological and artistic evidence from S. Maria Antiqua, the "Oratory of the Forty Martyrs," and S. Teodoro date them to the late sixth to seventh centuries. The first textual references to these churches, however, occur only in the Einsiedeln compilation and in the lives of eighth-century popes in the *Liber Pontificalis*: the first reference to S. Maria Antiqua is in the papal biography of John VII (r. 705–707): LP 88.2, ed. Duchesne, 1: 385; the first reference to SS. Sergio e Bacco is in that of Hadrian (r. 772–795): LP 97.90, ed. Duchesne, 1: 512; the first reference to S. Teodoro is in that of Leo III (r. 795–816): LP 98.45 and 75, ed. Duchesne, 2: 12 and 21. By the late eighth century S. Maria Antiqua, S. Teodoro, and SS. Sergio e Bacco were *diaconiae*, but we cannot be sure that they were all established as such. Regarding the "Oratory of the Forty Martyrs," not mentioned by this name in any source, see the later discussion in this chapter.

54. Coates-Stephens, "Byzantine Building Patronage," 149. Evidence from Ravenna might also support this view. As in Rome, most of the evidence in Ravenna for the construction of new churches comes from a text describing the activities of Ravenna's bishops (Agnel-

lus's ninth-century *Book of Pontiffs*). However, as discussed by Deliyannis, there are some hints, both in Agnellus's text and in surviving inscriptions, of patronage by members of the Byzantine administration or private laymen, and absent in Agnellus's text are foundation notices for a significant number of churches, monasteries, and smaller chapels: Deliyannis, *Ravenna*, 219–20 and 292–93.

55. The *Liber Pontificalis* specifies that Pope Honorius's (r. 625–638) reuse of bronze tiles (for the roof of St. Peter's) from the roof of the Temple of Venus and Rome in the Forum Romanum was done with imperial permission: LP 72.2, ed. Duchesne, 1: 323.

56. The scholarship on this church is extensive; fundamental are G. McN. Rushforth, "The Church of S. Maria Antiqua," *PBSR* 1 (1902): 1–119; Wladimir de Grüneisen et al., *Sainte Marie Antique* (Rome: M. Bretschneider, 1911); Eva Tea, *La basilica di Santa Maria Antiqua* (Milan: Vita e Pensiero, 1937); Pietro Romanelli and Per Jonas Nordhagen, *S. Maria Antiqua* (Rome: Istituto poligrafico dello Stato, Libreria dello Stato, 1964); John Osborne, J. Rasmus Brandt, and Giuseppe Morganti, eds., *Santa Maria Antiqua al Foro Romano: cento anni dopo. Atti del Colloquio internazionale, Roma, 5–6 maggio 2000* (Rome: Campisano Editore, 2005). Regarding the frescoes see also Beat Brenk, "Kultgeschichte versus Stilgeschichte: von der 'raison d'être' des Bildes im 7. Jahrhundert in Rom," in *Uomo e spazio nell'alto medioevo*, Settimane 50 (Spoleto: La sede del Centro, 2003), 971–1054. Painted photographs of the frescoes were published by Josef Wilpert, *Die römischen Mosaiken und Malereien der kirchlichen Bauten vom IV. bis XIII. Jahrhundert* (Freiburg im Breisgau: Herder, 1917).

57. The lack of consensus was evident in the recent conference at the British School in Rome, "Santa Maria Antiqua: 'The Sistine Chapel of the 8th Century' in Context. A Consideration of the Site from the 4th–9th Century," Dec. 4–6, 2013, that assembled many of the leading scholars on the church. The conference proceedings are forthcoming.

58. Regarding another level of frescoes, possibly including a representation of Mary under the "Maria Regina," see Giulia Bordi, "Santa Maria Antiqua: prima di Maria Regina," in *L'officina dello sguardo: scritti in onore di Maria Andaloro*, ed. G. Bordi (Rome: Gangemi Editore, 2014), 285–90.

59. I am grateful to Maria Lidova for sharing with me her forthcoming article, "Maria Regina on the 'Palimpsest Wall' in S. Maria Antiqua Church in Rome: Historical Context and Imperial Connotations of the Early Byzantine Image," *Iconographica* (2017).

60. This was first argued by Krautheimer: CBCR 2: 249–74 (R. Krautheimer, W. Frankl, S. Corbett, "S. Maria Antiqua"), here 266–68; discussed further by Coates-Stephens, "Byzantine Building Patronage," 155–58.

61. Coins from the reign of Justin II (r. 565–578) found under one of the columns establish a terminus post quem for these changes.

62. Averil Cameron, "The Theotokos in Sixth-Century Constantinople: A City Finds Its Symbol," *Journal of Theological Studies* 29 (1978): 79–108.

63. Bishop Ecclesius: Agnellus, *Liber pontificalis ecclesiae Ravennatis*, 57, ed. Deliyannis, 224–25. S. Maria in Cosmedin: Agnellus, 86, ed. Deliyannis, 253.

64. A dedication to Mary (S. Maria in Cannapara), which was located in the Basilica Julia in the Forum Romanum, might also have been established by the Byzantine administration. The evidence regarding this dedication is complicated, but it appears that the initial phase of the church may have dated to somewhere between the sixth to eighth centuries: Cristina Gennaccari, "Le chiese di Santa Maria in Cannapara," in *Ecclesiae urbis: atti del Congresso internazionale di studi sulle chiese di Roma (IV–X secolo), Roma, 4–10 settembre 2000*, eds. F. Guidobaldi and A. Guiglia Guidobaldi (Vatican City: Pontificio Istituto di archeologia cristiana, 2002), 419–39. The Byzantine general Belisarius also dedicated a *xenodochium* on the via Lata that, at least according to later evidence, had an oratory dedicated to Mary: LP 61.2, ed. Duchesne, 1: 293; Riccardo Santangeli Valenzani, "Pellegrini, senatori e papi: gli xenodochia a

Roma tra il V e il IX secolo," *Rivista dell'Istituto nazionale di archeologia e storia dell'arte* 19–20 (1996–1997): 203–26 at 210. Further evidence for Marian dedications in Rome and throughout Italy in the period are discussed by Robert Coates-Stephens, "Sulla fondazione di S. Maria in Domnica," in *Scavi e scoperte recenti nelle chiese di Roma: atti della giornata tematica dei Seminari di archeologia cristiana (Roma, 13 marzo 2008)*, eds. H. Brandenburg and F. Guidobaldi (Vatican City: Pontificio Istituto di archeologia cristiana, 2012), 77–91 at 81–91.

65. Agnellus, *Liber pontificalis ecclesiae Ravennatis*, 86, ed. Deliyannis, 253; Deliyannis, *Ravenna*, 154.

66. Siegmund, *Überlieferung*, 226 dates these translations to the period from the seventh to the mid-ninth centuries.

67. In a paper "Oratory of the Forty Martyrs," presented at the 2013 S. Maria Antiqua conference cited in n. 57. See also Coates-Stephens, "Byzantine Building Patronage," 157.

68. Life of Leo III (r. 795–816): LP 98.83, ed. Duchesne, 2: 26.

69. Francis Dvornik, *The Idea of Apostolicity in Byzantium and the Legend of the Apostle Andrew* (Cambridge, MA: Harvard University Press, 1958).

70. Per Jonas Nordhagen, "S. Maria Antiqua: The Frescoes of the Seventh Century," *ActaIRNorv* 8 (1978): 89–142 at 133–35; Nordhagen, "The Earliest Decorations in Santa Maria Antiqua and their Date," *ActaIRNorv* 1 (1962): 53–72 at 63.

71. *Passio* of the Forty Martyrs, Greek (BHG 1201), Latin (BHL 7537–42); Siegmund, *Überlieferung*, 249–50. BHL 7539: AASS Mar. II: 19D–21F. BHL 7538 (unedited) has been characterized as the "Roman" version of the *passio*. The saints were also celebrated in sermons by the well-known late antique Cappadocian Church fathers, Basil of Caesarea and Gregory of Nyssa: Christopher Walter, *The Warrior Saints in Byzantine Art and Tradition* (Aldershot: Ashgate, 2002), 170–80.

72. Gregor Kalas, "Topographical Transitions: The Oratory of the Forty Martyrs and Exhibition Strategies in the Early Medieval Roman Forum," in Osborne et al., *Santa Maria Antiqua al Foro Romano*, 191–211 at 199.

73. Kirsti Gulowsen, "Some Iconographic Aspects of the Relationship Between Santa Maria Antiqua and the Oratory of the Forty Martyrs," in Osborne et al., *Santa Maria Antiqua al Foro Romano*, 187–97; Nordhagen, "S. Maria Antiqua," 131–32; Nordhagen, "Earliest Decorations," 63.

74. Procopius, *Buildings*, 1.7.

75. *The Chronicle of Theophanes Confessor*, AM 6082, trans. Cyril Mango and Roger Scott, p. 390; Janin, 498–501, no. 3 and no. 6, which, according to Mango and Scott, are the same church.

76. Paul Magdalino, "Medieval Constantinople," in *Studies on the History and Topography of Byzantine Constantinople* (Aldershot: Ashgate, 2006), 1–111 at 36–38.

77. CBCR 4: 279–88 (R. Krautheimer and S. Corbett, "S. Teodoro"); Claudia Bolgia, "Il mosaico absidale di San Teodoro a Roma: problemi storici e restauri attraverso disegni e documenti inediti," *PBSR* 69 (2001): 317–51; Alessandra Milella, "San Teodoro alle pendici del Palatino: considerazioni sulle origini della diaconia," *Archeologia classica* 55 (2004): 203–33.

78. Euchaïta was raised to the rank of an archbishopric by the Emperor Anastasius (r. 491–518) and continued thereafter to be known for its cult site for Theodore: John Haldon, *A Tale of Two Saints: The Martyrdoms and Miracles of Saints Theodore 'the Recruit' and 'the General'* (Liverpool: Liverpool University Press, 2016); Maraval, *Lieux saints*, 376; Bernhard Kötting, *Peregrinatio Religiosa: Wallfahrten in der Antike und das Pilgerwesen in der alten Kirche* (Münster: Regensberg, 1950), 160–66. For Theodore's cult see also Walter, *Warrior Saints*, 44–66. I am grateful to John Haldon for sharing materials prior to publication.

79. Janin, 157–58, no. 9; Procopius, *Buildings*, 1.4.28. By the sixth century there was a second dedication to Theodore in Constantinople near the forum of Constantine: Janin, 159–60, no. 12.

80. See n. 65.

81. This may be the second Theodore, also associated with Euchaïta whose legend developed later. However, Coates-Stephens, "Byzantine Building Patronage," 161, also proposes de Rossi's earlier suggestion that this was the Byzantine official who dedicated the church.

82. Reported by the late sixth-century ecclesiastical history of Evagrius, *Historia Ecclesiastica*, 4.28, ed. A. Hübner, 2: 504–7.

83. Gregory of Tours, *Historiae*, 7.31, eds. Krusch and Levison, MGH SS rer. Merov. 1.1: 350–51. As early as the fifth century sanctuaries were dedicated to the saints throughout Syria and Mesopotamia: Maraval, *Lieux saints*, 330–35, 348–50, 352; Elizabeth Key Fowden, *The Barbarian Plain: Saint Sergius Between Rome and Iran* (Berkeley: University of California Press, 1999); Walter, *Warrior Saints*, 146–62.

84. Procopius, *Buildings*, 1.4.1–9; Janin, 466–70; Müller-Wiener et al., *Bildlexikon*, 177–83. The initial dedication, as recorded in the inscription, was to St. Sergius, but sources from the sixth century report the church's dedication to both saints.

85. Procopius, *Buildings*, 1.4.8, ed. and trans. H. B. Dewing, 49: "οὕτω δὲ ἄμφω ἀγαστὰ τὰ ἱερὰ τάδε ξυμβαίνει εἶναι ὥστε διαφανῶς τῆς τε πόλεως ὅλης καὶ οὐχ ἥκιστα τῶν βασιλείων ἐγκαλλώπισμα τυγχάνει ὄντα."

86. Vasiliev, *Justin*, 378.

87. In 1972, Mango proposed that the church of Sts. Sergius and Bacchus was built for the community of refugees; the issue has been much debated: Cyril Mango, "The Church of Saints Sergius and Bacchus at Constantinople and the Alleged Tradition of Octagonal Palatine Churches," *Jahrbuch der Österreichischen Byzantinistik* 21 (1972): 189–93; Richard Krautheimer, "Again Saints Sergius and Bacchus at Constantinople," *Jahrbuch der Österreichischen Byzantinistik* 23 (1974): 251–53; T. F. Matthews, "Architecture et liturgie dans les premières églises palatiales de Constantinople," *Revue de l'art* 24 (1974): 22–29; Cyril Mango, "The Church of Sts. Sergius and Bacchus Once Again," *Byzantion* 68 (1975): 385–92; Jonathan Bardill, "The Church of Sts. Sergius and Bacchus in Constantinople and the Monophysite Refugees," *DOP* 54 (2000): 1–11; Brian Croke, "Justinian, Theodora, and the Church of Saints Sergius and Bacchus," *DOP* 60 (2006): 25–63.

88. Codex Einsidlensis 326, f. 80r: Itinerary no. 1, ed. Walser, 145, "s(an)c(t)i sergii. ubi umbilicu(m) romae," see also 151; Mariangela Marinone, "SS. Sergius et Bacchus, Diaconia," LTUR 4: 303–4; Mara Bonfioli, "La diaconia dei SS. Sergio e Bacco nel foro romano: fonti e problemi," *RACr* 50 (1974): 55–85.

89. Filippo Coarelli, "Umbilicus Romae," LTUR 5: 95–96; Zaccaria Mari, "Miliarium Aureum," LTUR 3: 250–51.

90. *Passio* of Sergius and Bacchus, Greek (BHG 1624: ed. I. van den Gheyn, "Passio antiquior SS. Sergii et Bacchi graece nunc primum edita," *AB* 14 [1895]: 373–95), Latin (BHL 7599–606). BHL 7599: AASS Oct. III: 863D–70F. The evidence for the Roman origins of BHL 7599 is that this version is included in the Weissenburger Legendar, Brussels, Koninklijke Bibliotheek van België, 7984; as discussed in Chapter 7, relics of Sergius and Bacchus were translated from Rome to Weissenburg in the first half of the ninth century and their *passio* accompanied them. There are other manuscript versions, but only the so-called Roman type has been printed: Siegmund, *Überlieferung*, 250.

91. *Passio*, 4, AASS Oct. III: 864A.

92. *Passio*, 7, AASS Oct. III: 864E: "Indignatus itaque imperator mutavit vultum suum, & jussit confestim zonas eorum incidi, & exutos clamidibus & quæque erant miliciæ vestes, simul & torques aureas de cervicibus eorum auferri, & induit eos colubilia muliebria, & ita per mediam civitatem usque ad palatium pertrahi gravissimas in cervicibus catenas portantes. Cumque Sancti Dei traherentur per medium forum, cantantes simul dicebant: Si ambulaverimus in medio umbræ mortis, non timebimus mala, quoniam tu nobiscum es; & verbum illud Apostolicum: Quatenus abnegantes omnem impietatem & sæcularem cupiditatem & exuto

veteris hominis habitu, nudi in fide exultemus in te, Domine, quia induisti nos vestimento salutis, & tunica lætitiæ circumdedisti nos."

93. Stefano De Angeli, "Iuppiter Optimus Maximus Capitolinus, Aedes (Fasi Tardo-Rep. e Imp.)," LTUR 3: 148–53.

94. Ps. 22[23].4 (KJV, modified to fit the Latin text); see n. 92.

95. Richard Brilliant, "Arcus: Septimius Severus (Forum)," LTUR 1: 103–5.

96. Whether Constantine ascended the Capitoline is unclear; Eusebius's account suggests that he did not. Certainly Constantius II on his visit to Rome in 357 did not: Ammianus Marcellinus, 16.10.

97. Coates-Stephens, "The Forum Romanum," 397–401; Bauer, *Stadt*, 44–46; Kalas, *Restoration*, 96–99; Patrizia Verduchi, "Columna Phocae," LTUR 1: 307.

98. CIL VI 1200.

99. Coates-Stephens, "The Forum Romanum," 397–99; Bauer, *Stadt*, 44–46, 158–62.

100. LP 69.2, ed. Duchesne, 1: 317.

101. LP 72.1, ed. Duchesne, 1: 323 (Honorius's family background); LP 72.6, ed. Duchesne, 1: 324: "Fecit ecclesiam beati Adriani in Tribus Fatis, quam et dedicavit, et dona multa optulit."

102. LP 72, ed. Duchesne, 1: 323–24; Anton Thanner, *Papst Honorius I (625–638)* (St. Ottilien: EOS Verlag, 1989). Honorius's epitaph claims for him the honor of having brought an end to the Three Chapters schism (although in fact it continued after his death); in a letter that was to be harshly condemned by subsequent popes, Honorius acquiesced to attempts by Constantinople's patriarch to end eastern opposition to the Council of Chalcedon.

103. The shrine of St. Andrew in St. Peter's received lavish gifts; a basilica was built for St. Apollinaris in the portico of St. Peter's, and the connection was further reinforced by the institution of a weekly procession from S. Apollinare to St. Peter's.

104. Shrines or cemeteries on four extramural roads in different directions from Rome (the via Nomentana, the via Labicana, the via Ostiense, and the via Aurelia) were all recipients of papal gifts. Similarly, Honorius's dedications within the walls were not clustered in one area, but were located throughout the city.

105. See n. 112.

106. Janin, 13–14.

107. Regarding the church see Silvana Episcopo, "S. Hadrianus, ecclesia," LTUR 3: 8–9; Nino Lamboglia, "Uno scavo didattico dietro la 'Curia Senatus' e la topografia del Foro di Cesare," *RendPontAcc*, 3rd ser., 37 (1964–1965): 105–36; Adele Mancini, "La chiesa medioevale di S. Adriano nel foro romano," *RendPontAcc*, 3rd ser., 40 (1967–1968): 191–245; Chiara Morselli and Edoardo Tortorici, *Curia, Forum Iulium, Forum Transitorium* (Rome: De Luca, 1989), 15–33 and 257–58; Kalas, "Sacred Image/Urban Space," 25–80.

108. See especially the accounts of Bartoli who conducted the excavations: Alfonso Bartoli, *Curia Senatus: lo scavo e il restauro* ([Rome]: Istituto di studi romani, 1963); idem., "Il monumento della perpetuità del Senato," *Studi romani* 11 (1954): 129–37.

109. Edoardo Tortorici, "Curia Iulia," LTUR 1: 332–34.

110. Mancini, "La chiesa medioevale."

111. The last surviving attestation of the Roman senate in session occurs in Procopius, *Gothic Wars*, 1.19–20, but the senate's acclamation (at the Lateran) of the imperial portraits of Phocas (r. 602–610) and his wife is recorded: see Chapter 3, n. 12. A "senate" reappears in late eighth-century papal sources. For further discussion see especially Girolamo Arnaldi, "Rinascita, fine, reincarnazione e succesive metamorfosi del Senato romano (secoli V–XII)," *ASRSP* 105 (1982): 5–56. Bartoli, "Il monumento," 136 argued that the minimal changes carried out in converting the Senate house into a church indicated that the senate continued to meet in S. Adriano, but there is no direct evidence to support this interpretation.

112. *Passio* of Hadrian: Greek (BHG 27), Latin (BHL 3744–45). The Greek text (with Latin translation) is printed in AASS Sept. III: 218A–231A. BHL 3744: Mombritius, 1: 22–30. See also Siegmund, *Überlieferung*, 236–37. The Latin and Greek editions read "Maximianus/ Μαξιμιανὸς," although since the *passio* takes place in Nicomedia we would expect "Maximinus" (Maximinus Daia).

113. *Passio*, ed. Mombritius, 23: "Adrianus uero nomine qui erat prior officii uidens constantiam et magnanimitatem eorum aduersus tormenta dixit ad martyres Christi: Adiuro uos per deum uestrum: pro quo haec patimini: dicite mihi inueritate [*sic*]: quae est remuneratio uestra quam expectatis pro his tormentis."

114. *Passio*, ed. Mombritius, 23: "Scriptum est enim de illa gloria sic: Oculus non uidit: et auris non audiuit: nec in cor hominis ascendit: quae praeparauit dominus dilligentibus se," 1 Corinthians 2:9 (KJV, but modified to fit the Latin text, which has added *de illa gloria*).

115. For the challenges posed by traditional Roman notions of wealth in late antique Christian contexts, see Peter Brown, *Through the Eye of a Needle: Wealth, the Fall of Rome, and the Making of Christianity in the West, 350–550 AD* (Princeton, NJ: Princeton University Press, 2012).

116. *Passio*, ed. Mombritius, 24: "Beatus es domine meus Adriane: quia inuenisti diuitias: quas tibi non dimiserunt parentes tui: quoniam sic benedicetur omnis homo: qui timet dominum. Vere dominus meus nunc congregasti diuitias in iuuentute tua: quas non poteras inuenire in senectute tua. Vere ita securus perges ad illud saeculum: recondens tibi diuitias: quas inuenies in tempore necessitatis: quibus egent hi: qui multa possident: et abundabunt hi: qui sunt paupures."

117. *Passio*, ed. Mombritius, 28–29.

118. *Passio*, ed. Mombritius, 27: "Maximianus dixit: ergo nunc confitere deos: ut tibi propicientur: et ut te honorificient: et in locum tuum te restituant: Non enim similis illis exs [*sic*, read: es] qui tecum uincti sunt. Tu enim bene nati et magni filius: licet sis iuuenis: tamen honoribus dignus es: illi autem rusticani et filii stultorum sunt et pauperes. cui Adrianus: Noui quia scis patriam meam vel genus nec non et auos meos: Si autem nunc cognosceres illorum sanctorum bene nationem uel diuitias aut patriam quam expectant: statim caderes ad pedes eorum prouolutus: et deprecareris eos ut orarent pro te."

119. *Passio*, ed. Mombritius, 22.

120. *Passio*, ed. Mombritius, 24: "Non insanio Rex: sed ex multa insania ad sanam mentem reuertor."

121. The church is first mentioned in the papal biography of Pope Hadrian (r. 772–795): LP 97.51 and 97.96, ed. Duchesne, 1: 501 and 514. However, a now-destroyed apse mosaic in the church seems to have included Pope Honorius: Franchi De'Cavalieri, "S. Martina," at 222–23.

122. *Passio* of Martina, Greek (BHG 1176), Latin (BHL 5587–90). BHL 5587–88: AASS Ian. I: 11–18.

123. François Halkin, "Sainte Tatiana: légende grecque d'une 'martyre romaine,'" *AB* 89 (1971): 265–309; idem., *Légendes grecques de "martyres romaines"* (Brussels: Société des Bollandistes, 1973).

124. *Passio* of Hadrian, ed. Mombritius, 22.

125. Ps. 140[141].9 (KJV, modified); *Passio* of Martina, 43, AASS Ian. I: 16: "Tunc Alexander iratus iussit Sanctam in carcerem retrudi. Impulsa autem gratia Christi ambulabat dicens: . . . Custodi me a laqueo quem statuerunt mihi, & ab scandalis operantium iniquitatem."

126. Ps. 33.2[34.1] (KJV); *Passio* of Theodore, 6, AASS Nov. IV: 35D: "Beatus autem Theodorus nichil respondit praesidi sed psallebat dicens: Benedicam Dominum in omni tempore, semper laus eius in ore meo."

127. Ps. 118[119].14 (KJV, modified to fit the Latin text); *Passio* of Sergius and Bacchus, 12, AASS Oct. III: "Ambulantes autem psallebant simul & orabant tamquam ab uno ore sic ambo dicentes: In via testimoniorum tuorum delectati sumus, sicut in omnibus divitiis . . ."; *Passio* of Cosmas and Damian, 4, AASS Sept. VII: 471E: "Tunc alligaverunt omnes milites cathenis: & ducebant, ut mitterent eos in mare. Martyres vero euntes cum gaudio psallebant dicentes: In via testimoniorum tuorum, Domine, delectati sumus, sicut in omnibus divitiis."

128. Ps. 11.2[12.1] (KJV); *Passio* of the Forty Martyrs, 10, AASS Mar. II: 21C: "Et cœpit psallere. Saluum me fac, Domine, quoniam defecit sanctus &c."

129. Ps. 123[124].7 (KJV); *Passio* of the Forty Martyrs, 11, AASS Mar. II: 21C: "Cum autem confringerentur crura eorum & animas redderent, dicebant: Anima nostra sicut passer erepta est de laqueo venantium: laqueus contritus est, & nos liberati sumus; adiutorium nostrum in nomine Domini, qui fecit cælum & terram."

130. This procession was instituted by Pope Sergius (r. 687–701) for the Marian feast days: the Annunciation (March 25), the Dormition (August 15), the Nativity (September 8), and the Hypapante (February 2): LP 86.14, ed. Duchesne, 1: 376; Saxer, "L'utilisation," 1000–1002 (Appendix VI).

131. Described in the "Ordo qualiter in Purificatione sanctae Mariae agendum est": Ordo XX, ed. Andrieu, *Les ordines romani*, 3: 235–36, here 235.

132. LP 95.6, ed. Duchesne, 1: 465.

133. S. Adriano: LP 97.73, ed. Duchesne, 1: 508; SS. Cosma e Damiano: LP 97.76, ed. Duchesne, 1: 508; SS. Sergio e Bacco: LP 97.90, ed. Duchesne, 1: 512.

134. John Osborne, "The Atrium of S. Maria Antiqua, Rome: A History in Art," *PBSR* 55 (1987): 186–223 at 194–96.

135. The so-called Catalogue of 807, LP 98.69–81, ed. Duchesne, 2: 18–25, here LP 98.69, ed. Duchesne, 2: 18, "Hic vero praecipuus praesul ex largitatem omnipotentis Dei et beati Petri apostoli clavigeri regni caelorum obtulit per universas sanctorum sacras ecclesias huius alme Rome, ob veniam facinorum suorum, coronas vel etiam canistros ex argento purissimo, videlicet." Regarding the text, see especially Herman Geertman, *More veterum: il Liber Pontificalis e gli edifici ecclesiastici di Roma nella tarda antichità e nell'alto medioevo* (Groningen: H.D. Tjeenk Willink, 1975), 82–129.

136. S. Maria Antiqua already contained frescoes of Cosmas and Damian, as well as Sergius and Bacchus; relics of Cosmas and Damian, as well as of Theodore, are included in Theodotus's inscription (see Appendix 2); enumerated in the "Catalogue of 807" are a monastery dedicated to Sts. Cosmas and Damian near S. Maria Maggiore and an oratory for Sts. Cosmas and Damian in the *xenodochium* called Tucium; two monasteries dedicated to Sts. Sergius and Bacchus (one near the Lateran and one in the Subura); and a monastery dedicated to St. Hadrian that had been restored by Pope Hadrian, near S. Maria Maggiore. Also, according to the *Liber Pontificalis*, Pope Gregory III (r. 731–741) enlarged what had been an oratory for Sergius and Bacchus by St. Peter's, turning it into a *diaconia*: LP 92.13, ed. Duchesne, 1: 420. But this dedication is not listed in the "Catalogue of 807."

Chapter 3. St. Caesarius on the Palatine

1. Daniela Bruno, "Regione X. *Palatium*," in Carandini and Carafa, *Atlante di Roma antica*, 1: 215–80.

2. Throughout this chapter I rely on the work of Andrea Augenti, *Il Palatino nel medioevo: archeologia e topografia (secoli VI–XIII)* (Rome: Erma di Bretschneider, 1996); English summary in Andrea Augenti, "Continuity and Discontinuity of a Seat of Power: The Palatine Hill from the Fifth to the Tenth Century," in Smith, *Early Medieval Rome*, 43–53. See also Santangeli

Valenzani, "Il Palatino," in Meneghini and Santangeli Valenzani, *Roma nell'altomedioevo*, 207–11.

3. It appears that in the early Middle Ages at least three routes were accessible: the so-called clivus Palatinus, which led from the vicinity of the Arch of Titus to the Domus Augustana; a ramp from the Atrium Vestae; and a ramp from S. Maria Antiqua to the Domus Tiberiana: Augenti, *Palatino*, 16.

4. Ibid., 36–40.

5. Jonathan Bardill, "Visualizing the Great Palace of the Byzantine Emperors at Constantinople: Archaeology, Text, and Topography," in *Visualisierungen von Herrschaft: frühmittelalterliche Residenzen. Gestalt und Zeremoniell*, ed. Franz Alto Bauer (Istanbul: Ege Yayınları, 2006), 5–46; Cyril Mango, "Great Palace," *ODB*; Müller-Wiener et al., *Bildlexikon*, 229–37; Jean Ebersolt, *Le grand palais de Constantinople et le Livre des cérémonies* (Paris: E. Leroux, 1910); J. B. Bury, "The Great Palace," *BZ* (1912): 210–25.

6. Flavius Cresconius Corippus, *In laudem Iustini Augusti minoris*, 3.13–17, ed. and trans. A. Cameron, 61 (Latin) and 102–3 (English): "gemmis,/ tempore quas prisco Romana potentia cepit,/ quas viridis Nereus, quas protulit Indica tellus,/ et quas Memphitica Caesar perduxit ab aula,/ quas supplex Cleopatra dedit."

7. Raymond Janin, *Constantinople byzantine* (Paris: Institut français d'études byzantines, 1964), 115–17; Ebersolt, *Le grand palais*, 77–83. According to later sources this hall was commissioned by Emperor Justin II (although alternate traditions exist).

8. See Chapter 2, n. 16.

9. Augenti, *Palatino*, 44–45.

10. Ibid., 46–48; a seal from the exarch Paul (r. 723–726) was found in the Domus Augustana.

11. Otto Treitinger, *Die oströmische Kaiser- und Reichsidee nach ihrer Gestaltung im höfischen Zeremoniell* (Darmstadt: Gentner Verlag, 1956), 204–11.

12. Gregory the Great, *Registrum*, ed. D. Norberg, 2: 1101, Appendix VIII: "Venit autem icona suprascriptorum Focae et Leontiae Augustorum Romae septimo Kalendarum Maiarum, et acclamatum est eis in Lateranis in basilica Iulii ab omni clero uel senatu: 'Exaudi Christe! Focae Augusto et Leontiae Augustae vita!' Tunc iussit ipsam iconam domnus beatissimus et apostolicus Gregorius papa reponi eam in oratorio sancti Cesarii intra palatio." Discussed by Mark Humphries, "From Emperor to Pope? Ceremonial, Space and Authority at Rome from Constantine to Gregory the Great," in Cooper and Hillner, *Religion, Dynasty, and Patronage*, 21–58. The renowned archaeologist of Christian Rome Christian Hülsen argued that this passage refers to a chapel in the Lateran, not on the Palatine, and questioned the very existence of a chapel for St. Ceasarius on the Palatine: Christian Hülsen, "Die Kirchen des heil. Caesarius in Rom," in *Miscellanea Francesco Ehrle: Scritti di storia e paleografia* (Rome: Biblioteca Apostolica Vaticana, 1924), 2: 377–403. However, Duchesne's evidence that the term "palatium" only refers to the Lateran from the ninth century onward is a convincing argument against this interpretation: Louis Duchesne, "Le Palatin chrétien," *Nuovo bullettino di archeologia cristiana* 6 (1900): 17–28 at 23–24.

13. Augenti, *Palatino*, 50–55. Alfonso Bartoli, "Scoperta dell'oratorio e del monastero di S. Cesario sul Palatino," *Nuovo bollettino di archeologia cristiana* 13 (1907): 191–204, proposed a specific location on the basis of inconclusive fragmentary fresco remains, but there is no clear evidence. See also Laura Iamurri and Simona Ciofetta, "Santa Maria Antiqua e San Cesareo," *Roma sacra* 1.3 (1995): 26–31; Anna Laura Trinci, "S. Caesareus, Oratorium," LTUR 1: 213.

14. By the end of the fifth century the Great Palace in Constantinople had chapels for St. Stephen and St. Michael: regarding the former see the later discussion.

15. *Acta Petri et Pauli* (BHG 1490–91), 13, eds. Lipsius and Bonnet, *Acta Apostolorum Apocrypha*, 1: 178–222, here 184–85: "ἐξελθὼν δὲ ἀπὸ Γαΐτας ἦλθεν εἰς καστέλλιον λεγόμενον

Ταρακίνας, καὶ ἔμεινεν ἐκεῖ ἡμέρας ἑπτὰ εἰς τὸν οἶκον Καισαρίου τοῦ διακόνου, ὃν ἐχειροτόνησεν Πέτρος." Eastman, *Ancient Martyrdom Accounts*, provides a translation, 271–315, and discussion of the text, 221–27. The text has been argued to date to the fifth or sixth century and appears to be a translation from the Latin (although the surviving Latin text does not include the travels of Paul before his arrival in Rome).

16. Giovanni Uggeri, "Lautulae," in *Brill's New Pauly Online*.

17. CIL X 6850–51.

18. For example Procopius, *Gothic Wars*, 5.2.1, describes imperial troops stationed there. Scholarship (following Lugli's suggestion in 1926) has typically interpreted Terracina's walls as a Byzantine construction, but Christie and Rushworth have argued that they are more likely to date from the first half of the fifth century: Neil J. Christie and Alan Rushworth, "Urban Fortification and Defensive Strategy in Fifth and Sixth Century Italy: The Case of Terracina," *Journal of Roman Archaeology* 1 (1988): 73–87.

19. Silvio Gheroni, *La cattedrale di Terracina* (Turin: S.A.L.E., 1931); regarding medieval Terracina, see also Clara Rech, ed., *Terracina e il medioevo: un punto di osservazione sul primo millennio alla fine del secondo millennio* (Rome: Quasar, 1989).

20. André Guillou, "Inscriptions du duché de Rome," *MEFRM* 83.2 (1971): 149–58. See also Maria Rosaria Coppola, "Il foro emiliano di Terracina: rilievo, analisi tecnica, vicende storiche del monumento," *MEFRA* (1984): 325–77.

21. "Ὀρθοδόξ(ων) κ(αὶ) νηκ(η)τ(ῶν) / β(ασιλέων) πολλὰ τὰ ἔτη," cited in Guillou, "Inscriptions," 150.

22. "Mundificatus / est forus iste / tenp(ore) d(o)m(in)i Georgii / consul et dux," cited in ibid., 152.

23. The *passio* of Caesarius survives in four versions of varying length: *passio minima* (BHL 1515), *parva* (BHL 1512–13), *major* (BHL 1511), and *maxima* (BHL 1514): for discussion see AASS Nov. I: 84A–89F. The major difference in content concerns whether these stories focus on the pagan rite of self-immolation (BHL 1512–13) or the vengeance wrought on Caesarius's persecutor by a snake (BHL 1515); BHL 1511 and 1514 include both, but BHL 1514 also includes the martyrdom of Nereus, Achilleus, and Domitilla. My summary of the story here is based on the widely circulating BHL 1511: AASS Nov. I: 105A–117C. There is also a Greek version of the *passio*: BHG 284. The legend is conventionally dated to the fifth or sixth century: Lanéry, "Hagiographie," 238–46. The legend must have been fairly well known by the later seventh century, when Bede incorporated it into his martyrology.

24. *Passio*, 2, AASS Nov. I: 106B; 5, 107D.

25. *Passio*, 10, AASS Nov. I: 108B: "Hoc cum vidisset Cæsarius diaconus, cœpit clamare dicens: *Væ reipublicæ et principibus, qui cruciatibus adflectuntur et effusione sanguinum saginantur.*"

26. *Passio*, 20, AASS Nov. I: 111E–122A: "Eadem hora clamabat Cæsarius diaconus, dicens: *Audite, fratres, si justum est ut homo timeatur magis quam Deus creator omnium rerum, et in morte sanguinis hominum purificetur civitas vestra, vos judicate.*"

27. The development of the legend of Caesarius is analyzed by Dufourcq, *Étude*, 1: 139–42, 255–58, 305–307. See also Francesco Lanzoni, "A proposito della passione di San Cesario di Terracina," *RACr* 1 (1924): 145–48.

28. See n. 15.

29. *Passio* of Nereus and Achilleus (BHL 6058–59, 6061–64, 6066): AASS Maii III: 6E–13B: here §25, 13A: "Altera namque die veniens sanctus Diaconus, nomine Cæsarius, invenit corpora Virginum immaculata: in facies enim suas prostratæ, orantes Dominum, recesserunt. Quarum corpora sanctus Cæsarius in sarcophago novo simul condiens, in profundo terræ infodiens sepelivit."

30. See Appendix 3.

31. The exact sequence of events is unclear: Holger A. Klein, "Sacred Relics and Imperial Ceremonies at the Great Palace of Constantinople," in Bauer, *Visualisierungen von Herrschaft*, 79–99, here 88; Klein, *Byzanz, der Westen und das "wahre" Kreuz: die Geschichte einer Reliquie und ihrer künstlerischen Fassung in Byzanz und im Abendland* (Wiesbaden: Reichert, 2004), 32–47.

32. Klein, "Sacred Relics"; idem., "Eastern Objects and Western Desires: Relics and Reliquaries Between Byzantium and the West," *DOP* 58 (2004): 283–314; Otto Meinardus, "A Study of the Relics of the Saints of the Greek Orthodox Church," *Oriens christianus* 54 (1970): 130–278; Jean Ebersolt, *Sanctuaires de Byzance* (Paris: E. Leroux, 1921), 88–94.

33. Cyril Mango, "Constantine's Mausoleum and the Translation of Relics," *BZ* 83.1 (1990): 51–62.

34. Klein, "Sacred Relics," 83.

35. The Trier Ivory is variously dated from the fifth to the later ninth or early tenth century: Leslie Brubaker and John F. Haldon, *Byzantium in the Iconoclast Era (c. 680–850): A History* (Cambridge: Cambridge University Press, 2011), 132–35, 347–48.

36. Ioli Kalavrezou, "Helping Hands for the Empire: Imperial Ceremonies and the Cult of Relics at the Byzantine Court," in *Byzantine Court Culture from 829 to 1204*, ed. H. Maguire (Washington, DC: Dumbarton Oaks, 1997), 53–79 at 57–59.

37. Kenneth G. Holum and Gary Vikan, "The Trier Ivory, 'Adventus' Ceremonial, and the Relics of St. Stephen," *DOP* 33 (1979): 113–33.

38. For the relics in the Great Palace, most of a later date, see Ebersolt, *Sanctuaires*, 17–30.

39. For a more skeptical attitude, see Robert Ousterhout, "Sacred Geographies and Holy Cities: Constantinople as Jerusalem," in *Hierotopy: The Creation of Sacred Space in Byzantium and Medieval Russia*, ed. A. Lidov (Moscow: Progress-Tradition, 2006), 98–116.

40. The city did possess some "imperial" relics, but these were few in number and their legends not well developed. Constantine's mother, Empress Helena, was closely associated with the Sessorian basilica that became S. Croce in Gerusalemme and, by the later fourth century, with the discovery of the True Cross. However, no surviving legend explicitly connects S. Croce's cross relics with Helena: Blaauw, "Jerusalem." Also, a tradition developed (although no fully elaborated version of the legend survives from before the twelfth century) according to which Empress Eudoxia acquired the chains of St. Peter in Jerusalem and dedicated the church of S. Pietro in Vincoli with them: Kate Cooper, Julia Hillner, and Conrad Leyser, "Dark Age Rome: Towards an Interactive Topography," in *Social and Political Life in Late Antiquity*, eds. W. Bowden et al. (Leiden: Brill, 2006), 311–77.

41. In contrast, Justinian's jurists preferred to construe the primacy of the Roman Church in terms of its status as the ancient capital of the empire: Demacopoulos, *Invention of Peter*, 121–23.

42. Gregory the Great, *Registrum*, 4.30, ed. Norberg, 1: 248–50; Leyser, "Temptations of Cult"; John M. McCulloh, "From Antiquity to the Middle Ages: Continuity and Change in Papal Relic Policy from the 6th to the 8th Century," in *Pietas: Festschrift für Bernhard Kötting*, eds. E. Dassman and K. S. Frank (Münster: Aschendorff, 1980), 312–24.

43. Richard Price, *The Acts of the Lateran Synod of 649* (Liverpool: Liverpool University Press, 2014); Phil Booth, *Crisis of Empire: Doctrine and Dissent at the End of Late Antiquity* (Berkeley: University of California Press, 2013), 278–328; Catherine Cubitt, "The Lateran Council of 649 as an Ecumenical Council," in *Chalcedon in Context: Church Councils 400–700*, eds. R. Price and M. Whitby (Liverpool: Liverpool University Press, 2009), 133–47.

44. LP 76.4–7, ed. Duchesne, 1: 337–38.

45. Wolfram Brandes, "'Juristische' Krisenbewältigung im 7. Jahrhundert? Die Prozesse gegen Martin I. und Maximos Homologetes," in *Fontes Minores* 10, ed. L. Burgmann (Frankfurt am Main: Klostermann, 1998), 141–212.

46. Rushforth, "Church," 67–73; Nordhagen, "S. Maria Antiqua," 97–100.

47. The frescoes are not mentioned in the *Liber Pontificalis*, making papal involvement unlikely. Brenk, "Kultgeschichte versus Stilgeschichte," 1021, argues that the frescoes date to the period of 649–653 when the exarch Olympius changed sides to support the pope. But there is to my knowledge no clinching argument for such an early date (as opposed to a date after 680–681, when the frescos would not have been in opposition to the position of the imperial administration in Constantinople).

48. A Greek *vita* of Pope Martin, perhaps composed in eighth-century Rome, likewise indicates interest in cultivating the pope's memory: Bronwen Neil, *Seventh-Century Popes and Martyrs: The Political Hagiography of Anastasius Bibliothecarius* (Turnhout: Brepols, 2006), 105–9.

49. Pasquale Corsi, *La spedizione italiana di Costante II* (Bologna: Pàtron, 1983).

50. LP 78.2–4, ed. Duchesne, 1: 343–44.

51. LP 78.3, ed. Duchesne, 1: 343; trans. Davis, *Book of Pontiffs*, 70: "omnia quae erant in aere ad ornatum civitatis deposuit; sed et ecclesiae sanctae Mariae ad martyres quae de tigulis aereis erant discoperuit et in regia urbe cum alia diversa quas deposuerat direxit."

52. Ernest Walter Brooks, "The Sicilian Expedition of Constantine IV," *BZ* 17 (1908): 455–59.

53. LP 86.2, ed. Duchesne, 1: 371; trans. Davis, *Book of Pontiffs*, 81 (modified): "Cumque unus alio locum non cederet, sed utrique inmaniter perdurarent ut unus alium superaret, inito consilio primati iudicum et exercitus Romane militiae vel cleri, si dici est, plurima pars et praesertim sacerdotum, atque civium multitudo ad sacrum palatium perrexerunt."

54. LP 86.2, ed. Duchesne, 1: 371; trans. Davis, *Book of Pontiffs*, 81: "eumque de medio populi tollentes in oraculum beati Caesarii Christi martyris, quod est intro suprascriptum palatium, introduxerunt, et exinde in Lateranense episcopio cum laude adclamationibus deduxerunt."

55. LP 86.3–5, ed. Duchesne, 1: 372.

56. T. S. Brown, *Gentlemen and Officers: Imperial Administration and Aristocratic Power in Byzantine Italy, A.D. 554–800* ([London]: British School at Rome, 1984), 64–69.

57. See George Nedungatt and Michael Featherstone, eds., *The Council in Trullo Revisited* (Rome: Pontificio Istituto orientale, 1995), 42–186, for Greek and Latin text and English translation by M. Featherstone; also, in the same volume, Heinz Ohme, "Die sogennanten 'antirömischen' Kanones des Concilium Quinisextum," 307–21.

58. LP 86.7, ed. Duchesne, 1: 373, trans. Davis, *Book of the Pontiffs*, 82: "eligens ante mori quam novitatum erroribus consentire."

59. Ibid. (translation modified): "excitatum est cor Ravennatis militiae, ducatus etiam Pentapolitani et circumquaque partium, non permittere pontificem apostolicae sedis in regiam ascendere urbem."

60. LP 86.7–9, ed. Duchesne, 1: 373–74.

61. The inscription was formerly located in S. Anastasia at the foot of the Palatine, where it was copied by Petrus Sabinus in the late fifteenth century; it no longer survives. ICUR II.1: 442, no. 152: "Ultima Funereo persolvens munia busto. / Quo pater Illustris membra locanda dedit / Adiecit Titulos proles veneranda Joannes / Ne tantus quovis esset honore minor. / Hic Iacet ille plato qui multa per agmina lustrans / Et maris undisoni per freta longa volans / Claruit Insignis regno, Gratusque minister / Celebremque sua praestitit esse manu. / Post ergo multiplices quas prisca palatia Romae / Praestiterant Curas Longo refecta gradu / Pergit ad Aeterni Divina palatia Regis / Sumere cum meritis praemia firma Dei / PLATO·V(ir)· ill(ustris)· Cura palatii Urbis Romae"; Alexander Kazhdan, "Kouropalates," *ODB*. I am grateful to Gregor Kalas for sharing his article, "Acquiring the Antique in Early Medieval Rome: The Economics of Architectural Reuse at S. Maria Antiqua," in *Reuse and Renovation in Roman Material Culture:*

Functions, Aesthetics, Interpretations, eds. D. Ng and M. Swetnam-Burland (Cambridge University Press, forthcoming).

62. Two stamped bricks with the name Ἰωάννης were found in the Atrium Vestae suggesting the renovation of the ramp leading to there, but the ramp to S. Maria Antiqua is also a likely candidate: Augenti, *Palatino*, 56–58.

63. ICUR II.1: 442, no. 153.

64. Alexander Kazhdan, "Rhaiktor," *ODB*.

65. LP 88.2. ed. Duchesne, 1: 385: "Basilicam itaque sanctae Dei genetricis qui Antiqua vocatur pictura decoravit, illicque ambonem noviter fecit et super eandem ecclesiam episcopium quantum ad se construere maluit, illicque pontificati sui tempus vitam finivit."

66. Augenti, *Palatino*, 56–58.

67. LP 88.2, ed. Duchesne, 1: 385: "Fecit vero et imagines per diversas ecclesias quas, quicumque nosse desiderat in eis eius vultum depictum repperiet."

68. Per Jonas Nordhagen, "The Frescoes of John VII, A.D. 705–707, in S. Maria Antiqua in Rome," *ActaIRNorv* 3 (1968): 1–125 at 15–54, 87–98.

69. Pope John may also have had a copy of the earlier depictions of the Church fathers with their scrolls added to the façade of the "Oratory of the Forty Martyrs": ibid., 84.

70. Per Jonas Nordhagen, "John VII's Adoration of the Cross in S. Maria Antiqua," *Journal of the Warburg and Courtauld Institutes* 30 (1967): 388–90; Nordhagen, "Frescoes of John VII," 50–54; James D. Breckenridge, "Evidence for the Nature of Relations Between Pope John VII and the Byzantine Emperor Justinian II," *BZ* 65.2 (1972): 364–74.

71. See the summary in Nordhagen, "Frescoes of John VII," 95–98.

72. LP 88.5, ed. Duchesne, 1: 386: "Sed hic, humana fragilitate timidus, hos nequaquam emendans per suprafatos metropolitas direxit ad principem."

73. Augenti, *Palatino*, 57–58, emphasizes that the symbolic associations of the site articulated a new position of power for the papacy in Rome; Jean-Marie Sansterre, "Jean VII (705–7): idéologie pontificale et realisme politique," in *Rayonnement grec: hommages à Charles Delvoye*, eds. L. Hadermann-Misguich et al. (Brussels: Editions de l'Université de Bruxelles, 1982), 377–88, esp. 386, argues that the Lombard threat had made the Lateran unsafe.

74. Here I follow the *Sanatio Gallae et translatio S. Caesarii Romam* (BHL 1517–18): AASS Nov. I: 126B-129C. See Appendix 3 for further discussion of the text.

75. LP 46.6, ed. Duchesne, 1: 234.

76. In fact, Licinia Eudoxia was the daughter of Theodosius II, not Theodosius I; Theodosius I was responsible for S. Paolo.

77. Maraval, *Lieux saints*, 382–83; Gregory of Tours, *Liber in Gloria Martyrum*, 101, ed. B. Krusch, MGH SS rer. Merov. 1.2: 105.

78. *Sanatio Gallae*, 5, AASS Nov. I: 129: "qui locus usque hodie multa miracula præstat."

79. Saxer, "L'utilisation," 1002 (Appendix VI). As attested by the Sacramentary of Trent, a ninth-century sacramentary associated with Salzburg, whose base text derives from a late seventh-century sacramentary from Rome: *Sacramentarium Tridentinum*, eds. F. Dell'Oro and H. Rogger, *Fontes liturgici libri sacramentorum*: 75–416, here 252, nos. 774–77; Cyrille Vogel, *Medieval Liturgy: An Introduction to the Sources*, rev. and trans. William G. Storey and Niels Krogh Rasmussen with the assistance of John K. Brooks-Leonard (Washington, DC: Pastoral Press, 1986), 97–102.

80. In 778 the pope complained to Charlemagne about the wicked Beneventans who, together with the inhabitants of Gaieta and Terracina, were inciting his subjects in Campania to revolt. In a subsequent letter from 779 or 780, the pope complains about the wicked Neapolitans, who together with evil Greeks sent by the *patricius* of Sicily, attacked the city of Terracina. As reconstructed by Gay, in the interval between these letters Hadrian had sent an expedition to Terracina, conquering the city, but then lost it again to the combined Beneventan and Neapolitan forces.

The letter itself seeks Frankish help in recovering the town: *Codex Carolinus*, nos. 61 and 64, ed. W. Grundlach, MGH Epp. 3: 588–89 and 591–92; Jules Gay, "L'État pontifical, les Byzantins et les Lombards sur le littoral campanien (d'Hadrien Ier à Jean VIII)," *MEFR* 21 (1901): 487–508; Noble, *Republic*, 163.

81. Alexander Kazhdan, "Triklinos of Justinian," *ODB*; Ebersolt, *Sanctuaires*, 95–97.

82. LP 96.9, ed. Duchesne, 1: 470, "Et considerantes melius se posse salvari in vestiario, ascenderunt illuc, intus oratorium sancti Caesarii ingredientes." The specific location or origins of this oratory are unknown.

83. LP 104.25, ed. Duchesne, 2: 93; trans. Davis, *Lives of the Ninth-Century Popes*, 86.

84. LP 98.77, ed. Duchesne, 2: 23. Also included in the "Catalogue of 807" (which includes neither the oratory on the Palatine nor that in the Lateran) is an oratory for St. Caesarius in the monastery "de Corsas," located on the via Appia across from S. Sisto. Based on its name it has been speculated that the *monasterium de Corsas* could have been founded by Corsicans fleeing Arab raids in the eighth century. As refugees these monks may have chosen a patron saint increasingly supported by the papacy—but the idea has no further evidence to support it: Ferrari, *Early Roman Monasteries*, 96–99.

85. Martin Heinzelmann, "Einhards 'Translatio Marcellini et Petri': eine Hagiographische Reformschrift von 830," in *Einhard: Studien zu Leben und Werk. Dem Gedenken an Helmut Beumann gewidmet*, ed. H. Schefers (Darmstadt: Hessische Historische Kommission, 1997), 269–98; Julia M. H. Smith, "'Emending Evil Ways and Praising God's Omnipotence': Einhard and the Uses of Roman Martyrs," in *Seeing and Believing: Conversion in Late Antiquity and the Early Middle Ages*, eds. K. Mills and A. Grafton (Rochester, NY: University of Rochester Press, 2003), 189–223.

86. Einhard, *Translatio et miracula sanctorum Marcellini et Petri*, 1.5, ed. G. Waitz, MGH SS 15.1: 238–264; trans. P. E. Dutton, *Charlemagne's Courtier: The Complete Einhard*, 69–91. Regarding the intentional verisimilitude of Einhard's *translatio* see Hans Reinhard Seeliger, "Einhards römische Reliquien: zur Übertragung der Heiligen Marzellinus und Petrus ins Frankenreich," *RQ* 83 (1988): 58–75.

87. Anxiety over papal opposition to the theft is emphasized when on the return journey, in Pavia, the report of traveling papal ambassadors causes the group to deliberate how best to avoid their notice: Einhard, *Translatio*, 1.7, ed. Waitz, 241.

88. Einhard, *Translatio*, 1.5, ed. Waitz, 242; trans. Dutton (modified), 75: "Noverat enim, neminem a se Romanum inveniri posse, qui sibi ad hoc ullum ferret auxilium, sed ne talem quidem, cui haec animi sui secreta auderet ostendere. In hac cordis anxietate constitutus, repperit quendam monachum peregrinum nomine Basilium, qui ante biennium de Constantinopoli Romam venerat atque ibi in monte Palatino apud alios Graecos, qui eiusdem professionis erant, cum quattuor discipulis suis hospitium habebat. Hunc adiit atque ei quam patiebatur sollicitudinem aperuit. Tum consiliis eius animatus et orationibus fretus, tantam accepit in corde suo constantiam, ut statueret rem, quamvis cum periculo capitis sui, celerrime experiri."

89. LP 105.35, ed. Duchesne, 2: 114.

90. LP 105.28, ed. Duchesne, 2: 112.

91. LP 105.66, ed. Duchesne, 2: 122, lines 18–19; trans. Davis, *Lives of Ninth-Century Popes*, 137, which repeats LP 105.65, ed. Duchesne, 2: 122, lines 7–8: "Ipse quidem venerabilis pontifex fecit in basilica sancti Cesari, qui ponitur in Terracina, veste de quadrapulo ornata in circuitu de blatta, habente in medio crucem de chrisoclabo, legente de nomine domni Leoni quarti pape."

92. Barbara M. Kreutz, *Before the Normans: Southern Italy in the Ninth and Tenth Centuries* (Philadelphia: University of Pennsylvania Press, 1991), esp. Ch. 2. That the raids continued is indicated by a letter from Pope John VIII to Emperor Louis II in 875 reporting a victory over

Saracens in Fondi and Terracina and requesting additional help: *Fragmenta registri Iohannis VIII*, no. 49, ed. E. Caspar, MGH Epp. 7: 303.

93. Duchesne, "Palatin," 25–27; Ferrari, *Early Roman Monasteries*, 88–91.

94. *Vita* of Blasios (BHG 278): AASS Nov. IV: 657C–669D; Hippolyte Delehaye, "A propos de Saint-Césaire," *RendPontAcc*, 3rd ser., 3 (1925): 45–48; Henri Grégoire, "La Vie de saint Blaise d'Amorium," *Byzantion* 5 (1929–1930): 391–414; McCormick, *Origins of the European Economy*, 203–7. The text, which is in verse, survives in a single manuscript: Paris, BnF, gr. 1491 (tenth century). In Rome no evidence survives of Blasios's extended stay on the Palatine. Grégoire argued that Blasios's stay in Rome roughly corresponded with the Photian schism, suggesting that he may have been a monk who defied Photios and was thus obliged to leave Constantinople. However, as discussed by Sansterre, *Moines grecs*, 1: 45, the redating of Blasios's travels by Denise Papachryssanthou, *Actes du Prôtaton* (Paris: P. Lethielleux, 1975), 51–52, makes this unlikely; Blasios probably left as a pilgrim, as his life affirms, although he may have decided to extend his stay in Rome because of the Photian schism.

95. *Vita* of Sabas (BHG 1611): ed. G. Cozza-Luzi, *Historia et laudes SS. Sabae et Macarii iuniorum e Sicilia auctore Oreste Patriarcha Hierosolymitano*, 5–70, 137–42, here §48, pp. 65–66.

96. The monastery, at times referred to in medieval documents as S. Caesarii Graecorum, is mentioned for the last time in the early fifteenth century; precisely how long it remained in existence is unknown: Hülsen, *Chiese*, 232–33.

97. LP 168, ed. Duchesne, 2: 386: "apud monasterium sancti Cesarii, ubi omnes fratres propter metum senatorum et populi Romani consurgentis ad arma convenerant in unum"; *Mirabilia Urbis Romae*, 25, eds. Valentini and Zucchetti, *CTCR* 3: 57–58: "Infra Palatium est templum Iuliani. In fronte Palatii templum Solis. In eodem Palatio templum Iovis, quod vocatur Casa Maior. Ubi est Sanctus Caesarius, fuit Auguratorium Caesaris."

Chapter 4. Miraculous Charity Along the Tiber's Banks

1. Filippo Coarelli, "Forum Boarium," LTUR 2: 295–97; idem, "Forum Holitorium," LTUR 2: 299; Federico Guidobaldi and Claudia Angelelli, "Velabrum," LTUR 5: 101–8; Paolo Liverani, "Velabrum (Età Tardoantica)," LTUR 5: 108–9; Chiara Bariviera, "Regione XI. *Circus Maximus*," in Carandini and Carafa, *Atlante di Roma antica*, 1: 421–45. See also, with caution, Giuseppe Marchetti Longhi, "Il quartiere greco-orientale di Roma nell'antichità e nel medio evo," in *Atti del IV Congresso nazionale di studi romani* (Rome: Istituto di studi romani, 1938), 1: 169–85.

2. CIL VI 1035: "ARGENTARI ET NEGOTIANTES BOARI"; see the later discussion.

3. Codex Einsidlensis 326, f. 68v, ed. Walser, 21, no. 12; discussion 71–72.

4. Gregorovius, *Geschichte der Stadt Rom*, 13.7.5, ed. Kampf, 3: 336.

5. Saguì, "Roma e il Mediterraneo."

6. Most scholars, including Jean Durliat, *De la ville antique à la ville byzantine: le problème des substances* (Rome: École française de Rome, 1990), 137–48, date the end of the *annona* to the early seventh century, but the evidence for its continuation in the period after the Gothic Wars is weak.

7. Scholars, especially Jean Lestocquoy, "Administration de Rome et diaconies du VIIe au IXe siècle," *RACr* 7 (1930): 261–98, have long noted the degree to which the institution of the *diaconia* is reminiscent of Rome's *annona*. Durliat, *De la ville antique*, 163–83, has demonstrated that the *diaconiae* were, both in origin and function, independent of the *annona*. However, it seems exaggerated to deny any similarity, especially since *diaconiae* multiplied in the very period (later sixth or early seventh century) that the *annona* ceased.

8. An argument first made by René Vielliard, *Recherches sur les origines de la Rome chrétienne: les églises romaines et leur rôle dans l'histoire et la topographie de la ville depuis la fin du monde antique jusqu'à la formation de l'Etat pontifical. Essai d'urbanisme chrétien* (Macon, France: Protat Frères, 1941), 117–22; see also Raimund Hermes, "Die stadtrömischen Diakonien," *RQ* 91 (1996): 1–120 at 35–38. It appears that in general Rome's early *diaconiae* were located along the Tiber banks, while later *diaconiae* tended to be located along Rome's most prominent thoroughfares, often on streets leading out of the city's gates. This shift correlates well with the changing patterns of Rome's grain supply: throughout the seventh and particularly the eighth centuries, Rome's grain increasingly came from the Italian peninsula, rather than from abroad.

9. John of Ephesus, *Life of Paul of Antioch*, ed. and trans. E. W. Brooks, *Lives of the Eastern Saints (II)*, 671–76 at 675; see also John of Ephesus, *Life of Isaac*, ed. and trans. Brooks, *Lives of the Eastern Saints (II)*, 668–71 at 669. John of Ephesus, in his ecclesiastical history, also mentions various *diaconiae* for men and women in Constantinople: *The Third Part of the Ecclesiastical History of John, Bishop of Ephesus*, trans. R. Payne Smith (Oxford: University Press, 1860), Part 3, 2.15–16: 113–17. See Hermes, "Die stadtrömischen Diakonien," 17–20, for an overview of the comparative evidence.

10. The manuscript reads "*pryqy*" (Africa), corrected by Nöldeke to "*prws*," taken by Brooks to mean "Prusias," a suburb of Constantinople. The geographical context suggests that it may refer to Prusa (modern Bursa).

11. The evidence for Naples and Ravenna is less clear-cut. Those passages might be understood as referring to *diaconia*, "aid," as an abstract concept, rather than to specific institutions: Gregory the Great, *Registrum*, 5.25, ed. Norberg, 1: 292–93 (Pesaro); 10.8, 2: 833–34 (Naples); 11.17, 2: 886 (Ravenna).

12. For further discussion and bibliography see Maya Maskarinec, "Foreign Saints at Home in Eighth- and Ninth-Century Rome: The Patrocinia of *Diaconiae*, *Xenodochia* and Greek Monasteries," in *Cuius Patrocinio Tota Gaudet Regio: Saints' Cults and the Dynamics of Regional Cohesion*, eds. S. Kuzmová et al. (Zagreb: Hagiotheca, 2014), 21–37.

13. CBCR 2: 277–307 (R. Krautheimer, W. Frankl, S. Corbett, "S. Maria in Cosmedin"); Giovanni Battista Giovenale, *La basilica di S. Maria in Cosmedin* (Roma: Sansaini, 1927).

14. The church was rebuilt under Pope Hadrian (r. 772–795; see later discussion), renovated under Pope Nicholas (r. 858–867), remodeled in the twelfth century, and restored to its twelfth-century form (stripping the later baroque decoration) in 1892–1899 under the direction of G. B. Giovenale.

15. Brick stamps of Theoderic (r. 493–526) and Athalaric (r. 526–534) were found in the roof: CBCR 2: 279. There is no proof that this building served as a *diaconia* in its earliest instantiation: the earliest secure evidence for a *diaconia* here is the mid-eighth-century inscription of Eustathius; see later discussion.

16. The identification of the porticus as part of the *statio annonae* is based on three inscriptions found nearby that record dedications by the *praefectus annonae* or the *praefectus urbi*. Coarelli has argued against this interpretation, proposing that the structure was instead the *consaeptum sacellum*, a sacred precinct associated with the nearby altar of Hercules: Filippo Coarelli, *Il Foro Boario: dalle origini alla fine della repubblica* (Rome: Edizioni Quasar, 1988), 61–77.

17. This is suggested by sixth-century chancel screens and a capital "supposedly of Ravennate origin": CBCR 2: 303.

18. Filippo Coarelli, "Hercules Invictus, Ara Maxima," LTUR 3: 15–17.

19. Especially the masonry technique ("alternating brick and tufa voussoirs in the arches of the intermediate zone") is unusual for Rome, but it finds parallels in contemporaneous buildings in Sicily and southern Italy: CBCR 2: 303–4.

20. The toponym is first reported in the *Liber Pontificalis*'s Life of Hadrian (r. 772–795) but as a name predating the events described; see later discussion.

21. Cyril Mango, "On the Cult of Saints Cosmas and Damian at Constantinople," in *Θυμίαμα στη Μνήμη της Λασκαρίνας Μπούρα* (Athens: Mouseio Benake, 1994), 189–92. See also Chapter 2, n. 26.

22. The church of S. Maria in Cosmedin (today S. Maria di Portanova) in Naples is first attested (as already in existence) in the late eighth century: *Gesta Episcoporum Neapolitanorum*, ed. G. Waitz, MGH SS rer. Lang. 404; its first attestation as a *diaconia* dates from the eleventh century, but it is likely that it was established as a *diaconia* at an earlier date: Henri-Irénée Marrou, "L'origine orientale des diaconies romaines," *MEFR* 57 (1940): 95–142 at 103–4. What had once been the Arian baptistery in Ravenna is described by the ninth-century Agnellus of Ravenna as the "monasterium beatae uirginis Mariae qui uocatur Cosmiti," *Liber pontificalis ecclesiae Ravennatis*, 157, ed. Deliyannis, 335; cf. 86, p. 253.

23. The Constantinopolitan Cosmidion was damaged when Constantinople was besieged in 626, which might suggest that the Italian imitations were built before that date: Mango, "On the Cult," 192.

24. *Passio* of Sebastian (BHL 7543): AASS Jan. II: 265–78, here §88, 278; Massimiliano Ghilardi, "Martiri e cloache: intersezioni tra agiografia e archeologia," in *La Cloaca Maxima e i sistemi fognari di Roma dall'antichità ad oggi*, ed. E. Bianchi (Rome: Palombi Editori, 2014), 191–200. The *passio* of Sebastian is conventionally dated to between the fifth and sixth centuries.

25. The present building largely dates to the ninth-century reconstruction, although the portico in front of the church, with its four columns and Gothic inscription, and the bell tower date to the thirteenth century. The church was restored in 1924–1925 by A. Muñoz (using a thick layer of plaster that has hindered subsequent archaeological investigations): Antonio Muñoz, *Il restauro della basilica di S. Giorgio al Velabro in Roma* (Rome: Società editrice d'arte illustrata, 1926).

26. CBCR 1: 242–63 (R. Krautheimer, "S. Giorgio in Velabro"); Maurizio Castelli, "La chiesa di San Giorgio al Velabro," *Bullettino della Commissione archeologica comunale di Roma* 96 (1995): 125–64; Coates-Stephens, "Dark Age Architecture," 184–86; *La chiesa di San Giorgio in Velabro a Roma. Storia, documenti, testimonianze del restauro dopo l'attentato del luglio 1993*, Bollettino d'arte, volume speciale (2002). Regarding the later medieval church see also Peter Cornelius Claussen, Daniela Mondini, and Darko Senekovic, *Die Kirchen der Stadt Rom im Mittelalter 1050–1300, 3. G–L* (Stuttgart: Franz Steiner, 2010), 15–58.

27. LP 82.5, ed. Duchesne, 1: 360, footnote to "obtulit" (line 12): "Huius almi pontificis iussu aecclesiam iuxta Velum aureum in honore beati Sebastiani edificata est, necnon in honore martiris Georgii." Coates-Stephens, "Byzantine Building Patronage," 184–86, points out that the term "at his bidding (*iussu*)" indicates this was not a papal construction, perhaps explaining why the account was not included in most versions of the *Liber Pontificalis*.

28. CBCR 1: 258–59.

29. See Appendix 4.

30. "ΑΓΙΕ ΚΩΝΟΝ, ΑΓΙΕ ΓΕΩΡΓΙ": cited in A. Nibby, *Roma nell'anno MDCCCXXXVIII* (Rome: Tipografia delle Belle Arti, 1838), 150. See also Dey, *Aurelian Wall*, 55–61, 295–97; Joseph-Marie Sauget, "San Conone l'ortolano," BS 4: 152–54.

31. S. Georgius *ad forum* (or *ad mercatum*): the *diaconia* is first attested in Naples in the early tenth century, but was likely founded much earlier: Marrou, "L'origine orientale," 104.

32. The foundational work regarding the development of the legend remains Hippolyte Delehaye, *Les légendes grecques des saints militaires* (Paris: Alphonse Picard, 1909): 45–76. Particularly helpful in charting out the different Latin versions and their relationships is Wolfgang Haubrichs, *Georgslied und Georgslegende im frühen Mittelalter: Text und Rekonstruktion*

(Königstein/Ts.: Scriptor, 1979), 205–305. It should be noted that the story of St. George and the dragon was a much later medieval addition.

33. The oldest surviving text of the legend is a Greek palimpsest, Vienna, Österreichische Nationalbibliothek (ÖNB), Cod. 954, edited by Karl Krumbacher, *Der heilige Georg in der griechischen Überlieferung* (Munich: Verlag der Königlich Bayerischen Akademie der Wissenschaften, 1911), 1–3. As interpreted by Haubrichs, following earlier scholarship, there are three primary Latin text families of the George legend. However, the complexity of the manuscript tradition cannot be overemphasized. Different versions developed early and circulated widely.

34. Haubrichs, *Georgslied und Georgslegende*, 406–73 (Appendix I) offers an edition of X-lat, which I follow here. X-lat is the version that includes the most miraculous events; this is a translation of the Greek X type.

35. *Passio* of George, X-lat, 5, ed. Haubrichs, 415: the Lord appears to George in prison after his first torments to prophesy his resurrection to him, revealing also that he will become the greatest saint in heaven; 20, pp. 465–71: George's prayers and the cremation of all the assembled kings.

36. *Passio* of George, X-lat, 7, ed. Haubrichs, 418–19: contest with the magician; 12, pp. 432–33: resurrection of an ox; 14, pp. 438–41: causes bread to appear for the poorest widow and cures the blindness of her son.

37. *Passio* of George, X-lat, 13, ed. Haubrichs, 433–48.

38. *Passio* of George, Y-Version, ed. Haubrichs, 474–99 (Appendix 2), discussion 261–77. Type Y is hypothesized to have been originally translated in Rome because versions of it are found in passionaries based on Roman models.

39. Armellini and Cecchelli, *Chiese*, 2: 778.

40. Jaś Elsner, "Sacrifice and Narrative on the Arch of the Argentarii at Rome," *Journal of Roman Archaeology* 18 (2005): 83–98.

41. Massimo Pallottino, *L'arco degli argentari* (Rome: Danesi, 1946), 31–38.

42. Filippo Coarelli, "Ianus Quadrifons," LTUR 3: 94; Domenico Palombi, "Arcus Divi Constantini," LTUR 1: 91. The "Arch of Janus" appears to be the *arcus divi Constantini*, only known from its mention in the regional catalogs (after the indication *Velabrum*).

43. For the late fourth- to sixth-century developments that laid the groundwork for this expansion of papal prerogatives see Kristina Sessa, *The Formation of Papal Authority in Late Antique Italy: Roman Bishops and the Domestic Sphere* (New York: Cambridge University Press, 2012).

44. LP 83.5, ed. Duchesne, 1: 364; LP 84.5, 1: 367; LP 85.5, 1: 369.

45. Noble, *Republic*, 15–60.

46. LP 90.4–7, ed. Duchesne, 1: 389–91.

47. LP 90.10, ed. Duchesne, 1: 392; trans. Davis, *Book of Pontiffs*, 89: "Hisdem temporibus cum statuisset populus Romanus nequaquam heretici imperatoris nomen aut chartas vel figuram solidi susciperent, unde nec eius effigies in ecclesia introducta est, nec suum nomen ad missarum solemnia proferebatur."

48. Noble, *Republic*, 28–40.

49. LP 91.17 and 24, ed. Duchesne, 1: 403–4 and 409. What was actually going on in Constantinople is less clear; see most recently Brubaker and Haldon, *Byzantium in the Iconoclast Era*. For Roman reactions see Arnold Angenendt, "Der römische und gallisch-fränkische Anti-Ikonoklasmus," *Frühmittelalterliche Studien* 35 (2001): 201–25.

50. Walls: LP 91.2, ed. Duchesne, 1: 396 (this passage only occurs in the later recension of the life); churches and monasteries: LP 91.2–3, ed. Duchesne, 1: 397; *diaconiae*: LP 91.25, ed. Duchesne, 1: 410 (this passage only occurs in the later recension of the life). Bougard dates this later recension to the 740s: François Bougard, "Composition, diffusion et réception des parties

tardives du 'Liber pontificalis' romain (VIIIe–IXe siècles)," in *Liber, Gesta, histoire: écrire l'histoire des évêques et des papes*, eds. F. Bougard and M. Sot (Turnhout: Brepols, 2009), 127–52 at 137.

51. LP 91.9, ed. Duchesne, 1: 402. The LP does not report which churches were chosen, but later sacramentaries specify these churches.

52. Andrieu suggests that the station of S. Giorgio may have been added after the others, because the mass included for it in the *Hadrianum* is not (as for the other Thursday stations) part of the materials taken from the Gelasian sacramentary: Michel Andrieu, "Les messes des jeudis de carême et les anciens sacramentaires," *Revue des sciences religieuses* 9 (1929): 343–75 at 347.

53. Regarding the synod see further Chapter 6.

54. The *diaconia* of S. Maria Aquiro (in the Campus Martius region) and the *diaconia* dedicated to Sergius and Bacchus near the Vatican: LP 92.12–13, ed. Duchesne, 1: 419–20.

55. Embassies to Liutprand, see especially LP 93.13, ed. Duchesne, 1: 429–30; Ratchis's conversion: LP 93.22–23, ed. Duchesne, 1: 433–34.

56. LP 93.18, ed. Duchesne, 1: 432; trans. Davis, *Lives of the Eighth-Century Popes*, 43: "et per ascendentes scalas in superioribus super eandem turrem triclinium et cancellos aereos construxit, ubi et orbis terrarum descriptione depinxit."

57. LP 93.24, ed. Duchesne, 1: 434; trans. Davis, *Lives of the Eighth-Century Popes*, 47 (modified): "Huiusdemque temporibus magnum thesaurum dominus Deus noster in hac Romana urbe per eundem almificum pontificem propalare dignatus est. In venerabile itaque patriarchio sacratissimum beati Georgii martyris hisdem sanctissimus papa in capsa reconditum repperit caput; in qua et pittacium pariter invenit, litteris exaratum grecis, ipsud esse significantes. Qui sanctissimus papa omnino satisfactus, ilico adgregato huius Romane urbis populo, cum hymnis et canticis spiritalibus in venerabili diaconia eius nomini, sitam in hac Romana civitate, regione secunda, ad Velum aureum, illud deduci fecit, ubi immensa miracula et beneficia omnipotens Deus ad laudem nominis sui per eundem sacratissimum martyrem operare dignatur."

58. Jan Willem Drijvers, *Helena Augusta: The Mother of Constantine the Great and the Legend of Her Finding of the True Cross* (Leiden: Brill, 1992), 79–180 (Part 2); Neil B. McLynn, *Ambrose of Milan: Church and Court in a Christian Capital* (Berkeley: University of California Press, 1994), 211–17.

59. LP 86.7–10, ed. Duchesne, 1: 373–74.

60. To the contrary, Bauer, *Das Bild der Stadt Rom*, 59–60, argues that the cult of George in Rome did not predate Zacharias's find, but that Zacharias instituted the *diaconia* in conjunction with his discovery as a purposeful attempt to usurp Constantinople's cult. However, the *Liber Pontificalis* (see n. 57) clearly indicates that the Roman *diaconia* dedicated to George predated Zacharias's discovery.

61. Janin, 74–83. According to later tradition, a church in Constantinople in the "Hieron" quarter dated from the time of Constantine (Janin, no. 2). Another church dedicated to George "ἐν τῷ Ξηροκέρκῳ" also existed by the early sixth century (Janin, no. 6). The church for George "τοῦ Συκεώτου" (Janin, no. 8) had relics of the saint. According to a tradition (albeit first recorded in the second half of the ninth century in Nicephorus's encomium of Theodore of Sykeon), the Emperor Heraclius (r. 610–641) had the relics of Theodore, and presumably also of George, brought to Constantinople after Theodore's death. A pious aristocratic woman built a sanctuary dedicated to George and Theodore for the relics, which were to protect the city from Persian attack. Tellingly, according to Nicephorus's encomium, Constantine V had been responsible for the destruction of the sanctuary dedicated to George and Theodore in Constantinople, although the legend later reports that the emperor had been forced to reconstruct it under popular pressure: *Nicephori Sceuophylacis Encomium in S. Theodorum Siceotam*

(BHG 1749), 44–48, ed. C. Kirch, *AB* 20 (1901): 249–72 at 268–70; Michel Kaplan, "Les sanctuaires de Théodore de Sykéon," in *Les saints et leur sanctuaire: Byzance: textes, images et monuments*, eds. C. Jolivet-Lévy et al. (Paris: Publications de la Sorbonne, 1993), 65–79 at 75–76. Thus, both eastern and western tradition remembered the mid-eighth century as a critical period for George's cult, even as each city would continue to assert its close association with George.

62. See n. 57.

63. See n. 52.

64. Saxer, "L'utilisation," 1000 (Appendix VI).

65. Matt. 8:5–13 (Vulg./KJV), here 8:9: "Nam et ego homo sum sub potestate constitutus, habens sub me milites, et dico huic: Vade, et vadit: et alii: Veni, et venit: et servo meo: Fac hoc, et facit"; *Capitulare Evangeliorum*, ed. T. Klauser, 65, no. 62 (*Λ*); 107, no. 58 (note) (*Σ*).

66. A similar message is conveyed by the reading for St. George's feast day, as prescribed by the *Capitulare Evangeliorum*: ed. Klauser, 25, no. 101 (note) and no. 104 (note) (*Π*); 71, no. 116 (*Λ*); 112, no. 112 (*Σ*); 151, no. 124 (note) (*Δ*). These are lines from Luke 21:14–19 that commend patience and trust in God. Despite calamities, God will protect.

67. From a longer-term perspective this development may be compared to the increasing papal involvement in Rome's *tituli* throughout Late Antiquity that likewise rendered highly localized communities more dependent on the pope: Sessa, *Formation*, 230–55.

68. *Liber Diurnus*, 5.88, ed. H. Foerster, 168–69; 5.95, 173–75; *diaconiae* are also mentioned in 5.71, 127–28, and 5.98, 178–79.

69. Not discussed here is a second ecclesiastical foundation in the neighborhood, S. Maria in Portico (in the seventeenth century renamed S. Galla and destroyed in 1928–1930), which might also have been initially founded as a *diaconia* in the early Middle Ages. The reason to consider this possibility is that S. Maria in Portico eventually became one of the churches of cardinal-deacons (*cardinales diaconi*), suggesting it was earlier a *diaconia*. However, the earliest written attestation of S. Maria in Portico is an inscription from 1073, and there is no archaeological or inscriptional evidence in support of dating the church before the eleventh century: Hermes, "Die stadtrömischen Diakonien," 44–46.

70. Niccolò Del Re, "Nicola di Mira. 1. Fonti, 2. Leggenda e Reliquie, 3. Culto," in BS 9: 923–39. The earliest full *vita* and the florescence of St. Nicholas's cult date to the ninth century, but there is substantial evidence for an earlier interest in him.

71. Raymond Janin, "Les églises byzantines Saint-Nicolas à Constantinople," *Echos d'Orient* 31 (1932): 403–18. According to Procopius, Justinian had a church erected in honor of Sts. Priscus and Nicholas outside the walls of Constantinople: *Buildings*, 1.6.4.

72. Gustav Anrich, *Hagios Nikolaos: der heilige Nikolaus in der griechischen Kirche* (Leipzig: Teubner, 1913–1917), 2: 415–20.

73. The *Liber Pontificalis*'s Life of Hadrian (r. 772–795) describes how the chamberlain Calvulus (and others), accused of having ordered the murder of a papal official, was put on trial at the prison: LP 97.12, ed. Duchesne, 1: 490: "Deductique Elefanto, in carcere publico, illic quoram universo populo examinati sunt." For further discussion of the toponym "in carcere" see Alfonso Bartoli, "I templi del Foro Olitorio e la diaconia di S. Nicola 'in carcere,'" *RendPontAcc*, 3rd ser., 5 (1926–1927): 213–26.

74. This story is found in the Greek sixth-century *Praxis de Stratelatis* (BHG 1350), ed. G. Anrich in Anrich, *Hagios Nikolaos*, 1: 67–91, discussion in 2: 368–77; Latin translation (BHL 6119), ed. K. Meisen, *Nikolauskult und Nikolausbrauchtum im Abendlande: eine kulturgeographisch-volkskundliche Untersuchung* (Düsseldorf: L. Schwann, 1931), 527–30. According to Siegmund the Latin translation likely dates to the eighth century: Siegmund, *Überlieferung*, 243.

75. Apparently in the sixteenth century the *diaconia* dedicated to S. Nicola possessed the privilege of freeing a prisoner on the feast day of St. Nicholas: Bartoli, "I templi del Foro Olitorio," 224–25.

76. Regarding the date see Anna Campese Simone, "Alle origini di S. Nicola in Carcere: due epigrafi altomedievali incise su una colonna," in Guidobaldi and Guiglia Guidobaldi, *Ecclesiae urbis*, 295–317; Nicolette Gray, "The Paleography of Latin Inscriptions in the Eighth, Ninth and Tenth Centuries in Italy," *PBSR* 16 (1948): 38–162 at 84, no. 55.

77. See Appendix 5.

78. "DE DONIS D(e)I ET S(an)C(t)E D(e)I GENETRICI<s> MARIE / S(an)C(t)E ANNE S(an)C(ti)S SIMEON ET S(an)C(t)E / LVCIE EGO ANASTASIVS MA / IORDOMV<s> OF<f>ERO BOBIS PRO NATA / LICIES BESTRE." Dale Kinney, "Making Mute Stones Speak: Reading Columns in S. Nicola in Carcere and S. Maria in Aracoeli," in *Architectural Studies in Memory of Richard Krautheimer*, eds. J. S. Ackerman and C. L. Striker (Mainz: Zabern, 1996), 83–86 at 83 n. 6, translates this as "Of the gifts of God and of St. Mary Mother of God. To St. Anna, St. Simeon and St. Lucy, I Anastasius, majordomus, offer to you on your anniversary." In contrast, Campese Simone, "Alle origini," 306 interprets this as a gift to a church of Sts. Mary, Anna, Simeon, and Lucy. The positioning of the conjunctions would suggest Kinney's reading.

79. Campese Simone, "Alle origini," 304: "<H>IC REQVIESCIT IN ANTE."

80. Luke 2:25–36. As attested by the *Synaxarion*, Simeon and Anna were venerated on February 3 in Constantinople; Ado's mid-ninth-century martyrology (see Chapter 8) gives October 8 as the feast day of Simeon and September 1 as the feast day of Anna.

81. S. Lucia *in Orphea* (also known as S. Lucia *in Selcis*) and S. Lucia *in Septem Vias* are both included among the *diaconiae* to which Pope Leo III (r. 795–816) gave gifts: Hermes, "Die stadtrömischen Diakonien," 61–62 (S. Lucia *in Selcis*) and 64–65 (S. Lucia *in Septem Vias*). In an attempt to make sense of the set of saints G. Battista Proja, *S. Nicola in Carcere* (Rome: Istituto di studi romani, 1981), 35–37, and Andreina Palombi, *La basilica di San Nicola in Carcere: il complesso architettonico dei tre templi del Foro Olitorio* (Rome: Istituto nazionale di studi romani, 2006), 68 n. 38, have proposed that the choice of St. Lucy (who was often associated with light) was the result of the reference to light in the passage of Luke that narrates Simeon's recognition of Christ, as well as the symbolism of light central to the feast of the Hypapante (also known as the Purification of the Virgin), on February 2. This was a feast that commemorated the presentation of Christ in the temple and was celebrated in early medieval Rome with a procession from S. Adriano to S. Maria Maggiore.

82. Campese Simone, "Alle origini," 311, describes the term as more or less equivalent to an *oeconomus*.

83. Cf. Lorenzo Bianchi, "*Surgit in astra domus sublimis*: note sulla topografia antica e medievale fra Tevere e Foro Boario," *Bollettino del Centro di studi per la storia dell'architettura* 45–52 (2008–2015): 11–37.

84. The term is attested in a diploma of Otto III from 996 confirming the property of the Aventine monastery of SS. Bonifacio e Alessio: no. 209, ed. T. Sickel, MGH DD O III: 620, lines 37–38: "seu in ripa Greca vel in Aventino."

85. Bavant, "Le duché byzantin."

86. LP 93.13, ed. Duchesne, 1: 429.

87. "Κύριε βοήθει τῷ δούλῳ σου Στεφάνῳ πατρικίῳ καὶ δουκὶ Ῥώμης": Bavant, "Le duché byzantin," 77. This seal was found in Blera (in Latium) in 1882; the second, now in the Vatican, is similar, but does not mention Rome.

88. In Naples a Greek inscription from 721–722 also attests to the restoration of the *diaconia SS. Iohannis et Pauli* by a dux: Marrou, "L'origine orientale," 105–7.

89. See Chapter 1 and Appendix 1.

90. *Codex Carolinus*, no. 49, ed. Grundlach, MGH Epp. 3: 567–569 at 569: "nam et iudices ad faciendas iustitias omnibus vim patientibus in eadem Ravennantium urbe residendum ab hac Romana urbe direxit, Philippum videlicet illo in tempore presbiterum simulque et Eustachium quondam ducem." This is a letter sent by Pope Hadrian to Charlemagne in 774.

91. De Rubeis, "Epigrafi a Roma," 119–20, nos. 11a and 11b: "+Haec tibi praeclara Vir- / go caelestis Regina s(an)c(t)a su- / per exaltata et gloriosa Do- / mina mea D(e)i Genetrix Maria / de tua tibi offero dona ego / humillimus servulus tuus / Eustathius inmeritus dux / quem tibi deserviri et huic / s(an)c(t)ae tuae diac(oniae) dispensato- / rem effici iussisti tradens / de propriis meis facultati- / bus in usu <i>stius s(an)c(t)ae diac(oniae) pro / sustentatione Chr(ist)i pauper(um), / et omnium hic deservient[i]- / um diaconitar(um)."

92. CBCR 2: 301–2.

93. LP 97.72, ed. Duchesne, 1: 507: "Diaconia vero sanctae Dei genetricis semperque virginis Mariae quae appellatur Cosmidin, dudum breve in edificiis existens, sub ruinis posita, maximum monumentum de Tubertinos tufos super ea dependens, per annum circuli plurima multitudo populi congregans, multorumque lignorum struem incendens, demolivit. Simulque collectio ruderum mundans, a fundamentis aedificans, praedictam basilicam ultro citroque spatiose largans, tresque absidas in ea construens praecipuus antistes, veram Cosmidin amplissima noviter reparavit."

94. Sansterre, *Moines grecs*, 1: 47; 2: 102–4 n. 388, and, with caution, Charles Diehl, *Études sur l'administration byzantine dans l'Exarchat de Ravenne (568–751)* (Paris: Thorin, 1888), 278–79. The *schola Grecorum* is attested only in a handful of sources, primarily from the ninth century.

95. See Chapter 1. Regarding the multiple significations of "Greek" in eighth- and ninth-century Rome, see Clemens Gantner, *Freunde Roms und Völker der Finsternis: die päpstliche Konstruktion von Anderen im 8. und 9. Jahrhundert* (Vienna: Böhlau Verlag, 2014), esp. 88–100.

96. Hilduin, *Ex Hilduini Abbatis Libro de S. Dionysio*, ed. G. Waitz, MGH SS 15.1: 3.

97. Codex Einsidlensis 326, ff. 83v–84r: Itinerary no. 10, ed. Walser, 153: "DE PORTA APPIA USQ(UE) SCOLA GRECA IN VIA APPIA"; f. 77v: Itinerary no. 12 (included among the inscriptions), ed. Walser, 57, no. 72: "Inde p(er) scola(m) grecor(um). ibi in sinistra aeclesia grecoru(m)."

98. Sansterre, *Moines grecs*, 2: 102–4 n. 388.

99. *Annales Fuldenses*, 896, ed. F. Kurze, MGH SS rer. Germ. 7: 128: "Omnis namque senatus Romanorum necnon Grecorum scola cum vexillis et crucibus ad pontem Malvium venientes regem honorifice cum ymnis et laudibus suscipientes ad urbem perduxerunt." Similarly, the *Liber Pontificalis* reports that Pope Sergius (r. 844–847) sent the *scholae* and "other most learned Greeks of the *militia* (*aliosque militiae edoctissimos Grecos*)" to meet Louis: LP 104.9, ed. Duchesne, 2: 88.

100. "Sancta Maria quid est?" in Ordo L.49, ed. Andrieu, *Les ordines romani*, 5: 359–62, here 361, line 10: "Dat scola greca melos" (repeated, line 12). This is a hymn that (according to the *ordo*) was sung during the procession that carried the icon of Christ through Rome.

101. LP 103.14, ed. Duchesne, 2: 76.

102. The epitaph, which was once a floor tomb, survives in two badly effaced pieces: Pierre Batiffol, "Inscriptions byzantines de Saint-Georges au Vélabre," *MEFR* 7 (1887): 419–31 at 426–29. There also survives a monogram that seems to be John's: 430.

103. "Ὄλβον βραβεύων [μαθητείας] τοῖς πᾶσι," ibid., 427. Only a few letters of the word reconstructed by Batiffol as μαθητείας are clearly legible.

104. Ibid., 429.

105. This text survives in four fragments, which do not complete each other, but which appear to belong together: ibid., 424–26, line 1: "Θεσγῶον [*sic*; Batiffol proposes the reading θέσμιον] θρῆνον προσγράφω σοι τῷ τάφῳ"; line 3: "Οὐδὲν γὰρ πένθους ἄτερ πέλει ἐν βίῳ."

106. Ibid., 431.

107. Very little is known about this transformation because there are few references to Rome's *diaconiae* throughout the tenth and even early eleventh centuries. Regarding the *cardinales diaconi* see Tommaso Di Carpegna Falconieri, *Il clero di Roma nel medioevo: istituzioni e politica cittadina (secoli VIII–XIII)* (Rome: Viella, 2002), 128–35.

Chapter 5. Fashioning Saints for the Affluent on the Aventine Hill

1. For an introduction to the Aventine from antiquity to the present, see Vincenzo Di Gioia, *L'Aventino: un colle classico tra antico e moderno* (Rome: Istituto poligrafico e Zecca dello Stato, Libreria dello Stato, 2004).

2. Maddalena Andreussi, "Aventinus Mons," LTUR 1: 147–50; Daniela Bruno, "Regione XIII. *Aventinus*," in Carandini and Carafa, *Atlante di Roma antica*, 388–420.

3. M. J. Vermaseren and Carel Claudius van Essen, *The Excavations in the Mithraeum of the Church of Santa Prisca in Rome* (Leiden: Brill, 1965); Felix Marie Dominique Darsy, *Recherches archéologiques à Sainte-Sabine sur l'Aventin: géologie, topographie, sanctuaires archaïques, culte isiaque, ensemble architectural paléochrétien* (Vatican City: Pontificio Istituto di archeologia cristiana, 1968), 30–55.

4. Bowes, *Private Worship*, 63–103. Also see Sessa, *Formation*, and many of the contributions to Cooper and Hillner, *Religion, Dynasty, and Patronage.*

5. Jerome, *Epistulae*, Ep. 127, ed. Hilberg, 3: 145–56; for discussion, see Stefan Rebenich, *Jerome* (London: Routledge, 2002), 58; see also Ep. 47, 1: 345–37, in which Jerome refers friends to Marcella's household as a place to find copies of his texts.

6. Bowes, *Private Worship*, 76–96.

7. If the *titulus Crescentiana* may be identified with S. Sisto Vecchio (which is disputed), this would add a fourth *titulus* to the area: Margherita Cecchelli, "Crescentiana, Titulus," LTUR 1: 325.

8. I am grateful to Julia Hillner for access to her unpublished research materials about the *titulus Sabinae.* The alliance of these clans was the result of the marriage, ca. 345, of Caecina Lolliana and Gaius Caeionius Rufius Volusianus Lampadius; their daughter was named Sabina: PLRE I Sabina (2), perhaps the same as Sabina (3): André Chastagnol, "La famille de Caecinia Lolliana, grande dame païenne du IVe siècle après J.-C.," *Latomus* 20.4 (1961): 744–58.

9. André Chastagnol, "Le sénateur Volusien et la conversion d'une famille de l'aristocratie romaine au Bas-Empire," *Revue des études anciennes* 58 (1956): 241–53 at 252.

10. Michele Renee Salzman, *The Making of a Christian Aristocracy: Social and Religious Change in the Western Roman Empire* (Cambridge, MA: Harvard University Press, 2002); Brown, *Through the Eye of a Needle*, especially 241–307.

11. Kate Cooper, "Poverty, Obligation and Inheritance: Roman Heiresses and the Varieties of Senatorial Christianity in Fifth-Century Rome," in Cooper and Hillner, *Religion, Dynasty, and Patronage*, 165–89.

12. Julia Hillner points to evidence for the Caecinae's activity at sites on the Aventine Hill in the fifth century. An inscription, found near S. Sabina, was erected for the emperors Honorius and Arcadius by Caecina Decius Albinus iunior in the early fifth century: CIL VI 1192. Other inscriptions suggest a fifth-century family estate on the Aventine, near the present-day SS. Bonifacio e Alessio and S. Sabina: Federico Guidobaldi, "Domus: Caecina Decius Albinus iunior," LTUR 2: 29.

13. CBCR 4: 72–98 (R. Krautheimer and S. Corbett, "S. Sabina"); Richard Krautheimer, "Congetture sui mosaici scomparsi di S. Sabina a Roma," *RendPontAcc*, 3rd ser., 60 (1987–1988): 171–87 and, more recently, Julia Hillner, "Clerics, Property and Patronage: The Case of the

Roman Titular Churches," *Antiquité tardive* 14 (2006): 59–68 at 67, propose this distinction between the foundation of the *titulus* and the construction of the monumental basilica. Regarding S. Prisca, see CBCR 3: 260–76 (R. Krautheimer, S. Corbett, and W. Frankl, "S. Prisca").

14. For an overview of S. Sabina's history see Felix Marie Dominique Darsy, *Santa Sabina* (Rome: Marietti, 1961).

15. Peter is called a presbyter in Sta. Sabina's dedicatory inscription; the *Liber Pontificalis* records the construction of the church and baptistery by the bishop Peter during the pontificate of Celestine's successor, Sixtus III (r. 432–440). Presumably construction of the church began during the pontificate of Celestine but was only completed during that of Sixtus III: LP 46.8, ed. Duchesne, 1: 235.

16. ILCV 1: 347, no. 1778a: "CVLMEN APOSTOLICVM CVM CAELESTINVS HABERET / PRIMVS ET IN TOTO FVLGERET EPISCOPVS ORBE, / HAEC QVAE MIRARIS FVNDAVIT PRESBYTER VRBIS / ILLYRICA DE GENTE PETRVS, VIR NOMINE TANTO / DIGNVS, AB EXORTV CHRISTI NVTRITVS IN AVLA, / PAVPERIBVS LOCVPLES, SIBI PAVPER, QVI BONA VITAE / PRAESENTIS FVGIENS MERVIT SPERARE FVTVRAM."

17. *Codex Theodosianus*, 16.2.45 (421 Iul. 14), addressed to Philippus, praetorian prefect of Illyria, ed. Mommsen, 852; Charles Piétri, *Roma Christiana: recherches sur l'Église de Rome, son organisation, sa politique, son idéologie de Miltiade à Sixte III (311–440)* (Paris: École française de Rome, 1976), 1105–30; see also Geoffrey D. Dunn, "The Church of Rome as a Court of Appeal in the Early Fifth Century: The Evidence of Innocent I and the Illyrian Churches," *Journal of Ecclesiastical History* 64 (2013): 679–99.

18. Gal. 2:7–8; Franz Nikolasch, "Zur Deutung der 'Dominus-legem-dat'-Szene," *RQ* 64 (1969): 35–73 at 48–63.

19. Krautheimer, "Congetture."

20. Santangeli Valenzani, "Aventino," in Meneghini and Santangeli Valenzani, *Roma nell'altomedioevo*, 145–49; Maria Richiello, "Cenni topografici dell'Aventino dal sacco di Alarico (410 d.C.) ai giorni nostri," in Oliva Muratore et al., *La storia e il restauro del complesso conventuale dei Santi Bonifacio e Alessio all'Aventino* (Rome: E. de Rosa, 2004), 23–34. These studies build on (and correct) the foundational work of Giuseppe Marchetti Longhi, *L'Aventino nel medio evo* (Rome: Istituto di studi romani, 1947).

21. See Chapter 1.

22. In the synod of 499 two presbyters from the *titulus* referred to themselves as presbyters of the *titulus Sabinae*: *Acta Synhodi a. CCCCXCVIIII*, ed. T. Mommsen, MGH AA 12: 412, no. 30; 414, no. 58. In the synod of 595 its presbyters referred to it as the *titulus sanctae Sabinae*: ed. G. D. Mansi, *Sacrorum conciliorum nova*, 10: 488–89. The *natale* of St. Sabina is found in the earliest forms of the *capitulare evangeliorum*, which date from the mid-seventh century onward: *Capitulare Evangeliorum*, ed. Klauser, 36, no. 185 (*Π*); 82, no. 208 (*Λ*); 122, no. 210 (*Σ*); 161, no. 247 (*Δ*).

23. Matt. 13:44–52 (Vulg.): "Simile est regnum caelorum thesauro abscondito . . . de thesauro suo noua uetera."

24. Matt. 13:45–46 (Vulg.): "Iterum simile est regnum caelorum homini negotiatori, quaerenti bonas margaritas. Inventa autem una pretiosa margarita, abiit, et vendidit omnia quae habuit, et emit eam."

25. Saxer, "L'utilisation," 1000–1008 (Appendices VI–VII); all versions of the *capitulare evangeliorum* include the station at S. Sabina: *Capitulare Evangeliorum*, ed. Klauser, 19, no. 54 (*Π*); 65, no. 61 (*Λ*); 107, no. 58 (*Σ*); 146, no. 69 (*Δ*).

26. Matt. 6:16–21, here 21 (Vulg./KJV). The first lines of this reading address the question of how to fast; the last ones (19–21) the question of wealth: "Nolite thesaurizare vobis thesauros in terra: ubi ærugo, et tinea demolitur: et ubi fures effodiunt, et furantur. Thesaurizate

autem vobis thesauros in cælo, ubi neque ærugo, neque tinea demolitur, et ubi fures non effodiunt, nec furantur. Ubi enim est thesaurus tuus, ibi est et cor tuum."

27. *Passio* of Sabina (BHL 7407), *passio* of Serapia (BHL 7586): AASS Aug. VI: 500A–504E. The *passiones* of the two saints are part of the same narrative; however, since the women are martyred separately on different days, the legend was often divided in two, and the two *passiones* are already found independent of each other in ninth-century manuscripts arranged by the liturgical year. Even where they appear separately, however, both saints' *passiones* make specific reference to the other saint (Sabina's *passio* begins with Sabina collecting Serapia's relics), making it clear that, at least in the form in which the legend survives today, one *passio* was divided into two, not vice versa. Lanéry, "Hagiographie," 305–6, dates the legend to between the late sixth and the late eighth century, but this assessment predates the discovery of the S. Sabina fresco (see the later discussion), which suggests that some version of the legend was in existence by the early eighth century. Dufourcq, *Étude*, 1: 313–18, dated the *passio Sabinae et Serapiae* to the time of Pope Hormisdas (r. 514–523) because of the phrase *in unitate Spiritus Sancti*, which he argued reflects Hormisdas's theological position—an insistence on the distinct natures of Christ, united without confusion—in the Acacian schism. To my mind this reads too much into a single phrase, whose Christological resonance would also have been appreciated in the context of the monothelete controversy (see n. 43). Dufourcq furnishes no other evidence for such an early dating of the *passio*.

28. Some scholars (because of the legend's associations with S. Sabina on the Aventine) interpret the *oppidum Vendinensium* as a location in Rome, but there is no evidence in Rome either for an *oppidum Vendinensium* or for the subsequent landmarks mentioned in the text: the *arcus Bini*, *arcus Faustini*, and the *area Vindicani*. Kirsch, *Die römischen Titelkirchen*, 165, suggested that "Vendinensium" is a corruption of "Aventinensium." The more commonly accepted opinion identifies the site with an obscure village inhabited by the Vindinates, in Umbria, mentioned only in Pliny's first-century A.D. *Natural History* and in an inscription found near Terni: CIL XI 4209 (*Vindenatium*); see, in particular, Giovanni Nino Verrando, "Reciproche influenze tra Roma e il Martirologio e Passionario Umbri," in *L'Umbria meridionale fra tardoantico ed altomedioevo: atti del Convegno di studio, Acquasparta 6–7 maggio 1989*, ed. G. Binazzi (Perugia: Università degli studi, [1991]), 99–110.

29. The rare term "metallarius," is used in the Justinianic Code to refer to those who work in mines; in the *Scriptores Historiae Augustae* (Divus Claudius, 15.4) the usage "curator Illyrici met<al>larius" suggests that it could also refer to those responsible for overseeing mines; cited in ThLL 8 (M): 869.

30. *Passio*, 1, AASS Aug. VI: 500B: "quæ fuit uxor Valentini & filia Herodis quondam Metallarii, quæ sub Vespasiano augusto ter in urbe Roma candidam dedit Romanis." Such an aristocratic background is not uncommon, although by no means ubiquitous, among the legends associated with the founders of Rome's *tituli*; the *passio* of Prisca (BHL 6926), eventually associated with the nearby *titulus Priscae*, describes her as coming from a noble and wealthy family: AASS Jan. II: 184–87.

31. *Passio*, 1, AASS Aug. VI: 500B.

32. *Passio*, 12, AASS Aug. VI: 503E–504A.

33. *Passio*, 12, AASS Aug. VI: 503E: "Et non cessabat ex eo die facere eleemosynas multas, confidens in nomine Christi Jesu, & permanens in fide, quam ei tradiderat sancta virgo Serapia. Studebat autem quotidie visitare infirmos & in carceribus inclusos, præstans eis omnia, quæ necessaria erant, abunde."

34. *Passio*, 1, AASS Aug. VI: 500B: "Cum dies itaque metuendus persecutionis innotuisset Christianis, multi etiam per orbem terrarum subirent in nomine Christi martyria."

35. *Passio*, 1, AASS Aug. VI: 500B: "erat sancta virgo Serapia apud oppidum Vendinensium civis Antiochena in domo Sabinæ."

36. I am grateful to John Osborne for sharing with me his article "Rome and Constantinople About the Year 700: The Significance of the Recently Uncovered Mural in the Narthex of Santa Sabina," in *L'officinia dello sguardo: scritti in onore di Maria Andaloro. 1. I luoghi dell'arte*, eds. G. Bordi et al. (Rome: Gangemi, 2014), 327–34. When the fresco was first revealed to the public in 2010, it was accompanied by a brief volume: Claudia Tempesta, ed., *L'icona murale di Santa Sabina all'Aventino* (Rome: Gangemi, 2010); see also Manuela Gianandrea, "Un'inedita committenza nella chiesa romana di Santa Sabina all'Aventino: il dipinto altomedievale con la Vergine e il Bambino, santi e donatori," in *Medioevo: i committenti. Atti del Convegno internazionale di studi, Parma, 21–26 settembre 2010*, ed. A. C. Quintavalle (Milan: Electa, 2011), 399–410 (these predate the uncovering of the final part of the upper inscription).

37. Gianandrea, "Un'inedita committenza," 404.

38. "TH<e>ODORVS ARCHIP(res)B(yter) VNACVM GEORGIO P(res)B(ytero) BOTVM SO["; Manuela Gianandrea, "Lettura iconografica e stilistica del dipinto murale," in Tempesta, *L'icona murale*, 25–30 at 26.

39. Osborne, "Rome and Constantinople," 330–31.

40. LP 90.1, ed. Duchesne, 1: 389.

41. The *Liber Pontificalis* enumerates some of the Roman delegates by name: "Theodorum et Georgium presbiteros, Iohannem diaconum, Constantinum subdiaconum"; 81.3, ed. Duchesne, 1: 350. The papal legate Theodore, twice an unsuccessful candidate for the papacy, is known to have become an archpresbyter between 686 and 687; the subdeacon Constantine likely became Pope Constantine.

42. Gianandrea, "Lettura iconografica."

43. *Passio*, 1, AASS Aug. VI: 500C: "Dicit ad eam Sabina: Filia mea & domina mea, virgo Serapia, aut vivere tecum aut mori tecum debeo, non te dimittam." The use of the phrase "in unitate Spiritus sancti," in the concluding prayer, both after the death of Serapia (11: 503A) and of Sabina (15: 504A), based on which Dufourcq argued that the *passio* dates to the time of the early sixth-century Acacian schism (see n. 27), might also indicate an interest in emphasizing Chalcedonian Christology: Bernard Botte, "In unitate Spiritus Sancti," *La Maison-Dieu* 23 (1950): 49–63.

44. "Sancta synodus sexta generalis. Constantinopolitana tertia," ed. Mansi, *Sacrorum conciliorum nova*, 11: 195–922; Francis-Xavier Murphy, *Konstantinopel II und III* (Mainz: Matthias-Grünewald, 1990), 230–66.

45. Relegation to a monastery by Pope Leo II (r. 682–683): LP 92.3, ed. Duchesne, 1: 359; the Acts of the Seventh Ecumenical Council of 787 (Nicaea II) describe how Pope Benedict II sent his *consularius*, a certain Boniface, to visit Macarius daily to convert him from the monothelete heresy: ed. Mansi, *Sacrorum conciliorum nova*, 12: 959–1154, here 1035–38; *Interpretatio Synodi VII*, in Anastasius Bibliothecarius, *Opera omnia*, 3, PL 129: 195–512, here 227A (Anastasius Bibliothecarius's Latin translation).

46. Silvana Episcopo, "S. Bonifacius, Basilica," LTUR 1: 201–2; CBCR 1: 40–41 (R. Krautheimer, "SS. Alessio e Bonifacio"); for the later history of the site, see Muratore et al., *La storia*. Current scholarship remains heavily indebted to the early work of A. Monaci, "Regesto dell'abbazia di S. Alessio all'Aventino," *ASRSP* 27 (1904): 351–98; *ASRSP* 28 (1905): 151–200, 395–499.

47. Certain recensions of the *Liber Pontificalis* mention a monastery dedicated to Boniface and Alexius during the pontificate of Sixtus (r. 432–440); according to Duchesne, this is a twelfth-century interpolation: Duchesne, "Notes sur la topographie de Rome au Moyen-Âge," *MEFR* 10 (1890): 225–50 at 233 n. 2.

48. The site is included in itineraries of Rome, see n. 56, and in the *Liber Pontificalis*'s Life of Leo III (r. 795–816), specifically named as a *diaconia*: LP 98.29, ed. Duchesne, 2: 9; 98.75, ed. Duchesne, 2: 21. A manuscript of the martyrology ascribed to Jerome (the eighth-century Bern,

Burgerbibliothek, Bongars 289) also attests to the veneration of Boniface in Rome on May 14: *Martyrologium Hieronymianum*, eds. G. B. de Rossi and L. Duchesne, AASS Nov. II.1: 60.

49. C. E. Bosworth, "Ṭarsūs," *EI*[2].

50. This is a frequently cited conclusion; for example, D. J. Constantelos, "The Moslem Conquests of the Near East as Revealed in the Greek Sources of the Seventh and Eighth Centuries," *Byzantion* 4 (1972): 325–57, and the works cited in the subsequent two notes. However, it should be emphasized that the scale of this phenomenon is unknown.

51. Michael Lapidge, "The Career of Archbishop Theodore," in *Archbishop Theodore: Commemorative Studies on his Life and Influence*, ed. M. Lapidge (Cambridge: Cambridge University Press, 1995), 1–29.

52. Franklin, *Latin Dossier.*

53. In the Synod of 649 it is referred to as the *Monasterium de Cilicia qui ponitur in Aquas Salvias*; Bede's *Chronica* refers to it as the *Monasterium S. Pauli ad Aquas Salvias*: see the sources cited in Ferrari, *Early Roman Monasteries*, 33–36.

54. Robert Coates-Stephens, "San Saba and the *Xenodochium de Via Nova*," *RACr* 83 (2007): 223–56.

55. "Sancta synodus sexta generalis. Constantinopolitana tertia," ed. Mansi, *Sacrorum conciliorum nova*, 11: 624, 629–30; cited in Coates-Stephens, "San Saba," 226 n. 5.

56. *Istae verae ecclesiae*, eds. Valentini and Zucchetti, *CTCR* 2: 118–31 at 130: "Basilica Sancti Bonifaci martyris, ubi ipse dormit." Likewise, the itinerary found in William of Malmesbury's twelfth-century *Gesta Regum Anglorum* (whose model arguably dates from as early as the later seventh century) reports on the presence of Boniface in his church: William of Malmesbury, *Gesta Regum Anglorum*, eds. Valentini and Zucchetti, *CTCR* 2: 138–53 at 152–53.

57. In its list of intramural churches, the *Istae vero ecclesiae* reports only one other instance of such a claim. This is SS. Giovanni e Paolo, a *titulus* whose founders were believed to have been martyred and buried in their house, which subsequently became a church: *Istae verae ecclesiae*, eds. Valentini and Zucchetti, *CTCR* 2: 124. Ecclesiastical foundations could and did possess relics of their patron (or other) saints (whether in the form of primary relics or, more frequently, secondary contact-relics). Before the mid- to late eighth century, however, few of Rome's intramural churches were "publicized" so explicitly as pilgrimage sites—in contrast to the extramural shrines with the bodies of Rome's martyrs, which were meticulously enumerated in itineraries of Rome.

58. Caroline J. Goodson, "Building for Bodies: The Architecture of Saint Veneration in Early Medieval Rome," in *Roma Felix: Formation and Reflections of Medieval Rome*, eds. É. Ó. Carragáin and C. L. Neuman de Vegvar (Aldershot: Ashgate, 2007), 51–79.

59. *Passio* of Boniface, Greek (BHG 280: ed. T. Ruinart, *Acta primorum martyrum sincera & selecta*, 284–91), Latin (BHL 1413: AASS Maii III: 280F–284A). In what follows I quote from the very similar Greek and Latin versions.

60. Pio Franchi De'Cavalieri, "Dove fu scritta la leggenda di S. Bonifazio?," *Nuovo bollettino di archeologia cristiana* 6 (1900): 205–34. Franchi De'Cavalieri argued, however, that the *passio* was written outside of Rome, a claim I contest. For discussion, see Appendix 6.

61. *Passio*, 1, AASS Maii III: 280F: "Temporibus Diocletiani quater & Maximiani ter impiissimorum Imperatorum." From here on out the two texts are nearly identical.

62. *Passio*, 1, ed. Ruinart, 284: "Ἦν τις ἐν τῇ Ῥώμῃ γυνὴ μεγάλῃ [read μεγάλη?], ὀνόματι Ἀγλαΐς, θυγάτηρ Ἀκακίου, γένους Κλάρου, ἀπὸ ἀνθυπάτου γενομένου. αὕτη δὲ τρίτον κάνδιδα ἔπραξεν ἐν τῇ Ῥώμῃ, καὶ ἐπαρχότητα [perhaps read ἐπαρχότητι?], ἔχουσα ὑφ' ἑαυτὴν ἑβδομήκοντα τρεῖς φροντιστὰς εἰς τὴν κτῆσιν αὐτῆς." *Passio*, 2, AASS Maii III: 281A: "In illis igitur temporibus erat quædam in urbe Roma mulier magna, nomine Aglaes, filia quidem Acacii, genere autem Clari, quondam Proconsulis. Hæc ergo ter candidam egerat

apud urbem Romam Expræfecturam, habens sub se septuaginta & tres procuratores." The editors of the AASS suggest emending this to "Hæc <erat vidua N. qui> ter candidam egerat apud urbem Romam & Præfecturam" (282A n. k), on the grounds that a woman would not have been a candidate for office.

63. See Appendix 6, n. 6.

64. Regarding the hagiographical theme of a celibate marriage (which in the *passio* of Boniface and Aglaës takes a particularly unusual form since the two are never married and their celibacy is achieved only by Boniface's martyrdom), see Dyan Elliott, *Spiritual Marriage: Sexual Abstinence in Medieval Wedlock* (Princeton, NJ: Princeton University Press, 1993); Anne P. Alwis, *Celibate Marriages in Late Antique and Byzantine Hagiography: The Lives of Saints Julian and Basilissa, Andronikos and Athanasia, and Galaktion and Episteme* (New York: Continuum, 2011).

65. *Passio*, 1, ed. Ruinart, 284: "ἦν δὲ οὗτος μεθυστὴς, καὶ πόρνος, καὶ πάντων φίλος ὧν μισεῖ κύριος ὁ Θεός"; *Passio*, 2, AASS Maii III: 281A: "Erat autem hic ebriosus & adulter, & amicus peccatorum, quæ odit Dominus Deus."

66. *Passio*, 1, ed. Ruinart, 284: "τρία δὲ εἶχε κατορθώματα, φιλόξενος ἦν, καὶ εὐμετάδοτος, καὶ ἐλεήμων, εἴ ποτε γὰρ ἴδεν [edition; read εἶδεν] ξένον, ἢ ὁδοιπόρον, μετὰ πάσης σπουδῆς καὶ προθυμίας προτρεπόμενος διηκόνει αὐτῷ, καὶ νυκτὸς περιάγων τὰς πλατείας καὶ ῥύμας, διεδίδου τοῖς δεομένοις τὰ πρὸς τὴν χρείαν"; *Passio*, 2, AASS Maii III: 281A: "tria autem habebat rectitudinis opera, hospitalitatem scilicet, largitatem, & misericordiam. Qui si aliquando videret peregrinum aut de itinete venientem, cum omni festinatione & alacritate adhortans in hospitium suum introire, ministrabat ei. Noctibus autem circuibat plateas & vicos civitatis, tribuens pauperibus omnia quæ necessaria erant."

67. *Passio*, 16, ed. Ruinart, 290, "καὶ παραλαβοῦσα κληρικοὺς εὐλαβεῖς μετὰ λιτῆς, καὶ κηρῶν, καὶ θυμιαμάτων ὑπήντησαν τῷ ἁγίῳ λειψάνῳ, καὶ ἀπέθετο ὡς ἀπὸ σταδίων πεντήκοντα τῆς πόλεως Ῥώμης, εὐκτήριον οἰκοδομήσασα οἶκον ἄξιον τῆς ἀθλήσεως τοῦ καλλινίκου μάρτυρος"; *Passio*, 12, Maii III: 283C: "Et consurgens Aglaës confestim accepit secum Clericos & viros religiosos, & sic cum hymnis & canticis spiritalibus, & omni veneratione obviavit sancto corpori, & reposuit illud ad stadia Urbis Romæ quinque, in via quæ Latina nuncupatur, ædificans ei domum dignam passione ejus."

68. *Passio*, 2, ed. Ruinart, 284–5: "καὶ νῦν ἀκήκοα Χριστιανῶν λεγόντων, ὅτι εἴ τις ἐξυπηρετήσεται τοῖς ἁγίοις, τοῖς διὰ Χριστὸν ἀγωνισαμένοις καὶ ἀθλήσασιν ὑπὲρ αὐτοῦ, συμμέτοχος αὐτῶν γίνεται ἐν τῇ φοβερᾷ ἡμέρᾳ τῆς δικαιοκρισίας τοῦ Θεοῦ"; *Passio*, 3, AASS Maii III: 281B: "Et nunc audivi quosdam Christianorum dicentium, quoniam si quis ministraverit Sanctis, qui propter nomen Domini Jesu Christi agonizantur, & certamen sumpserunt propter eum, consors eorum siet in die illa terribilis judicii Dei." The word ὅτι can mean "because," but here it introduces a quotation; the Latin's *quoniam* ("because") is a mistranslation of the Greek.

69. *Passio*, 2, ed. Ruinart, 285: "πορευθεὶς οὖν φέρε ἡμῖν λείψανα ἁγίων μαρτύρων, εἴ πως ἐξυπηρετησάμενοι τούτοις, καὶ εὐκτηρίους οἴκους οἰκοδομήσαντες ἀξίως τῆς ἀθλήσεως αὐτῶν, σωθῶμεν δι' αὐτῶν, καὶ ἡμεῖς καὶ ἄλλοι πολλοί"; *Passio*, 3, AASS Maii III: 281B: "Perge igitur ad illas partes, & affer nobis reliquias, id est corpora sanctorum Martyrum, si quomodo servientes atque ministrantes eis, nec non & oratorias domos ædificantes eis dignas, per sanctas passiones eorum salvemur, tam nos quam & alii multi." The specification that *reliquiae* are the physical bodies of the saints is noteworthy in that the term also referred to contact-relics: John M. McCulloh, "The Cult of Relics in the Letters and 'Dialogues' of Pope Gregory the Great: A Lexicographical Study," *Traditio* 32 (1976): 145–84 at 153–56. The Latin text is very concerned to identify the relics as corporeal, a claim that resonates well with the itineraries that specify that the *diaconia* possessed the body of Boniface. Franchi De'Cavalieri, "Dove fu scritta," 212, refers to this passage as an example suggesting that the Latin text post-

dates the Greek. The Greek text refers to λείψανα, which refers to a corpse (frequently with reference to a saint's relics): Lampe s.v. Accordingly Franchi De'Cavalieri suggests that the translator added the additional phrase to adequately translate the Greek.

70. *Passio*, 3, ed. Ruinart, 285: "Ἔλαβε δὲ ὁ παῖς χρυσίον ἱκανὸν, ὥστε ἀγοράσαι λείψανα ἁγίων μαρτύρων, καὶ εἰς διάδοσιν τῶν πτωχῶν, καὶ δώδεκα ἱππεῖς, καὶ τρία λεκτίκια"; *Passio*, 3, AASS Maii III: 281B: "Accepit autem puer Bonifacius aurum satis multum ad comparationem corporum Sanctorum, & ad ministrationem egenorum, & duodecim equites, & tres basternas." The *passio*'s reference (here and elsewhere) to Boniface, a grown man, as "the boy" indicates that he is a (managerial) slave.

71. *Passio*, 5, ed. Ruinart, 286: "Ἐλθὼν οὖν δι' ἡμερῶν τινῶν ἐν Ταρσῷ τῇ πόλει"; *Passio*, 5, AASS Maii III: 281D: "Adveniens igitur post dies aliquot in Tarsum civitatem."

72. *Passio*, 15, ed. Ruinart, 290: "οὗτός ἐστιν ὃν ζητοῦμεν, δεόμεθά σου, δώρησαι ἡμῖν αὐτόν. λέγει αὐτοῖς ὁ ταξεώτης· ἐγὼ δωρεὰν τὸ λείψανον ἀπολῦσαι ὑμῖν οὐ δύναμαι. οἱ δὲ δεδωκότες αὐτῷ νομίσματα πεντακόσια, ἔλαβον τὸ λείψανον τοῦ ἁγίου μάρτυρος"; *Passio*, 11, AASS Maii III: 283C: "Et dicunt ad Officialem: Iste est quem quærimus; petimus te, da nobis eum. Dicit eis ille: Ego gratis corpus ejus dare non possum vobis. Illi autem dantes ei solidos quingentos, acceperunt corpus sancti Martyris."

73. Margherita Trinci Cecchelli, *La diocesi di Roma*, 4: *La I regione ecclesiastica* (Spoleto: Centro italiano di studi sull'alto medioevo, 1976), 69–70, no. 18, plates X, XC. The piece is now located in the garden behind the apse of SS. Bonifacio e Alessio. For Eugene's generosity to the church, see LP 101.3, ed. Duchesne, 2: 69.

74. "S]ẸRAPHIEMARTYRỊḄṾ(s)["; Cecchelli, *La diocesi di Roma*, 4: 69 n. 1, notes that the last letter, difficult to read, may be an I-B ligature with an abbreviation mark above, indicating *martyribus*—suggesting the reconstruction "[Sabine et S]ẹraphie martyrịḅụ(s)." A cornice piece, now located on the wall in S. Sabina, appears to be derived from the same *ciborium*: ibid., 228, no. 261, plate LXXXVII.

75. CBCR 4: 75: "SVMMA PAPATVS EVGENIVS ARCE LOCATVS / CORPVS ALEXANDRI PRAESVLIS EGREGII / NEC NON THEODOLI SIMVL ET TE MARTYR EVENTI / JVXTA SAVINAM SERAPHIAMQVE PIAM / AEDE SVB HAC POSVIT." For an image and description of the inscription see Darsy, *Santa Sabina*, 112–13, Fig. 29.

76. LP 98.29, ed. Duchesne, 2: 9; 98.75, ed. Duchesne, 2: 21.

77. Riccardo Santangeli Valenzani, "L'iscrizione di Teodora da Santa Sabina: una nuova ipotesi di interpretazione," in *για το φίλο μας: scritti in ricordo di Gaetano Messineo*, eds. E. Mangani and A. Pellegrino (Monte Compatri, RM: Espera, 2016), 345–54.

78. The *passio* of Adalbert has recently been translated into English by Cristian Gaşpar in *Saints of the Christianization Age of Central Europe (Tenth–Eleventh Century)*, ed. G. Klaniczay (Budapest: Central European University Press, 2012), 95–182; regarding Adalbert and Bruno see Gaşpar's preface, 79–94, and, in the same volume, Ian Wood, "The Hagiography of Conversion," 1–16.

79. As attested by a 996 diploma of Otto for "Leo venerabilis abbas monasterii Sancti martiris Bonifatii atque Alexii, quod situm est in Aventino": Ferrari, *Early Roman Monasteries*, 79 n. 6.

80. In the early ninth century (in the *Liber Pontificalis*'s Life of Leo III) the *diaconia* is mentioned as dedicated to Boniface. Santangeli Valenzani, "L'iscrizione di Teodora da Santa Sabina," 351–53, argues that the site was already dedicated to both saints when Theodora restored it in the early tenth century.

81. Aleksander Gieysztor, "'Pauper sum et peregrinus': la légende de saint Alexis en Occident: un idéal de pauvreté," in *Etudes sur l'histoire de la pauvreté (Moyen Âge–XVI*[e] *siècle)*, ed. M. Mollat du Jourdin (Paris: Publications de la Sorbonne, 1974), 125–39.

82. My summary of Alexius' *passio* is based on AASS Jul. IV: 251E–254C (BHL 286). For the cult of St. Alexius in Rome see especially Duchesne, "Notes," 234–50.

83. *Passio*, 2, AASS Jul. IV: 252A: "Cum autem ad tempus adolescentiæ accessisset, & eum nuptialibus infulis aptum judicassent, elegerunt ei puellam ex genere imperiali, & ornaverunt thalamum, & impositæ sunt eis singulæ coronæ in templo S. Bonifacii martyris per manus honoratissimorum sacerdotum, & sic cum gaudio, & lætitia lætum duxerunt diem."

84. *Passio*, 5, AASS Jul. IV: 252E: "& isdem homo Dei ab hominibus venerari cœpisset, humanam fugiens gloriam, occulte exiit de civitate Edessa, & venit Laodiciam, ibique navem ascendens volebat in Tharsum Ciliciæ ire, ut in templo S. Pauli, quod ibidem est, maneret incognitus. Deo itaque dispensante rapta est navis vento, & ducta est ad Romanum portum."

85. *Passio*, 11, AASS Jul. IV: 253D: "& sic cum magno labore ad templum sancti Bonifacii martyris perduxerunt, & illic per septem dies in Dei laudibus persistentes operati sunt monumentum de auro, & gemmis pretiosis, in quo sacratissimum illud corpus cum magna veneratione collocaverunt die XIV mensis Julii." Duchesne, "Notes," 240–41.

Chapter 6. Collectivities of Sanctity in Early Medieval Rome

1. Cf. Thunø, *The Apse Mosaic*, who demonstrates how post-apostolic saints were positioned as building blocks of the Church community in Roman apse mosaics commissioned by popes (including the S. Venanzio chapel discussed later).

2. *Passio* of the Quattro Coronati (BHL 1837): AASS Nov. III: 765B–779D. In the oldest and, according to the editor H. Delehaye, best manuscripts the text is entitled "Incipit passio sanctorum Simproniani, Claudii, Nicostrati, Castorii et Simplicii" (*Passio* 1, AASS Nov. III: 765B). There also exists a Greek translation of the older *passio*, printed in the *Acta Sanctorum*; this, according to the judgment of Delehaye, was likely an Italo-Greek translation.

3. The core of the text (chs. 1–21) takes place in Pannonia, while a single rather discrete section takes place in Rome (ch. 22); accordingly, the text may be interpreted as an older, Pannonian text that was expanded in Rome. Alternatively (especially given the evidence for the early veneration of similarly named saints in Rome), the whole text may be interpreted as a Roman creation. An introduction to the difficulties of reconstructing where and when these saints began to be venerated (and a complex solution) is offered by Jean Guyon, "Les Quatre Couronnés et l'histoire de leur culte des origines au milieu du IXe siècle," *MEFRA* 87.1 (1975): 505–61. The text was intensively studied in the nineteenth and early twentieth centuries, and its origins and reliability continue to be the subject of scholarly controversy.

4. *Passio*, 1, AASS Nov. III: 765E: "Ventum quodam die inperante Dioclitiano, ut simulacrum Solis cum quadriga ex lapide taso artifices cum omni argumento currum equos vel omnia ex uno lapide sculpirent."

5. *Passio*, 6–7, AASS Nov. III: 768–69.

6. *Passio*, 21, AASS Nov. III: 779C–D: "Tunc beatus Sevastianus noctu cum Militiadem episcopum collegit corpora et sepelivit in via Labicana, miliario ab urbe tertio, cum sanctis aliis in arenario."

7. *Passio*, 21, AASS Nov. III: 779D: "Quod dum eodem tempore sed post duos annos evenisset, id est sextum idus novembris, et nomina eorum repperire minime potuissent, iussit beatus Militiades episcopus ut sub nomina sanctorum Claudii, Nicostrati, Simproniani et Castorii [et Simplicii: add. A 2] anniversaria dies eorum recolatur."

8. The *Depositio Martyrum* includes on November 7 "Clementis, Semproniani, Claudi, Nicostrati, in Comitatum," eds. Valentini and Zucchetti, *CTCR* 2: 17–28 at 27. A much more similar set of saints (Claudius, a *commentariensis*, a notary/secretary/prison-keeper; his son, Symphorianus; Nicostratus, a *primiscrinius*, "the chief of an official department"; and his brother Castor) appears in the *passio* of Sebastian (BHL 7543): AASS Ian. II: 265–78. This *passio* reports that the saints were drowned and does not record the recovery of their bodies. Early sacramentaries

also contain names of similar or identical saints who at times, particularly in later sources, are also referred to as the *Quattuor Coronati*. The evidence is extensively detailed by Guyon, "Les Quatre Couronnés," 508–14 and Table 1.

9. Lia Barelli, *The Monumental Complex of Santi Quattro Coronati in Rome*, trans. C. McDowall (Rome: Viella, 2009); CBCR 4: 1–36 (R. Krautheimer and S. Corbett, "SS. Quattro Coronati").

10. *De locis*, eds. Valentini and Zucchetti, *CTCR* 2: 113, on the via Labicana: "IIII Coronati, id est Claudius, Nicostratus, Simpronianus, Castorius, Simplicius"; *Notitia*, eds. Valentini and Zucchetti, *CTCR* 2: 83, under via Labicana: "et in tercio IIII Coronatos." The *De locis* does not maintain the *passio*'s careful distinction that the Roman saints were commemorated with the "names" of the Pannonian saints; this is a confusion/conflation that is found in later sources.

11. LP 105.41, ed. Duchesne, 2: 115–16: "Nam et corpora sanctorum martyrum IIII Coronatorum sollerti cura inquirens repperit . . . eorumque sacratissima corpora cum Claudio, Nicostrato, Simphroniano atque Castorio et Simplicio, necnon Severo, Severiano, Carpoforo et Victorino, IIII fratribus . . . pariter sub sacro altare recondens locavit." There is an alternate reading "scilicet" instead of "cum," which was rejected by Duchesne on the authority of the manuscripts, but which some scholars prefer. The first reading suggests that nine bodies (and then also Severus etc.) were translated from the catacombs to the church; the alternate suggests that the four Roman and five Pannonian saints had been thoroughly equated. Depending on the reading of the text, then, either Leo had brought all five Pannonian saints as well as the four Roman soldiers from the catacombs to SS. Quattro Coronati, or else the identities of Pannonian and Roman martyrs had so completely merged that the Pannonian martyrs themselves were now buried in Rome.

12. AASS Nov. III: 755–56. One inscription records Pope Paschal II's (r. 1099–1118) discovery of the relics under the altar (in the context of renovating the church). Another, undated inscription, probably of the same date (closely following the wording in the *Liber Pontificalis*) records Leo IV's placement of the saints' relics under the church's altar. The inscriptions are now located on the wall to the left of the altar.

13. Gillian Mackie, "The San Venanzio Chapel in Rome and the Martyr Shrine Sequence," *Revue d'art canadienne* 23 (1996): 1–13.

14. LP 73.4, ed. Duchesne, 1: 329: "Et post dies aliquantos ingressus est Isacius patricius in episcopio Lateranense et fuit ibi per dies VIII, usque dum omnem substantiam illam depraedarent. Eodem tempore direxit exinde parte ex ipsa substantia in civitate regia ad Heraclium imperatorem."

15. Francesco Borri, "La Dalmazia altomedievale tra discontinuità e racconto storico (secc. VII–VIII)," *Studi veneziani*, n.s., 58 (2009): 15–52.

16. LP 74.1–2, ed. Duchesne, 1: 330; trans. Davis, *Book of Pontiffs*, 64–65 (modified): "Iohannes, natione Dalmata, ex patre Venantio scolastico, sedit ann. I mens. VIIII dies XVIIII. Hic temporibus suis misit per omnem Dalmatiam seu Histriam multas pecunias per sanctissimum et fidelissimum Martinum abbatem propter redemptionem captivorum qui depraedati erant a gentibus. Eodem tempore fecit ecclesiam beatis martyribus Venantio, Anastasio, Mauro et aliorum multorum martyrum, quorum reliquias de Dalmatias et Histrias adduci praeceperat, et recondit eas in ecclesia suprascripta, iuxta fontem Lateranensem, iuxta oratorium beati Iohannis evangelistae."

17. For further discussion see especially Goodson, "Building for Bodies," 70–71.

18. LP 34.13, ed. Duchesne, 1: 174.

19. LP 48.2, ed. Duchesne, 1: 242. Two of these chapels, for the two saints John, survive, although only parts of their original furnishings are preserved. For a discussion of the function of these chapels see Gillian Mackie, *Early Christian Chapels in the West: Decoration, Function and Patronage* (Toronto: University of Toronto Press, 2003), 195–211.

20. The *Liber Pontificalis* reports that in his letters Pope Hilarius "confirmed the dominion and preeminence of the holy catholic and apostolic see"; trans. Davis, *Book of the Pontiffs*, 37; LP 48.2, ed. Duchesne, 1: 242: "Hic fecit decretalem et per universam Orientem exparsit, et epistulas de fide catholica, confirmans III synodos Niceni, Epheseni et Calcedonense, vel tomum sancti episcopi Leonis; et damnavit Eutychem et Nestorium vel omnes sequaces eorum et vel omnes hereses; et confirmans dominationem et principatum sanctae sedis catholicae et apostolicae."

21. Joseph D. Alchermes, "Petrine Politics: Pope Symmachus and the Rotunda of St. Andrew at Old St. Peter's," *Catholic Historical Review* 81.1 (1995): 1–40.

22. LP 53.7, ed. Duchesne, 1: 261–62.

23. Thunø, *The Apse Mosaic*, esp. 23–24, 41–42, 191.

24. Ibid., 74–76.

25. Maurus is the only of these saints associated with Istria, but he is not differentiated as such in the mosaic.

26. For text and translation see Thunø, "Inscription and Divine Presence," 290.

27. The bones did not include either skulls or long bones. The investigation was undertaken at the request of the bishops of Split and Poreč: Makso Peloza, "Rekognicija relikvija dalmatinskih i istarskih mučenika u oratoriju svetog Venancija kod baptisterija Lateranske bazilike u Rimu 1962.–1964. godine [Reconnaissance des reliques des martyrs dalmates et istriens dans l'oratoire de St. Venance au baptistère de St. Jean de Latran à Rome (1962–1964)]," *Vjesnika za arheologiju i historiju dalmatinsku=Bulletin d'archéologie et d'histoire dalmate* 63.3 (1961–1962): 163–80, with a summary in French on p. 180. The acts of the recognition are now kept in the Archivio Capitolare in Rome.

28. For a summary see Emilio Marin, "Il mosaico della cappella di S. Venanzio al Battistero Lateranense: status questionis," in *Il cristianesimo in Istria fra tarda antichità e alto medioevo: novità e riflessioni. Atti della giornata tematica dei Seminari di archeologia cristiana, Roma, 8 marzo 2007*, eds. E. Marin and D. Mazzoleni (Vatican: Pontificio Istituto di archeologia cristiana, 2009), 209–15.

29. Hippolyte Delehaye, "Saints d'Istrie et de Dalmatie," *AB* 18 (1899): 368–411.

30. LP 92.6, ed. Duchesne, 1: 417; trans. Davis, *Lives of the Eighth-Century Popes*, 22: "Hic fecit oratorium intro eandem basilicam, iuxta arcum principalem, parte virorum, in quo recondivit in honore Salvatoris sanctaeque eius genetricis reliquias sanctorum apostolorum vel omnium sanctorum martyrum ac confessorum, perfectorum iustorum, toto in orbe terrarum requiescentium."

31. Bauer, *Das Bild der Stadt Rom*, 53–58; Blaauw, *Cultus et decor*, 2: 571–72.

32. Franz Alto Bauer, "St. Peter's as a Place of Collective Memory in Late Antiquity," in Behrwald and Witschel, *Rom in der Spätantike*, 155–70; Alan T. Thacker, "Popes, Emperors and Clergy at Old Saint Peter's from the Fourth to the Eighth Century," in *Old Saint Peter's, Rome*, eds. R. McKitterick et al. (Cambridge: Cambridge University Press, 2013), 137–56.

33. Beat Brenk, "Der Kultort, seine Zugänglichkeit und seine Besucher," in *Akten des XII. Internationalen Kongresses für christliche Archäologie*, eds. E. Dassmann and J. Engemann (Münster: Aschendorff, 1995), 69–122 at 79–81.

34. Michael Borgolte, *Petrusnachfolge und Kaiserimitation: die Grablegen der Päpste, ihre Genese und Traditionsbildung* (Göttingen: Vandenhoeck & Ruprecht, 1989), 49–119, 346–51.

35. Blaauw, *Cultus et decor*, 2: 566–80.

36. *Notitia ecclesiarum urbis Romae*, eds. Valentini and Zucchetti, *CTCR* 2: 95–99. It should be noted that this description of St. Peter's (which immediately follows a description of Milanese saints omitted in the edition) is significantly later in date (of initial composition) than the preceding sections of the itinerary describing extramural shrines in Rome.

37. Ibid., 95–96: "Intrante [te] in porticum Sancti Andreae, occurit tibi in sinistra manu altare Sancti Laurenti, deinde Sancti Viti, deinde Sancti Cassiani, deinde ipsius Andreae in medio rotundae."

38. The *Notitia* also names an altar for "Sancti Syxti," but this appears to be the result of a confusion with the altar of "Sossii" otherwise attested, but not named here.

39. The *Notitia* mentions these three altars; there is also evidence for an altar dedicated to St. Anastasia.

40. Ibid., 96–97.

41. Ibid., 97: "pervenies per cryptam ad caput beati Petri principis apostolorum, et exinde pervenies ad altare maius eiusque confessionem, et exinde, post fusas poenitentiae lacrimas, vadis."

42. Hubert Mordek, "Rom, Byzanz und die Franken im 8. Jahrhundert: zur Überlieferung und kirchenpolitischen Bedeutung der Synodus Romana Papst Gregors III. vom Jahre 732 (mit Edition)," in *Person und Gemeinschaft im Mittelalter: Karl Schmid zum fünfundsechzigsten Geburtstag*, eds. G. Althoff et al. (Sigmaringen: Thorbecke, 1988), 123–56.

43. LP 92.3, ed. Duchesne, 1: 416; trans. Davis, *Lives of the Eighth-Century Popes*, 20: "adversus eandem venerationem sacrarum imaginum . . . depositor atque destructor et profanator vel blasphemus extiterit." Regarding the synod see Herrin, *Formation of Christendom*, 347–48.

44. LP 92.6, ed. Duchesne, 1: 417: "Quam institutionem in eodem oratorio tabulis lapideis conscribere fecit." The text was most recently edited by Mordek, "Rom, Byzanz," 147–54, who includes the version found in the manuscripts, as well as the stone fragments. Since the former is more complete, that is the text from which I quote later.

45. Mordek, "Rom, Byzanz," 128.

46. Fragments of this tablet survive and were transcribed in the late fifteenth century.

47. Mordek, "Rom, Byzanz," 152–54.

48. LP 92.6, ed. Duchesne, 1: 417: "Quorum festa vigiliarum a monachis trium monasteriorum illic servientium cotidie per ordinem existentia atque nataliciorum missas in eodem loco celebrare, instituens in canone ita a sacerdote dicendum: *Quorum solemnitas hodie in conspectu tue maiestatis celebratur, domine Deus noster, toto in orbe terrarum.*" Precisely how these arrangements are to be understood is debatable; see especially Sebastian Scholz, *Politik, Selbstverständnis, Selbstdarstellung: die Päpste in karolingischer und ottonischer Zeit* (Stuttgart: Franz Steiner, 2006), 34–35. What is clear, as emphasized by John Hennig, is that the decree does *not* establish an anniversary of the chapel's dedication, that is, a day each year in honor of All Saints: John Hennig, "The Meaning of All the Saints," *Mediaeval Studies* 10 (1948): 147–61. For the development of this liturgical celebration see Chapter 8. Regarding these masses and in particular their Frankish transmission, see also Leo Eizenhöfer, "Die Marmormessen Gregors III," *Ephemerides liturgicae* 67 (1953): 112–28.

49. "His expletis presbiter, qui in ebdoma fuerit, post prima, quae in sacro corpore beati Petri fecerit missa, secunda in eodem oratorio in honore salvatoris, dei genetricis, sanctorum apostolorum, martyrum, confessorum, perfectorum iustorum, quorum natalicia fuerint, assidue a catholica et apostolica ecclesia celebrentur, sicut a nobis coram beati Petri corpore confirmatur"; ed. Mordek, "Rom, Byzanz," 149.

50. "sed et diem natalicium celebrantes sanctorum tuorum martyrum ac confessorum, perfectorum iustorum, quorum hodie sollemnitas in conspectu gloriae tuae celebratur"; ed. Mordek, "Rom, Byzanz," 150.

51. Rushforth, "Church," 28–36; de Grüneisen et al., *Sainte Marie Antique*, 108–15; Tea, *La basilica*, 271–80. This fresco, like so many found in S. Maria Antiqua, is unique. A possible comparandum is a fresco from S. Saba (dated to the first half of the ninth century), but its

fragmentary state makes a detailed comparison impossible: Wilpert, *Die römischen Mosaiken*, Pl. 193.

52. Rushforth, "Church," 29.

53. Tea, *La basilica*, 99–100.

54. Rushforth, "Church," 73–74.

55. Ibid., 25–28, 81–82.

56. Serena La Mantia, "'Santi su misura': la parete di Paolo I a Santa Maria Antiqua," in *L'VIII secolo: un secolo inquieto. Atti del Convegno internazionale di studi, Cividale del Friuli, 4–7 dicembre 2008*, ed. V. Pace (Cividale del Friuli, Udine: Comune di Cividale del Friuli, 2010), 149–61.

57. Maureen C. Miller, *Clothing the Clergy: Virtue and Power in Medieval Europe, c. 800–1200* (Ithaca: Cornell University Press, 2014), esp. 13–35, 96–108. I am grateful to Maureen Miller for sharing her manuscript with me prior to publication.

58. These details are observed by Rushforth, "Church," 35.

59. Regarding the Mt. Sinai icon see Kurt Weitzmann, *The Monastery of Saint Catherine at Mount Sinai: The Icons. 1: From the Sixth to the Tenth Century* (Princeton, NJ: Princeton University Press, 1976), 48–49 (icon B.24) and Pl. 20.

60. Depicted in order (moving away from Christ) are St. Clement, a bishop of Rome attentive to his flock and a martyr who promoted the conversion of new peoples; St. Sylvester, famed for converting the emperor Constantine, his mother Helena, and thousands of Romans; St. Leo, whose embassy to Attila the Hun was said to have preserved Rome from destruction; Pope Alexander, whose *passio* recounts that he converted the greater part of Rome's senatorial aristocracy (BHL 266: AASS Maii I: 371C–375F); and the Roman presbyters, Valentine and Abundius, both of whose *passiones* feature miraculous cures that succeed in converting prominent Romans: *passio* of Valentine (BHL 8465): AASS Feb. II: 753C–754D; *passio* of Abundius (BHL 17): AASS Sept. V: 300E–303A.

61. Depicted in order (away from Christ) are John Chrysostom, Gregory of Nazianzus, and Basil of Caesarea (all three of whom were commonly depicted together in Byzantine iconography and who had all been depicted previously in S. Maria Antiqua); Peter, patriarch of Alexandria and a martyr under Diocletian; Cyril, patriarch of Alexandria; Epiphanius, bishop of Constantia (Salamis) in Cyprus; Athanasius of Alexandria; Nicholas of Myra; and Erasmus of Formia, Italy.

62. John Chrysostom died in exile after Empress Eudoxia had him banished; Gregory of Nazianzus was known (among his many writings) for his invectives against the pagan emperor Julian; Cyril was famous for his opposition to the Christology of Nestorius, patriarch of Constantinople; Athanasius of Alexandria was exiled five times by the imperial court for his staunch views against Arianism.

63. The empress Eudoxia traveled out to the desert to meet Euthymius; Sabas went on a mission to Constantinople. The Roman bishop labeled Gregory is presumably Gregory the Great, although Rushforth, "Church," 31, suggested that it might be Gregory III (r. 731–741), who according to the *Liber Pontificalis* (LP 92.14, ed. Duchesne, 1: 420) had enlarged a preexisting oratory for Sergius and Bacchus near St. Peter's. On the other side of the door, lay saints seem to have continued the panorama of sanctity. Although the first saint is unidentifiable, the second is likely Mammes, a child-martyr of Caesarea.

64. Bauer, *Das Bild der Stadt Rom*, 90–94.

65. Julia M. H. Smith, "Care of Relics in Early Medieval Rome," in *Rome and Religion in the Early Middle Ages: Studies in Honor of Thomas F. X. Noble*, eds. V. Garver and O. Phelan (Farnham: Ashgate, 2014), 179–205. I am grateful to Julia Smith for providing me with a copy of her article prior to its publication. As attested by the relic authentics, which are written in

hands dating from the seventh or eighth century through the thirteenth century, the origins of this collection may date back as early as the seventh century.

66. Guido Cordini, "'Non est in toto sanctior orbe locus': Collecting Relics in Early Medieval Rome," in *Treasures of Heaven: Saints, Relics and Devotion in Medieval Europe*, ed. M. Bagnoli (New Haven: Yale University Press, 2010), 69–78.

67. Bruno Galland and Jean Vezin, *Les authentiques de reliques du Sancta Sanctorum* (Vatican City: Biblioteca Apostolica Vaticana, 2004).

68. Some medieval descriptions of the collection's contents do survive, but these are not complete, instead focusing on "high-profile" relics or more recent acquisitions. For details see the introduction in Galland and Vezin, *Les authentiques de reliques.*

69. The following is my count based on Galland and Vezin, *Les authentiques de reliques.*

70. Old Testament figures: Amos, Isaac, and the archangel Michael (included on two relic authentics); New Testament figures: John the Baptist, Zacharias (presumably John the Baptist's father), Martha, and Cornelius of Caesarea; Roman saints: Peter, Paul (twice), Abdon and Sennen, Lawrence, Anastasia, and Justin (Galland interprets this as Justin of Rome, although it could well be a different saint: no. 57, ed. Galland, 113).

71. Included are Arsenius, Cosmas and Damian, Constantine, Domnius, George, Jerome, Lucy, Nicholas, Stephen, and Sergius and Bacchus. Saints whose identity is less clear are Charitos, abbot of Palestine, under Aurelian (?); Teobtistus, likely Theoctistus, a Palestinian monk and companion of St. Euthymius; and Epifanius, likely Epiphanius, bishop of Constantia (Salamis) in Cyprus, fourth century (included in S. Maria Antiqua's panorama of saints, see n. 61). Also included are one North African saint, Cyprian (but who was venerated at an early date in Rome) and one saint from north of the Alps, Aldegund. Regarding the collection as a whole (not merely the seventh- to ninth-century authentics) see Smith, "Care of Relics," 183 and Appendix.

72. Cosmas and Damian: no. 30, ed. Galland, 103; Sergius and Bacchus: no. 98, p. 131.

73. George: no. 57, ed. Galland, 113; Stephen: no. 49, p. 110.

74. Domninus: no. 83, ed. Galland, 124: the label dates to the eighth or ninth century. Galland, however, identifies this saint as the companion of Philemon of Rome.

75. Constantine: no. 90, ed. Galland, 127: the label dates to the seventh or eighth century. Also included are relics of Constantine labeled in an undated Greek hand.

76. This is discussed by Julia M. H. Smith, "Portable Christianity: Relics in the Medieval West (*c.*700–1200)," *Proceedings of the British Academy* 181 (2012): 143–67.

77. Galland and Vezin, *Les authentiques de reliques*, 55.

78. There is one straightforward example of this. A seventh- or eighth-century hand labeled four Holy Land relics, as well as Lucy and Cyprian, both saints well known in early medieval Rome; Group E: nos. 20–25.

79. The other saints included are the Old Testament saint Isaac, the archangel Michael, and the healing saints Cosmas and Damian: Group C: nos. 28–31.

80. Reliquary no. IV: nos. 1–8, 50, 51, and 70. See Galland and Vezin, *Les authentiques de reliques*, 28.

81. Reliquary no. III: nos. 35–38 and 41. See ibid., 28.

82. For Theodotus's inscription see Chapter 1 and Appendix 2. Galland identifies Sisinnius as the companion of Saturninus of Rome, but given the Greek label and that the saint appears on his own, I prefer to identify him as Sisinnius of Antioch, known as a protector of children: Walter, *Warrior Saints*, 241–42. Alternatively, the saint might be identified as Sisinnius, bishop of Cyzicus.

83. Reliquary no. XXIII: nos. 33–34. See Galland and Vezin, *Les authentiques de reliques*, 30. Included were the teeth of Jerome (labeled in Greek in a ninth-century hand) and John the Baptist (labeled in Greek in a tenth-century hand). This reliquary also included a small silk

bag depicting Samson fighting with a lion, two wooden tablets with Peter and Paul, and some bones and cloth fragments.

84. These relics were cataloged by Father Louis-Antoine as a group, but he did not specify where they were found. Group Δ11: nos. 20, 29–32, 49, 56, 57, 67, 71, 83, 84, 92 and 104. See Galland and Vezin, *Les authentiques de reliques*, 28.

85. Relics included in Group Δ11 are (by date): seventh/eighth century: Lucy, Isaac, Cosmas and Damian, Michael; eighth century: Stephen, Iuenius confessor (Galland interprets this to be Justin martyr), Arsenius (desert father), Lawrence; eighth/ninth: Domninus; ninth century: George; tenth century: Andrew, Pope Stephen; eleventh century: daughters of St. Sophia; undated: Constantine (labeled in Greek).

86. See n. 79.

87. See n. 78. The last of this seventh- to eighth-century group of relic authentics written in the same hand, that of Cyprian (no. 22), was left separate in the box.

88. I am grateful to Hendrik Dey for suggesting discussion of this point.

89. Silvana Casartelli Novelli, "La 'nuova Gerusalemme' generata dal Cristo: il cantus firmus dell'immaginario di Roma 'capitale Cristiana,'" in Pani Ermini, *Christiana loca*, 1: 153–71 and catalog in 2: 253–313 (esp. 258–69).

90. Dey, *Aurelian Wall*, 142–49.

91. Goodson, *Rome of Pope Paschal*, 154–58, 232–34; Thunø, *The Apse Mosaic*, 164–70.

Chapter 7. Carolingian Romes Outside of Rome

1. One place to begin is Arnold Angenendt and Rudolf Schieffer, *Roma—caput et fons: zwei Vorträge über das päpstliche Rom zwischen Altertum und Mittelalter* (Opladen: Westdeutscher Verlag, 1989).

2. Gregory the Great, *Registrum*, 6.6, ed. Norberg, 1: 373–74.

3. Rosamond McKitterick, *History and Memory in the Carolingian World* (Cambridge: Cambridge University Press, 2004), 133–55.

4. Yitzhak Hen, "The Romanization of the Frankish Liturgy: Ideal, Reality, and the Rhetoric of Reform," in Bolgia et al., *Rome Across Time and Space*, 111–24. Regarding the question of "Roman" books see also Donald A. Bullough, "Roman Books and Carolingian Renovatio," in *Carolingian Renewal: Sources and Heritage* (Manchester: Manchester University Press, 1991), 1–33.

5. Einhard, *Vita Karoli Magni*, 26, ed. G. Waitz, MGH SS rer. Germ. 25: 30–31.

6. As in the "Karolus magnus et Leo papa," an anonymous poem from ca. 800, ed. E. Dümmler, MGH Poetae 1: 368, line 94.

7. See especially Klaus Herbers, "Rom im Frankenreich: Rombeziehung durch Heilige in der Mitte des 9. Jahrhunderts," in *Mönchtum, Kirche, Herrschaft, 750–1000*, eds. D. R. Bauer and J. Semmler (Sigmaringen: J. Thorbecke Verlag, 1998), 133–69.

8. Mayke de Jong, "Carolingian Monasticism: The Power of Prayer," in *The New Cambridge Medieval History. 2:* c.*700*–c.*900*, ed. R. McKitterick (Cambridge: Cambridge University Press, 1995), 622–53 at 651.

9. Karl Schmid, "Die Frage nach den Anfängen der Mönchsgemeinschaft in Fulda," in *Die Klostergemeinschaft von Fulda im früheren Mittelalter*, ed. K. Schmid (Munich: W. Fink, 1978), 108–35.

10. Richard Krautheimer, "The Carolingian Revival of Early Christian Architecture," *Art Bulletin* 24.1 (1942): 1–38.

11. Geary, *Furta sacra*, 47.

12. Janneke E. Raaigmakers, "Fulda, eine Heilige Stadt: Hrabanus Maurus und die Reliquienstranslationen (835–838)," in *Hrabanus Maurus in Fulda, mit einer Hrabanus Maurus-*

Bibliographie (1979–2009), eds. M.-A. Aris and S. Bullido del Barrio (Frankfurt am Main: Josef Knecht, 2010), 219–38.

13. Rudolf of Fulda, *Miracula sanctorum in Fuldenses ecclesias translatorum*, ed. G. Waitz, MGH SS 15.1: 328–41.

14. The oldest library catalogs from Fulda are all fragmentary, but the later collection and the catalogs of other contemporary monasteries of similar stature give a sense of the riches it must have possessed: Paul Lehmann, "Die alte Klosterbibliothek Fulda und ihre Bedeutung," *Aus der Landesbibliothek Fulda* 2 (1928): 5–12; Karl Christ, *Die Bibliothek des Klosters Fulda im 16. Jahrhundert: die Handschriften-Verzeichnisse* (Leipzig: O. Harrassowitz, 1933), 64–66.

15. Klaus Gugel, *Welche erhaltenen mittelalterlichen Handschriften dürfen der Bibliothek des Klosters Fulda zugerechnet werden? 1. Die Handschriften* (Frankfurt am Main: Verlag Josef Knecht, 1995), 60–61, no. 326. In the thirteenth century, this ninth-century compilation was rebound with a diverse range of later texts. The entire manuscript has been digitized and is freely available online at "e-codices: Virtual Manuscript Library of Switzerland": www.e-codices.unifr.ch/. The compilation's quires are III, V, IV, I, III–1: all pages are ruled the same with twenty lines per page and written in the same hand. After the first section (inscriptions), none of the beginnings of the sections (itineraries, wall description, liturgical description, and poem collection) corresponds to the beginning of a quire.

16. Significant in shifting focus away from the Einsiedeln compilation as a "real" usable itinerary toward an understanding of it as a mental map are Franz Alto Bauer, "Das Bild der Stadt Rom in karolingischer Zeit: der Anonymus Einsidlensis," *RQ* 92 (1997): 190–228; Riccardo Santangeli Valenzani, "L'itinerario di Einsiedeln," in Arena et al., *Roma dall'antichità al medioevo*, 154–60. Neither of these articles addresses the liturgical description or poetry collection included in the manuscript.

17. ff. 67r–79r.

18. See Chapter 1, n. 8.

19. ff. 79v–85r. There are ten itineraries within the city. An eleventh itinerary exclusively lists sites outside of the city. Another "itinerary" is found in the inscription collection (f. 77v–78r) but has not been visually rearranged in the manner of the other itineraries.

20. ff. 85r–86r. See Chapter 1, n. 7.

21. ff. 86v–88v. See Chapter 1, n. 98.

22. ff. 88v–97v. The poems are identified and, in part, transcribed by Theodor Mommsen, "Handschriftliches zur Lateinischen Anthologie," *Rheinisches Museum für Philologie*, n.s., 9 (1854): 296–301. Mommsen's references to folio numbers do not precisely correspond to the manuscript's present-day foliation.

23. ff. 78v–79r, nos. 76–80, ed. Walser, 61–63, discussion 133–41.

24. The poem collection begins on f. 88v (directly after the last line of the liturgical description). It continues onto the last two pages of the quaternion. At this point the compiler had not quite finished copying the "Conflictus veris et hiemis." Then the compiler added a bifolium but by the end had not finished copying another text which he had started (the *Tituli Historiarum*). A ternion was then added (which is now missing the last page and, presumably, the end of the epitaph for Bernard).

25. ff. 88v–89r: "Quadam nocte niger," ed. Mommsen, 298; also ed. K. Strecker, in MGH Poetae 4.2: 1119–20.

26. ff. 89r–89v: "Monastica de erumnis XII Heruclis" (Ausonius): no. 24, ed. S. Prete, *Decimi Magni Ausonii Burdigalensis opuscula*, 112–13.

27. Lawrence Nees, *A Tainted Mantle: Hercules and the Classical Tradition at the Carolingian Court* (Philadelphia: University of Pennsylvania Press, 1991), 28–32.

28. ff. 89v–91r: "Conflictus veris et hiemis" (Alcuin): ed. and discussed in René Martin, "Au confluent des traditions antique, germanique et chrétienne: le 'Conflictus Veris et Hiemis'

d'Alcuin," *Revue des études latines* 72 (1994): 177–91; translation in P. Godman, *Poetry of the Carolingian Renaissance* (Norman: University of Oklahoma Press, 1985), 145–49, no. 14.

29. "Tum respondit ouans sublimi e sede Palemon / et Dafnis pariter, pastorum et turba piorum," ed. Martin, 179.

30. f. 91r, ed. Mommsen, 298: "Iustius invidia nihil est quae protinus ipsum / Corrodit auctorem excruciatque animam." This couplet slightly modifies lines quoted in Jerome's *Commentary on Galatians*, 3, commentary on 5.19–21, PL 26: 417.

31. f. 91r, ed. Mommsen, 299: "Titire tu fido recubans sub tegmine Christi"; ed. Ferrua, *Epigrammata Damasiana*, 87–88, no. 2; cf. Virgil, *Eclogues*, 1.1, ed. R. Coleman, 43: "Tityre, tu patulae recubans sub tegmine fagi / silvestrem." These verses are ascribed to Pope Damasus in a tenth-century manuscript.

32. ff. 91r–91v, ed. Mommsen, 299: "Anima pro diversis actibus diversa nomina sortitur. Dum ergo vivificat corpus, anima est; dum vult, animus est; dum scit, mens est; dum recolit, memoria est; dum rectum iudicat, ratio est; dum spirat, spiritus est; dum aliquid sentit, sensus est." Cf. Isidore's *Etymologies*, 11.1.13, ed. W. M. Lindsay.

33. f. 91v, ed. Mommsen, 299: "Decipies alios verbis vultuque benigno / Nam mihi iam notus dissimulator eris." These lines are taken from one of Martial's epigrams: *Epigrams*, 4.88, ed. and trans. W. Ker, 1: 290–91. In the Einsiedeln compilation the verses are labeled "Ad Septitianum."

34. ff. 91v–97v; translation and commentary in Renate Pillinger, *Die Tituli Historiarum oder das sogennante Dittochaeon des Prudentius* (Vienna: Österreichischen Akademie der Wissenschaften, 1980).

35. f. 97v, ed. Mommsen, 299–300. The epitaph of Gerold is also edited by E. Dümmler, MGH Poetae 1: 114, no. 10.

36. Epitaph of Gerold, ed. Dümmler, 114: "Mole sub hac magni servantur membra Geroldi, / Huius iura loci cunctis qui viribus auxit, / Pannoniis vera ecclesiae pro pace peremptus." The Einsiedeln compilation has "vita" instead of "iura."

37. Epitaph of Bernald, ed. Mommsen, 300: "Nobileque ornavit vita modesta genus."

38. Literally, "the rewards of merits which await the pious," as contrasted, in the next line, to the insignificance of the graves for their corporeal remains: epitaph of Bernald, ed. Mommsen, 300: "Quamvis magna piis meritorum praemia restent, / Parva tamen functis sunt loca corporibus."

39. Epitaph of Gerold, ed. Dümmler, 114: "Sideribusque animam dedit."

40. Alcuin, *De animae ratione liber ad Eulaliam virginem*, PL 101: 639–50; Marie-Hélène Jullien and Françoise Perelman, *Clavis scriptorum latinorum medii aevi: auctores Galliae 735–987. 2: Alcuin* (Turnhout: Brepols, 1999), 121–25 (ALC 17). For discussion see Malcolm R. Godden, "Anglo-Saxons on the Mind," in *Learning and Literature in Anglo-Saxon England: Studies Presented to Peter Clemoes on the Occasion of His Sixty-Fifth Birthday*, eds. M. Lapidge and H. Gneuss (Cambridge: Cambridge University Press, 1985), 271–98 at 271–74. Regarding Alcuin see, most recently, Douglas Dales, *Alcuin: Theology and Thought* (Cambridge: Cambridge University Press, 2013). Near the end of his life, Alcuin asked the monastic community at Fulda to remember him in their prayers.

41. Alcuin, *De animae ratione*, 7, PL 101: 642: "Nunc autem consideremus miram velocitatem animae in formandis rebus, quae percipit per carnales sensus, a quibus quasi per quosdam nuntios, quidquid rerum sensibilium cognitarum vel incognitarum percipit, mox in seipsa earum ineffabili celeritate format figuras, informatasque in suae thesauro memoriae recondit. Sicut enim qui Romam vidit, Romam enim [*Forte*, etiam] fingit in animo suo, et format qualis sit. Et dum nomen audierit vel rememorat Romae, statim recurrit animus illius ad memoriam, ubi conditam habet formam illius, et ibi recognoscit [eam ad memoriam], ubi recondidit illam." Alcuin distinguishes the different parts of the soul, a definition very similar to that included

in the Einsiedeln compilation, although Alcuin also includes "voluntas" (11: 644). However, throughout his treatise he uses *anima*, *animus*, and *mens* fairly interchangeably, the mind being the principal part of the soul; see Godden, "Anglo-Saxons on the Mind," 272.

42. Alcuin, *De animae ratione*, 7, PL 101: 642: "Et adhuc mirabilius est, quod incognitarum rerum, si lectae vel auditae erunt in auribus, anima statim format figuram ignotae rei. Sicut forte Jerusalem quisquam nostrum habet in anima sua formatam, qualis sit: quamvis longe aliter sit, quam sibi anima fingit, dum videtur."

43. Alcuin, *De animae ratione*, 7, PL 101: 642: "Muros et domos et plateas non fingit in eo, sicut in Jerusalem facit, [sed] quidquid in aliis civitatibus vidit sibi cognitis, hoc fingit in Jerusalem esse posse; ex notis enim speciebus fingit ignota: nec enim in civitate Jerusalem fingit hominis membra, sed aedificia civitatibus consueta." "In eo" here refers back to the figure of Abraham, Alcuin's previous example.

44. Alcuin, *De animae ratione*, 8, PL 101: 642: "Ex qua velocitate animae, quo in se sic omnia fingit audita vel visa, aut sensa, aut odorata, aut gustata, iterumque inventa recognoscit, mira Dei potentia et naturae efficacia [Al., efficientia], utcunque cognosci poterit."

45. Alcuin, *De animae ratione*, 8, PL 101: 642: "Dum de Jerusalem cogito, non eo momento de Roma possum cogitare."

46. Alcuin, *De animae ratione*, 14, PL 101: 646: "Hic est thesaurus desiderabilis, qui requiescit in ore prudentis, et abundat in corde sapientis. Haec in Virgiliacis non invenietur mendaciis, sed in evangelica affluenter reperietur veritate."

47. Alcuin, *De animae ratione*, 9, PL 101: 643: "Sciendum est certissime, animam, si in ea nobilitate permansisset qua condita est a Creatore, omnimodis immortalem esse, sicut sanctorum animae sunt."

48. Alcuin, *De animae ratione*, 14, PL 101: 647: "quia non est in sermone tantummodo regnum Dei, sed in virtute sancti Spiritus et sanctorum perfecta meritorum claritate."

49. Médard Barth, *Handbuch der elsässischen Kirchen im Mittelalter*, Archives de l'Église d'Alsace, n.s., 11–13 (Strasbourg: Société d'histoire de l'Église d'Alsace, 1960–1963), 1678–712.

50. Hans J. Hummer, *Politics and Power in Early Medieval Europe: Alsace and the Frankish Realm, 600–1000* (Cambridge: Cambridge University Press, 2005), 177–80; Franz Staab, "Erzbischof Otgar (826–847)," in *Handbuch der Mainzer Kirchengeschichte. 1. Christliche Antike und Mittelalter*, ed. F. Jürgensmeier (Würzburg: Echter, 2000), 153–62.

51. Ferrari, *Early Roman Monasteries*, 295–98.

52. Hrabanus Maurus, "Versus in tumulo S. Sergii," ed. E. Dümmler, MGH Poetae 2: 219, no. 55.1: "Martyribus sanctis honor extat maximus orbe. / Nomine pro Christi qui meruere mori. / Excellens inter quos gaudet Sergius almus, / Qui cum fratre Bacho supplicia arcta luit. / Romulea ex urbe hos praesul Otgarius ambos / Advexit, tantum Sergium et hic posuit."

53. Hrabanus Maurus, "Super confessionem ipsius sepulchri," ed. Dümmler, MGH Poetae 2: 219, no. 55.3: "Quisquis dona velit rite impetrare tonantis, / Supplex poscat opem hic, martyrum et auxilium."

54. Surviving manuscript evidence from the monastery of Weissenburg attests to the presence of their *passio*; a Weissenburg manuscript of a Bible glossary from the second half of the ninth century also contains hymns for a few martyrs including, right before the Roman martyr Lawrence, a hymn for Sergius and Bacchus: Weissenburg 66, in Hans Butzmann, *Die Weissenburger Handschriften* (Frankfurt am Main: Vittorio Klostermann, 1964), 211–13.

55. The hymn was traditionally attributed to Walafrid Strabo, *Hymnus de S. Sergio et Bacho*, ed. E. Dümmler, MGH Poetae 2: 418–19, no. 83.

56. Ibid., no. 83.3: "Athletae. . . . superastis arma / hostis antiqui trucis atque cosmi / carnis agone"; no. 83.5: "miles radians"; no. 83.6: "tacma caelestis Solimae supernae."

57. Ibid., no. 83.2: "Sergius, Bachus sotii corona / carnis a claustro pariter migrando / sydera supra."

58. Ibid., no. 83.8: "Inde vos saecli precium sequentes, / quaesumus, nobis meritis favete, / nosos ut vestris nequeat nocere / civibus istis"; no. 83.9: "Hic topus vester vocitatur alba / civitas sacris decorata gazis, / quem sacrosancti cineres adornant, / somata sancta"; no. 83.12: "Vos crucis Christi socios rogate, / qui dei patris comitantur agnum, / intra caelorum mereamur urbis / septa subire."

59. The editor, Ernst Dümmler, notes borrowings from Virgil and Horace.

60. *Translatio Sergii et Bacchi*, ed. W. Levison, MGH SS 30.2: 1340–42.

61. *Translatio Sergii et Bacchi*, ed. Levison, 1342: "Deinde venerabiles eorum exuvias illa urbium nobilissima et mundi domina obtinuit Roma, quae postmodum, per venerabilem Otgarium Mogontinum episcopum ad Gallias translatae, in civitate Leucopolitana quae et Wizenburch vocatur honestissimae sepulturae sunt commendatae. Hic nimirum fratrum suorum completionem et magnae resurrectionis expectant diem, quando illorum gaudii perfectio corporum in quibus triumphaverunt glorifica erit resurrectio."

62. A. Bernard, "Der Reliquienschatz der ehemaligen Abtei Weißenburg," *Archiv für elsässische Kirchengeschichte* 12 (1937): 73–82; regarding the tympanum see Franz Xaver Kraus, *Kunst und Alterthum in Elsass-Lothringen: beschreibende Statistik. 1. Kunst und Alterthum im Unter-Elsass* (Strassburg: C. F. Schmidts Universitäts-Buchhandlung, 1876), 613.

63. Caesarius's feast day is typically mentioned in Carolingian martyrologies and calendars and was included in the widespread sacramentary, the *Hadrianum*: *Der karolingische Reichskalendar und seine Überlieferung bis ins 12. Jahrhundert*, ed. A. Borst, 2.3: 1455 (November 1); Jean Deshusses, *Le sacramentaire grégorien: ses principales formes d'après les plus anciens manuscrits. 1. Le sacramentaire, le supplément d'Aniane* (Fribourg: Éditions universitaire, 1971), 283.

64. To my knowledge, the earliest attestation of a translation of St. Caesarius's relics from Rome is in the later tenth century, when Bishop Anno of Cologne (r. 1056–1075) obtained, in Rome, an arm of the saint: *Vita Annonis archiepiscopi Coloniensis*, 34–35, ed. R. Koepke, MGH SS 11: 481–82.

65. "Romae Caesarii"; *Der karolingische Reichskalendar*, ed. Borst, 2.3: 1457, no. 7.

66. Wolfgang Haubrichs, *Die Kultur der Abtei Prüm zur Karolingerzeit: Studien zur Heimat des althochdeutschen Georgsliedes* (Bonn: Ludwig Röhrscheid, 1979), especially 22–23, 56–59, 116–22.

67. *Historia translationis reliquiarum martyrum sanctorum Chrysanthi et Dariae ex urbe Roma in Galliam* (BHL 1793): AASS Oct. XI: 490B–495A; here 1.1: 490B: "ut alicujus præclarissimi martyris corpus ei dari deberet famæ celebrioris, de cujus passione ac veneratione nullus fidelium posset ambigere." The imperial letter was addressed to Pope Gregory IV, but by the time Marcward arrived in Rome, Gregory had died, and his request was granted by Gregory's successor, Sergius II: Heinrich Joseph Floß, "Romreise des Abtes Markward von Prüm und Übertragung der hl. Chrysanthus und Daria nach Münstereifel im Jahre 844," *Annalen des Historischen Vereins für den Niederrhein* 20 (1869): 96–217 at 107.

68. Wandalbert, *Martyrologium*, ed. E. Dümmler, MGH Poetae 2: 578–603; Jacques Dubois, "Le Martyrologe métrique de Wandelbert: ses sources, son originalité, son influence sur le Martyrologe d'Usuard," *AB* 79 (1961): 257–93, especially 277–79.

69. Jacques Dubois, *Les martyrologes du Moyen Âge latin*, Typologie des sources du Moyen Âge occidental 26 (Turnhout: Brepols, 1978), 18–19, 40–42.

70. Wandalbert, *Martyrologium*, lines 709–710, ed. Dümmler, 598: "Caesarius prima designat fronte Novembrem. / Eximio cuius laetatur Roma triumpho." Cf. Renaud and Dubois, *Edition pratique*, 199, no. 4. Another example is St. Hadrian (Sept. 8), whom Wandelbert, again unlike Florus, associates with Rome: Wandalbert, *Martyrologium*, line 548, ed. Dümmler, 593: "Martyr et Adrianus Romam tunc sanguine comit."

71. "Elle [la Passion de S. Georges] nous fait l'effet d'être une sorte de *Monte Testaccio*, formé par des débris de toute provenance et sans cohésion," in his review of F. Cumont's article

"La plus ancienne légende de saint Georges," in *AB* 57 (1939): 134–36, here 135, cited in part in Walter, *Warrior Saints*, 111.

72. Ernst von Dobschütz, ed., *Das Decretum Gelasianum de libris recipiendis et non recipiendis* (Leipzig: J. C. Hinrichs, 1912), 21–60; Rosamond McKitterick, *The Carolingians and the Written Word* (Cambridge: Cambridge University Press, 1989), 203–4.

73. *Decretum Gelasianum*, 4.4, ed. Dobshütz, 39–42 (about *gesta*); 5.8, ed. Dobschütz, 57, line 331 (about the *passio Georgii* specifically); here 4.4, ed. Dobschütz, 40–41, lines 210–12: "et ab infidelibus et idiotis superflua aut minus apta quam rei ordo fuerit esse putantur."

74. The following discussion draws primarily from the conclusions of Wolfgang Haubrichs, "St. Georg auf der frühmittelalterlichen Reichenau: Hagiographie, Hymnographie, Liturgie und Reliquienkult," in *Herrschaft, Kirche, Kultur: Beiträge zur Geschichte des Mittelalters. Festschrift für Friedrich Prinz zu seinem 65. Geburtstag*, ed. G. Jenal (Stuttgart: Hiersemann, 1993), 505–35.

75. *Martyrologium Hieronymianum*, eds. de Rossi and Duchesne, AASS Nov. II, 1: 49 (VII Kal. Mai./April 25).

76. Deshusses, *Le sacramentaire grégorien*, 210; H. Delehaye, *Commentarius in Martyrologium Hieronymianum*, AASS Nov. II, 2: 204–9; *Der karolingische Reichskalendar*, ed. Borst, 2.2: 806–15.

77. Notker, *Martyrologium*, IX Kal. Mai. (April 23), PL 131: 1025–1164 at 1069: "In Perside, civitate Diospoli, passio sancti Georgii martyris . . . Cujus gesta passionis, etsi inter apocryphas connumerantur scripturas, tamen illustrissimum ejus martyrium inter coronas martyrum Ecclesia Dei venerabiliter honorat." Cf. Chapter 8, n. 44. The martyrology survives in a single incomplete tenth-century manuscript: St. Gallen, Stiftsbibliothek, Cod. Sang. 456, which is available at "e-codices": www.e-codices.unifr.ch/.

78. Notker, *Martyrologium,* VII Kal. Mai. (April 25), PL 131: 1070: "In Perside S. Georgii martyris, juxta Kalendarium sagacissimi Hieronymi. Cujus passio apud Romanos et pene alios omnes IX Kalendarum Maiarum, ut superius notatum est, celebris habetur. Quod idcirco significandum putavi, ut patriarcha noster Hatto Magontiacensis, qui hoc anno item ab incarnatione Domini, caput ejus et aliud quoddam membrum cum plurimis et maximis sanctorum reliquiis in Alemanniam ad novum monasterium suum a Formoso apostolico impetratis asportavit. In ejus solemnitate, S. Georgii videlicet, indicenda, caute se agat, quia et plures in hac die ipsius natalitia celebrare consueverunt."

79. A. Gerlich, "Hatto, I., Ebf. v. Mainz," in LexMa, 4: 1957–58.

80. Walter Berschin, *Reichenauer Wandmalerei 840–1120: Goldbach, Reichenau-Oberzell St. Georg, Reichenau-Niederzell St. Peter und Paul* (Heidelberg: Mattes, 2012), 30–68; Dörthe Jakobs, *Sankt Georg in Reichenau-Oberzell: der Bau und seine Ausstattung. Bestand, Veränderungen, Restaurierungsgeschichte*, 3 vols. (Stuttgart: Theiss, 1999).

81. *Breviarium Richenoviense* (Zürich, Zentralbibliothek, Ms. Rh. hist. 28, ff. 127r–154v), ed. de Rossi and Duchesne, *Martyrologium Hieronymianum*, AASS Nov. II, 1. A digital version of this manuscript is available at the Carolingian Culture at Reichenau and St. Gall Project: www.stgallplan.org/en/index_library.html. The other feasts marked in majuscules are Mary; Albanus, the patron of the monastery in Mainz of which Hatto was archbishop; and the Roman saints Pancratius and Marianus, and Chrysanthus and Daria: Wolfgang Haubrichs, "Neue Zeugnisse zur Reichenauer Kultgeschichte des 9. Jahrhunderts," *Zeitschrift für die Geschichte des Oberrheins* 126 (1978): 1–43 at 18–20.

82. Feast of St. George: *Breviarium Richenoviense* (Zürich, Zentralbibliothek, Ms. Rh. hist. 28, f. 136r), ed. de Rossi and Duchesne, AASS Nov. II, 1: 47 (VIIII Kal. Mai.). The martyrology also includes an entry for the feast of St. George "in persida ciuitate. diospoli" on April 25 (VII Kal. Mai.): f. 136v, ed. de Rossi and Duchesne, 47; and marks November 18 (XIIII Kal. Decembr.) as the dedication of the church to St. George in Reichenau: "Et dedicatio.

aeccl(esi)ae. sci georgii martyris. In / cella. quae d(icitu)r Hathonis": f. 152r, ed. de Rossi and Duchesne, 144. Neither of these feasts is marked in majuscules.

Chapter 8. A Universalizing Rome Through the Lens of Ado of Vienne

1. Wilhelm Kremers, *Ado von Vienne: sein Leben und seine Schriften* (Steyl: Missionsdruckerei, 1911).

2. Jacques Dubois and Geneviève Renaud, eds., *Le Martyrologe d'Adon, ses deux familles, ses trois recensions: texte et commentaire* (Paris: Éditions du Centre national de la recherche scientifique, 1984), XX–XXVIII; Henri Quentin, *Les martyrologes historiques du Moyen Âge: étude sur la formation du Martyrologe romain* (Paris: J. Gabalda, 1908), 465–681; Herbers, "Rom im Frankenreich," 158–60.

3. MGH Capit. 1, ed. A. Boretius, no. 170 (Capitulare Monasticum 817. Iul. 10.): 343–49. For discussion see Jong, "Carolingian Monasticism."

4. For discussion of Jerome's martyrology, see Felice Lifshitz, *The Name of the Saint: The Martyrology of Jerome and Access to the Sacred in Francia, 627–827* (Notre Dame, IN: University of Notre Dame Press, 2006); for an introduction and translation of Bede's martyrology (ca. 725–731), see Felice Lifshitz, "Bede, Martyrology," in *Medieval Hagiography: An Anthology*, ed. T. Head (New York: Routledge, 2000), 167–97.

5. These include the martyrologies of the Anonymous of Lyon (before 806), Florus of Lyon (ca. 825–840), Wandelbert (ca. 848), Hrabanus Maurus (before 857), Usuard (ca. 860), Wolfhard (before 895), and Notker (before 912): see Dubois, *Les martyrologes*, 37–59.

6. Ado, eds. Dubois and Renaud, XXV: "Ne putes me in hoc opere in vacuum laborasse, et rem non necessariam exsecutum fuisse, breviter tibi causam facti aperiam. Primum fuit imperium ac iussio sanctorum virorum, ut supplerentur dies, qui absque nominibus martyrum in Martyrologio (quod venerabilis Flori studio in labore domini Bedae accreverat) tantum notati erant. Deinde collecti undecunque passionum codices animum in tantum suscitaverunt, ut non solum praeteritas dierum festivitates, verum et aliorum, qui per totum annum ibi notatim positi erant, latius et paulo apertius describerem, infirmioribus fratribus, et minus legere valentibus serviens, ad laudem omnipotentis Dei; ut in memoriis martyrum haberent compendiosam lectionem, atque in parvo codicillo, quod multo labore alii per plures codices exquirunt."

7. Ibid., XXI. For a detailed comparison see Quentin, *Les martyrologes historiques*, 481–85. The martyrologies of Bede and Florus are edited in Renaud and Dubois, *Edition pratique*.

8. According to Quentin's statistics, 51 of the 475 notices from Florus included in the *venerabile et perantiquum martyrologium* (which Ado claims as the basis for his martyrology and whose dates uniformly correspond to Ado's own martyrology) were displaced to different days: Quentin, *Les martyrologes historiques*, 456.

9. Ado, eds. Dubois and Renaud, XXV: "Huic operi, ut dies martyrum verissimo notarentur, qui confusi in Kalendis satis inveniri solent, adiuvit venerabile et perantiquum Martyrologium ab urbe Roma Aquileiam cuidam sancto episcopo a pontifice Romano directum, et mihi postmodum a quodam religioso fratre aliquot diebus praestitum. Quod ego diligenti cura transcriptum, positus apud Ravennam, in capite huius operis ponendum putavi."

10. Roman Martyrology, ed. Quentin, *Les martyrologes historiques*, 414–51 (referred to by Quentin as the *Vetus/Parvum Romanum*); discussion at 409–64 and 649–72. The earliest surviving manuscript copy of the Roman Martyrology, St. Gallen, Stiftsbibliothek, Cod. Sang. 454 is available at "e-codices": www.e-codices.unifr.ch/.

11. In St. Gallen, Stiftsbibliothek, Cod. Sang. 454, p. 2: it begins, "INCIP(IT) MARTYROLOGIVM ROMANVM" (ed. Quentin, 414).

12. Roman Martyrology, April 1, ed. Quentin, 423: "KL. APR. Romae theodorae, sororis martyris hermetis. quae sub aureliano martyrizavit. sepultae via salaria."

13. Quentin, *Les martyrologes historiques.*

14. Ado, *De sex aetatibus mundi*: full edition in PL 123: 23–138; partial edition by G. Pertz in MGH SS 2: 315–23.

15. These sources were meticulously identified by Quentin, whose conclusions I follow throughout this section: Quentin, *Les martyrologes historiques*, 458–64 and 485–649.

16. For an overview and additional bibliography see Giles Brown, "Introduction: The Carolingian Renaissance," in *Carolingian Culture: Emulation and Innovation*, ed. R. McKitterick (Cambridge: Cambridge University Press, 1994), 1–51; McKitterick, *The Carolingians and the Written Word.*

17. Roman Martyrology, Feb. 2, ed. Quentin, 417 (IIII NON.): "Caesareae cornelii centurionis. ipsius urbis episcopi" (discussion, 591); May 24, ed. Quentin, 428 (VIIII KL.): "Et iohannae uxoris chuzae" (discussion, 593).

18. Max Buchner, "Zur Überlieferungsgeschichte des 'Liber pontificalis' und zu seiner Verbreitung im Frankenreiche im 9. Jahrhundert," *RQ* 34 (1926): 141–66.

19. Quentin, *Les martyrologes historiques*, 102–4 (for Bede) and 318–20 (Florus).

20. Ibid., 641–49.

21. The term *gesta martyrum* is used by scholars to refer to a large group of hagiographical texts of saints martyred or otherwise associated with Rome, which A. Dufourcq and other early scholars believed had formed a late antique corpus of texts. Because of textual similarities it is clear that many of these texts were likely composed in similar contexts, in Rome, starting in the fifth and sixth centuries, but there is no evidence to support the theory that these texts were ever transmitted together as an established corpus; see Cooper, "The Martyr, the *Matrona* and the Bishop," 305–8 and Clare Pilsworth, "Dating the *Gesta Martyrum*: A Manuscript-Based Approach," *EME* 9.3 (2000): 309–24.

22. Quentin, *Les martyrologes historiques*, 645–49.

23. Lifshitz, *The Name of the Saint.*

24. Roman Martyrology, Sept. 9, ed. Quentin, 439 (V ID.): "*Nicomediae dorothei et gorgonii martyrum.* quorum unus id est *gorgonius romam* transfertur." (Italics refer to text derived from Florus; note that Quentin's convention is the inverse of that of Dubois and Renaud for Ado's martyrology). This notice is repeated and expanded in Ado's own martyrology: Ado, Sept. 9, eds. Dubois and Renaud, 306–7, here 307: "*Interiecto tempore beatus Gorgonius Romam transfertur, positusque est venerabiliter via Latina, inter duas lauros.*" (Italics refer to Ado's additions to, or radical alterations of, Florus). For discussion see Quentin, *Les martyrologes historiques*, 613–15.

25. Florus's martyrology, May 6, eds. Dubois and Renaud, 82: "Natale sancti Johannis apostoli, ante portam Latinam"; Bede, *Chronica*, ed. T. Mommsen, MGH AA 13: 285.

26. Roman Martyrology, May 6, ed. Quentin, 426 (PRID. NON.): "*Sancti iohannis apostoli.* quando *ante portam latinam* in ferventis olei dolium missus est"; Ado's martyrology, May 6, eds. Dubois and Renaud, 149. Discussion: Quentin, *Les martyrologes historiques*, 632 and 661.

27. This and the following statistics derive from word counts of Rome based on the edition of H. Rosweyde reprinted in the PL 123: 143–78, which is very similar, although not identical, to Quentin's edition. The number of saints associated with Rome is much greater than this number suggests since often multiple saints are associated with Rome without repeating the specification "Rome."

28. There are notices for approximately 50 saints (or groups of saints) from locations in Italy, 60 from Africa, 50 from Asia Minor, 40 from the Levant, and 25 from Greece.

29. These cities all appear four or five times in the martyrology. Also appearing equally frequently are Spoleto and the regions of Tuscany and Mauritania.

30. Roman Martyrology, Aug. 5, ed. Quentin, 435 (NONIS): "*In rhetia civitate augusta sanctae afrae martyris*"; March 17, ed. Quentin, 421 (XVI KL.): "*Sancti patricii episcopi. qui primos* apud *scottos predicavit.*"

31. Vitus: Roman Martyrology, June 15, ed. Quentin, 430; Ado's martyrology, June 15, eds. Dubois and Renaud, 195–96; Theodore: Roman Martyrology, Nov. 9, ed. Quentin, 446; Ado's martyrology, Nov. 9, eds. Dubois and Renaud, 378; Sergius and Bacchus: Roman Martyrology, Oct. 7, ed. Quentin, 442; Ado's martyrology, Oct. 7, eds. Dubois and Renaud, 347–49; in contrast to surviving versions of the *passio*, however, Ado narrates how soon after his death the body of Bacchus (martyred separately) was moved to be near to that of Sergius. See Quentin, *Les martyrologes historiques*, 571–72.

32. Florus's martyrology (following Bede), March 9, eds. Dubois and Renaud, 47; Roman Martyrology, March 11, ed. Quentin, 421; Ado's martyrology, March 11, eds. Dubois and Renaud, 101–3 (first family of manuscripts). But in the second family of manuscripts of Ado's martyrology (a later version of his martyrology, likely undertaken after his death), the Forty Martyrs have been moved back again to March 9: Ado's martyrology, March 9, eds. Dubois and Renaud, 100 (second family of manuscripts).

33. Bede's martyrology, Nov. 1, eds. Dubois and Renaud, 199.

34. Ado's martyrology, Nov. 1, eds. Dubois and Renaud, 371–72.

35. Roman Martyrology, Nov. 1, ed. Quentin, 445 (KL. NOV.): "*Romae caesarii diaconi.*" Perhaps Ado had intended "Romae" to be read as part of the preceding phrase regarding the feast of all saints, but at least the scribe of the ninth-century St. Gallen, Stiftsbibliothek, Cod. Sang. 454, p. 19, clearly associated it with Caesarius.

36. Florus's martyrology, Nov. 8, eds. Dubois and Renaud, 203.

37. Ado's martyrology, Nov. 8, eds. Dubois and Renaud, 376. Similarly, the Roman Martyrology includes both groups of saints—the stonemasons, Claudius, Nicostratus, Simpronianus, Castorius and Simplicius, and the soldiers, the Quattro Coronati—under the heading "Romae," with no mention of Pannonia: Nov. 8, ed. Quentin, 446. Ado, based on a misreading of the passage of the *Liber Pontificalis* that describes how Pope Leo IV translated the saints' relics to SS. Quattro Coronati, also provides the names of the Quattro Coronati.

38. Ado's martyrology, Sept. 27, eds. Dubois and Renaud, 329–31, here 331: "*Duorum autem fratrum Cosmae et Damiani memoriam Roma etiam, templo praeclaro opere nomini eorum aedificato, solemniter agit.*"

39. Ado's martyrology, Sept. 9, eds. Dubois and Renaud, 307 (an entry based on a passage from the *Liber Pontificalis*).

40. Florus' martyrology, Sept. 8, eds. Dubois and Renaud, 165; Quentin, *Les martyrologes historiques*, 486–88.

41. Ado's martyrology, Sept. 8, eds. Dubois and Renaud, 303–6, here 306: "*Non longo post tempore beati Adriani corpus Romam etiam translatum, honorabili quoque templo exornatum est.*" The version of Hadrian's *passio* Ado was working with likely did not specify the date of Hadrian's martyrdom; accordingly, Ado interpreted Florus's notice for Hadrian as indicating the date of Hadrian's death. As demonstrated by Quentin, the choice of this date (Sept. 8), already found in Bede, likely derives from the fact that this is the feast of the birth of Mary, the liturgical procession for which began at S. Adriano.

42. Ado's martyrology, March 4, eds. Dubois and Renaud, 98; Sept. 8, eds. Dubois and Renaud, 303: "*Romae, festivitas sepulturae*, sancti Adriani martyris, qui apud Nicomediam, cum

aliis viginti tribus *passus est IIII Non. Mar.*" (This is the second family of manuscripts of Ado's martyrology; italics not in Usuard.)

43. Quentin, *Les martyrologes historiques*, 636; Florus's martyrology, April 23, eds. Dubois and Renaud, 69.

44. Roman Martyrology, April 23, ed. Quentin, 425 (VIIII KL.): "*Perside civitate diospoli georgii martyris*"; Ado's martyrology, April 23, eds. Dubois and Renaud, 132, "In Perside, civitate Diospoli, passio sancti Georgii martyris, *cuius gesta passionis, etsi inter apocryphas connumeratur scripturas, tamen illustrissimum martyrium eius inter coronas martyrum ecclesia Dei venerabiliter honorat.*" Cf. Chapter 7, n. 77.

45. Ado's martyrology, March 15, eds. Dubois and Renaud, 106: "*Romae, Zachariae pontificis, qui Romae sedit annos decem. Hic in patriarcho beati Georgii martyris caput reperit in capsa reconditum in qua pittacium pariter invenit, hoc ipsum graecis litteris exaratum. Sepultus est in ecclesia sancti Petri apostoli*" (second recension).

46. Roman Martyrology, Jan. 1, ed. Quentin, 414; Ado's martyrology, Jan. 1, eds. Dubois and Renaud, 40–41.

47. Roman Martyrology, June 5, ed. Quentin, 429: "NONIS. Bonefacii martyris. apud tarsum XIIII^{mo} die maii mensis passi. romae. Nonis iunii sepulti"; Ado's martyrology, June 5, eds. Dubois and Renaud, 184–85.

48. Quentin, *Les martyrologes historiques*, 496.

49. Ado's martyrology, May 14, eds. Renaud and Dubois, 160: "*Eodem die, passio sancti Bonifacii martyris, apud Tarsum, XIIII. die mensis Maii passi, Romae Nonas Iulii sepulti, quando et celebrior dies eius agitur ubi eius passio adnotata est.*" (This is the second family of manuscripts of Ado's martyrology; italics not in Usuard.)

50. Ado's martyrology, June 5, eds. Renaud and Dubois, 184: "*Eodem die, natale (festivitas II) sancti Bonifacii martyris sub Diocletiano et Maximiano apud Tarsum civitatem passi (apud Tarsum civitatem sub Diocletiano et Maximiano passi II) sed Romae in via quae Latina nuncupatur, sepulti.*" ("II" refers to variants in the second family). Ado also included an entry for the saints with whom Boniface was martyred on the subsequent day: Ado, June 6, eds. Dubois and Renaud, 186; some versions of the Roman Martyrology also include an entry for these saints: ed. Quentin, 429 (VII ID. note b).

51. Florus's martyrology, Aug. 29, eds. Renaud and Dubois, 160: "Romae, in Aventino, sanctae Sabinae virginis atque martyris." The saint's association with Rome is also found in other Carolingian martyrologies and calendars: *Der karolingische Reichskalendar*, ed. Borst, 2.2: 1238, nos. 6–8 (29. Aug.).

52. Quentin, *Les martyrologes historiques*, 570–71 and 658–59.

53. Roman Martyrology, Aug. 29, ed. Quentin, 438 (IIII KL.): "*Romae* ad arcum faustini *sabinae martyris*"; Sept. 3, ed. Quentin, 438: "III NON. Romae seraphiae virginis. IIII Kalendas augusti passae. pridie Kalendas sepultae. III Nonas septembris memoria passionis eius celebrior." Quentin suggested that Ado's choice of September 3 for the feast of St. Serapia was motivated by the fact that this day only contained a very brief notice in Florus's martyrology, while the date given for their martyrdom already contained other notices.

54. Ado's martyrology, Aug. 29, eds. Dubois and Renaud, 292–93; Sept. 3, eds. Dubois and Renaud, 297–98.

55. Ado's martyrology, Nov. 1, eds. Dubois and Renaud, 371: "Festivitas sanctorum omnium. Petente namque papa Bonifacio, iussit Phocas imperator, in veteri fano quod Pantheon vocabatur *et a Domitiano prius factum erat*, ablatis idolatriae sordibus, ecclesiam beatae semperque virginis Mariae et omnium Martyrum fieri: ut ubi quondam omnium, non deorum, sed daemoniorum cultus agebatur, ibi deinceps omnium fieret memoria sanctorum." This text (as well as the following passage) is found in all three recensions of the first family, as well as in the second family, of Ado's text.

56. Ado's martyrology, Nov. 1, eds. Dubois and Renaud, 371: "*quae ab illo tempore Kalendis novembris in urbe* Roma *celebris et* generalis *agitur. Sed et in Galliis, monente sanctae recordationis*

Gregorio pontifice, piissimus Ludovicus imperator, omnibus regni et imperii sui episcopis consentientibus, statuit ut solemniter festivitas omnium sanctorum in praedicta die annuatim perpetuo ageretur. Quasi sanctam constitutionem reverenti amore suscepit omnis Ecclesia."

57. Pierre Jounel, "Le culte collectif des saints à Rome du VIIe au IXe siècle," *Ecclesia orans* 6 (1989): 285–300.

58. Jacques Dubois, *Le martyrologe d'Usuard* (Brussels: Société des Bollandistes, 1965).

59. Giuseppe Antonio Guazzelli, "Baronio attraverso il *Martyrologium Romanum*," in *Cesare Baronio tra santità e scrittura storica*, eds. G. A. Guazzelli et al. (Rome: Viella, 2012), 67–110.

60. *Martyrologium romanum ad novam kalendarii rationem, et ecclesiasticae historiae veritatem restitutum. Gregorii XIII. Pont. Max. iussu editum. Accesserunt notationes atque Tractatio de Martyrologio romano: auctore Caesare Baronio sorano Congregationis Oratorii presbytero* (Rome: ex typ. Dominici Basae, 1586), Nov. 1, p. 493: "Festivitas omnium sanctorum, quam in honorem beatae Dei genitricis virginis Mariae & sanctorum Martyrum Bonifacius Papa quartus, dedicato templo Pantheon, celebrem & generalem instituit agi quotannis in Vrbe Roma. Sed & Gregorius item quartus postmodum decreuit, eamdem festiuitatem, quae variis modis iam in diuersis ecclesiis celebrabatur, in honore omnium Sanctorum solemniter hac die ab vniuersa Ecclesia perpetuo obseruari."

61. Quentin, *Les martyrologes historiques*, 4–5. H. Rosweyde published the text in 1613 as the *Vetus Romanum Martyrologium hactenus a Cardinale Baronio desideratum* (Antwerp: ex officina Plantiniana, 1613).

62. Rosweyde, *Vetus Romanum Martyrologium*, Preface, "SANCTISSIMO DOMINO NOSTRO PAVLO V. PONT. MAX. BEATITATEM PP. Romam redit, SANCTISSIME PATER, quod Romæ olim conceptum, quod Româ profectum, quod Romam ad originis suæ sedem anhelabat. VETVS id est ROMANVM MARTYROLOGIVM: quod Praedecessores vestri summâ curâ in Vrbe collectum, singulari fide conscriptum, maximo beneficio in Romani orbis diœceses transmiserunt."

Epilogue

1. Martin Maischberger, *Marmor in Rom: Anlieferung, Lager- und Werkplatz in der Kaiserzeit* (Wiesbaden: Ludwig Reichart Verlag, 1997), 61–93.

2. Aristides, *To Rome*, 13, ed. W. Dindorf, 1: 327: "ὅ τι δ' ἂν μὴ ἐνταῦθα ἴδῃ τις, οὐκ ἔστι τῶν γενομένων, ἢ γιγνομένων"; quoted in Catharine Edwards and Greg Woolf, "Cosmopolis: Rome as World City," in *Rome the Cosmopolis* (Cambridge: Cambridge University Press, 2003), 1–20, here 5.

Appendix 1. Saints from Abroad Venerated in Rome, ca. 500–800

1. Lifshitz, *The Name of the Saint.*

2. Siegmund, *Überlieferung*, situates the translation of many more hagiographical texts in Rome, based on the assumption that this was the most likely location for such translations to occur in this period, but further study is needed.

Appendix 2. Theodotus and S. Angelo in Pescheria

1. De Rubeis, "Epigrafi a Roma," 118–19, no. 10; Luca Cardin, *Epigrafia a Roma nel primo medioevo (secoli IV–X)* (Rome: Jouvence, 2008), 83–84.

Appendix 3. The *Translatio* of St. Caesarius from Terracina to Rome

1. Duchesne, "Palatin," 22: "La langue, la composition et divers autres indices conseillent d'en placer la rédaction au VIe siècle, et cette date est confirmée par ce que nous savons d'ailleurs sur l'âge des documents romains du même genre."

2. Suitbert Benz, "Zur Geschichte der römischen Kirchweihe nach den Texten des 6. bis 7. Jahrhunderts," in *Enkainia: gesammelte Arbeiten zum 800-jährigen Weihegedächtnis der Abteikirche Maria Laach am 24. August 1956*, ed. H. Emonds (Düsseldorf: Patmos-Verlag, 1956), 62–109.

3. AASS Nov. I: 90A.

4. Claudia Rapp, *Holy Bishops in Late Antiquity* (Berkeley: University of California Press, 2005), 299.

Appendix 4. The Spread of St. George's Cult

1. The earliest surviving Latin account is Theodosius, *De situ terrae sanctae*, 4, ed. P. Geyer, *Itineraria et Alia Geographica*, 113–25 at 116. The late sixth-century anonymous pilgrim from Piacenza in Northern Italy mentions Diospolis as the location of St. George's tomb and notes that many miracles of George occur in the province: Antoninus of Piacenza, *Itinerarium*, 25, ed. Geyer, *Itineraria et Alia Geographica*, 127–74, at 142 and 166. See also Maraval, *Lieux saints*, 298–99.

2. Haubrichs, *Georgslied und Georgslegende*, 225–32, provides a list of the earliest churches dedicated to St. George. From this he concludes (pp. 232–33) that in the fourth and fifth centuries the cult of George was focused in a number of eastern centers (Melitene, Saccaea-Maximianopolis, perhaps Lydda). In the sixth century, dedications to George became more frequent, especially in southern Syria, Arabia, Palestine and throughout Byzantium.

3. Janin, 74–83, esp. 81, no. 6. Walter, *Warrior Saints*, 109–44.

4. Eugen Ewig, "Die Verehrung orientalischer Heiliger im spätrömischen Gallien und im Merowingerreich," in *Festschrift Percy Ernst Schramm zu seinem siebzigsten Geburtstag von Schülern und Freunden zugeeignet*, eds. Peter Classen and Peter Scheibert (Wiesbaden: Franz Steiner, 1964), 385–400, esp. 392.

5. Venantius Fortunatus, *Carmina*, 2.12, "De basilica sancti Georgi," ed. M. Reydellet, *Venance Fortunat: Poèmes*, 1: 69, here line 2: "cuius in hunc mundum spargitur altus honor."

6. Venantius Fortunatus, *Carmina*, 2.12, ed. Reydellet, lines 5–6: "Qui uirtute potens orientis in axe sepultus / ecce sub occiduo cardine praebet opem."

7. Gregory of Tours, *Liber in gloriam martyrum*, 100, ed. Krusch, MGH SS rer. Merov. 1.2: 104–5.

8. Gregory the Great, *Registrum*, 9.7, ed. Norberg, 2: 569.

Appendix 5. An Early Medieval *Diaconia* Dedicated to St. Nicholas?

1. Cited in Armellini and Cecchelli, *Chiese*, 2: 768–70.

2. Palombi, *La basilica*, 66–72. Palombi (p. 61) also cites fifteenth-century reports of Greek inscriptions found reused as paving stones in the church's crypt.

3. Kinney, "Making Mute Stones Speak," assumes the column was moved into the church after it was inscribed; Campese Simone, "Alle origini," 316–17 and Palombi, *La basilica*, 67–68, argue that this need not be the case. Certainly the fluted green *cipollino* column is, like all the other columns in the church, a reused column.

4. Campese Simone, "Alle origini," 312. Regarding Eustathius's inscription see Chapter 4, n. 91.

5. Hermes, "Die stadtrömischen Diakonien," 44–45.

6. Vincenzo Golzio, *San Nicola in Carcere e i tre templi del Foro Olitorio* (Rome: Libreria Fratelli Treves, [1928]); Hülsen, *Chiese*, 392; Armellini and Cecchelli, *Chiese*, 2: 765–71.

7. Kinney, "Making Mute Stones Speak," 83 n. 7; Campese Simone, "Alle origini," 306.

8. Proja, *S. Nicola*, 39: "Abbiamo detto poc'anzi che la dedica originaria della basilica era al ss.mo Salvatore, ma essa non appare in nessun documento ufficiale. Lo affermano autori medioevali e rinascimentali." Proja, however, does not cite any of these medieval or Renaissance sources. He does cite a nineteenth-century inscription, which was erected after restoration work carried out under Pope Pius IX in 1846–1867 but describes the reconsecration of the church under Pope Honorius II in the early twelfth century. However, the inscription does not in fact claim that the church was originally dedicated to the Savior. It reads, "AEDEM VETVSTISSIMAM / DEO SERVATORI / IN HONOREM NICOLAI MAGNI / PONTIFICIS MYRENSIVM / ANTIQVITVS DEDICATAM"—"An ancient seat for God the Savior, dedicated of old in honor of the great Nicolas, bishop of Myra." Palombi, *La basilica*, 26 n. 52 and 68 n. 38, cites Proja regarding the church's original dedication to the Savior, without further elaborating on the evidence for this claim, except to suggest its plausibility by pointing out that, as described in Luke, when Simeon recognizes Jesus, he gives praise to God thanking him that he has merited to behold God's salvation (Luke 2:25–32).

Appendix 6. The *Passio* of St. Boniface of Tarsus

1. Franchi De'Cavalieri, "Dove fu scritta"; his conclusion is accepted by Siegmund, *Überlieferung*.

2. McCormick, *Origins of the European Economy*, 68–71; Dietrich Claude, "Spätantike und frühmittelalterliche Orientfahrten: Routen und Reisende," in *Voyages et voyageurs à Byzance et en Occident du VIe au XIe siècle*, eds. A. Dierkens and J.-M. Sansterre (Geneva: Droz, 2000), 235–53.

3. Duchesne, "Notes," 229 argued, based on the style of the Latin *passio* of Boniface ("trop correct pour le septième ou le huitième siècle") that it did not date to before the ninth century.

4. AASS Maii III: 283, endnote l.

5. No churches for Boniface are included in Gabriele Mietke, "Monumentalisierung christlicher Heiliger in Kilikien in frühbyzantinischer Zeit," *Olba* 17 (2009): 117–40; Stephen Hill, *The Early Byzantine Churches of Cilicia and Isauria* (Aldershot: Variorum, 1996); Raymond Janin, *Les églises et les monastères des grands centres byzantins (Bithynie, Hellespont, Latros, Galèsios, Trébizonde, Athènes, Thessalonique)*, La géographie ecclésiastique de l'empire Byzantin 2 (Paris: Institut français d'études byzantines, 1975).

6. In the form in which these two texts survive, they share certain words and phrases, in particular the rare expression: "ter in urbe Roma candidam dedit" (in Greek "τρίτον κάνδιδα ἔπραξεν ἐν τῇ Ῥώμῃ"). The *candida* is "a game or play exhibited by a candidate for office" (Lewis and Short). (The Greek expression is also found in the Greek *passio* of Eleutherius, discussed by Franchi De'Cavalieri as one of the texts similar to the *passio* of Boniface.) In the *passio* of Sabina and Serapia, Serapia says, "credo enim ego, etsi indigna & peccatrix sum, quod dignam me faciat Dominus meus Jesus Christus Sanctis suis ancillam suam," which is similar to Aglaës's comment in the *passio* of Boniface: "Ego autem peccatrix, etsi indigna sum" (in the Greek Aglaës says, "ἐγὼ δὲ ἡ ἁμαρτωλός," but more similar is Boniface's statement "διότι εἰ καὶ ἀνάξιός εἰμι, καὶ ἁμαρτωλός") although Serapia, unlike Aglaës and Boniface, has little reason to make such a comment. These similarities were first observed by Dufourcq, *Étude*, 1:

164–68, 318–21. Dufourcq argued (contra the earlier conclusions of Duchesne) that the *passio* of Boniface derived from that of Sabina and Serapia (both of which were, according to him, likely written by monks on the Aventine) and thus that the Latin *passio* of Boniface predated its Greek version. Yet as Franchi De'Cavalieri conclusively showed, the Greek text certainly predates the Latin text. In essence, then, the legends are quite distinct and unrelated. In my opinion, however, Franchi De'Cavalieri goes too far in dismissing any similarity between the legends of Boniface and Sabina/Serapia; the similar expressions used in the two texts seem unlikely to be coincidental and could be explained by imagining the joint evolution of the two texts on the seventh- to eighth-century Aventine.

7. Hippolyte Delehaye, "Hagiographie napolitaine," *AB* 57 (1939): 5–64 at 22 (May, no. 14).

8. Boniface appears in the *Synaxarion* of Constantinople under December 19 (a date not found in either his Greek or Latin *passiones*): *Synaxarium ecclesiae Constantinopolitanae*, Dec. 19, ed. H. Delehaye, 325, no. 1. His Greek *passio* circulated in both the earlier version (BHG 280) and in a subsequent Metaphrastic (tenth-century) redaction (BHG 281): PG 115: 241–58. A Greek sermon about Boniface, attributed to Ephrem the Syrian, is preserved in a late Mount Athos manuscript: Mount Athos, Iviron, Cod. 4887.767, ff. 44v–54v, ed. K. G. Phrantzolas, *Ὁσίου Ἐφραίμ τοῦ Σύρου ἔργα*, 7: 187–98, but there does not seem to be any reason to believe the attribution to Ephrem. Its account of Boniface is very similar to the Greek *passio*.

Bibliography

Primary Sources

Entries are arranged by author (or title) rather than modern editor. Hagiographical texts edited in the AASS or Mombritius are not listed individually.

Acta apostolorum apocrypha. Edited by Richard Lipsius and Max Bonnet. 2 vols. Leipzig: Mendelssohn, 1891–1903.

Acta primorum martyrum sincera & selecta. Edited by Thierry Ruinart. 2nd ed. Amsterdam: ex officina Wetsteniana, 1713.

Acta Synhodi a. CCCCXCVIIII. Edited by Theodor Mommsen. MGH AA 12: 399–415.

Ado. *Le Martyrologe d'Adon, ses deux familles, ses trois recensions: texte et commentaire*. Edited by Jacques Dubois and Geneviève Renaud. Paris: Éditions du Centre national de la recherche scientifique, 1984.

Agathias. *Histories*. Translated by J. D. Frendo. Corpus fontium historiae Byzantinae 2A. Berlin: Walter de Gruyter, 1975.

Agnellus. *Liber pontificalis ecclesiae Ravennatis*. Edited by Deborah M. Deliyannis. CCCM 199. Turnhout: Brepols, 2006. Translated by Deborah M. Deliyannis, *The Book of Pontiffs of the Church of Ravenna* (Washington, DC: Catholic University Press, 2004).

Ambrose. *De virginibus*. Edited by Egnatius Cazzaniga. Turin: Paraviae, 1948.

Ammianus Marcellinus. With an English translation by John C. Rolfe. 3 vols. Loeb Classical Library. Cambridge, MA: Harvard University Press, 1963–1964.

Annales Fuldenses. Edited by Friedrich Kurze. MGH SS rer. Germ. 7.

Aristides, Aelius. Edited by Wilhelm Dindorf. Leipzig: G. Reimer, 1829.

Ausonius. *Decimi Magni Ausonii Burdigalensis Opuscula*. Edited by Sextus Prete. Leipzig: Teubner, 1978.

Bede. *Chronica*. Edited by Theodor Mommsen. MGH AA 13. *Chronica Minora* 3: 223–333.

———. *Martyrology*. See *Edition pratique*. Translated in Lifshitz, "Bede."

Capitulare Evangeliorum. Edited by Theodor Klauser, *Das römische Capitulare Evangeliorum: Texte und Untersuchungen zu seiner ältesten Geschichte*. Münster in Westfalen: Aschendorff, 1935.

Codex Carolinus. Edited by Wilhelm Grundlach. MGH Epp. 3. *Epistolae Merowingici et Karolini aevi* 1: 469–657.

Codex Einsidlensis 326. Edited by Gerold Walser, *Die Einsiedler Inschriftensammlung durch Rom*. Stuttgart: Franz Steiner, 1987.

Codex Justinianus. Edited by Paul Krueger. Berlin: Weidmann, 1877.

Codex Theodosianus. Edited by Theodor Mommsen and Paul Martin Meyer, *Theodosiani libri XVI cum constitutionibus Sirmondianis et leges novellae ad Theodosianum pertinentes*. Berlin: Weidmann, 1905.

Corippus, Flavius Cresconius. *In laudem Iustini Augusti minoris*. Edited and translated by Averil Cameron. London: Athlone Press, 1976.

Damasus. *Epigrammata Damasiana*. Edited by Antonio Ferrua. Vatican City: Pontificio Istituto di archeologia cristiana, 1942.

———. *S. Damasi papæ opera quæ extant et vita ex codicibus MSS*. Edited by Martius Milesius Sarazanius. Paris: Billaine, 1672.

Das Decretum Gelasianum de libris recipiendis et non recipiendis. Edited by Ernst von Dobschütz. Leipzig: J. C. Hinrichs, 1912.

Edition pratique des martyrologues de Bède, de l'Anonyme lyonnais et de Florus. Edited by Geneviève Renaud and Jacques Dubois. Paris: Centre national de la recherche scientifique, 1976.

Einhard. *Vita Karoli Magni*. Edited by Georg Waitz. MGH SS rer. Germ. 25.

———. *Translatio et miracula sanctorum Marcellini et Petri*. Edited by Georg Waitz. MGH SS 15.1: 238–64.

Ephrem the Syrian. *Ὁσίου Ἐφραίμ τοῦ Σύρου ἔργα*. Edited by Konstantinos G. Phrantzolas. 7 vols. Thessaloniki: Ekdoseis To Perivoli tes Panagias, 1988.

Evagrius. *Historia Ecclesiastica*. Edited by Adelheid Hübner. 2 vols. Fontes Christiani 57. Turnhout: Brepols, 2007.

Excerpta Valesiana. Edited by Jacques Moreau and Velizar Velkow. Leipzig: Teubner, 1968.

Florus. *Martyrology*. See *Edition pratique*.

Fragmenta registri Iohannis VIII. Edited by Erich Caspar. MGH Epp. 7. *Epistolae Karolini aevi* 5: 273–312.

Gesta Episcoporum Neapolitanorum. Edited by Georg Waitz. MGH SS. rer. Lang. 398–436.

Gregory of Tours. *Historiae*. Edited by Bruno Krusch and Wilhelm Levison. MGH SS rer. Merov. 1.1. *Gregorii Turonensis Opera* 1.

———. *Liber in gloriam martyrum*. Edited by Bruno Krusch. MGH SS rer. Merov. 1.2. *Gregorii Turonensis Opera* 2: 34–111 [484–561]. Translated by Raymond Van Dam, *Glory of the Martyrs*. Liverpool: Liverpool University Press, 1988.

Gregory the Great. *Grégoire le Grand. Dialogues*. Edited by Adalbert de Vogüé. 3 vols. Sources chrétiennes 251, 260, 265. Paris: Les éditions du Cerf, 1978–1980.

———. *S. Gregorii Magni Registrum Epistularum*. Edited by Dag Norberg. 2 vols. CCSL 140–140A. Turnhout: Brepols, 1982.

Hilduin. *Ex Hilduini Abbatis Libro de S. Dionysio*. Edited by Georg Waitz. MGH SS 15.1: 2–3.

Historia et laudes SS. Sabae et Macarii iuniorum e Sicilia auctore Oreste Patriarcha Hierosolymitano. Edited by Giuseppe Cozza-Luzi. Rome: Typis vaticanis, 1893.

Hrabanus Maurus. "Versus in tumulo S. Sergii"; "Super confessionem ipsius sepulchri." Edited by Ernst Dümmler. MGH Poetae 2: 219, no. 55.1–3.

Isidore. *Isidori Hispalensis episcopi Etymologiarum sive originum libri XX*. Edited by W. M. Lindsay. 2 vols. Oxford: Clarendon, 1911.

Itineraria et Alia Geographica. CCSL 175. Turnhout: Brepols, 1965.

Jerome. *Sancti Eusebii Hieronymi epistulae*. Edited by Isidor Hilberg. 3 vols. CSEL 54–56. Vienna: F. Tempsky, 1910–1918.

John of Ephesus. *Lives of the Eastern Saints (II)*. Edited and translated by E. W. Brooks. Patrologia Orientalis 18: 513–698. Paris: Firmin-Didot, 1924.

———. *The Third Part of the Ecclesiastical History of John, Bishop of Ephesus*. Translated by R. Payne Smith. Oxford: University Press, 1860.

Der karolingische Reichskalender und seine Überlieferung bis ins 12. Jahrhundert. Edited by Arno Borst. 3 vols. MGH Libri memoriales 2.1–3. 2001.

"Karolus magnus et Leo papa." Edited by Ernst Dümmler. MGH Poetae 1: 366–80.

Leo the Great. *Sancti Leonis Magni romani pontificis tractatus septem et nonaginta*. Edited by Antoine Chavasse. CCSL 138–138A. Turnhout: Brepols, 1973.

Liber Diurnus Romanorum Pontificum. Edited by Hans Foerster. Bern: Francke Verlag, 1958.

Martial. *Epigrams*. Edited and translated by Walter C. A. Ker. London: Heinemann, 1925.

Martyrologium Hieronymianum. Edited by Giovanni Battista de Rossi and Louis Duchesne. AASS Nov. II.1 (1894; repr. 1971): 1–156.

Martyrologium romanum ad novam kalendarii rationem, et ecclesiasticae historiae veritatem restitutum. Gregorii XIII. Pont. Max. iussu editum. Accesserunt notationes atque Tractatio de Martyrologio romano: auctore Caesare Baronio sorano Congregationis Oratorii presbytero. Rome: ex typ. Dominici Basae, 1586.

Nicephori Sceuophylacis Encomium in S. Theodorum Siceotam (BHG 1749). Edited by C. Kirch. *AB* 20 (1901): 249–72.

Novellae. Edited by Rudolf Schoell and Wilhelm Kroll. Corpus Iuris Civilis 3. Berlin: Weidmann, 1928.

Passio antiquior SS. Sergii et Bacchi graece nunc primum edita. Edited by I. van den Gheyn. *AB* 14 (1895): 373–95.

Passio of Saint Adalbert Bishop of Prague and Martyr. Edited and translated by Cristian Gaşpar. In Klaniczay, *Saints*, 95–182.

Procopius. Edited and translated by H. B. Dewing. 7 vols. Loeb Classical Library. Cambridge, MA: Harvard University Press, 1914–1940.

Prudentius. Edited and translated by Jeffrey Henderson Thomson. Loeb Classical Library. Cambridge, MA: Harvard University Press, 2014.

"Quadam nocte niger." Edited by Karl Strecker. MGH Poetae 4.2: 1119–20.

"Roman Martyrology." *Parvum Romanum*. Edited by Henri Quentin. In *Les martyrologes historiques du Moyen Âge*, 414–51. Older edition: *Vetus Romanum Martyrologium hactenus a Cardinale Baronio desideratum*. Edited by Heribert Rosweyde. Antwerp: ex officina Plantiniana, 1613.

Rudolf of Fulda. *Miracula sanctorum in Fuldenses ecclesias translatorum*. Edited by Georg Waitz. MGH SS 15.1: 328–41.

Le sacramentaire grégorien: ses principales formes d'après les plus anciens manuscrits. 1. Le sacramentaire, le supplément d'Aniane. Edited by Jean Deshusses. Fribourg: Éditions universitaires, 1971.

Sacramentarium Tridentinum. Edited by F. Dell'Oro and H. Rogger. In *Fontes liturgici libri sacramentorum*. Trent: Società studi trentini di scienze storiche, 1985.

Sacrorum conciliorum nova et amplissima collectio. Edited by Giovan Domenico Mansi et al. Paris: H. Welter, 1901–1927.

Synaxarium ecclesiae Constantinopolitanae: Propylaeum ad Acta sanctorum Novembris. Edited by Hippolyte Delehaye. Brussels: apud Socios Bollandianos, 1902.

Theophanes. *The Chronicle of Theophanes Confessor: Byzantine and Near Eastern History, AD 284–813*. Translated by Cyril Mango and Roger Scott. Oxford: Clarendon Press, 1997.

Translatio sancti Viti martyris: Übertragung des hl. Märtyrers Vitus. Edited and translated by Irene Schmale-Ott. Münster: Aschendorff, 1979.

Translatio Sergii et Bacchi. Edited by Wilhelm Levison. MGH SS 30.2: 1340–42.

Usuard. *Le Martyrologe d'Usuard*. Edited by Jacques Dubois. Brussels: Société des Bollandistes, 1965.

Venantius Fortunatus. *Venance Fortunat: Poèmes*. Edited and translated by Marc Reydellet. 3 vols. Paris: Les Belles Lettres, 1994–2004.

Virgil. *Eclogues*. Edited by Robert Coleman. Cambridge: Cambridge University Press, 1977.

Vita Annonis archiepiscopi Coloniensis. Edited by Rudolf Koepke. MGH SS 11. *Historiae aevi Salici*: 462–518.

Walafrid Strabo. *Hymnus de S. Sergio et Bacho*. Edited by Ernst Dümmler. MGH Poetae 2: 418–19, no. 83.

Wandalbert of Prüm. *Martyrologium*. Edited by Ernst Dümmler. MGH Poetae 2: 578–603.

Secondary Sources

Alchermes, Joseph D. "Petrine Politics: Pope Symmachus and the Rotunda of St. Andrew at Old St. Peter's." *Catholic Historical Review* 81.1 (1995): 1–40.

Alwis, Anne P. *Celibate Marriages in Late Antique and Byzantine Hagiography: The Lives of Saints Julian and Basilissa, Andronikos and Athanasia, and Galaktion and Episteme*. New York: Continuum, 2011.

Andrieu, Michel. "Chronique d'archéologie chrétienne: les églises de Rome au Moyen-Âge." *Revue des sciences religieuses* 9 (1929): 540–74.

———. "Les messes des jeudis de carême et les anciens sacramentaires." *Revue des sciences religieuses* 9 (1929): 343–75.

———. *Les ordines romani du Haut Moyen Âge*. 5 vols. Spicilegium sacrum Lovaniense 11, 23, 24, 28, 29. Louvain: Spicilegium sacrum Lovaniense, 1931–1961.

Angenendt, Arnold. "Der römische und gallisch-fränkische Anti-Ikonoklasmus." *Frühmittelalterliche Studien* 35 (2001): 201–25.

Angenendt, Arnold, and Rudolf Schieffer. *Roma—caput et fons: zwei Vorträge über das päpstliche Rom zwischen Altertum und Mittelalter*. Opladen: Westdeutscher Verlag, 1989.

Anrich, Gustav. *Hagios Nikolaos: der heilige Nikolaus in der griechischen Kirche*. Leipzig: Teubner, 1913–1917.

Arena, Maria Stella, Paolo Delogu, Lidia Paroli, Marco Ricci, Lucia Saguì, and Laura Vendittelli, eds. *Roma dall'antichità al medioevo: archeologia e storia nel Museo Nazionale Romano Crypta Balbi*. Milan: Electa, 2001.

Armellini, Mariano, and Carlo Cecchelli. *Le chiese di Roma dal sec. IV al XIX*. 2nd ed. 2 vols. Rome: N. Ruffolo, 1942.

Arnaldi, Girolamo. "Rinascita, fine, reincarnazione e succesive metamorfosi del Senato romano (secoli V–XII)." *ASRSP* 105 (1982): 5–56.

Arnold, Jonathan J. *Theoderic and the Roman Imperial Restoration*. Cambridge: Cambridge University Press, 2014.

Augenti, Andrea. "Continuity and Discontinuity of a Seat of Power: The Palatine Hill from the Fifth to the Tenth Century." In Smith, *Early Medieval Rome*, 43–53.

———. *Il Palatino nel medioevo: archeologia e topografia (secoli VI–XIII)*. Rome: Erma di Bretschneider, 1996.

Azzara, Claudio. *L'ideologia del potere regio nel papato altomedievale: secoli VI–VIII*. Spoleto: Centro italiano di studi sull'alto medioevo, 1997.

Bardill, Jonathan. "The Church of Sts. Sergius and Bacchus in Constantinople and the Monophysite Refugees." *DOP* 54 (2000): 1–11.

———. "Visualizing the Great Palace of the Byzantine Emperors at Constantinople: Archaeology, Text, and Topography." In Bauer, *Visualisierungen von Herrschaft*, 5–46.

Barelli, Lia. *The Monumental Complex of Santi Quattro Coronati in Rome*. Translated by Christopher McDowall. Rome: Viella, 2009.

Barth, Médard. *Handbuch der elsässischen Kirchen im Mittelalter*. Archives de l'Église d'Alsace, n.s., 11–13. Strasbourg: Société d'histoire de l'Église d'Alsace, 1960–1963.

Bartlett, Robert. *Why Can the Dead Do Such Great Things? Saints and Worshippers from the Martyrs to the Reformation*. Princeton, NJ: Princeton University Press, 2013.

Bartoli, Alfonso. *Curia Senatus: lo scavo e il restauro*. [Rome]: Istituto di Studi Romani, 1963.

———. "I templi del Foro Olitorio e la diaconia di S. Nicola 'in carcere.'" *RendPontAcc*, 3rd ser., 5 (1926–1927): 213–26.

———. "Il monumento della perpetuità del Senato." *Studi romani* 11 (1954): 129–37.

———. "Scoperta dell'oratorio e del monastero di S. Cesario sul Palatino." *Nuovo bollettino di archeologia cristiana* 13 (1907): 191–204.

Bassett, Sarah E. *The Urban Image of Late Antique Constantinople*. Cambridge: Cambridge University Press, 2004.

Batiffol, Pierre. "Inscriptions byzantines de Saint-Georges au Vélabre." *MEFR* 7 (1887): 419–31.

Bauer, Franz Alto. *Das Bild der Stadt Rom im Frühmittelalter: Papststiftungen im Spiegel des Liber Pontificalis von Gregor dem Dritten bis zu Leo dem Dritten*. Wiesbaden: L. Reichert, 2004.

———. "Das Bild der Stadt Rom in karolingischer Zeit: der Anonymus Einsidlensis." *RQ* 92 (1997): 190–228.

———. "St. Peter's as a Place of Collective Memory in Late Antiquity." In Behrwald and Witschel, *Rom in der Spätantike*, 155–70.

———. *Stadt, Platz und Denkmal in der Spätantike: Untersuchungen zur Ausstattung des öffentlichen Raums in den spätantiken Städten Rom, Konstantinopel und Ephesos*. Mainz am Rhein: P. von Zabern, 1996.

———, ed. *Visualisierungen von Herrschaft: frühmittelalterliche Residenzen. Gestalt und Zeremoniell*. Istanbul: Ege Yayınları, 2006.

Bavant, Bernard. "Le duché byzantin de Rome: origine, durée et extension géographique." *MEFRM* 91.1 (1979): 41–88.

Behrwald, Ralf, and Christian Witschel, eds. *Rom in der Spätantike: historische Erinnerung im städtischen Raum*. Stuttgart: Franz Steiner Verlag, 2012.

Bellardini, Donatella, and Paolo Delogu. "*Liber Pontificalis* e altre fonti: la topografia di Roma nell'VIII secolo." In *Atti del Colloquio internazionale: il Liber Pontificalis e la storia materiale (Roma, 21–22 febbraio 2002)*, edited by H. Geertman, 205–23. Assen, the Netherlands: Koninklijke Van Gorcum, 2003.

Belting, Hans. "Eine Privatkapelle im frühmittelalterlichen Rom." *DOP* 41, Studies on Art and Archeology in Honor of Ernst Kitzinger on His Seventy-Fifth Birthday (1987): 55–69.

Benz, Suitbert. "Zur Geschichte der römischen Kirchweihe nach den Texten des 6. bis 7. Jahrhunderts." In *Enkainia: gesammelte Arbeiten zum 800-jährigen Weihegedächtnis der Abteikirche Maria Laach am 24. August 1956*, edited by Hilarius Emonds, 62–109. Düsseldorf: Patmos-Verlag, 1956.

Bernard, A. "Der Reliquienschatz der ehemaligen Abtei Weißenburg." *Archiv für elsässische Kirchengeschichte* 12 (1937): 73–82.

Berschin, Walter. *Reichenauer Wandmalerei 840–1120: Goldbach, Reichenau-Oberzell St. Georg, Reichenau-Niederzell St. Peter und Paul*. Heidelberg: Mattes, 2012.

Bertolini, Ottorino. *Roma di fronte a Bisanzio e ai Longobardi*. Bologna: L. Cappelli, 1941.

———. "Per la storia delle diaconie romane nell'alto medioevo sino alla fine del secolo VIII." *ASRSP* 70 (1947): 1–145.

Bianchi, Lorenzo. "*Surgit in astra domus sublimis*: note sulla topografia antica e medievale fra Tevere e Foro Boario." *Bollettino del Centro di studi per la storia dell'architettura* 45–52 (2008–2015): 11–37.

Birch, Debra J. *Pilgrimage to Rome in the Middle Ages: Continuity and Change*. Woodbridge: Boydell Press, 1998.

Blaauw, Sible de. *Cultus et decor: liturgia e architettura nella Roma tardoantica e medievale: Basilica Salvatoris, Sanctae Mariae, Sancti Petri*. Vatican City: Biblioteca Apostolica Vaticana, 1994.

———. "Jerusalem and the Cult of the Cross." In *Pratum Romanum: Richard Krautheimer zum 100. Geburtstag*, edited by Renate L. Colella, 55–73. Wiesbaden: Reichert, 1997.

———. "L'altare nelle chiese di Roma come centro di culto e della committenza papale." In *Roma nell'alto medioevo*, 969–89.

Boesch Gajano, Sofia. "La proposta agiografica dei 'Dialogi' di Gregorio Magno." *Studi medievali*, 3rd ser., 21 (1980): 623–64.

Bolgia, Claudia. "Il mosaico absidale di San Teodoro a Roma: problemi storici e restauri attraverso disegni e documenti inediti." *PBSR* 69 (2001): 317–51.

Bolgia, Claudia, Rosamond McKitterick, and John Osborne, eds. *Rome Across Time and Space: Cultural Transmissions and the Exchange of Ideas,* c. *500–1400*. Cambridge: Cambridge University Press, 2011.

Bonfioli, Mara. "La diaconia dei SS. Sergio e Bacco nel foro romano: fonti e problemi." *RACr* 50 (1974): 55–85.

Booth, Phil. *Crisis of Empire: Doctrine and Dissent at the End of Late Antiquity*. Berkeley: University of California Press, 2013.

———. "Orthodox and Heretic in the Early Byzantine Cult(s) of Saints Cosmas and Damian." In *An Age of Saints? Power, Conflict and Dissent in Early Medieval Christianity*, edited by Peter Sarris et al., 114–28. Leiden: Brill, 2011.

Bordi, Giulia. "Santa Maria Antiqua: prima di Maria Regina." In *L'officina dello sguardo: scritti in onore di Maria Andaloro*, edited by Giulia Bordi, 285–90. Rome: Gangemi Editore, 2014.

Borgolte, Michael. *Petrusnachfolge und Kaiserimitation: die Grablegen der Päpste, ihre Genese und Traditionsbildung*. Göttingen: Vandenhoeck & Ruprecht, 1989.

Borri, Francesco. "La Dalmazia altomedievale tra discontinuità e racconto storico (secc. VII–VIII)." *Studi veneziani*, n.s., 58 (2009): 15–52.

Botte, Bernard. "In unitate Spiritus Sancti." *La Maison-Dieu* 23 (1950): 49–63.

Bougard, François. "Composition, diffusion et réception des parties tardives du 'Liber pontificalis' romain (VIIIe–IXe siècles)." In *Liber, Gesta, histoire: écrire l'histoire des évêques et des papes*, edited by François Bougard and Michel Sot, 127–52. Turnhout: Brepols, 2009.

Bowersock, G. W., Peter Brown, and Oleg Grabar. *Late Antiquity: A Guide to the Postclassical World*. Cambridge, MA: Belknap Press, 1999.

Bowes, Kimberly Diane. *Private Worship, Public Values, and Religious Change in Late Antiquity*. Cambridge: Cambridge University Press, 2008.

Brandes, Wolfram. "'Juristische' Krisenbewältigung im 7. Jahrhundert? Die Prozesse gegen Martin I. und Maximos Homologetes." In *Fontes Minores* 10, edited by Ludwig Burgmann, 141–212. Frankfurt am Main: Klostermann, 1998.

Brandt, Olof, and Philippe Pergola, eds. *Marmoribus vestita: miscellanea in onore di Federico Guidobaldi*. Vatican City: Pontificio Istituto di archeologia cristiana, 2011.

Breckenridge, James D. "Evidence for the Nature of Relations Between Pope John VII and the Byzantine Emperor Justinian II." *BZ* 65.2 (1972): 364–74.

Brenk, Beat. "Der Kultort, seine Zugänglichkeit und seine Besucher." In *Akten des XII. Internationalen Kongresses für christliche Archäologie*, edited by Ernst Dassmann and Josef Engemann, 69–122. Münster: Aschendorff, 1995.

———. "Kultgeschichte versus Stilgeschichte: von der 'raison d'être' des Bildes im 7. Jahrhundert in Rom." In *Uomo e spazio nell'alto medioevo*, 971–1054. Settimane 50. Spoleto: La sede del Centro, 2003.

———. "Zur Einführung des Kultes der heiligen Kosmas und Damian in Rom." *Theologische Zeitschrift* 62.2 (2006): 303–20.

Brockett, Clyde. "Processing from Lateran to Hierusalem and Back: A Unique Ritual for the Cross Relic." In *Cantus Planus: International Musicological Society Study Group. Papers Read at the 16th Meeting, Vienna, Austria, 2011*, edited by Robert Klugseder, 78–83. Purkersdorf: Hollinek, 2012.

Brooks, Ernest Walter. "The Sicilian Expedition of Constantine IV." *BZ* 17 (1908): 455–59.

Brown, Giles. "Introduction: The Carolingian Renaissance." In *Carolingian Culture: Emulation and Innovation*, edited by Rosamond McKitterick, 1–51. Cambridge: Cambridge University Press, 1994.

Brown, Peter. *The Cult of the Saints: Its Rise and Function in Latin Christianity*. Haskell Lectures on the History of Religions, n.s., 2. Chicago: University of Chicago Press, 1981.

———. *The Rise of Western Christendom: Triumph and Diversity, A.D. 200–1000*. Malden, MA: Blackwell, 1995.

———. *Through the Eye of a Needle: Wealth, the Fall of Rome, and the Making of Christianity in the West, 350–550 AD*. Princeton, NJ: Princeton University Press, 2012.

Brown, T. S. *Gentlemen and Officers: Imperial Administration and Aristocratic Power in Byzantine Italy, A.D. 554–800*. [London]: British School at Rome, 1984.

Brubaker, Leslie, and John F. Haldon. *Byzantium in the Iconoclast Era (c. 680–850): A History*. Cambridge: Cambridge University Press, 2011.

Buchner, Max. "Zur Überlieferungsgeschichte des 'Liber pontificalis' und zu seiner Verbreitung im Frankenreiche im 9. Jahrhundert." *RQ* 34 (1926): 141–66.

Budriesi, Roberta. *La basilica dei SS. Cosma e Damiano a Roma*. Bologna: R. Pàtron, 1968.

Bullough, Donald A. "Roman Books and Carolingian Renovatio." In *Carolingian Renewal: Sources and Heritage*, 1–33. Manchester: Manchester University Press, 1991.

Burgarella, Filippo. "Presenze greche a Roma: aspetti culturali e religiosi." In *Roma fra Oriente e Occidente*, 943–98. Settimane 49. Spoleto: La sede del Centro, 2002.

Bury, J. B. "The Great Palace." *BZ* (1912): 210–25.

Butzmann, Hans. *Die Weissenburger Handschriften*. Frankfurt am Main: Vittorio Klostermann, 1964.

Cameron, Averil. "The Theotokos in Sixth-Century Constantinople: A City Finds Its Symbol." *Journal of Theological Studies* 29 (1978): 79–108.

Campese Simone, Anna. "Alle origini di S. Nicola in Carcere: due epigrafi altomedievali incise su una colonna." In Guidobaldi and Guiglia Guidobaldi, *Ecclesiae urbis*, 295–317.

Carandini, Andrea, and Paolo Carafa, eds. *Atlante di Roma antica: biografia e ritratti della città*. Milan: Electa, 2012.

Cardin, Luca. *Epigrafia a Roma nel primo medioevo (secoli IV–X)*. Rome: Jouvence, 2008.

Carlà, Filippo. "Milan, Ravenna, Rome: Some Reflections on the Cult of the Saints and on Civic Politics in Late Antique Italy." *Rivista di storia e letteratura religiosa* 46 (2010): 197–272.

Casartelli Novelli, Silvana. "La 'nuova Gerusalemme' generata dal Cristo: il cantus firmus dell'immaginario di Roma 'capitale cristiana'." In Pani Ermini, *Christiana loca*, 1: 153–71.

Castelli, Maurizio. "La chiesa di San Giorgio al Velabro." *Bullettino della Commissione archeologica comunale di Roma* 96 (1995): 125–64.

Cecchelli, Carlo. "Continuità storica di Roma antica nell'alto medioevo." In *La città nell'alto medioevo*, 89–149. Settimane 6. Spoleto: La sede del Centro, 1959.

Cecchelli, Margherita Trinci. *La diocesi di Roma*. 4: *La I regione ecclesiastica*. Spoleto: Centro italiano di studi sull'alto medioevo, 1976.

———. "Santa Susanna." In Arena et al., *Roma dall'antichità al medioevo*, 641–43.

Chastagnol, André. "La famille de Caecinia Lolliana, grande dame païenne du IVe siècle après J.-C." *Latomus* 20.4 (1961): 744–58.

———. "Le sénateur Volusien et la conversion d'une famille de l'aristocratie romaine au Bas-Empire." *Revue des études anciennes* 58 (1956): 241–53.

Chavasse, Antoine. "L'organisation stationnale du carême romain, avant le VIIIe siècle: une organisation 'pastorale.'" *Revue des sciences religieuses* 56 (1982): 17–32.

———. *Le Sacramentaire Gélasien, Vaticanus reginensis 316: Sacramentaire presbytéral en usage dans les titres romains au VIIe siècle*. Tournai: Desclée, 1958.

La chiesa di San Giorgio in Velabro a Roma. Storia, documenti, testimonianze del restauro dopo l'attentato del luglio 1993. Bollettino d'arte, volume speciale. Rome: Istituto poligrafico e Zecca dello Stato, Libreria dello Stato, 2002.

Christ, Karl. *Die Bibliothek des Klosters Fulda im 16. Jahrhundert: die Handschriften-Verzeichnisse.* Leipzig: O. Harrassowitz, 1933.

Christie, Neil J., and Alan Rushworth. "Urban Fortification and Defensive Strategy in Fifth and Sixth Century Italy: The Case of Terracina." *Journal of Roman Archaeology* 1 (1988): 73–87.

Claude, Dietrich. "Spätantike und frühmittelalterliche Orientfahrten: Routen und Reisende." In *Voyages et voyageurs à Byzance et en Occident du VIe au XIe siècle*, edited by Alain Dierkens and Jean-Marie Sansterre, 235–53. Geneva: Droz, 2000.

Claussen, Peter Cornelius. *Die Kirchen der Stadt Rom im Mittelalter 1050–1300, 1. A–F.* Stuttgart: Franz Steiner, 2002.

Claussen, Peter Cornelius, Daniela Mondini, and Darko Senekovic. *Die Kirchen der Stadt Rom im Mittelalter 1050–1300, 3. G–L.* Stuttgart: Franz Steiner, 2010.

Coarelli, Filippo. *Il Foro Boario: dalle origini alla fine della repubblica.* Rome: Edizioni Quasar, 1988.

Coates-Stephens, Robert. "Byzantine Building Patronage in Post-reconquest Rome." In *Les cités de l'Italie tardo-antique, IVe–VIe siècle: institutions, économie, société, culture et religion*, edited by Massimiliano Ghilardi et al., 149–66. Rome: École française de Rome, 2006.

———. "Dark Age Architecture in Rome." *PBSR* 65 (1997): 177–232.

———. "The Forum Romanum in the Byzantine Period." In Brandt and Pergola, *Marmoribus vestita*, 385–408.

———. "San Saba and the *Xenodochium de Via Nova*." *RACr* 83 (2007): 223–56.

———. "Sulla fondazione di S. Maria in Domnica." In *Scavi e scoperte recenti nelle chiese di Roma: atti della giornata tematica dei Seminari di archeologia cristiana (Roma, 13 marzo 2008)*, edited by Hugo Brandenburg and Federico Guidobaldi, 77–91. Vatican City: Pontificio Istituto di archeologia cristiana, 2012.

Conant, Jonathan P. "Europe and the African Cult of Saints, circa 350–900: An Essay in Mediterranean Communications." *Speculum* 55 (2010): 1–46.

Constantelos, D. J. "The Moslem Conquests of the Near East as Revealed in the Greek Sources of the Seventh and Eighth Centuries." *Byzantion* 4 (1972): 325–57.

Cooper, Kate. "The Martyr, the *Matrona* and the Bishop: The Matron Lucina and the Politics of Martyr Cult in Fifth- and Sixth-Century Rome." *EME* 8.3 (1999): 297–317.

———. "Poverty, Obligation and Inheritance: Roman Heiresses and the Varieties of Senatorial Christianity in Fifth-Century Rome." In Cooper and Hillner, *Religion, Dynasty, and Patronage*, 165–89.

Cooper, Kate, and Julia Hillner, eds. *Religion, Dynasty, and Patronage in Early Christian Rome, 300–900.* Cambridge: Cambridge University Press, 2007.

Cooper, Kate, Julia Hillner, and Conrad Leyser. "Dark Age Rome: Towards an Interactive Topography." In *Social and Political Life in Late Antiquity*, edited by William Bowden et al., 311–77. Leiden: Brill, 2006.

Coppola, Maria Rosaria. "Il foro emiliano di Terracina: rilievo, analisi tecnica, vicende storiche del monumento." *MEFRA* (1984): 325–77.

Cordini, Guido. "'Non est in toto sanctior orbe locus': Collecting Relics in Early Medieval Rome." In *Treasures of Heaven: Saints, Relics and Devotion in Medieval Europe*, edited by Martina Bagnoli, 69–78. New Haven: Yale University Press, 2010.

Corsi, Pasquale. *La spedizione italiana di Costante II.* Bologna: Pàtron, 1983.

Costambeys, Marios, and Conrad Leyser. "To Be the Neighbour of St Stephen: Patronage, Martyr Cult, and Roman Monasteries, *c.*600–*c.*900." In Cooper and Hillner, *Religion, Dynasty, and Patronage*, 262–87.

Croke, Brian. "Justinian, Theodora, and the Church of Saints Sergius and Bacchus." *DOP* 60 (2006): 25–63.

Cubitt, Catherine. "The Lateran Council of 649 as an Ecumenical Council." In *Chalcedon in Context: Church Councils 400–700*, edited by Richard Price and Mary Whitby, 133–47. Liverpool: Liverpool University Press, 2009.

Dales, Douglas. *Alcuin: Theology and Thought*. Cambridge: Cambridge University Press, 2013.

Dal Santo, Matthew J. *Debating the Saints' Cults in the Age of Gregory the Great*. Oxford: Oxford University Press, 2012.

Darsy, Felix Marie Dominique. *Recherches archéologiques à Sainte-Sabine sur l'Aventin: géologie, topographie, sanctuaires archaïques, culte isiaque, ensemble architectural paléochrétien*. Vatican City: Pontificio Istituto di archeologia cristiana, 1968.

———. *Santa Sabina*. Rome: Marietti, 1961.

de Certeau, Michel. *The Practice of Everyday Life*. Translated by Steven Rendall. Berkeley: University of California Press, 1984.

de Gaiffier, Baudouin. "La lecture des passions des martyrs à Rome avant le IXe siècle." *AB* 87 (1969): 63–78.

de Grüneisen, Wladimir, Christian Hülsen, Giovanni Giorgis, Vincenzo Federici, and Joseph David. *Sainte Marie Antique*. Rome: M. Bretschneider, 1911.

De Rubeis, Flavia. "Epigrafi a Roma dall'età classica all'alto medioevo." In Arena et al., *Roma dall'antichità al medioevo*, 104–121.

Delehaye, Hippolyte. "A propos de Saint-Césaire." *RendPontAcc*, 3rd ser., 3 (1925): 45–48.

———. *Étude sur le légendier romain: les saints de novembre et de décembre*. Brussels: Société des Bollandistes, 1936.

———. "Hagiographie napolitaine." *AB* 57 (1939): 5–64.

———. "La légende de Saint Eustache." *Bulletin de la Classe des lettres et des sciences morales et politiques*, 5th ser., 5 (Brussels: Académie royale de Belgique, 1919): 175–210.

———. *Les légendes grecques des saints militaires*. Paris: Alphonse Picard, 1909.

———. Review of F. Cumont, "La plus ancienne légende de saint Georges." In *AB* 57 (1939): 134–36.

———. "Saints d'Istrie et de Dalmatie." *AB* 18 (1899): 368–411.

Deliyannis, Deborah Mauskopf. *Ravenna in Late Antiquity*. Cambridge: Cambridge University Press, 2010.

Della Valle, Giuseppina. "Teodorico e Roma." *Rendiconti della Accademia di archeologia, lettere e belle arti di Napoli* 34 (1959): 119–76.

Delogu, Paolo. "Il passaggio dall'antichità al medioevo." In *Storia di Roma dall'antichità a oggi. 2. Roma medievale*, edited by André Vauchez, 3–40. Rome: Laterza, 2001.

Demacopoulos, George E. *Gregory the Great: Ascetic, Pastor, and First Man of Rome*. Notre Dame, IN: University of Notre Dame Press, 2015.

———. *The Invention of Peter: Apostolic Discourse and Papal Authority in Late Antiquity*. Philadelphia: University of Pennsylvania Press, 2013.

Deshusses, Jean. *Le sacramentaire grégorien: ses principales formes d'après les plus anciens manuscrits. 1. Le sacramentaire, le supplément d'Aniane*. Fribourg: Éditions universitaire, 1971.

Deubner, Ludwig. *Kosmas und Damian*. Leipzig: B. G. Teubner, 1907.

Dey, Hendrik W. *The Aurelian Wall and the Refashioning of Imperial Rome, A.D. 271–855*. Cambridge: Cambridge University Press, 2011.

———. "*Diaconiae*, *Xenodochia*, *Hospitalia* and Monasteries: 'Social Security' and the Meaning of Monasticism in Early Medieval Rome." *EME* 16.4 (2008): 398–422.

Di Carpegna Falconieri, Tommaso. *Il clero di Roma nel medioevo: istituzioni e politica cittadina (secoli VIII–XIII).* Rome: Viella, 2002.

Di Gioia, Vincenzo. *L'Aventino: un colle classico tra antico e moderno.* Rome: Istituto poligrafico e Zecca dello Stato, Libreria dello Stato, 2004.

Diehl, Charles. *Études sur l'administration byzantine dans l'Exarchat de Ravenne (568–751).* Paris: Thorin, 1888.

Donckel, Emil. "Außerrömische Heilige in Rom von den Anfängen unter Liberius bis Leo IV. (847): ein Beitrag zur Entwicklung des stadtrömischen Festkalenders." PhD diss., Hermann, 1938.

Drijvers, Jan Willem. *Helena Augusta: The Mother of Constantine the Great and the Legend of Her Finding of the True Cross.* Leiden: Brill, 1992.

Dubois, Jacques. "Le Martyrologe métrique de Wandelbert: ses sources, son originalité, son influence sur le Martyrologe d'Usuard." *AB* 79 (1961): 257–93.

———. *Les martyrologes du Moyen Âge latin.* Typologie des sources du Moyen Âge occidental 26. Turnhout: Brepols, 1978.

Duchesne, Louis. "Notes sur la topographie de Rome au Moyen-Âge." *MEFR* 10 (1890): 225–50.

———. "Le Palatin chrétien." *Nuovo bullettino di archeologia cristiana* 6 (1900): 17–28.

Dufourcq, Albert. *Étude sur les Gesta martyrum romains.* Paris: Fontemoig, 1900.

Dunn, Geoffrey D. "The Church of Rome as a Court of Appeal in the Early Fifth Century: The Evidence of Innocent I and the Illyrian Churches." *Journal of Ecclesiastical History* 64 (2013): 679–99.

Durliat, Jean. *De la ville antique à la ville byzantine: le problème des substances.* Rome: École française de Rome, 1990.

Dutton, Paul Edward. *Charlemagne's Courtier: The Complete Einhard.* Peterborough, Ontario: Broadview Press, 1998.

Duval, Noël, et al., eds. *Actes du XIe Congrès international d'archéologie chrétienne: Lyon, Vienne, Grenoble, Genève et Aoste (21–28 Septembre 1986).* Rome: École française de Rome, 1989.

Dvornik, Francis. *The Idea of Apostolicity in Byzantium and the Legend of the Apostle Andrew.* Cambridge, MA: Harvard University Press, 1958.

Eastman, David L. *The Ancient Martyrdom Accounts of Peter and Paul.* Atlanta: SBL Press, 2015.

Ebersolt, Jean. *Le grand palais de Constantinople et le Livre des cérémonies.* Paris: E. Leroux, 1910.

———. *Sanctuaires de Byzance.* Paris: E. Leroux, 1921.

Edwards, Catharine, and Greg Woolf. "Cosmopolis: Rome as World City." In *Rome the Cosmopolis,* edited by Catherine Edwards and Greg Woolf, 1–20. Cambridge: Cambridge University Press, 2003.

Eizenhöfer, Leo. "Die Marmormessen Gregors III." *Ephemerides liturgicae* 67 (1953): 112–28.

Ekonomou, Andrew J. *Byzantine Rome and the Greek Popes: Eastern Influences on Rome and the Papacy from Gregory the Great to Zacharias, A.D. 590–752.* Lanham, MD: Lexington Books, 2007.

Elliott, Dyan. *Spiritual Marriage: Sexual Abstinence in Medieval Wedlock.* Princeton, NJ: Princeton University Press, 1993.

Elsner, Jaś. "Sacrifice and Narrative on the Arch of the Argentarii at Rome." *Journal of Roman Archaeology* 18 (2005): 83–98.

Ewig, Eugen. "Die Verehrung orientalischer Heiliger im spätrömischen Gallien und im Merowingerreich." In *Festschrift Percy Ernst Schramm zu seinem siebzigsten Geburtstag von Schülern und Freunden zugeeignet,* edited by Peter Classen and Peter Scheibert, 385–400. Wiesbaden: Franz Steiner, 1964.

Falesiedi, Ugo. *Le diaconie: i servizi assistenziali nella Chiesa antica*. Rome: Istituto Patristico Augustinianum, 1995.

Favro, Diane G. "Moving Events: Curating the Memory of the Roman Triumph." In *Memoria Romana: Memory in Rome and Rome in Memory*, edited by Karl Galinsky, 85–102. Ann Arbor: University of Michigan Press for the American Academy in Rome, 2014.

———. *The Urban Image of Augustan Rome*. Cambridge: Cambridge University Press, 1996.

Ferrari, Guy. *Early Roman Monasteries: Notes for the History of the Monasteries and Convents at Rome from the V through the X Century*. Vatican City: Pontificio Istituto di archeologia cristiana, 1957.

Flaccomio, Gabriella, ed. *Il "tempio di Romolo" al foro romano*. Quaderni dell'Istituto di storia dell'architettura 26, fasc. 157–62. Rome: Multigrafica Editrice, 1981.

Floß, Heinrich Joseph. "Romreise des Abtes Markward von Prüm und Übertragung der hl. Chrysanthus und Daria nach Münstereifel im Jahre 844." *Annalen des Historischen Vereins für den Niederrhein* 20 (1869): 96–217.

Fowden, Elizabeth Key. *The Barbarian Plain: Saint Sergius Between Rome and Iran*. Berkeley: University of California Press, 1999.

Franchi De'Cavalieri, Pio. "Dove fu scritta la leggenda di S. Bonifazio?" *Nuovo bollettino di archeologia cristiana* 6 (1900): 205–34.

———. "S. Martina." *RQ* 17 (1903): 222–36.

Franklin, Carmela Vircillo. *The Latin Dossier of Anastasius the Persian: Hagiographic Translations and Transformations*. Toronto: Pontifical Institute of Mediaeval Studies, 2004.

Fux, Pierre-Yves. "Les patries des martyrs: doctrine et métaphores chez les poètes Damase, Ambroise, Paulin de Nola et Prudence." In *Mauritius und die thebäische Legion: Akten des internationalen Kolloquiums, Freiburg, Saint-Maurice, Martigny, 17–20 September 2003*, edited by Otto Wermelinger, 365–75. Fribourg: Academic Press Fribourg, 2005.

Galland, Bruno, and Jean Vezin. *Les authentiques de reliques du Sancta Sanctorum*. Vatican City: Biblioteca Apostolica Vaticana, 2004.

Gantner, Clemens. *Freunde Roms und Völker der Finsternis: die päpstliche Konstruktion von Anderen im 8. und 9. Jahrhundert*. Vienna: Böhlau Verlag, 2014.

Gatto, Ludovico. "Ancora sull'edilizia e l'urbanistica nella Roma di Teodorico." *Romanobarbarica* 12.3 (1992–1993): 311–80.

Gay, Jules. "L'État pontifical, les Byzantins et les Lombards sur le littoral campanien (d'Hadrien Ier à Jean VIII)." *MEFR* 21 (1901): 487–508.

Geary, Patrick J. *Furta Sacra: Thefts of Relics in the Central Middle Ages*. Princeton, NJ: Princeton University Press, 1978.

Geertman, Herman. *More veterum: il Liber Pontificalis e gli edifici ecclesiastici di Roma nella tarda antichità e nell'alto medioevo*. Groningen: H. D. Tjeenk Willink, 1975.

Gennaccari, Cristina. "Le chiese di Santa Maria in Cannapara." In Guidobaldi and Guiglia Guidobaldi, *Ecclesiae urbis*, 419–39.

Gheroni, Silvio. *La cattedrale di Terracina*. Turin: S.A.L.E., 1931.

Ghilardi, Massimiliano. "Martiri e cloache: intersezioni tra agiografia e archeologia." In *La Cloaca Maxima e i sistemi fognari di Roma dall'antichità ad oggi*, edited by Elisabetta Bianchi, 191–200. Rome: Palombi Editori, 2014.

Gianandrea, Manuela. "Lettura iconografica e stilistica del dipinto murale." In Tempesta, *L'icona murale*, 25–30.

———. "Un'inedita committenza nella chiesa romana di Santa Sabina all'Aventino: il dipinto altomedievale con la Vergine e il Bambino, santi e donatori." In *Medioevo: i committenti. Atti del Convegno internazionale di studi, Parma, 21–26 settembre 2010*, edited by A. C. Quintavalle, 399–410. Milan: Electa, 2011.

Gieysztor, Aleksander. "'Pauper sum et peregrinus': la légende de saint Alexis en Occident: un idéal de pauvreté." In *Etudes sur l'histoire de la pauvreté (Moyen Âge–XVIe siècle)*, edited by Michel Mollat du Jourdin, 125–39. Paris: Publications de la Sorbonne, 1974.

Gillett, Andrew. "Rome, Ravenna and the Last Western Emperors." *PBSR* 69 (2001): 131–67.

Giovenale, Giovanni Battista. *La basilica di S. Maria in Cosmedin*. Rome: Sansaini, 1927.

Godden, Malcolm R. "Anglo-Saxons on the Mind." In *Learning and Literature in Anglo-Saxon England: Studies Presented to Peter Clemoes on the Occasion of His Sixty-Fifth Birthday*, edited by Michael Lapidge and Helmut Gneuss, 271–98. Cambridge: Cambridge University Press, 1985.

Godman, Peter. *Poetry of the Carolingian Renaissance*. Norman: University of Oklahoma Press, 1985.

Golzio, Vincenzo. *San Nicola in Carcere e i tre templi del Foro Olitorio*. Rome: Libreria Fratelli Treves, [1928].

Goodson, Caroline J. "Building for Bodies: The Architecture of Saint Veneration in Early Medieval Rome." In *Roma Felix: Formation and Reflections of Medieval Rome*, edited by Éamonn Ó Carragáin and Carol L. Neuman de Vegvar, 51–79. Aldershot: Ashgate, 2007.

———. *The Rome of Pope Paschal I: Papal Power, Urban Renovation, Church Rebuilding and Relic Translation, 817–824*. Cambridge: Cambridge University Press, 2010.

Gorski, Gilbert J., and James E. Packer. *The Roman Forum: A Reconstruction and Architectural Guide*. New York: Cambridge University Press, 2015.

Gray, Nicolette. "The Paleography of Latin Inscriptions in the Eighth, Ninth and Tenth Centuries in Italy." *PBSR* 16 (1948): 38–162.

Greatrex, Geoffrey B. "Justin I and the Arians." *Studia Patristica* 34 (2001): 73–81.

Grégoire, Henri. "La Vie de saint Blaise d'Amorium." *Byzantion* 5 (1929–1930): 391–414.

Gregorovius, Ferdinand. *Geschichte der Stadt Rom im Mittelalter vom V. bis zum XVI. Jahrhundert* (1859–1872). Edited by Waldemar Kampf. 4 vols. Munich: C. H. Beck, 1978 (first Beck edition 1953–1957).

Grig, Lucy, and Gavin Kelly, eds. *Two Romes: Rome and Constantinople in Late Antiquity*. Oxford: Oxford University Press, 2012.

Guazzelli, Giuseppe Antonio. "Baronio attraverso il *Martyrologium Romanum*." In *Cesare Baronio tra santità e scrittura storica*, edited by Giuseppe Antonio Guazzelli et al., 67–110. Rome: Viella, 2012.

Guerrini, Paola. "Theodericus rex nelle testimonianze epigrafiche." *Temporis signa: archeologia della tarda antichità e del medioevo* 6 (2011): 133–74.

Gugel, Klaus. *Welche erhaltenen mittelalterlichen Handschriften dürfen der Bibliothek des Klosters Fulda zugerechnet werden? 1. Die Handschriften*. Frankfurt am Main: Verlag Josef Knecht, 1995.

Guidobaldi, Federico. "L'inserimento delle chiese titolari di Roma nel tessuto urbano preesistente: osservazioni ed implicazioni." In *Quaeritur inventus colitur: miscellanea in onore di Padre U. M. Fasola*, 381–96. Vatican City: Pontificio Istituto di archeologia cristiana, 1989.

Guidobaldi, Federico, and Alessandra Guiglia Guidobaldi, eds. *Ecclesiae urbis: atti del Congresso internazionale di studi sulle chiese di Roma (IV–X secolo), Roma, 4–10 settembre 2000*. Vatican City: Pontificio Istituto di archeologia cristiana, 2002.

Guillou, André. "Inscriptions du duché de Rome." *MEFRM* 83.2 (1971): 149–58.

Gulowsen, Kirsti. "Some Iconographic Aspects of the Relationship Between Santa Maria Antiqua and the Oratory of the Forty Martyrs." In Osborne et al., *Santa Maria Antiqua al Foro Romano*, 187–97.

Guyon, Jean. "Les Quatre Couronnés et l'histoire de leur culte des origines au milieu du IXe siècle." *MEFRA* 87.1 (1975): 505–61.

Haldon, John. *A Tale of Two Saints: The Martyrdoms and Miracles of Saints Theodore 'the Recruit' and 'the General'*. Liverpool: Liverpool University Press, 2016.

Halkin, François. *Légendes grecques de 'martyres romaines'*. Brussels: Société des Bollandistes, 1973.

———. "Sainte Tatiana: légende grecque d'une 'martyre romaine.'" *AB* 89 (1971): 265–309.

Hansen, Maria Fabricius. *The Eloquence of Appropriation: Prolegomena to an Understanding of Spolia in Early Christian Rome*. Rome: L'Erma di Bretschneider, 2003.

Haubrichs, Wolfgang. *Georgslied und Georgslegende im frühen Mittelalter: Text und Rekonstruktion*. Königstein/Ts.: Scriptor, 1979.

———. *Die Kultur der Abtei Prüm zur Karolingerzeit: Studien zur Heimat des althochdeutschen Georgsliedes*. Bonn: Ludwig Röhrscheid, 1979.

———. "Neue Zeugnisse zur Reichenauer Kultgeschichte des 9. Jahrhunderts." *Zeitschrift für die Geschichte des Oberrheins* 126 (1978): 1–43.

———. "St. Georg auf der frühmittelalterlichen Reichenau: Hagiographie, Hymnographie, Liturgie und Reliquienkult." In *Herrschaft, Kirche, Kultur: Beiträge zur Geschichte des Mittelalters. Festschrift für Friedrich Prinz zu seinem 65. Geburtstag*, edited by Georg Jenal, 505–35. Stuttgart: Hiersemann, 1993.

Heinzelmann, Martin. "Einhards 'Translatio Marcellini et Petri': eine Hagiographische Reformschrift von 830." In *Einhard: Studien zu Leben und Werk. Dem Gedenken an Helmut Beumann gewidmet*, edited by Hermann Schefers, 269–98. Darmstadt: Hessische Historische Kommission, 1997.

———. *Translationsberichte und andere Quellen des Reliquienkultes*. Turnhout: Brepols, 1979.

Hen, Yitzhak. "The Romanization of the Frankish Liturgy: Ideal, Reality, and the Rhetoric of Reform." In Bolgia et al., *Rome Across Time and Space*, 111–24.

Hennig, John. "The Meaning of All the Saints." *Mediaeval Studies* 10 (1948): 147–61.

Herbers, Klaus. "Rom im Frankenreich: Rombeziehung durch Heilige in der Mitte des 9. Jahrhunderts." In *Mönchtum, Kirche, Herrschaft, 750–1000*, edited by Dieter R. Bauer and Josef Semmler, 133–69. Sigmaringen: J. Thorbecke Verlag, 1998.

Hermes, Raimund. "Die stadtrömischen Diakonien." *RQ* 91 (1996): 1–120.

Herrin, Judith. *The Formation of Christendom*. Princeton, NJ: Princeton University Press, 1987.

Hill, Stephen. *The Early Byzantine Churches of Cilicia and Isauria*. Aldershot: Variorum, 1996.

Hillner, Julia. "Clerics, Property and Patronage: The Case of the Roman Titular Churches." *Antiquité tardive* 14 (2006): 59–68.

———. "Families, Patronage, and the Titular Churches of Rome, *c.*300–*c.*600." In Cooper and Hillner, *Religion, Dynasty, and Patronage*, 225–61.

Holum, Kenneth G., and Gary Vikan. "The Trier Ivory, 'Adventus' Ceremonial, and the Relics of St. Stephen." *DOP* 33 (1979): 113–33.

Hülsen, Christian. "Die Kirchen des heil. Caesarius in Rom." In *Miscellanea Francesco Ehrle: Scritti di storia e paleografia*, 2: 377–403. Rome: Biblioteca Apostolica Vaticana, 1924.

———. *La pianta di Roma dell'anonimo einsidlense*. Rome: E. Loescher, 1907.

———. *Le chiese di Roma nel medio evo, cataloghi ed appunti*. Firenze: L. S. Olschki, 1927.

Hummer, Hans J. *Politics and Power in Early Medieval Europe: Alsace and the Frankish Realm, 600–1000*. Cambridge: Cambridge University Press, 2005.

Humphries, Mark. "From Emperor to Pope? Ceremonial, Space and Authority at Rome from Constantine to Gregory the Great." In Cooper and Hillner, *Religion, Dynasty, and Patronage*, 21–58.

Iamurri, Laura, and Simona Ciofetta. "Santa Maria Antiqua e San Cesareo." *Roma sacra* 1.3 (1995): 26–31.

Jakobs, Dörthe. *Sankt Georg in Reichenau-Oberzell: der Bau und seine Ausstattung. Bestand, Veränderungen, Restaurierungsgeschichte*. 3 vols. Stuttgart: Theiss, 1999.

Janin, Raymond. *Constantinople byzantine*. Paris: Institut français d'études byzantines, 1964.

———. "Les églises byzantines Saint-Nicolas à Constantinople." *Echos d'Orient* 31 (1932): 403–18.

———. *Les églises et les monastères des grands centres byzantins (Bithynie, Hellespont, Latros, Galèsios, Trébizonde, Athènes, Thessalonique)*. La géographie ecclésiastique de l'empire Byzantin 2. Paris: Institut français d'études byzantines, 1975.

Jessop, Lesley. "Pictorial Cycles of Non-Biblical Saints: The Seventh- and Eighth-Century Mural Cycles in Rome and Contexts for Their Use." *PBSR* 67 (1999): 233–79.

Jong, Mayke de. "Carolingian Monasticism: The Power of Prayer." In *The New Cambridge Medieval History. 2:* c.*700*–c.*900*, edited by Rosamond McKitterick, 622–53. Cambridge: Cambridge University Press, 1995.

Jordan, Heinrich. *Topographie der Stadt Rom im Alterthum*. Berlin: Weidmann, 1871.

Jost, Michael. *Die Patrozinien der Kirchen der Stadt Rom vom Anfang bis in das 10. Jahrhundert*. Neuried: Ars Una, 2000.

Jounel, Pierre. "Le culte collectif des saints à Rome du VIIe au IXe siècle." *Ecclesia orans* 6 (1989): 285–300.

Jullien, Marie-Hélène, and Françoise Perelman. *Clavis scriptorum latinorum medii aevi: auctores Galliae 735–987. 2: Alcuin*. Turnhout: Brepols, 1999.

Kalas, Gregor. "Acquiring the Antique in Early Medieval Rome: The Economics of Architectural Reuse at S. Maria Antiqua." In *Reuse and Renovation in Roman Material Culture: Functions, Aesthetics, Interpretations*, edited by Diana Ng and Maria Swetnam-Burland. Cambridge University Press, forthcoming.

———. *The Restoration of the Roman Forum in Late Antiquity: Transforming Public Space*. Austin: University of Texas Press, 2015.

———. "Sacred Image/Urban Space: Image, Installations, and Rituals in the Early Medieval Roman Forum." PhD diss., Bryn Mawr College, 1999.

———. "Topographical Transitions: The Oratory of the Forty Martyrs and Exhibition Strategies in the Early Medieval Roman Forum." In Osborne et al., *Santa Maria Antiqua al Foro Romano*, 191–211.

Kalavrezou, Ioli. "Helping Hands for the Empire: Imperial Ceremonies and the Cult of Relics at the Byzantine Court." In *Byzantine Court Culture from 829 to 1204*, edited by Henry Maguire, 53–79. Washington, DC: Dumbarton Oaks, 1997.

Kaplan, Michel. "Les sanctuaires de Théodore de Sykéon." In *Les saints et leur sanctuaire: Byzance: textes, images et monuments*, edited by Catherine Jolivet-Lévy et al., 65–79. Paris: Publications de la Sorbonne, 1993.

Kinney, Dale. "Making Mute Stones Speak: Reading Columns in S. Nicola in Carcere and S. Maria in Aracoeli." In *Architectural Studies in Memory of Richard Krautheimer*, edited by James S. Ackerman and Cecil Lee Striker, 83–86. Mainz: Zabern, 1996.

———. "The *Praesepia* in S. Maria in Trastevere and S. Maria Maggiore." In Brandt and Pergola, *Marmoribus vestita*, 777–95.

Kirsch, Johann Peter. *Die römischen Titelkirchen im Altertum*. Paderborn: F. Schöningh, 1918.

Klaniczay, Gábor, ed. *Saints of the Christianization Age of Central Europe (Tenth–Eleventh Century)*. Budapest: Central European University Press, 2012.

Klein, Holger A. *Byzanz, der Westen und das 'wahre' Kreuz: die Geschichte einer Reliquie und ihrer künstlerischen Fassung in Byzanz und im Abendland*. Wiesbaden: Reichert, 2004.

———. "Eastern Objects and Western Desires: Relics and Reliquaries Between Byzantium and the West." *DOP* 58 (2004): 283–314.

———. "Sacred Relics and Imperial Ceremonies at the Great Palace of Constantinople." In Bauer, *Visualisierungen von Herrschaft*, 79–99.

Kötting, Bernhard. *Peregrinatio Religiosa: Wallfahrten in der Antike und das Pilgerwesen in der alten Kirche*. Münster: Regensberg, 1950.

Kraus, Franz Xaver. *Kunst und Alterthum in Elsass-Lothringen: beschreibende Statistik. 1. Kunst und Alterthum im Unter-Elsass*. Strassburg: C. F. Schmidts Universitäts-Buchhandlung, 1876.

Krautheimer, Richard. "Again Saints Sergius and Bacchus at Constantinople." *Jahrbuch der Österreichischen Byzantinistik* 23 (1974): 251–53.

———. "The Carolingian Revival of Early Christian Architecture." *Art Bulletin* 24.1 (1942): 1–38.

———. "Congetture sui mosaici scomparsi di S. Sabina a Roma." *RendPontAcc*, 3rd ser., 60 (1987/1988): 171–87.

———. "A Note on the Inscription in the Apse of Old St. Peter's." *DOP* 41, Studies on Art and Archeology in Honor of Ernst Kitzinger on His Seventy-Fifth Birthday (1987): 317–20.

———. *Rome, Profile of a City, 312–1308*. Princeton, NJ: Princeton University Press, 1980.

Kremers, Wilhelm. *Ado von Vienne: sein Leben und seine Schriften*. Steyl: Missionsdruckerei, 1911.

Kreutz, Barbara M. *Before the Normans: Southern Italy in the Ninth and Tenth Centuries*. Philadelphia: University of Pennsylvania Press, 1991.

Krumbacher, Karl. *Der heilige Georg in der griechischen Überlieferung*. Munich: Verlag der Königlich Bayerischen Akademie der Wissenschaften, 1911.

La Mantia, Serena. "'Santi su misura': la parete di Paolo I a Santa Maria Antiqua." In *L'VIII secolo: un secolo inquieto. Atti del Convegno internazionale di studi, Cividale del Friuli, 4–7 dicembre 2008*, edited by Valentino Pace, 149–61. Cividale del Friuli, Udine: Comune di Cividale del Friuli, 2010.

Lamboglia, Nino. "Uno scavo didattico dietro la 'Curia Senatus' e la topografia del Foro di Cesare." *RendPontAcc*, 3rd ser., 37 (1964–1965): 105–36.

Lanciani, Rodolfo. *L'itinerario di Einsiedeln e l'ordine di Benedetto Canonico*. Rome: Tipografia della R. Accademia dei Lincei, 1891.

Lanéry, Cécile. "Hagiographie d'Italie (300–550). I. Les Passions latines composées en Italie." In *Hagiographies: histoire internationale de la littérature hagiographique latine et vernaculaire en Occident des origines à 1550*, 5: 15–369. Turnhout: Brepols, 2010.

———. "La légende de sainte Agnès: quelques réflexions sur la genèse d'un dossier hagiographique (IVe–VIe s.)." *MEFRM* 126.1 (2014): 17–26.

Lanzoni, Francesco. "A proposito della passione di San Cesario di Terracina." *RACr* 1 (1924): 145–48.

Lapidge, Michael. "The Career of Archbishop Theodore." In *Archbishop Theodore: Commemorative Studies on His Life and Influence*, edited by Michael Lapidge, 1–29. Cambridge: Cambridge University Press, 1995.

Lehmann, Paul. "Die alte Klosterbibliothek Fulda und ihre Bedeutung." *Aus der Landesbibliothek Fulda* 2 (1928): 5–12.

Lestocquoy, Jean. "Administration de Rome et diaconies du VIIe au IXe siècle." *RACr* 7 (1930): 261–98.

Leyser, Conrad. "The Temptations of Cult: Roman Martyr Piety in the Age of Gregory the Great." *EME* 9.3 (2000): 289–307.

Lidova, Maria. "Maria Regina on the 'Palimpsest Wall' in S. Maria Antiqua Church in Rome: Historical Context and Imperial Connotations of the Early Byzantine Image." *Iconographica* (forthcoming).

Lifshitz, Felice. "Bede, Martyrology." In *Medieval Hagiography: An Anthology*, edited by Thomas Head, 167–97. New York: Routledge, 2000.

———. *The Name of the Saint: The Martyrology of Jerome and Access to the Sacred in Francia, 627–827.* Notre Dame, IN: University of Notre Dame Press, 2006.

Llewellyn, Peter. *Rome in the Dark Ages.* New York: Praeger, 1971.

Luciani, Roberto. "Le chiese mariane." In Pani Ermini, *Christiana loca*, 1: 131–45.

Lugli, Giuseppe. *Roma antica: il centro monumentale.* Rome: G. Bardi, 1946.

Mackie, Gillian. *Early Christian Chapels in the West: Decoration, Function and Patronage.* Toronto: University of Toronto Press, 2003.

———. "The San Venanzio Chapel in Rome and the Martyr Shrine Sequence." *Revue d'art canadienne* 23 (1996): 1–13.

Machado, Carlos. "Between Memory and Oblivion: The End of the Roman *Domus*." In Behrwald and Witschel, *Rom in der Spätantike*, 111–38.

Magdalino, Paul. "Medieval Constantinople." In *Studies on the History and Topography of Byzantine Constantinople*, 1–111. Aldershot: Ashgate, 2006.

Maischberger, Martin. *Marmor in Rom: Anlieferung, Lager- und Werkplatz in der Kaiserzeit.* Wiesbaden: Ludwig Reichart Verlag, 1997.

Mancini, Adele. "La chiesa medioevale di S. Adriano nel foro romano." *RendPontAcc*, 3rd ser., 40 (1967–1968): 191–245.

Mango, Cyril A. *The Brazen House: A Study of the Vestibule of the Imperial Palace of Constantinople.* Copenhagen: Munksgaard, 1959.

———. "The Church of Saints Sergius and Bacchus at Constantinople and the Alleged Tradition of Octagonal Palatine Churches." *Jahrbuch der Österreichischen Byzantinistik* 21 (1972): 189–93.

———. "The Church of Sts. Sergius and Bacchus Once Again." *Byzantion* 68 (1975): 385–92.

———. "Constantine's Mausoleum and the Translation of Relics." *BZ* 83.1 (1990): 51–62.

———. "La culture grecque et l'Occident au VIIIe siècle." In *I problemi dell'Occidente nel secolo VIII*, 693–721. Settimane 20. Spoleto: La sede del Centro, 1973.

———. *Le développement urbain de Constantinople, IVe–VIIe siècles.* Paris: De Boccard, 1985.

———. "On the Cult of Saints Cosmas and Damian at Constantinople." In *Θυμίαμα στη Μνήμη της Λασκαρίνας Μπούρα*, 189–92. Athens: Mouseio Benake, 1994.

Maraval, Pierre. *Lieux saints et pèlerinages d'Orient: histoire et géographie des origines à la conquête arabe.* Paris: Cerf, 1985.

Marchetti Longhi, Giuseppe. "Il quartiere greco-orientale di Roma nell'antichità e nel medio evo." In *Atti del IV Congresso nazionale di studi romani* (Rome: Istituto di studi romani, 1938) 1: 169–85.

———. *L'Aventino nel medio evo.* Rome: Istituto di studi romani, 1947.

Marin, Emilio. "Il mosaico della cappella di S. Venanzio al Battistero Lateranense: status quaestionis." In *Il cristianesimo in Istria fra tarda antichità e alto medioevo: novità e riflessioni. Atti della giornata tematica dei Seminari di archeologia cristiana, Roma, 8 marzo 2007*, edited by Emilio Marin and Danilo Mazzoleni, 209–15. Vatican City: Pontificio Istituto di archeologia cristiana, 2009.

Marrou, Henri-Irénée. "L'origine orientale des diaconies romaines." *MEFR* 57 (1940): 95–142.

Martin, René. "Au confluent des traditions antique, germanique et chrétienne: le 'Conflictus Veris et Hiemis' d'Alcuin." *Revue des études latines* 72 (1994): 177–91.

Maskarinec, Maya. "Foreign Saints at Home in Eighth- and Ninth-Century Rome: The Patrocinia of *Diaconiae*, *Xenodochia* and Greek Monasteries." In *Cuius Patrocinio Tota Gaudet Regio: Saints' Cults and the Dynamics of Regional Cohesion*, edited by Stanislava Kuzmová, Ana Marinković, and Trpimir Vedriš, 21–37. Zagreb: Hagiotheca, 2014.

Matthews, T. F. "Architecture et liturgie dans les premières églises palatiales de Constantinople." *Revue de l'art* 24 (1974): 22–29.

Matthiae, Guglielmo. *SS. Cosma e Damiano e S. Teodoro.* Rome: Danesi, 1948.

Mayer, Wendy. "Antioch and the Intersection Between Religious Factionalism, Place and Power." In *The Power of Religion in Late Antiquity*, edited by Andrew Cain and Noel Lenski, 357–67. Aldershot: Ashgate, 2009.

McCormick, Michael. *Eternal Victory: Triumphal Rulership in Late Antiquity, Byzantium, and the Early Medieval West*. Cambridge: Cambridge University Press, 1990.

———. *Origins of the European Economy: Communications and Commerce, A.D. 300–900*. Cambridge: Cambridge University Press, 2001.

McCulloh, John M. "The Cult of Relics in the Letters and 'Dialogues' of Pope Gregory the Great: A Lexicographical Study." *Traditio* 32 (1976): 145–84.

———. "From Antiquity to the Middle Ages: Continuity and Change in Papal Relic Policy from the 6th to the 8th Century." In *Pietas: Festschrift für Bernhard Kötting*, edited by Ernst Dassman and Karl Suso Frank, 312–24. Münster: Aschendorff, 1980.

McKitterick, Rosamond. *The Carolingians and the Written Word*. Cambridge: Cambridge University Press, 1989.

———. *History and Memory in the Carolingian World*. Cambridge: Cambridge University Press, 2004.

McLynn, Neil B. *Ambrose of Milan: Church and Court in a Christian Capital*. Berkeley: University of California Press, 1994.

Meinardus, Otto. "A Study of the Relics of the Saints of the Greek Orthodox Church." *Oriens christianus* 54 (1970): 130–278.

Meisen, Karl. *Nikolauskult und Nikolausbrauchtum im Abendlande: eine kulturgeographisch-volkskundliche Untersuchung*. Düsseldorf: L. Schwann, 1931.

Meneghini, Roberto, and Riccardo Santangeli Valenzani. *Roma nell'altomedioevo: topografia e urbanistica della città dal V al X secolo*. Rome: Istituto poligrafico e Zecca dello Stato, Libreria dello Stato, 2004.

Mietke, Gabriele. "Monumentalisierung christlicher Heiliger in Kilikien in frühbyzantinischer Zeit." *Olba* 17 (2009): 117–40.

Milella, Alessandra. "San Teodoro alle pendici del Palatino: considerazioni sulle origini della diaconia." *Archeologia classica* 55 (2004): 203–233.

Miller, Maureen C. *Clothing the Clergy: Virtue and Power in Medieval Europe, c. 800–1200*. Ithaca: Cornell University Press, 2014.

———. "The Sources of Textiles and Vestments in Early Medieval Rome." In *Rome and Religion in the Medieval World: Studies in Honor of Thomas F.X. Noble*, edited by Valerie L. Garver and Owen Michael Phelan, 83–100. Farnham: Ashgate, 2014.

Mommsen, Theodor. "Handschriftliches zur Lateinischen Anthologie." *Rheinisches Museum für Philologie*, n.s., 9 (1854): 296–301.

Monaci, A. "Regesto dell'abbazia di S. Alessio all'Aventino [1]." *ASRSP* 27 (1904): 351–98.

———. "Regesto dell'abbazia di S. Alessio all'Aventino [2]." *ASRSP* 28 (1905): 151–200, 395–499.

Moralee, Jason. "A Hill of Many Names: The Capitolium from Late Antiquity to the Middle Ages." *ActaIRNorv* 26 (2013): 47–70.

Mordek, Hubert. "Rom, Byzanz und die Franken im 8. Jahrhundert: zur Überlieferung und kirchenpolitischen Bedeutung der Synodus Romana Papst Gregors III. vom Jahre 732 (mit Edition)." In *Person und Gemeinschaft im Mittelalter: Karl Schmid zum fünfundsechzigsten Geburtstag*, edited by Gerd Althoff et al., 123–56. Sigmaringen: Thorbecke, 1988.

Morselli, Chiara, and Edoardo Tortorici. *Curia, Forum Iulium, Forum Transitorium*. Rome: De Luca, 1989.

Müller-Wiener, Wolfgang, Nezih Firatli, Renate Schiele, and Wolf Schiele. *Bildlexikon zur Topographie Istanbuls: Byzantion-Konstantinopolis-Istanbul bis zum Beginn des 17. Jahrhunderts*. Tübingen: E. Wasmuth, 1977.

Muñoz, Antonio. *Il restauro della basilica di S. Giorgio al Velabro in Roma*. Rome: Società editrice d'arte illustrata, 1926.

Muratore, Oliva, Maria Richiello, and Paolo Barbato. *La storia e il restauro del complesso conventuale dei Santi Bonifacio e Alessio all'Aventino*. Rome: E. de Rosa, 2004.

Murphy, Francis-Xavier. *Konstantinopel II und III*. Mainz: Matthias-Grünewald, 1990.

Nedungatt, George, and Michael Featherstone, eds. *The Council in Trullo Revisited*. Rome: Pontificio Istituto orientale, 1995.

Nees, Lawrence. *A Tainted Mantle: Hercules and the Classical Tradition at the Carolingian Court*. Philadelphia: University of Pennsylvania Press, 1991.

Neil, Bronwen. *Seventh-Century Popes and Martyrs: The Political Hagiography of Anastasius Bibliothecarius*. Turnhout: Brepols, 2006.

Nibby, A. *Roma nell'anno MDCCCXXXVIII*. Rome: Tipografia delle Belle Arti, 1838.

Nikolasch, Franz. "Zur Deutung der 'Dominus-legem-dat'-Szene." *RQ* 64 (1969): 35–73.

Noble, Thomas F. X. *The Republic of St. Peter: The Birth of the Papal State, 680–825*. Philadelphia: University of Pennsylvania Press, 1984.

Nora, Pierre. "Between Memory and History: Les Lieux de Mémoire." *Representations* 26, Special Issue: Memory and Counter-Memory (Spring 1989): 7–24.

Nordhagen, Per Jonas. "The Earliest Decorations in Santa Maria Antiqua and their Date." *ActaIRNorv* 1 (1962): 53–72.

———. "The Frescoes of John VII, A.D. 705–707, in S. Maria Antiqua in Rome." *ActaIRNorv* 3 (1968): 1–125.

———. "John VII's Adoration of the Cross in S. Maria Antiqua." *Journal of the Warburg and Courtauld Institutes* 30 (1967): 388–90.

———. "S. Maria Antiqua: The Frescoes of the Seventh Century." *ActaIRNorv* 8 (1978): 89–142.

Ohme, Heinz. "Die sogenannten 'antirömischen Kanones' des Concilium Quinisextum (692): Vereinheitlichung als Gefahr für die Einheit der Kirche." In Nedungatt and Featherstone, *The Council in Trullo Revisited*, 307–21.

Osborne, John. "The Atrium of S. Maria Antiqua, Rome: A History in Art." *PBSR* 55 (1987): 186–223.

———. "The Roman Catacombs in the Middle Ages." *PBSR* 53 (1985): 278–328.

———. "Rome and Constantinople About the Year 700: The Significance of the Recently Uncovered Mural in the Narthex of Santa Sabina." In *L'officinia dello sguardo: scritti in onore di Maria Andaloro. 1. I luoghi dell'arte*, edited by Giulia Bordi et al., 327–34. Rome: Gangemi, 2014.

Osborne, John, J. Rasmus Brandt, and Giuseppe Morganti, eds. *Santa Maria Antiqua al Foro Romano: cento anni dopo. Atti del Colloquio internazionale, Roma, 5–6 maggio 2000*. Rome: Campisano Editore, 2005.

Ousterhout, Robert. "Sacred Geographies and Holy Cities: Constantinople as Jerusalem." In *Hierotopy: The Creation of Sacred Space in Byzantium and Medieval Russia*, edited by Alexei Lidov, 98–116. Moscow: Progress-Tradition, 2006.

Palombi, Andreina. *La basilica di San Nicola in Carcere: il complesso architettonico dei tre templi del Foro Olitorio*. Rome: Istituto nazionale di studi romani, 2006.

Pani Ermini, Letizia, ed. *Christiana loca: lo spazio cristiano nella Roma del primo millennio*. 2 vols. Rome: Fratelli Palombi, 2000–2001.

———. "Spazio cristiano e culto dei santi orientali a Roma." In *Oriente cristiano e santità: figure e storia di santi tra Bisanzio e l'Occidente*, edited by Sebastiano Gentile, 85–92. Milan: Centro Tibaldi, 1998.

Papachryssanthou, Denise. *Actes du Prôtaton*. Paris: P. Lethielleux, 1975.

Pallottino, Massimo. *L'arco degli argentari*. Rome: Danesi, 1946.

Peloza, Makso. "Rekognicija relikvija dalmatinskih i istarskih mučenika u oratoriju svetog Venancija kod baptisterija Lateranske bazilike u Rimu 1962.–1964. godine [Reconnaissance des reliques des martyrs dalmates et istriens dans l'oratoire de St. Venance au baptistère de St. Jean de Latran à Rome (1962–1964)]." *Vjesnika za arheologiju i historiju dalmatinsku=Bulletin d'archéologie et d'histoire dalmate* 63.3 (1961–1962): 163–80.

Perraymond, Myla. "Le scholae peregrinorum nel borgo di San Pietro." *Romanobarbarica* 4 (1979): 183–200.

———. "Linee di diffusione del culto dei Santi Anargiri attraverso le testimonianze monumentali ed epigrafiche del VI secolo." In *Acta XIII Congressus internationalis archaeologiae christianae (Split-Poreč 25 settembre–1 ottobre 1994)*, 673–87. Vatican City: Pontificio Istituto di archeologia christiana, 1998.

Pietrangeli, Carlo, ed. *San Giovanni in Laterano.* Firenze: Nardini Editore, 1990.

Piétri, Charles. *Roma Christiana: recherches sur l'Église de Rome, son organisation, sa politique, son idéologie de Miltiade à Sixte III (311–440).* Paris: École française de Rome, 1976.

Pilara, Gianluca. *La città di Roma fra chiesa e impero durante il conflitto gotico-bizantino.* Rome: Aracne, 2006.

Pillinger, Renate. *Die Tituli Historiarum oder das sogennante Dittochaeon des Prudentius.* Vienna: Österreichischen Akademie der Wissenschaften, 1980.

Pilsworth, Clare. "Dating the *Gesta Martyrum*: A Manuscript-Based Approach." *EME* 9.3 (2000): 309–24.

Pohlkamp, Wilhelm. "Kaiser Konstantin, der heidnische und der christliche Kult in den Actus Silvestri." *Frühmittelalterliche Studien* 18 (1984): 357–400.

Price, Richard. *The Acts of the Lateran Synod of 649.* With contributions by Phil Booth and Catherine Cubitt. Liverpool: Liverpool University Press, 2014.

Proja, G. Battista. *S. Nicola in Carcere.* Rome: Istituto di studi romani, 1981.

Quentin, Henri. *Les martyrologes historiques du Moyen Âge: étude sur la formation du Martyrologe romain.* Paris: J. Gabalda, 1908.

Raaigmakers, Janneke E. "Fulda, eine Heilige Stadt: Hrabanus Maurus und die Reliquienstranslationen (835–838)." In *Hrabanus Maurus in Fulda, mit einer Hrabanus Maurus-Bibliographie (1979–2009)*, edited by Marc-Aeilko Aris and Susanna Bullido del Barrio, 219–38. Frankfurt am Main: Josef Knecht, 2010.

Rapp, Claudia. *Holy Bishops in Late Antiquity.* Berkeley: University of California Press, 2005.

Rea, Rossella. "Il Colosseo: destrutturazione e riuso tra IV e VIII secolo." *MEFRM* 111 (1999): 183–95.

Rebenich, Stefan. *Jerome.* London: Routledge, 2002.

Rech, Clara, ed. *Terracina e il medioevo: un punto di osservazione sul primo millennio alla fine del secondo millennio.* Rome: Quasar, 1989.

Reekmans, Louis. "L'implantation monumentale chrétienne dans la paysage urbain de Rome de 300 à 850." In Duval et al., *Actes du XIe Congrès*, 861–915.

Rettner, Arno. "Dreimal Theodotus? Stifterbild und Grabstiftung in der Theodotus-Kapelle von Santa Maria Antiqua in Rom." In *Für irdischen Ruhm und himmlischen Lohn: Stifter und Auftraggeber in der mittelalterlichen Kunst*, edited by Hans-Rudolf Meier et al., 31–46. Berlin: Dietrich Reimer, 1995.

Richiello, Maria. "Cenni topografici dell'Aventino dal sacco di Alarico (410 d.C.) ai giorni nostri." In Muratore et al., *La storia*, 23–34.

Röckelein, Hedwig. "'Die Hüllen der Heilige': zur Materialität des hagiographischen Mediums." In *Reliquiare im Mittelalter*, edited by Bruno Reudenbach and Gia Toussaint, 75–88. Berlin: Akademie Verlag, 2005.

———. *Reliquientranslationen nach Sachsen im 9. Jahrhundert: Über Kommunikation, Mobilität und Öffentlichkeit im Frühmittelalter.* Stuttgart: Thorbecke, 2002.

Roma nell'alto medioevo, Settimane 48. Spoleto: Centro italiano di studi sull'alto medioevo, 2001.

Romanelli, Pietro, and Per Jonas Nordhagen. *S. Maria Antiqua*. Rome: Istituto poligrafico dello Stato, Libreria dello Stato, 1964.

Rushforth, G. McN. "The Church of S. Maria Antiqua." *PBSR* 1 (1902): 1–119.

Sághy, Marianne. "Martyr Cult and Collective Identity in Fourth-Century Rome." In *Identity and Alterity in Hagiography and the Cult of Saints*, edited by Ana Marinkovic and Trpimir Vedriš, 17–34. Zagreb: Hagiotheca, 2010.

Saguì, Lucia. "Roma e il Mediterraneo: la circolazione delle merci." In Arena et al., *Roma dall'antichità al medioevo*, 62–68.

Salzman, Michele Renee. *The Making of a Christian Aristocracy: Social and Religious Change in the Western Roman Empire*. Cambridge, MA: Harvard University Press, 2002.

Sansterre, Jean-Marie. "Jean VII (705–7): idéologie pontificale et realisme politique." In *Rayonnement grec: hommages à Charles Delvoye*, edited by Lydie Hadermann-Misguich et al., 377–88. Brussels: Editions de l'Université de Bruxelles, 1982.

———. *Les moines grecs et orientaux à Rome aux époques byzantine et carolingienne: milieu du VIème s.–fin du IXème s.* Brussels: Palais des Académies, 1983.

Santangeli Valenzani, Riccardo. *Edilizia residenziale in Italia nell'altomedioevo*. Rome: Carocci, 2011.

———. "Hosting Foreigners in Early Medieval Rome: From *Xenodochia* to *Scholae Peregrinorum*." In *England and Rome in the Early Middle Ages: Pilgrimage, Art, and Politics*, edited by Francesca Tinti, 69–88. Turnhout: Brepols, 2014.

———. "L'iscrizione di Teodora da Santa Sabina: una nuova ipotesi di interpretazione." In *για το φίλο μας: scritti in ricordo di Gaetano Messineo*, edited by Elisabetta Mangani and Angelo Pellegrino, 345–54. Monte Compatri, RM: Espera, 2016.

———. "L'itinerario di Einsiedeln." In Arena et al., *Roma dall'antichità al medioevo*, 154–60.

———. "Pellegrini, senatori e papi: gli xenodochia a Roma tra il V e il IX secolo." *Rivista dell'Istituto nazionale di archeologia e storia dell'arte* 19–20 (1996–1997): 203–26.

Saxer, Victor. "La chiesa di Roma dal V al X secolo: amministrazione centrale e organizzazione territoriale." In *Roma nell'alto medioevo*, 493–632.

———. "L'utilisation par la liturgie de l'espace urbain et suburbain: l'exemple de Rome dans l'Antiquité et le Haut Moyen Âge." In Duval et al., *Actes du XIe Congrès*, 917–1033.

Scheidel, Walter and Elijah Meeks. *Orbis: The Stanford Geospatial Network Model of the Roman World*. 2012. orbis.stanford.edu.

Schmid, Karl. "Die Frage nach den Anfängen der Mönchsgemeinschaft in Fulda." In *Die Klostergemeinschaft von Fulda im früheren Mittelalter*, edited by Karl Schmid, 108–35. Munich: W. Fink, 1978.

Scholz, Sebastian. *Politik, Selbstverständnis, Selbstdarstellung: die Päpste in karolingischer und ottonischer Zeit*. Stuttgart: Franz Steiner, 2006.

Schramm, Percy Ernst. *Kaiser, Rom und Renovatio: Studien und Texte zur Geschichte des römischen Erneuerungsgedankens vom Ende des karolingischen Reiches biz zum Investiturstreit*. Leipzig: B. G. Teubner, 1929.

Seeliger, Hans Reinhard. "Einhards römische Reliquien: zur Übertragung der Heiligen Marzellinus und Petrus ins Frankenreich." *RQ* 83 (1988): 58–75.

Sessa, Kristina. *The Formation of Papal Authority in Late Antique Italy: Roman Bishops and the Domestic Sphere*. New York: Cambridge University Press, 2012.

Siegmund, Albert. *Die Überlieferung der griechischen christlichen Literatur in der lateinischen Kirche bis zum zwölften Jahrhundert*. Munich-Pasing: Filser Verlag, 1949.

Smith, Julia M. H. "Care of Relics in Early Medieval Rome." In *Rome and Religion in the Early Middle Ages: Studies in Honor of Thomas F. X. Noble*, edited by Valerie Garver and Owen Phelan, 179–205. Farnham: Ashgate, 2014.

———. "Cursing and Curing, or the Practice of Christianity in Eighth-Century Rome." In *Italy and Medieval Europe: Papers for Chris Wickham on the Occasion of His 65th Birthday*, edited by Ross Balzaretti, Julia Barrow, and Patricia Skinner. Past and Present Supplement. Oxford: Oxford University Press, forthcoming.

———, ed. *Early Medieval Rome and the Christian West: Essays in Honour of Donald A. Bullough*. Leiden: Brill, 2000.

———."'Emending Evil Ways and Praising God's Omnipotence': Einhard and the Uses of Roman Martyrs." In *Seeing and Believing: Conversion in Late Antiquity and the Early Middle Ages*, edited by Kenneth Mills and Anthony Grafton, 189–223. Rochester, NY: University of Rochester Press, 2003.

———. "Old Saints, New Cults: Roman Relics in Carolingian Francia." In *Early Medieval Rome and the Christian West: Essays in Honour of Donald A. Bullough*, edited by J. M. H. Smith, 317–39. Leiden: Brill, 2000.

———. "Portable Christianity: Relics in the Medieval West (*c.*700–1200)." *Proceedings of the British Academy* 181 (2012): 143–67.

Spera, Lucrezia. "Trasformazioni e riassetti del tessuto urbano nel Campo Marzio centrale tra tarda antichità e medioevo." *MEFRM* 126.1 (2014): 47–74.

Staab, Franz. "Erzbischof Otgar (826–847)." In *Handbuch der Mainzer Kirchengeschichte. 1. Christliche Antike und Mittelalter*, edited by Friedhelm Jürgensmeier, 153–62. Würzburg: Echter, 2000.

Stoclet, Alain. *Autour de Fulrad de Saint-Denis (v. 710–784)*. Geneva: Droz, 1993.

Tea, Eva. *La basilica di Santa Maria Antiqua*. Milan: Vita e Pensiero, 1937.

Tempesta, Claudia, ed. *L'icona murale di Santa Sabina all'Aventino*. Rome: Gangemi, 2010.

Terry, Ann Bennett, and Henry Maguire. *Dynamic Splendor: The Wall Mosaics in the Cathedral of Eufrasius at Poreč*. 2 vols. University Park: Pennsylvania State University Press, 2007.

Teteriatnikov, Natalia. "For Whom Is Theodotus Praying? An Interpretation of the Program of the Private Chapel in S. Maria Antiqua." *Cahiers archéologiques: fin de l'Antiquité et Moyen Âge* 41 (1993): 37–46.

Thacker, Alan. T. "Martyr Cult Within the Walls: Saints and Relics in the Roman *Tituli* of the Fourth to Seventh Centuries." In *Text, Image, Interpretation: Studies in Anglo-Saxon Literature and its Insular Context in Honour of Éamonn Ó Carragáin*, edited by Alastair J. Minnis and Jane Roberts, 32–70. Turnhout: Brepols, 2007.

———. "The Origin and Early Development of Rome's Intramural Cults: A Context for the Cult of Sant'Agnese in Agone." *MEFRM* 126.1 (2014): 137–146.

———. "Popes, Emperors and Clergy at Old Saint Peter's from the Fourth to the Eighth Century." In *Old Saint Peter's, Rome*, edited by Rosamond McKitterick et al., 137–56. Cambridge: Cambridge University Press, 2013.

Thanner, Anton. *Papst Honorius I (625–638)*. St. Ottilien: EOS Verlag, 1989.

Thunø, Erik. *The Apse Mosaic in Early Medieval Rome: Time, Network, and Repetition*. New York: Cambridge University Press, 2015.

———. *Image and Relic: Mediating the Sacred in Early Medieval Rome*. Rome: Erma di Bretschneider, 2002.

———. "Inscription and Divine Presence: Golden Letters in the Early Medieval Apse Mosaic." *Word & Image: A Journal of Verbal/Visual Enquiry* 27.3 (2011): 279–91.

Treitinger, Otto. *Die oströmische Kaiser- und Reichsidee nach ihrer Gestaltung im höfischen Zeremoniell*. Darmstadt: Gentner Verlag, 1956.

Van Dam, Raymond. *Rome and Constantinople: Rewriting Roman History During Late Antiquity*. Waco, TX: Baylor University Press, 2010.

Vasiliev, Alexander Alexandrovich. *Justin the First: An Introduction to the Epoch of Justinian the Great*. Cambridge, MA: Harvard University Press, 1950.

Vermaseren, M. J., and Carel Claudius van Essen. *The Excavations in the Mithraeum of the Church of Santa Prisca in Rome*. Leiden: Brill, 1965.

Verrando, Giovanni Nino. "Reciproche influenze tra Roma e il Martirologio e Passionario Umbri." In *L'Umbria meridionale fra tardo-antico ed altomedioevo: atti del Convegno di studio, Acquasparta 6–7 maggio 1989*, edited by Gianfranco Binazzi, 99–110. Perugia: Università degli studi, [1991].

Vielliard, René. *Recherches sur les origines de la Rome chrétienne: les églises romaines et leur rôle dans l'histoire et la topographie de la ville depuis la fin du monde antique jusqu'à la formation de l'Etat pontifical. Essai d'urbanisme chrétien*. Macon, France: Protat Frères, 1941.

Vitiello, Massimiliano. "Teoderico a Roma: politica, amministrazione e propaganda nell' 'adventus' dell'anno 500 (Considerazioni sull' 'Anonimo Valesiano II')." *Historia: Zeitschrift für Alte Geschichte* 53.1 (2004): 73–120.

Vogel, Cyrille. *Medieval Liturgy: An Introduction to the Sources*. Revised and translated by William G. Storey and Niels Krogh Rasmussen with the assistance of John K. Brooks-Leonard. Washington, DC: Pastoral Press, 1986.

Walter, Christopher. *The Warrior Saints in Byzantine Art and Tradition*. Aldershot: Ashgate, 2002.

Ward-Perkins, Bryan. "Old and New Rome Compared: The Rise of Constantinople." In *Two Romes*, edited by Lucy Grig and Gavin Kelly, 53–78. New York: Oxford University Press, 2012.

Weitzmann, Kurt. *The Monastery of Saint Catherine at Mount Sinai: The Icons. 1: From the Sixth to the Tenth Century*. Princeton, NJ: Princeton University Press, 1976.

Westall, Richard. "Theodoric Patron of the Churches of Rome?" *ActaIRNorv* 27 (2014): 119–37.

Wickham, Chris. *Framing the Early Middle Ages: Europe and the Mediterranean, 400–800*. Oxford: Oxford University Press, 2005.

———. *Medieval Rome: Stability and Crisis of a City, 900–1150*. Oxford: Oxford University Press, 2015.

Wilpert, Josef. *Die römischen Mosaiken und Malereien der kirchlichen Bauten vom IV. bis XIII. Jahrhundert*. Freiburg im Breisgau: Herder, 1917.

Wolf, Gerhard. "Icons and Sites: Cult Images of the Virgin in Mediaeval Rome." In *Images of the Mother of God: Perceptions of the Theotokos in Byzantium*, edited by Maria Vassilaki, 23–49. Aldershot: Ashgate, 2005.

Wood, Ian. "The Hagiography of Conversion." In Klaniczay, *Saints*, 1–16.

Index

Note: Entries for saints consist of the name followed by "Saint" (e.g., Damian, Saint). Entries for churches dedicated to saints often begin with "S." or "St." (e.g., S. Agnese, St. Peter's) or their plurals "SS." and "Sts."; entries beginning with "S." or the like appear before all other entries beginning with "s"; there, "St.," "SS.," and "Sts." are alphabetized as if they were "S." All buildings, monuments, and neighborhoods are in Rome unless otherwise indicated. Illustrations are indicated by page numbers in italic type.

Acknowledgments

I would especially like to thank Patrick Geary, Teofilo Ruiz, Diane Favro, Claudia Rapp, and Michael Maas for their encouragement, advice, and critique. Ra'anan Boustan, Robert Coates-Stephens, Sharon Gerstel, Caroline Goodson, Gerda Heydemann, Ronald Mellor, William North, Helmut Reimitz, and Chris Wickham provided helpful commentary and corrections along the way. Parts of the project benefited from discussion at seminars and workshops at the University of Vienna (2012); the German Historical Institute, London (2013); Oxford (2013); the University of Zurich (2013), in particular the comments of Sebastian Scholz; the University of Warsaw (2013), in particular the comments of Robert Wiśniewski; and with Irene San Pietro, Catherine Chin, Martin Eisner, and Patrick Nold at the American Academy in Rome (2013–2014). Caroline Goodson, John Haldon, Julia Hillner, Kristine Iara, Erik Inglis, Gregor Kalas, Maria Lidova, Maureen Miller, John Osborne, and Julia Smith all kindly shared unpublished work with me. The publication process was facilitated by Ruth Mazo Karras, and the book manuscript benefited significantly from the suggestions of Jerome Singerman, George Demacopoulos, and Hendrik Dey.

The research for this project was assisted by the support of the Jacob K. Javits Fellowships Program (2011–2012), the Institut für Byzantinistik und Neogräzistik at the University of Vienna (Spring 2012), the American Academy in Rome (2013–2014), the Andrew W. Mellon Foundation and the American Council of Learned Societies (2014–2015), and the Institute for the Study of the Ancient World, New York University (2016–2017). Access to monuments in Rome was facilitated by Giulia Barra at the American Academy in Rome. Bruno Angeli, Matthew Brennan, Prisca Brülisauer, Maria Castellino, Maria Daniela Donninelli, Bernie Frischer, Julia Gearhart, Father Justin, Liz Kurtulik Mercuri, Justinus Pagnamenta, Marga Sanchez, Maria Sole, and Gabriele Wohlgemuth assisted with the acquisition of images and permissions, and Gordie Thompson redrew the maps. Marion Riggs kindly took pictures in Rome. David Luljak prepared the index, Gail Naron Chalew copyedited the manuscript, and Brian Ostrander served as production editor. The

Art History Publication Initiative provided subvention for the images and the color illustrations.

The credit and the blame for embarking on such a project must go to my parents and my sister, Malika. May it find a contented reader in Alex.